D0762539

OUR LADY OF GUADALUPE

Aparición De la imagen de nuestra Sⁱ,
guadalupe de Mexico

Our Lady of Guadalupe

The Origins and Sources of a
Mexican National Symbol,
1531–1797

by

Stafford Poole, C. M.

THE UNIVERSITY OF ARIZONA PRESS

Tucson

Third printing 1997
The University of Arizona Press
Copyright © 1995
Arizona Board of Regents
All rights reserved

♾ This book is printed on acid-free, archival-quality paper.
Manufactured in the United States of America

00 99 98 97   6 5 4 3

Library of Congress Cataloging-in-Publication Data
Poole, Stafford.
    Our Lady of Guadalupe : the origins and sources of a
Mexican national symbol, 1531–1797 / by Stafford Poole.
        p.   cm.
    Includes bibliographical references and index.
    ISBN 0-8165-1526-3 (alk. paper)
    ISBN 0-8165-1623-5 (pbk. : alk. paper)
    1. Guadalupe, Our Lady of—History.   2. Mexico—
Religious life and customs.   I. Title.
BT660.G8P66   1995
232.91′7′097253—dc20   94-18724
                                                            CIP

British Library Cataloguing-in-Publication Data
A catalogue record for this book is available from the British
Library.

Frontispiece: Appearance of the image of Our Lady of
Guadalupe on the cloak of Juan Diego. Engraving from
Imagen de la Virgen Maria, Madre de Dios de Guadalupe (1648)
by Miguel Sánchez. Courtesy of the John Carter Brown
Library at Brown University.

To

Jennifer Walsh

8 December 1974–19 January 1994

Juventud, divino tesoro,
Ya te vas para no volver;
Cuando quiero llorar, no lloro,
Y a veces lloro sin querer.

—Rubén Darío

Huel nicnequi cenca niquelehuia inic nican
nechquechilizque noteocaltzin in oncan nicnextiz
nicpantlaçaz nitemacaz In ixquich notetlaçotlaliz
notepalehuiliz in notemanahuiliz, canel nehuatl in
namoicnohuacanantzin . . . ca oncan niquincaquiliz in
inchoquiz intlaocol inic nicyectiliz nicpatiz in ixquich
nepapan innetoliniz intonehuiz inchichinaquiliz.

I ardently wish and greatly desire that they build my church
for me here, where I will reveal, I will make known, and I
will give to people all my love, my compassion, my aid, and
my protection, for it is I who am your compassionate mother
. . . there I will hear their weeping and their sorrows in order
to remedy and heal all their various afflictions, their
miseries, and their torments.

—*Nican mopohua*

Quando de veritate scandalum sumitur, utilius permittitur
nasci scandalum, quam ut veritas relinquatur.

When scandal is taken at the truth, it is preferable to let the
scandal be born than to give up the truth.

—Saint Gregory the Great
on Ezekiel, book 1, homily 7

Contents

CONTENTS

xi

Acknowledgments

I would like to express my appreciation to all who helped in any way with this work. Thomas Anslow, C.M., John Rybolt, C.M., and Douglas Slawson gave me helpful criticisms on the early drafts and Professor John Frederick Schwaller did the same for the final draft. Professor Robert Ryal Miller offered numerous helpful comments during the progress of the work and also directed me to many important sources. Professor Jeannette Favrot Peterson provided valuable information on the Stradanus engraving of 1615 and the iconography of Guadalupe. Doctor Barry Sell generously shared the results of his research into Nahuatl sermons and also corrected the manuscript for errors of fact and Nahuatl grammar. Research in Mexico was made possible by a Travel to Collections grant from the National Endowment for the Humanities. Professor W. Michael Mathes generously shared his forthcoming Guadalupan bibliography. Thanks are expressed to the administration and staff of the Biblioteca Nacional, Mexico City; the administration and staff of the Biblioteca Nacional de Antropología e Historia, Mexico City; the administration and staff of the Archivo General de la Nación, Mexico City; Mme. Monique Cohen and the staff of the Département des Manuscrits, Division Orientale, Bibliothèque Nationale de France, Paris; the staff of special collections, University Research Library, the University of California at Los Angeles; Ms. Jane Garner, Benson Latin American Collection, University of Texas at Austin General Libraries; and Doctor Norman Fiering, director, Mr. Dan Slive, reference librarian, and the staff of the John Carter Brown Library, Providence, Rhode Island. Finally, a special word of thanks to Professor Susan Schroeder, who supported and encouraged this project from the beginning, and to Professor James Lockhart, who guided me into the beauties of Nahuatl.

OUR LADY OF GUADALUPE

Introduction

The hold that the devotion to Our Lady of Guadalupe has on the Mexican people is universally recognized. It permeates their lives; her picture is to be found throughout the republic. No visitor to the shrine at Tepeyac can fail to be impressed by the depth of faith that it arouses. Nor is this confined to Mexico, for the Empress of the Americas is venerated throughout the Western Hemisphere. Though immigrants have brought her to the United States, the devotion extends far beyond any single ethnic group. More than one predominantly Anglo parish in this country carries the name of the Dark Virgin, and her feast, 12 December, is observed in all dioceses in the United States. In the annals of Catholic Marian devotion Guadalupe has few, if any, equals.

This devotion is based on the story of the Virgin Mary's appearance to the newly converted Indian, Juan Diego, in December 1531, which is described in detail in chapter 2. The first known account of it, however, was not published until 1648 by the Oratorian priest Miguel Sánchez. In the following year another account, commonly known today by the Nahuatl name *Nican mopohua*, was published by the vicar of Guadalupe, Luis Laso de la Vega, with the Indians as its intended audience. Its impact on the Indians is unclear, and not unexpectedly it had none on the Spaniards. In contrast, Sánchez's account was responsible for the popularization and spread of the devotion among the criollos of Mexico City, that is, among those people of European stock who had been born in the New World. Though the only difference between criollos and peninsular Spaniards was in their place of birth, the criollos saw themselves as marginalized. Disdained by the peninsulars, excluded from the topmost positions of local government, and fettered by what they regarded as second-class citizenship, they reacted by developing a strong sense of group and regional identity. Known as the "sons of the land" in the sixteenth century, they were, in the late seventeenth century, calling themselves *indianos* and *americanos*. Sánchez's publication of the story of the apparitions came at an opportune moment in the development of criollo consciousness. It struck an immediate, sympathetic chord.

Sánchez's book was not just a devotional treatise that narrated still another Marian apparition among the hundreds that were to be found throughout the Spanish dominions. It was a florid, complex celebration of *criollismo*. Downplaying the Indian dimension of the apparition account and devotion, Sánchez saw Guadalupe as a proof of special divine favor toward the criollos, a sign that the woman prophesied in the twelfth chapter of the book of Revelation (Apocalypse) had come to fulfill that prophecy in Mexico City. The Virgin Mary had revealed herself to the criollos, even if through the agency of a lowly Nahua. This sense of uniqueness and special election was embodied in the well-known story of how Pope Benedict XIV, after hearing the apparition account and seeing a copy of the image in the mid–eighteenth century, supposedly quoted Psalm 147, "Non fecit taliter omni nationi" [He has not done the like for any other nation].

The devotion spread rapidly, always with the same criollo emphasis. An abridged edition of Sánchez's work published in 1660 by the Jesuit Mateo de la Cruz made the story more accessible and had a wider impact than the original. In 1666 the cathedral chapter of Mexico City associated the diocesan Church structure with Guadalupe when it conducted a formal inquiry into the oral transmission of the account through successive generations of Indians, criollos, and peninsular Spaniards. Although the devotion to Guadalupe was originally centered in Mexico City, it quickly spread elsewhere in New Spain. Unlike similar devotions, Guadalupe did not remain exclusively local nor was it confined to Tepeyac. Between 1659 and 1669 a congregation of diocesan priests dedicated to Guadalupe was founded in Querétaro, where a church was dedicated to her in 1680. There is also evidence of a shrine outside of San Luis Potosí (1655–1665), a Franciscan convent dedicated to Guadalupe among the Manso Indians in what is now Ciudad Juárez (1659), an altar to Guadalupe in the chapel of the Franciscan convent of San Francisco in Tlaxcala, devotion to Guadalupe in Oaxaca (1666, 1674), and a perpetual endowment of masses in the cathedral of Guadalajara (1693).[1] Criollo preachers took up the new devotion with enthusiasm, with a resulting wealth of published sermons in the period from 1660 to 1800. All these celebrated the criollo nature of the devotion to the detriment of its Indian message. The apparitions themselves were infrequently described by these preachers and only occasionally did the figure of Juan Diego appear. The criollos were the new chosen people; no other people had a picture of the Virgin that she had personally painted; God had not done the like for any other nation.

Some authors, like Luis Becerra Tanco and Francisco de Florencia, did find a place for the Indians. They believed that the apparitions were heaven's way of affirming their humanity. Still, it was only in the eighteenth century that the story of Guadalupe began to take hold among the native population. The Franciscan missionary college founded at Zacatecas by fray Antonio Margil de Jesús in 1708 to prepare friars to work among the pagan natives bore the name of Guadalupe. There were unrealized attempts to translate the *Nican mopohua* into Spanish, one sponsored early in the eighteenth century by Lorenzo Botturini Benaduci, a second later in the century by Archbishop Francisco Antonio Lorenzana. The message that was preached to the natives, however, was not the same as that popularized among the criollos. Nahuatl sermons tended to stress the need for the natives to have devotion to the Virgin and to seek her help and protection. Only in the important sermons of Ignacio de Paredes (1759) and Antonio López Murto (1791) were there declarations that the Indians had been especially favored by Mary.

The devotion soon spread beyond New Spain. It reached the peninsula through the agency of Pedro de Gálvez, a former *visitador* in New Spain and a member of the Council of the Indies, who in 1662 subsidized publication in Spain of Mateo de la Cruz's version of the story. In 1743 Philip V established a Guadalupan congregation with himself and his successors as grand masters. Why a criollo devotion would have appealed to the Spanish king is not clear, unless it was an attempt to blunt its political potential. After the city of Mexico chose Guadalupe as its principal patron in 1737, this patronage was extended to all New Spain and Guatemala (1746) and later (1757) to all Spanish dominions throughout the world. In New Spain, however, criollismo continued to dominate popular preaching. At the end of the century it received one of its strongest expressions in the febrile and confused Guadalupan sermon of the Dominican fray Servando Teresa de Mier (1795).

The first truly political use of Guadalupe as a national symbol was in Miguel Hidalgo's revolution of 1810. The Dark Virgin appeared on his banners, while his troops proclaimed long life to her and death to the Spaniards. The longstanding rivalry between the Virgin of Guadalupe (La Criolla) and the Virgin of Remedios (La Conquistadora) became clearly marked along nationalist and political lines. The nuns of San Jerónimo dressed the statue of Remedios as a general, and the royalist army used it on their banners just as Hidalgo used Guadalupe. There is a story that at the same time the Virgin of Guadalupe was shot in effigy as a rebel by royal troops.[2] After independence Guadalupe emerged as the preeminent national symbol. This time, however, it was appropriated not by the criollos but by their successors, the ruling classes of the newly independent state, whether liberal or conservative. One of the great religious and national events of the nineteenth century was the coronation of the Guadalupe image in 1895, yet the Indians played a minimal role in it.

In the nineteenth century the ascendancy of Guadalupe faced a challenge, not from a rival devotion but from historians and critics. Although doubts had been expressed publicly about the apparitions since the eighteenth century, it was only in the latter part of the nineteenth century that there was a strong attack on their historicity. Critics included the priest and bibliographer Vicente de Paúl Andrade, Bishop Eduardo Sánchez Camacho of Tamaulipas (who was compelled to resign his bishopric in part because of his public denial of the apparitions), and bibliographer José María de Agreda y Sánchez. One reluctant combatant was Joaquín García Icazbalceta, the foremost historian in Mexico. After the publication of his classic biography of Archbishop Juan de Zumárraga in 1881, he was criticized for failing to mention the apparitions. The obvious response was that nothing in his sources mentioned them. When Archbishop Pelagio Antonio Labastida y Dávalos of Mexico City asked him to review the manuscript of a book on Guadalupe, he responded with his famous "Carta acerca del origen de la imagen de Nuestra Señora de Guadalupe de México" of October 1883, in which he examined at length the evidence for and against the historicity of the apparition account and concluded that it was no more than a pious drama. Although García Icazbalceta was a conservative Catholic, this did not spare him angry, even vicious, attacks from his fellow countrymen and co-religionists during his lifetime and after his death. It is easy to understand why he was unwilling to publish the letter on the grounds that he did not have the vocation to be a martyr.[3]

What precisely does Guadalupe symbolize? What has been and is the message that the Virgin of Tepeyac brings to the peoples of the Western Hemisphere? Equally important, what does it tell us about the society that so enthusiastically embraced it? The message has been a varied, even ambiguous one that has meant different things to different groups and that has been exploited to meet special needs and interests. For Hidalgo and his ragtag army of Indians bent on revenge for centuries of oppression, as for Emiliano Zapata's *sureños* fighting for land and liberty, Guadalupe symbolized liberation and native rights. For others Guadalupe has had various meanings: indigenism, religious syncretism, respect for cultural autonomy, the struggle for human dignity, or, conversely, submission and subjugation, whether of Indians or women. Most frequently Guadalupe is associated with *mexicanidad*. "Mexico was born at Tepeyac" aptly summarizes the role that the devotion has played in Mexican history.[4] "Apart from her religious significance," wrote Jiménez Moreno, "she is the most genuine symbol of Mexican culture, its visible trace." In the words of Eric Wolf, she is truly a "national symbol." This theme was echoed by Ena Campbell: "It is the Virgin of Guadalupe who expresses the sociopolitical uniqueness of the entire Mexican population." And in a bittersweet lament, Octavio Paz has observed, "The Mexican people, after more than two centuries of experiments and defeats, have faith only in the Virgin of Guadalupe and the National Lottery."[5]

This facet of Guadalupe has been aptly summarized by William B. Taylor.

> The story of the apparition in 1531, just ten years after the Aztec capital at
> Tenochtitlan fell to Cortés, *is* rich in providential possibilities—a dark-
> complected Virgin Mary appears to a lowly Indian at Tepeyac, the sacred place
> of a pre-Columbian mother goddess, leaving her beautiful image on the Indian's
> cloak. Then, in a spontaneous surge of Indian devotion, natives flock to the site
> of the miracle, embracing her image in their spiritual orphanhood as if she were
> a new mother restoring order in the supernatural world as well as in the here and
> now. She combines the Indian past with the Spanish present to make something
> new, a proto-Mexican Indian madonna who will gradually be accepted as well by
> American Spaniards and *mestizos* as their own, thus forming the spiritual basis of a
> national independence movement in the early 19th century.[6]

Out of the multitudinous writings on Guadalupe certain themes have
emerged, some of which have now reached mythic status. One of these is a close
association with Tonantzin, the mother goddess of the Mexica, whose temple
or center of devotion was at the hill of Tepeyac. The Virgin of Guadalupe is
viewed as a revenant or new incarnation of the pre-Hispanic deity, the result, it
is asserted, of an act of deliberate syncretism or substitution by the missionary
friars. Thus she brought comfort and motherhood to the Indians after a period
of total disruption; when all was lost for the them, she gave them renewal and
rebirth as a people. Guadalupe stands for both transformation and continuity
in Mexican religious and national life. As a result the Indians spontaneously
flocked to her in the aftermath of the conquest as a symbol of motherly love
and protection, and thousands were converted in the early days of the devotion.
In the process she melded the criollos and Indians into one people, the modern
Mexican. Both Church and state were thereby compelled to recognize the humanity of the Indians and accept the legitimacy of their cultures. Most of these
conclusions are based on an examination of the intrinsic meaning of myth
rather than the history of the origins and development of the apparition account
and the devotion based on it. Consequently for the most part they do not stand
up to close historical scrutiny.

The most comprehensive examination of Guadalupe as a national symbol in
recent years has been Jacques Lafaye's *Quetzalcoatl and Guadalupe: The Formation
of Mexican National Consciousness, 1531–1813*, which appeared in France in 1974
and in an English translation two years later. It is a complex, scholarly, and at
times dense work that uses a multidisciplinary approach to assess the place of
Guadalupe in the growth of Mexican national consciousness. Lafaye analyzes
the growth of the Guadalupe and Quetzalcoatl myths in the eighteenth century
and sees Guadalupe as the one common element in an otherwise fragmented
nation that lacks a natural focus of unity. A central facet of the growth of

Mexican national consciousness was the Hispanicization of Quetzalcoatl and the Indianization of Guadalupe. Lafaye's book has been praised for its analysis of the growth of the Quetzalcoatl and Guadalupe myths but also criticized for its unjustified generalizations and failure as a history of national consciousness.[7] As will be clear in the course of this work, I believe that Lafaye's weakness lies precisely in his flawed analysis of the growth and development of the apparition/devotion.

If Guadalupe is a powerful national symbol, it is also an ambiguous one. Like Tonantzin, she symbolizes destruction and the fulfillment of apocalyptic prophecies or, conversely, motherly protection and love. She represents both liberation and submission. This ambiguity was the theme of Mauro Rodríguez's book, *Guadalupe, ¿historia o símbolo?* published in 1980. He was led to undertake the study by the disparity between the message of Guadalupe—special election and blessings—and the tawdry realities of Mexican life. Rodríguez approaches the question of the tradition from the point of view of religious psychology. For him *guadalupanismo* and machismo have similar functions: personal affirmation, a protest against the father figure, and a refuge in the idealized mother image. For the Spaniards it was a way of assuaging the guilty consciences of the conquistadores and their descendants. For the Indians it was a means of giving up the past and becoming reconciled to the present. For the criollos it became the banner of independence. For the modern Mexicans the message of blessing, divine love, and special election is a comfort against the superiority of their northern neighbor. For the ecclesiastical hierarchy the Guadalupe symbol is a source of power. For the rich and powerful it is an opiate for the common people and suppresses revolutionary forces.

Despite these strong statements, Rodríguez does not repudiate Guadalupe. He believes that once the historic basis has been eliminated, its symbolic value remains. "Its character as a symbol does not depend on the apparitions."[8] The symbol, however, can be manipulated. Guadalupe can be an instrument of rule, a way to keep people resigned and infantile. Despite the claim of preachers that Guadalupe unites all Mexicans, the people remain strongly unequal. Interpreting Guadalupe as an ambiguous symbol, Rodriguez urges a reinterpretation of the religious nature of the shrine and devotion.

Some of Rodríguez's interpretations rest on questionable historical bases. Thus, for example, he assumes that the devotion of the sixteenth century is the same as that of today and that it was more or less universal among social and ethnic groups. Like Lafaye, he maintains that the flood of 1629 to 1634 marked the ascendancy of Guadalupe over all other Marian devotions in New Spain, though there is no real evidence for this. Rodríguez makes the erroneous statement that Bernardino de Sahagún testified that the image had been painted by an Indian, and though Rodríguez promises to discuss the matter in a later chapter, he does not do so.

The year after the publication of Rodríguez's work, Francisco de la Maza's *El guadalupanismo mexicano* appeared. After briefly surveying the history of the tradition, de la Maza concluded that it lacked any historical basis and was a legend. His book has been influential and is frequently cited, but it is of limited value. Aside from some research into criollo sermons and Guadalupan poetry, it contains little that is original. The absence of any scholarly apparatus, including bibliography and notes even for direct quotations, not only weakens it still more but makes it frustrating to the serious reader.

In a recent work, *Destierro de sombras*, published in 1986, Edmundo O'Gorman argues that Alonso de Montúfar, the second archbishop of Mexico (1551–1572), was the key figure in the development of the Guadalupe devotion. He dates the foundation of the chapel at Tepeyac to 1556, though he says that the present image may have been placed there in 1555 or 1556. He attempts to show that the name Guadalupe was imposed on the shrine and the image in 1556, thus removing its Indian character and making it a Spanish devotion. It was a way of legitimizing the Virgin for Spaniards. He accepts fully the identification of Antonio Valeriano, a famed native scholar and governor, as the author of the *Nican mopohua*, which because of its use of the name Guadalupe he dates to 1556. The purpose of the *Nican mopohua* was to re-Indianize the image as a means of exalting and affirming the Indians. It was also intended to show the Indians the special relationship that the Virgin had established with them. Montúfar, in turn, embraced the devotion as a means of removing the Indians from the influence of the mendicants, particularly the Franciscans, and bringing them under the control of the hierarchy. Hence the archbishop was the person responsible for the placing of the image—surreptitiously, says O'Gorman.[9]

O'Gorman's assertion that the archbishop saw the devotion as a means of gaining control over the Indians would be plausible were it not for the fact that the devotion of 1555 to 1556 was not the same as that known today. Although he assumes a continuum between the two, the former had nothing to do with the apparition account, as this study will make clear. O'Gorman's work also relies on other dubious assumptions. First among these would be his acceptance of Valeriano's authorship of the *Nican mopohua* and his dating it to 1556. Another is that the Spaniards imposed the name Guadalupe on the chapel in an act of deliberate appropriation. A third is that there was conscious manipulation in the founding and growth of both the shrine and devotion. I argue that Valeriano did not write the *Nican mopohua* and that it received its first and final form from Laso de la Vega or his native helpers. The obvious confusion that surrounded the origins of the shrine and the contradictory accounts of it make it clear that it is perilous to make absolute statements about how it originated. With regard to motivations, my study reveals not a deliberate or planned implementation of the devotion but a confused evolution prior to 1648. There is evidence that the shrine became identified with Guadalupe around 1556, but O'Gorman exaggerates the deliberate nature of the Spaniards' appropriation of the image and devotion.

The view of Guadalupe as a unifying and integrating force in Mexican society can be found in an interesting study by Donald Kurtz, "The Virgin of Guadalupe and the Politics of Becoming Human." Writing from an anthropological-sociological perspective, he sees the apparition/devotion as an important part of the dialectical process whereby the Indians gained a basic humanity (a position taken three centuries before by Becerra Tanco and Florencia) and the two separate societies of New Spain moved toward forming a whole that was more than its constituent parts. Although he says that "based on circumstantial evidence a case can be made that the Virgin of Guadalupe was a contrivance of the good bishop," he absolves Zumárraga of any conscious complicity in a hoax.[10] Kurtz sees the devotion as stemming from the contact of two societies disrupted or altered by the events of the conquest. His key concept is "liminality," by which populations "strive toward reorganization of society and establishment of normal modes of social action."[11] In this context "the Virgin of Guadalupe symbol was anticipatory to new dialectic processes."[12] Thus for Zumárraga and the Franciscans the Virgin of Guadalupe became a symbol to be used in the struggle to establish Indian humanness.

Kurtz offers intriguing insights into the mythical meaning of Guadalupe, but unfortunately they do not rest on a solid historical foundation. He accepts the tradition of the apparitions uncritically and bases his conclusions on it. He also makes some erroneous assertions; for example, that Zumárraga informed people in Spain of the event during his stay in 1532, that he actively supported the cult on his return, that he boasted that "in the five years following the apparition six times as many Indians were baptized as in the seven preceding years," that he collected money in New Spain to build the shrine, that he carried the image to it, and that he appointed Juan Diego as attendant at the shrine.[13] He makes the astounding statement that Cortés "had been appointed a judge of the second Audiencia" and that "he assisted Zumárraga in raising funds for the construction of the shrine of the Virgin."[14] He also associates the Franciscans with the propagation of the devotion in the sixteenth century. These assertions are demonstrably wrong and seriously undermine Kurtz's conclusions.

The differing impact that Guadalupe had on Indians and Spaniards in the process of constituting modern Mexican society has been studied by Patricia Harrington and Ena Campbell. According to Harrington, "At the beginning the Virgin of Guadalupe meant quite different things to these two groups. The Indians read the image as restoring to them a coherent world. To the Spaniards . . . she represented Roman Catholic orthodoxy and a continuation of Spanish traditions."[15] The cult of Guadalupe was closely associated with that of Tonantzin, whom Harrington describes as a relatively benevolent deity despite her demand for human sacrifice. "Teteoinnan, the Mother of the Gods, also called Toci and Tonantzin, was the patron of physicians and mid-wives, female fortune-tellers, and sweat houses—a goddess of birth, health, and the future."[16] Though the Guadalupe image was primarily Spanish in character, the devotion was overwhelmingly Indian in the beginning. It filled a void in the Indians' lives following the total disruption of the conquest. "[Miguel] Sánchez saw in Guadalupe a sign not of the apocryphal [sic] battle of the last days, but of the birth of a new world in the Mexican nation."[17] The sun and moon of Revelation 12 represented the apocalyptic and millennial aspirations of the criollos, but "to the Indians the same symbolism of sun and moon evoked not biblical prophecies, but the Aztec cyclical cosmogony with its expectation of periodic cataclysmic doom and rebirth. In the chaos and destruction of the colonial period, the image of Guadalupe/Tonantzin represented to the Indians a promise that the Great Goddess who guards over death and birth would shelter them and guarantee a new cycle of life."[18]

Campbell poses an important and basic question. "Why, then, was Guadalupe accepted so readily by the Indians? How did this figure, who was once identified with the religion of the conquerors, become a tutelary symbol for both the Indian and the Spanish populations?"[19] The answer was to be found in the fact that the Spaniards immediately identified Guadalupe with the Extremaduran Virgin of the same name, whereas the Indians saw her "as the miraculous incarnation of the Aztec earth and fertility goddess, Tonantsi [sic], Our Lady Mother, who, like Guadalupe, was associated with the moon."[20] Campbell pictures Tonantzin as a totally benevolent deity, in contrast with the destructive and malevolent Coatlicue. In this interpretation the temple to Tonantzin at Tepeyac was erected not by the Aztecs but by the Totonacs, who had grown weary of Aztec human sacrifice. In contrast with Harrington's assertion that Tonantzin demanded human sacrifice, Campbell says that Tonantzin "preferred the sacrifice of birds and small animals."[21] In her incarnation as Guadalupe "the loving Tonantsi continued to defend her children against the wrath of the Judeo-Christian god." "In a symbolic sense, Guadalupe represents the Indian mother goddess in the third and most benevolent transformation."[22] Thus Guadalupe as the new Tonantzin becomes the binding force of the Mexican nation. "As mother, protectress, and preserver of life, health, and happiness, the combined image of Guadalupe/Tonantsi transforms and binds together the diverse cultural streams of Mexican society at the level of their highest common, symbolic denominator."[23] She thus accepts the assertion that mass conversions followed the apparitions in 1531.

Like similar interpretations, those of Harrington and Campbell encounter difficulties vis-à-vis the historical evolution of Guadalupe. The very existence of a shrine or temple at Tepeyac dedicated to Tonantzin is open to question, as is the nature and identity of the mother goddess herself. If indeed Guadalupe became the binding force of the new nation, she did so not in 1531 but two hundred years later. My research shows clearly that for the first century of its existence, beginning in 1648, the devotion to Guadalupe based on the apparition story was a criollo phenomenon in which any Indian role was tangential. There was no spontaneous surge of Indians toward Guadalupe/Tonantzin in the sixteenth century, no mass conversions, no consoling acceptance of a new mother goddess. Rather, there seems to have been a more or less planned effort to propagate the devotion among the Indians only in the eighteenth century.

A revisionist approach has also been taken by Jeannette Favrot Peterson, who, in a study of the iconography of Guadalupe, deals with the vexed question of whether Guadalupe was a symbol of liberation or submission. Peterson's purpose is to challenge two myths, "first, that [Guadalupe's] cult spontaneously welded together all the strata of New Spain: and second, that Guadalupe from the sixteenth century on served as a symbol of freedom for the oppressed native populations. . . . Not until the nineteenth century did Guadalupe's cult gain in strength among a largely disenfranchised population. Moreover, only in the twentieth century has her image taken on new meaning compatible with her title 'Mother of the Mexicans.'"[24] By surveying the iconography of Guadalupe, she shows the criollo nature of the devotion and the ways in which it was manipulated by various classes to advance their interests. "For creole intellectuals, Guadalupe's apparition was an opportune sign that the Virgin Mary had chosen Mexico as her 'favored city' and Mexicans as the elect."[25] The criollos had an ambivalent attitude toward the Indians' role: the fictive Indian of the glories of the past Aztec empire versus the drunken, loutish native of criollo stereotypes. The Virgin, however, remained an ambiguous figure. On the one hand she encouraged the status quo, but in the revolution of 1810 "her image was used to symbolize the insurgent movement."[26] Peterson believes that it was only with the separation of Church and state that Guadalupe passed from being an institutional symbol to that of a popular culture. As will be apparent throughout, I reach similar conclusions.

In his study "The Virgin of Guadalupe: An Inquiry into the Social History of Marian Devotion," which has already been cited, William Taylor examines Guadalupe in the wider context of Marian devotion in the late colonial and early national periods. He rightly sees Guadalupe as a predominantly criollo devotion, "more popular among creole clergymen of the mid-17th century than among Indian villagers."[27] It was these clergymen who consciously sought to propagate the devotion among the Indians in the latter half of the eighteenth century. He finds evidence for this in judicial records where "from the late 1750s and 1760s on, concerted efforts by curates in rural Indian parishes of central Mexico to establish or increase popular veneration of the image of the Mexican Guadalupe appear."[28] The priests who appeared in these records as devotees of Guadalupe had been trained in Mexico City, had published sermons on the Virgin of Guadalupe, and had listed sermons at Tepeyac in their professional resumés. "Even at the end of the colonial period the prophetic appeal to an Indian past in the Guadalupe cult was promoted mainly by creole intellectuals."[29] Taylor is cautious about connecting the Mexican Guadalupe with any pre-Hispanic devotion. "Too little is known at present about the cult of Tonantzin to elaborate on this relationship."[30]

One of his most important contributions is a meticulous examination of selected baptismal records from approximately 1750 to 1840 to find a correlation between naming patterns and devotion to the Mexican Guadalupe. His conclusion is that in the latter half of the eighteenth century there was a growth in popularity among non-Indians but not among Indians. He also deals with the question of the Virgin Mary as a contradictory symbol of revolution and resignation. "The Virgin's messages of accommodation and liberation were not perceived as contradictory or as simple alternatives. The importance of each message waxed and waned, but neither meaning disappeared."[31] My research substantiates Taylor's conclusions.

In light of the numerous critiques and interpretations of Guadalupe, it is not surprising that many studies have been apologetic in nature; that is, defensive of the apparitions and hence of traditional Mexican values against critics and skeptics, modernists and anticlericals. One of the earliest and best analyses of the sources of the Guadalupe legend was made by the Mexican scholar and linguist Primo Feliciano Velázquez in his book *La aparición de Santa María de Guadalupe*, first published in 1931. Written from an apparitionist stance, it is a measured and balanced work, probably the most scholarly one to emerge from the apparitionist school. Another defender was the noted Nahuatl scholar Angel María Garibay K., who included analyses of sources, especially the Nahuatl *anales*, in several of his journal articles and books and wrote an especially defensive article for *The New Catholic Encyclopedia*. As will be seen in the course of this work, I disagree with many of his conclusions.

Other writers of this century, including Antonio Pompa y Pompa and Jesús García Gutiérrez, have risen to the defense of the apparition account. An especially stalwart defender of Guadalupe as a national and religious symbol has been the Jesuit historian Mariano Cuevas (1879–1949). Unfortunately, I feel that Cuevas's contributions to the controversy have not been positive. In addition to using sharply personal comments about critics of the apparition tradition, he showed himself to be tendentious and often careless in his interpretation and use of sources. He was responsible for perpetuating and popularizing the single greatest and most lasting error in the history of the tradition, the identification of Antonio Valeriano as the author of the *Nican mopohua*. In the controversy over the Guadalupe tradition, his assertions must be taken with great caution.[32] Within more recent years the foremost champion has been Lauro López Beltrán, who has been responsible for the publication of numerous works on Guadalupe, including a reprint of the original work of Miguel Sánchez. In 1982 Ernesto de la Torre Villar and Ramiro Navarro de Anda, both sympathetic to the apparitionist school, published the *Testimonios históricos guadalupanos*, which, despite lacunae and unevenness, reproduces the most important sources of the controversy.

As a religious symbol, Guadalupe also has ambiguities. A central feature of this symbolism has been the claim that there was a vast conversion of Indians in the aftermath of the apparitions in 1531.[33] There is no evidence for such an assertion, yet, like a similar claim that Guadalupe was an example of guided syncretism whereby the early missionaries enticed the Indians to Christianity, it shows no signs of dying out. Typical of the substitution argument is George C. Vaillant's statement, endorsed by Luis Weckmann, that the cult of Tonantzin, the mother goddess of the Mexica, "was transferred to the Virgin by the early missionaries, an act exemplifying their intelligent procedures in evangelizing the Aztecs."[34] Michael Candelaria echoes that claim. "Our Lady of Guadalupe was originally the Aztec fertility goddess Tonantzin, whom the Spanish conquerors baptized as Mary, the mother of Jesus, in an effort to evangelize and subjugate the Indians."[35] The fact that such assertions run contrary to the known evidence will probably not hinder their continued popularity.

Some nineteenth-century churchmen raised belief in Guadalupe almost to the status of a dogma, and at least one, the Jesuit Esteban Antícoli, maintained that no one who denied the apparitions could consider himself or herself a good Catholic. From the beginning, however, the institutional Church was cautious in giving formal approbation. There was a delay of some ninety years between the first request for a special feast and mass and the rather guarded concession of 1754. The real growth in ecclesiastical support came after 1895, the year in which the papacy permitted the Mexican hierarchy to have a solemn coronation of the image. In 1910 Pope Pius X proclaimed the Virgin of Guadalupe the patroness of all Latin America, and twenty-five years later Pius XI extended the patronage to the Philippines. This process accelerated in 1945, when Pius XII called her the Queen of Mexico and Empress of the Americas and declared that "according to the tradition, brushes that were not from here below left a most sweet image painted on the mantle of the poor Juan Diego."[36] The most definitive seal of approval was the beatification of Juan Diego in 1990. That event, a benevolent response to the desires of the Mexican hierarchy, raises serious questions about the procedures that were followed and the historical analyses that underlay them.[37] Equally troubling is the question of motivation in beatifying Juan Diego at such a late period in the history of the apparitions.

A contemporary view of the religious significance of Guadalupe is typified by Virgil Elizondo.

> In her, the people experience acceptance, dignity, love and protection . . . they dare to affirm life even when all others deny them life. . . . Were it not for Our Lady of Guadalupe there would be no Mexican or Mexican American people today. The great Mexican nations had been defeated by the Spanish invasion which came to a violent and bloody climax in 1521. The native peoples who had not been killed no longer wanted to live. Everything of value to them, including their gods, had been destroyed. Nothing was worth living for. With this colossal catastrophe, their entire past became irrelevant. . . . In sharp contrast to the total rupture with the past which was initiated by the conquest-evangelisation enterprise, Guadalupe provided the necessary *sense of continuity* which is basic to human existence. . . . Out of their own past and in close continuity with it, something truly sacred was now emerging.[38]

With all his hyperbole and historical inaccuracies, Elizondo exemplifies a contemporary Catholic attitude toward Guadalupe. This approach requires an uncritical acceptance of the Black Legend of Spanish cruelty, exploitation, and destruction in New Spain. In contrast, the Virgin of Tepeyac stands for indigenism and the continuity of religious thought. In this interpretation she brought the Church to a realization of the humanity of the Indians and a respect for their religious attitudes. The Indian who is a commoner (*macehualli*) becomes "my youngest child" (*noxocoyouh*) to the Virgin. Guadalupe symbolizes the reversal of roles: the woman who instructs the male-dominated Church, the Indian who evangelizes the Spaniard, the bishop who kneels in tears before the woman and the native, the conquered who vanquish the conqueror. "For not only did she call a poor man, native to the soil upon which she appeared, to stand before the colonizer and claim his personal and cultural legitimacy; but she spoke to him in his native Náhuatl language, one which was slowly being stolen from him and his people, along with their political, social and religious institutions. . . . Thus she restored to a conquered people a sense of worth and dignity, and laid for them a foundation for a revived religious and national identity."[39] Similar examples of this viewpoint can be multiplied endlessly, and many show the same sublime disregard for historical accuracy. Thus Guadalupe has been adapted to the needs of contemporary agendas. In a very real sense the Virgin of Tepeyac is reinvented by successive generations to meet the demands of a new orthodoxy.

Though this approach has obvious affinities with liberation theology, Guadalupe has not been adopted as a major symbol by liberation theologians. This may be due to the inherent ambiguities in the symbolism or because others, like Bartolomé de las Casas, are more potent symbols. Pope John Paul II somewhat tentatively allied himself with the liberationist symbolism in his address to the Mexican nation on the occasion of Juan Diego's beatification, 6 May 1990. The theme was explicitly embraced by journalist Peter Hebblethwaite, who saw in the beatification of Juan Diego an affirmation of liberation theology. His analysis, however, is weakened by demonstrable errors, such as describing Cuauhtitlan as a "Mexico City shantytown" and Nahuatl as "this proscribed 'pagan' language" and "the banned language of the humiliated people."[40]

Many of the interpretations cited above are flawed precisely because they rely on an inadequate or erroneous historical base. Divorced from that base they lose their credibility. Hence the essential question is that of the historical reality of the apparition account and its message. Are these indeed factual events or are they legends and pious invention? Is there an authentic tradition that connects the modern devotion with its manifold meanings to events that actually occurred in 1531? These questions cannot be avoided, as Mauro Rodríguez, Juan Bautista Muñoz, and some liberation theologians have attempted to do, by saying that the symbolism and meaning of the devotion are independent of the objective reality of the traditional account.[41] In Guadalupe history and symbolism are inextricably intertwined. Without that history the symbolism loses any objectivity it may have had and is at the mercy of propagandists and special interests. The basis must be examined closely, and that is something that has not yet been done in any comprehensive way.

Thirty years ago Charles Gibson observed of Guadalupe, "A complete history remains to be written."[42] More recently, Taylor has written, "More archival research needs to be done on how and where the cult of Guadalupe came into existence, who believed, what changed, and when."[43] This work is intended to fill this void in Guadalupan studies. It is not a study of the impact of guadalupanismo on Mexican society, culture, or national identity. The approach is historiographic rather than sociological, anthropological, or iconographic. It is a monograph, a species of detective work, that seeks to trace the development of the apparition tradition through an examination of its sources. For that reason a generally chronological framework has been followed so that the weight of the evidence, or lack thereof, may be clear. The study ends at 1797, with the letters of Servando Teresa de Mier to Juan Bautista Muñoz and the effective formulation of the antiapparitionist arguments. That year marks the close of the formative period of the tradition and the arguments against it.

The story of the development of the Guadalupe tradition is complex and tortuous in the extreme. There are gaps and lacunae in the sources, conflicting testimonies, and unanswered questions at almost every stage of the growth of the apparition tradition. This book is a journey through those stages, one that begins by examining the formation of the society in which tradition has placed the events of Tepeyac, that is, New Spain ten years after the Spanish conquest.

1

New Spain in 1531

When Fernando Cortés walked down the causeway to the Mexica capital
of Tenochtitlan on 8 November 1519 to meet the Emperor Moteucçoma II
Xocoyotzin, neither one could have foreseen the final outcome. Within two
years, after overcoming incredible obstacles, the Extremaduran captain and his
small force, aided by the Tlaxcalans and other native allies, would overthrow
the empire of the Mexica and establish Spanish rule in its place. On 13 August
1521, after a long and brutal siege, Tenochtitlan fell to the invaders, and that
part of modern Mexico was in Spanish hands.[1]

The Spanish conquest of Mexico was not, as it is often depicted on a popular
level, the wanton destruction of an ideal native society by an imperialistic, tech-
nologically more advanced one. It should rather be seen as the clash of two
imperialisms. The so-called Aztec empire, which was actually a confederation
of three Nahua city-states with Tenochtitlan as the leader, was militaristic and
expansionist. By a series of conquests it had subjugated most of present-day
central Mexico, with the exception of Tlaxcala and the Tarascan kingdom of
Michoacan. From these subject peoples it extracted tribute, often in the form
of victims for human sacrifice. These peoples were restive and some proved willing, with varying degrees of enthusiasm, to ally themselves with the enemy of
their enemy. Even with their help, however, the Spanish conquest was a prolonged, harrowing, and bloody affair. By 1531 only the Tarascans of Michoacan
and the Maya of southern Mexico, Yucatan, and Guatemala remained free of
Spanish rule. This rule ended just north of Mexico City. Only with the silver
strikes of midcentury were the Spaniards lured farther north.

The civil and military administration of the conquered territories was given
to Cortés when the crown appointed him governor and captain general in 1522.
A farsighted man with a vision of a Spanish-Indian empire in the New World,
Cortés began the reconstruction of the demolished Mexica capital. The result
was an emerging Spanish renaissance city called Mexico, a name that in colonial
times referred exclusively to the city district. The kingdom itself was called

New Spain.[2] Cortés also introduced the *encomienda* against the wishes of the crown. This was a system for rewarding the principal conquistadores by allotting them native communities from which they had the right to receive tribute both in kind and in labor. In return they were supposed to see to the evangelization of the Indians, especially by founding and supporting churches, and to constitute a militia in times of public disturbance. The encomienda was subject to appalling abuses and had already contributed to the destruction of the Indians in the Caribbean. Many humanitarians were beginning to raise an outcry against it, and the crown was uneasy with the power that it gave the conquistadores. It was brought under royal control by the end of the sixteenth century.

In 1524 Cortés left Mexico City in order to put down a supposed rebellion in Honduras. It was a costly error on his part. The trip to the south was beset by terrible difficulties and ultimately proved futile. In his absence his enemies, proclaiming that he was dead, came into the ascendancy and inaugurated an orgy of corruption and persecution of his followers. Order was restored with Cortés's return in 1526, but his position had been seriously undermined by a stream of denunciations forwarded to Spain. In order to regain his standing with the crown he left New Spain in 1527 and reached the mother country in the following year. He returned to New Spain two years later with the title of the marquess of the valley of Oaxaca, together with lands and encomiendas that made him the wealthiest man in the colony. Much to his disappointment, however, he no longer governed the kingdom he had won for Castile.

Already in 1527 the crown had appointed as the ruling body of New Spain a combination of law court and ruling council known to history as the first *audiencia*. Two of the original four judges died before beginning their rule and the other two proved inept. Effective control fell to the audiencia president, Nuño de Guzmán, one of the most venal and ruthless men in the history of New Spain. Fearing that he was losing royal favor, he led a military expedition to the west and north in the hope that success in the field would erase the memory of his crimes elsewhere. Beginning in 1529 he left a trail of blood and pillage through modern Jalisco and southern Sinaloa. He founded the outpost cities of Culiacan and Guadalajara (the latter named for his native city in Spain) and was still governor of the territory in 1531. In 1538 he would be recalled to Spain to spend the rest of his life under a form of house arrest. His conquests and settlements marked the northernmost limit of the Spanish advance until the great silver discoveries in Zacatecas at midcentury drew the Spaniards northward.

The Spanish population of New Spain in 1531 consisted predominantly of peninsulars, that is, persons born in the mother country. Very early, however, there emerged another class of Spaniards, the criollos, persons of Spanish or European blood who had been born in the New World. Though the only distinction between a peninsular and a criollo was in the place of birth, others were added by society. In general the peninsulars, no matter how lowly their station may have been in the mother country, felt themselves superior to the criollos. This snobbery was based on a conviction that the criollos were racially impure and physically and morally degenerate and was often justified by a deterministic view that life and the climate in New Spain had an intrinsically debilitating effect physically, mentally, and morally. A Spanish physician told the English Dominican Thomas Gage that "the climate of those parts had this effect, to produce a fair shew but little matter or substance," and Spanish cosmographer López de Velasco believed that the criollos would deteriorate in mind and body until they were indistinguishable from the Indians.[3]

The criollos were commonly excluded from the highest positions in Church and state, such as viceroy or archbishop of Mexico. The "sons of the land," as they called themselves, resented their subordinate status. The antagonism between the criollos and the peninsulars grew toward the end of the sixteenth century. The peninsulars regarded the criollos as presumptuous social climbers with wrongheaded aspirations to nobility. The enmity was strong in the religious orders, particularly the Franciscans, which by the second half of the century had a large proportion of criollos. These were viewed by the peninsulars as detrimental to the religious life, unable to live it rigorously, and given to license and laziness. By the middle of the seventeenth century this burgeoning *criollismo*, or criollo consciousness, had become articulated into what was almost a national identity. In the story of the Guadalupe apparitions the criollos would find a justification for an extravagant sense of divine election and messianic destiny.

The subject peoples adjusted in various ways to a new life and religion. Culture shock, obviously, was rampant. The disruption caused by the change of life, law, religion, language, calendar, and even proper names, had a devastating impact on much of the population. So also did the many epidemics that arrived with the conquerors. The use of alcohol, closely controlled under the Mexica rulers, became a major problem, if contemporary sources are to be believed. As Gibson has said, "In terms of their own tradition, Indians under Christianity were living a life deficient in controls."[4] Yet at the same time, as current research is showing, the discontinuity was not as marked as is often thought. In outlying areas the first Spaniards the natives saw were missionaries and civil servants, not conquistadores. There was a strong continuity in local political and social institutions, with the result that villages and towns often retained basic preconquest political structures under the rule of native dynasties or oligarchies. No serious attempt was made to suppress the native languages or impose Spanish. In preconquest times Nahuatl had served as a lingua franca in much of what is modern Mexico, and it continued to be dominant among the natives after the conquest. The missionary friars adapted the Latin alphabet to form written Nahuatl, and an elite of educated native scholars, teachers, chroniclers, and notaries took to writing with skill and exuberance. Frances Karttunen and James Lockhart have categorized three major stages in the evolution of the Nahuatl language after the conquest. Stage 1, roughly from 1519 until 1545/50, was characterized by little change in Nahuatl and few borrowings from Spanish. In Stage 2, approximately 1545/50 to 1640/50, Spanish nouns appeared as loan words incorporated into Nahuatl, but there was little other impact. Stage 3, 1640/50 to the present, saw a full range of change, of which the distinctive feature was the borrowing of verbs according to a set formula. Lockhart has also expanded the implication of these categories to fields other than language, for example, situating the Guadalupe devotion in Stage 3.[5]

In the Spanish imperial system, Christianity was an essential accompaniment to conquest. The conquering and colonizing ventures were as much missionary endeavors as military ones. The effective evangelization of New Spain began with the arrival of the Franciscans. Pedro de Gante (Peter of Ghent) and two companions were the first, in 1523. Fray Pedro was a Fleming and is often described as an illegitimate kinsman of Charles I, the king of Spain.[6] He would eventually undertake some of the most important ventures of the colonial period in the education of the Indians. In 1524 twelve Franciscans, under the leadership of fray Martín de Valencia, landed at Veracruz and walked the entire distance to Mexico City. The number, of course, was highly symbolic, and they became known as "The Twelve" or "The Twelve Apostles." One of them, fray Toribio de Benavente, saw the natives pointing to his tattered habit and exclaiming "motolinía." Told that the word meant "poor person," he took it as his surname and was henceforth known as Toribio de Motolinía. He achieved fame both as a missionary and as a historian of the Indies. When the friars arrived in Mexico City, the Indians were astounded to see Cortés and other conquistadores kneel to kiss their hands and the hems of their robes. What Robert Ricard called the "Spiritual Conquest of Mexico" had begun.

The mendicant orders played the major role in the evangelization of the newly conquered land. The Franciscans branched out from Mexico City very early after the conquest and soon evangelized large areas in the central plateau. They also took the lead in developing programs for preparing missionaries, especially in the native languages. The Dominicans, whose first arrivals also numbered twelve, reached New Spain in 1526. Their presence was less extensive and was centered in two areas, the valley of Mexico, including Puebla and Morelos, and the Zapotec and Mixtec lands, with the city of Oaxaca as their center. The Augustinians, the third major group of friars, came seven years later and had to content themselves with those localities that the other two orders had not yet occupied.

The diocesan structure—bishops, chapters, and diocesan, or secular, clergy—lagged behind that of the religious. The first bishopric in New Spain was erected in Tlaxcala in 1526, among the people whose support made the

Spanish conquest possible, with the Dominican Julián Garcés as bishop. Although it was the first chronologically, it yielded pride of place to Mexico City, whose first bishop was fray Juan de Zumárraga. In 1531 the diocesan structure was still inchoate. The missionary enterprise was dominated by the mendicants, who created what Ricard called the "Church of friars."[7] Later in the century the impact of the Catholic Reformation and the centrist policies of the Spanish crown strengthened the bishops. The friars, however, remained strong, and the hostility between them and the bishops seriously hampered the work of evangelization.

The great Spanish humanitarian movement of the sixteenth century was already launched on its crusade by 1531. It was inaugurated by the Dominican Antonio de Montesinos, who in a ringing sermon delivered on the island of Española in December 1511 condemned the Spaniards for their oppression of the Indians. The dispute that followed led to the first attempt at a legal alleviation of the natives' lot, the Laws of Burgos of 1512 to 1513. Although well intentioned, they had the unfortunate result of fastening the encomienda system on the Indies. In 1514 the movement received its foremost champion when Bartolomé de las Casas (1484–1566) underwent a conversion to the Indians' cause. He became an active lobbyist on their behalf at the Spanish court and undertook a number of experiments in peaceful conversion, unaccompanied by military conquest. In 1531, however, the pro-Indian movement was still in its early stages.

The religion preached to the newly conquered peoples was Castilian Roman Catholicism. The nationalistic modifier "Castilian" is essential to understanding religion in colonial Mexico. It was the religious system of a specific area of the Catholic world as it existed prior to the reforms of the Council of Trent (1545–1563), the reforming popes, or the founding of the Jesuits. Untouched by the religious upheavals following the revolt of Martin Luther in 1517, it reflected the nature, genius, and shortcomings of the people of Castile.

Spanish Catholicism, like the Spanish character itself, was molded during the seven-century struggle to drive the Moors (Arab and Berber Muslims from North Africa) from Iberian soil. In 711 the Moors, newly converted to Islam, invaded the Visigothic kingdom of Spain and within seven years had conquered all but a small northern area. In 718 the Christians (they did not call themselves Spaniards in their struggle with the infidel) began the long and costly process of recovery, now known as the *reconquista*. By the thirteenth century it was essentially complete. In the course of this struggle Catholicism and Spanish identity became fused both in reality and in myth. Militancy, a crusading spirit, intolerance, and the use of force for religious ends were among the legacies of the reconquest.

Like Catholicism throughout the world, the Church in Castile was structured and hierarchical. In the cities bishops reigned as spiritual, and sometimes civil, leaders. The two richest dioceses in the country were Seville and Toledo. The latter, the richest of all, had at the beginning of the sixteenth century "19,283 vassals, revenues of over 30,000 ducats, and a standing military force of over 2,000 men distributed in twenty fortified towns or castles in the arch- bishopric."[8] Below the bishops was a complex hierarchy composed of chapters, canons, chaplains, and parishes with their pastors and curates. The clergy had a clear status in society and, in spite of rather widespread anticlericalism, pres- tige. Many were graduates of the great Spanish universities, such as Salamanca and Valladolid, often with degrees in canon or civil law. Bishops and clerics frequently served the crown as royal officials, while others, especially outside the great cities, were often poorly educated or even illiterate.

Religion in Castile tended to be strongly local, especially in the rural areas.[9] It centered around the village, with its festivals and traditions, concerned more with devotion than dogma. In general ordinary Castilians were not well in- structed in their faith, which was often a folk religion mingled with supersti- tion and confined to the knowledge of a few prayers. There was little systematic instruction, and in the rural areas sermons were rare. When the Council of Trent legislated the preaching of sermons on Sundays, it was widely regarded as an intolerable innovation. Religion was often externalized and consisted of certain actions which, if repeated frequently enough or in the right way, would produce the desired result. On the other hand, the mystical element was strong and during the course of the sixteenth century would produce some of the greatest religious literature of modern times. Of special importance were the confraternities (cofradías) that were found throughout Castile. These brother- hoods sponsored charitable endeavors, founded and maintained chapels, pro- vided support and security for members, and gave townsfolk a strong identifi- cation with their religion.

Cult centered on local devotions. Attendance at mass was casual in a way that might shock a modern Catholic. People often walked about the church during services (there were no pews and few chairs, except for the upper classes), carrying on animated conversations and sometimes making assignations. Pil- grimages (romerías) and celebrations of saints' days were as important as the mass. Devotion was directed primarily to the Virgin Mary and the local patron saint. Christ was a more distant figure, often seen as a threatening judge whose wrath was turned aside by the tender and protective Virgin. Mary represented a compassionate approach to religion in contrast with her son, whose anger was directed toward a sinful world. In New Spain she was sometimes depicted in the Trinity, giving birth to the Holy Spirit.[10] As Allison Coudert has observed, "For many Catholics the real Trinity consisted of God, Christ, and Mary. Some went even farther. In the fifteenth century people kept statuettes of the virgin that opened to reveal the Trinity within."[11]

The Indians' reaction to Christianity varied, ranging from opposition to resignation, cryptopaganism, enthusiastic conversion, and multitudinous forms of adjustment. The Mexica, who had traditionally accepted gods from conquered peoples into their pantheon, did not actively resist Christianity, though they had difficulty in understanding the exclusive claims of the Christian god. Some form of religious syncretism or adaptation became common. By deliberate policy, formally enunciated at the First Mexican Provincial Council of 1555 though accepted much earlier, the Church evangelized the natives of New Spain in their own languages. This required a wholesale linguistic and cultural preparation for the missionaries. The Franciscans took the lead in language studies and in ethnohistorical studies designed to show the missionaries how to combat the evils of the old religions. The sixteenth century saw the publication of numerous instructional grammars (*artes*), dictionaries, catechisms, confessional manuals (*confesionarios*), and dramas. Even today the Nahuatl works of Andrés de Olmos, Bernardino de Sahagún, and Alonso de Molina are indispensable for the researcher.

The challenge posed by the native languages involved more than just translating prayers and sermons. The task of rendering Christian European concepts into differing tongues and cultures was daunting enough in itself, but it was made still more so by the fact that the Nahuas and Europeans were separated by a major cognitive and psychological gap. In this regard the Church in New Spain was replicating the experience of the Church in the first four centuries of its existence and the contemporary experience of the Jesuits in China. On a superficial level this challenge was met by simply incorporating Spanish words such as *dios*, *espíritu santo*, or *obispo* into the native languages. Sometimes Spanish and Nahuatl words were joined, as in *tlatoani obispo* (ruler bishop) or *yolli anima* (soul). At other times the missionaries adapted native terms to Christian usage, such as *tlacatecolotl* (person-owl, derived from pre-Hispanic usage) for demon or *mictlan* (land of the dead) for hell, but the results could cause confusion. Whereas the Europeans saw the concepts of order and chaos as antithetical, the Nahuas saw them as part of an ongoing dialectical process. The idea of sin as a personal, willful violation of a divine law that merited punishment was alien to their belief system. It was difficult to find a native word for sin or redemption when those concepts as European Christians understood them were not shared by the natives.[12] As will be seen further on in this work, missionaries like Bernardino de Sahagún and Martín de León condemned the use of certain terms as disguised forms of cryptopaganism.

Present-day research is showing the impact that translation into a native language had on religious belief. The very use of a native word subtly altered the religious concept toward the outlook, mentality, and worldview of the natives. In the case of New Spain this has been called the Nahuatilization of

Christianity.[13] It also carries the implication that the missionaries themselves were affected by these sometimes arcane changes. In the post–Vatican II Church the idea that the evangelizer is in some way evangelized by those to whom he or she preaches has gained some acceptance. In regard to New Spain Burkhart has defined it as "the friar whose sympathies come to lie with the Indians against the colonists and the ecclesiastical hierarchy, against an Old World perceived as corrupt, and who adopts Indian ways in order to fulfill his mission."[14] The missionaries themselves were often unaware of this identification, and consequently their acculturation was unwitting.

One important aspect of religious devotion in both Spain and New Spain was the apparition genre.[15] Stories of appearances by the Virgin Mary or a saint that resulted in the foundation of shrines and chapels were common in sixteenth-century Spain. These stories tended to follow a more or less standard formula, which served as a skeleton or framework, though the accounts varied in details. The Virgin or the saint appeared to an individual and commanded the building of a sanctuary or chapel on the site of the apparition. The recipient, or seer, of the apparition was almost always a poor person, representing the marginalized and helpless in society. In Spain this could be a shepherd, a swineherd, a woodsman, or a charcoal burner. In America the seer was more often an Indian, who not only represented the poor and oppressed but who also, like an Iberian herdsman, was closest to being a "wild" person.[16] Similarly, in modern times, the seer has most often been a child or a young person, usually from humble circumstances.

The visionary was sometimes skeptical in the beginning or, more commonly, fearful of not being believed. The Virgin would identify herself and comfort him (in the majority of cases it was a male) with assurances of motherly love and protection. In most accounts the ecclesiastical and civil authorities were initially skeptical but were converted after a dramatic miracle or sign. "The essential drama of the story is the rejection, then the vindication of the less credible, marginal seer in the face of the skepticism not only of the authorities, but often of their own families. . . . Power structures are surprised and converted; ultimately they assume control of the sacred enterprises they first refused to accept."[17] In this way the humble and marginalized prevailed over the rich and powerful, an idea that has ample precedent in the Bible. Quite often there was a dialogue between the image (or the image and the poor seer) on the one hand and the village or town with its lay and clerical authorities on the other. "In these situations the saint, usually Mary, has to make an effort so that she may eventually be of service to the community. . . . The poor or the powerless have the visions and the eventual imposition of their truth upon the town authorities is a sure way of showing that Mary or the saint has come to serve everybody."[18]

The emphasis in these accounts was almost exclusively on the Virgin or saint, not on God the Father or Christ, who were rarely mentioned. From the twelfth century on the Virgin Mary was identified with the woman of Revelation (Apocalypse) 12 and was often described as emitting a strong light.[19] The person who received the apparition or revelation achieved a degree of local sanctification but usually remained a secondary, even shadowy figure who served primarily as a conduit for the message. He or she rarely became the object of a cult, as has happened in more recent times with Bernadette Soubirous of the Lourdes apparitions or Catherine Labouré of the Miraculous Medal. The primary focus of attention was on the shrine or the image.

These apparitions were social in nature. They centered on the local village, parish, or shrine, usually in rural areas, and were a focus for uniting the people and giving them an identity. The devotions they spawned were also the means of dealing with the uncontrollable forces of nature. The Virgin or the saint, under the specific local patronage, was invoked against sickness, drought, flood, and the other dangers that made rural life precarious. These invocations were carried over to New Spain, especially in regard to epidemics, which were such a destructive part of colonial life. In Spain natural disasters had included raids by Moors, bandits, and unruly nobles; in New Spain they included subjugation and oppression.

Of the myriad apparition stories to be found in the Spanish empire in the sixteenth century, two are important for this study. The first was that of Our Lady of Guadalupe of Extremadura. That area of Spain was home to a large number of conquistadores, including Cortés, Pedro de Alvarado, Gonzalo de Sandoval, and the Pizarros, and provided a disproportionately large percentage of the first settlers of Mexico. The Extremaduran Guadalupe was popular throughout Spain, and the name Guadalupe appeared in Latin America even before 1531—the island of Guadaloupe in the Caribbean was named for this Virgin by Columbus. The story of her apparition followed the standard formula mentioned above, although it existed in several versions.[20] The image was supposed to have been given by Pope Saint Gregory the Great to Saint Leander of Seville. At the time of the Moorish invasion it was hidden in the mountains of Extremadura. It was rediscovered at the end of the thirteenth century by a herdsman or shepherd, who is sometimes given the name Gil Cordero, when he went in search of a stray cow. High in the Guadalupe range he found the cow dead, but as he started to skin it, it jumped up alive. Looking up, he saw the Virgin, who, in some versions, told him of the statue hidden in a nearby cave. He returned to Cáceres with the intention of reporting the wonder to the clerical authorities but was met by his wife, who told him that their son had died. The herdsman went to his home and as he was praying over the boy, the priests arrived for the funeral. The son was immediately returned to life as proof to the authorities of the authenticity of the herdsman's story. Accompanied by a cleric, the herdsman returned to the original site and found the image. In reality, the shrine antedated the story, but the story became associated with it as a miraculous explanation for its origin. A monastery was built at the site; in the sixteenth century it was under the direction of the Hieronymite friars (Jerónimos, the Order of Saint Jerome). The Virgin of Extremadura was to become closely linked to the history of the Virgin of Tepeyac.

The other devotion that had even closer links to the Mexican Guadalupe was that of the Virgin of los Remedios. This became the central devotion of the peninsulars in New Spain because of its association with the conquest. There were many versions of the story of the image.[21] It is a small (twenty-seven centimeters) statuette of Mary with the child Jesus in her left hand and a scepter in her right brought from Spain by one of Cortés's soldiers, who in some versions was named Juan Rodríguez de Villafuente. He carried it in a belt, and it accompanied the Spaniards on their campaigns against the Mexica. It was said that it was the image that Cortés placed in the temple of Huitzilopochtli on the great pyramid in Tenochtitlan. Together with the leather belt it was lost or hidden during the Noche Triste (1 July 1520, the "sad night," when the Spaniards were driven from Tenochtitlan by the Mexica) on the hill called Totoltepec. There it was found among some maguey plants by an Indian cacique named Cecuauhtli (One Eagle), whose Christian name was Juan de Tovar, though other versions say that it was an Indian neophyte or a Spaniard. Some versions of the story placed him among the Mexica warriors on the Noche Triste who were repulsed by a vision of the Virgin Mary in the sky above the Spaniards.[22] Various years were assigned for the discovery of the image: 1540, 1544, 1555.

Tovar took the image to his home, where he kept it for ten years. It then disappeared, but don Juan found it again on the hill where he had originally discovered it. He brought it back to his house, but it fled again. "He returned it to his home, repeating his complaints and asking the image why it was fleeing or what was lacking in his house that caused her discontent, and he was greatly afflicted that the statue did not answer him."[23] To keep the statue at home, and perhaps believing he had not been hospitable enough, he placed food before it. When it disappeared a third time and was found again on the hill, Tovar locked it in a chest. This availed nothing because the same thing happened twice again. (The refusal of images to move from the site where they had been discovered or revealed was a common motif in the apparition genre.)

Tovar consulted a member of the cathedral chapter in Mexico City who after a brief investigation decided that a small chapel should be built on the hill as a home for the Virgin. By 1574 it was in poor condition, and García de Albornoz, a city councilman (regidor) of Mexico City, persuaded the civil cabildo to take over its patronage. This was done, and it soon became a popular devotion under the special patronage of the civil government of Mexico City.

There were other variations of this basic account. One related that the shrine was built at the direct command of the Virgin, who appeared to the Indian.

Another was that Juan de Tovar was working on a church in Tacuba when a beam fell on him and he was fatally injured. The Virgin appeared to him and gave him a belt by which he was instantly healed and which he wore for the rest of his life. The Augustinians believed that this belt had originally belonged to Saint Augustine.[24] Another variation omitted the belt and related that after his injury he was taken to Guadalupe to be healed. There the Virgin appeared to him and after rebuking him for removing her from her house commanded him to build the shrine at Remedios.

Until the middle of the seventeenth century, the two devotions of Remedios and Guadalupe appear to have been closely linked. In the early seventeenth century the poet Angel Betancurt confused the two figures of Juan Diego and Juan de Tovar. In 1698 Agustín Vetancurt gave the name Juan Diego to the discoverer of Remedios, and in the mid–eighteenth century Botturini Benaduci called him Juan Bernardino de Tovar. The fact that the devotion of Remedios originated around midcentury, at a time that many believe also marked the origin of the chapel at Guadalupe, implies an even closer relationship, perhaps even a common provenance. Eventually, however, Remedios became the preferred devotion of the peninsulars and was called La Conquistadora or La Gachupina (in the later colonial period Gachupín was an opprobrious nickname for peninsular Spaniards), while Guadalupe was adopted by the criollos and was called La Criolla.

In summary, New Spain in 1531 was a newly conquered realm that had taken the first steps toward peace and stability. In the north Spanish rule ended just beyond Mexico City. In the south it extended to Chiapas and Guatemala, although the Tarascans of Michoacan and the Maya of Chiapas and Yucatan were still unconquered. Stable, secure, and effective civil government had been introduced by the second audiencia, beginning the process whereby the lawyers would supplant the conquistadores. Cortés was living in Cuernavaca, honored with a noble title and riches but shorn of any authority outside his *marquesado*. Zumárraga held the title of bishop of Mexico and governed as such, though he had not yet been consecrated. The mendicants, armed with missionary privileges from the papacy, were evangelizing the new land with the Castilian form of Roman Catholicism. This was the New Spain in which tradition has situated the story of the apparitions of Our Lady of Guadalupe.

2

The Events of Tepeyac

What many today consider to be the authoritative account of the apparitions of Our Lady of Guadalupe of Mexico, and the one on which most modern versions are based, was published in the year 1649 by the vicar of Guadalupe, a priest named Luis Laso de la Vega. It was written in Nahuatl, the predominant native language of the central plateau, and was titled *Huey tlamahuiçoltica* (By a great miracle, or Very miraculously). The actual description of the apparitions as found in this book is known by its opening words, *Nican mopohua* (Here is recounted). Although a similar account in Spanish had been published the year before by the Oratorian priest Miguel Sánchez, Laso de la Vega's version has become the accepted one, in part because of later claims that it was close to or even contemporaneous with the events narrated. Chapter 7 will deal with these two accounts in more detail. Here it will be enough to give a summary of the apparition account as found in the *Nican mopohua*.

Juan Diego was a recently converted Nahua who lived in the town of Cuauhtitlan.[1] Religious life in New Spain, however, was centered in the Franciscan house at Tlatelolco, where he went for instructions and devotions. On a Saturday in early December 1531, on his way to Tlatelolco, he passed the hill of Tepeyac, where he heard the sound of birds singing.[2] Overwhelmed by the beauty of their song, he thought he might be in the earthly paradise his ancestors had told him about. "Where am I? . . . In that place, then, of which the ancients, our ancestors, told us, in the land of flowers, in the land of abundance? There, then, in the heavenly land?"[3] When the birds' song ceased, he heard himself summoned to the top of the hill by a woman's voice.

On the hilltop he saw a resplendent vision of a woman who identified herself as the Virgin Mary, "the mother of the great true deity God, the giver of life, the creator of people, the lord of the universe, possessor of heaven and earth."[4] Addressing him tenderly, she told him to go to the bishop of Mexico and inform him of her wish that a church be built to her on the site. "I ardently wish and greatly desire that they build my temple for me here, where I will reveal, I will make known, and I will give to people all my love, my compassion, my aid, and my protection, for I am your compassionate mother. . . . There I will hear their weeping and their sorrows in order to remedy and heal all their various afflictions, their sufferings, and their sorrows." Juan Diego went immediately to the bishop's palace in Mexico City, but his audience with Juan de Zumárraga, the first bishop of Mexico, was delayed by the latter's servants. Eventually he was allowed to deliver his message. The bishop put him off, and Juan Diego realized that his words had not been believed. Sorrowfully, he returned to Tepeyac, where he found the Virgin waiting for him. He told her of his lack of success and asked her to send other messengers who would be believed. She, however, directed him to return to Zumárraga on the following day.

On that day, Sunday, he returned to Tlatelolco for mass and instruction. Afterward he went to the episcopal palace and after again experiencing rebuffs by the servants was allowed to enter. He informed Zumárraga of his new commission and was in turn questioned by him in some detail. This time the bishop asked for a sign to prove the truth of the communication. When Juan Diego left, Zumárraga sent his servants to follow him to discover where he went and with whom he spoke. The servants, however, lost him near the causeway leading to Tepeyac. Frustrated and angry, they returned to inform Zumárraga of what had happened.

On Monday Juan Diego did not return to Tepeyac.[5] His uncle, Juan Bernardino, was mortally ill and asked his nephew to summon one of the priests from Tlatelolco to hear his confession and prepare him for death. Very early on Tuesday morning, while it was still dark, Juan Diego left for Tlatelolco. On reaching Tepeyac he took a different route around the hill in order to avoid the Virgin and go directly for the priest. She found him, nevertheless, and he explained the reason for his detour. She replied, "Know, rest very much assured, my youngest child, let nothing whatever frighten you or worry you. Do not be concerned. Do not fear the illness or any illness or affliction. Am I, your mother, not here? Are you not under my shade and my shadow? Am I not your happiness? Are you not in my lap and in my carrying gear? Is there anything more that you need? Do not let anything worry you further or upset you. Do not let your uncle's illness worry you. He will not die of what is now upon him. Rest assured, for he is already well." He in reply asked for a sign to give to the bishop. The Virgin directed him to the top of the hill where he would find "every kind of precious Spanish flower" in a place where flowers did not grow and at a time when they would be out of season.[6] He did as directed and brought the flowers to the Virgin, who placed them in his cloak (*tilmatli*, now commonly called *tilma*). She told him to go to Zumárraga and open it only in his presence.

At the palace the servants again delayed him and attempted to see what was in the cloak. They saw the flowers, but when they tried three times to take some, they found only painted ones. Juan Diego was eventually summoned into Zumárraga's presence, where he told him of his conversation with the Virgin. When he unfolded his tilma, the flowers fell to the floor, and imprinted on the cloak was the picture of the Virgin. Zumárraga and those with him fell to their knees, and the bishop in tears begged forgiveness for his skepticism. He untied the mantle from Juan Diego's neck and carried it into his private oratory. He then made plans for the immediate erection of the chapel at Tepeyac.

Juan Diego returned home to find his uncle fully recovered. Juan Bernardino told of having also seen the Virgin, who healed him and told him of Juan Diego's mission. It was to Juan Bernardino, not Juan Diego, that the Virgin revealed that the title of the chapel was to be "the ever Virgin Saint Mary of Guadalupe." The uncle was taken to see Zumárraga to tell his story, and the two natives stayed in the palace for a few days. Zumárraga moved the image from his oratory to the principal church for public exposition. There the entire city came to venerate it for "no person on earth had painted her precious image."

That is the story as found in the *Nican mopohua*. It is told in typically Nahuatl style: poetic, with many doublets, reverential forms, inversions, and affectionate terms. It is a beautiful and poignant tale that has captivated generations, even of those who are not believers. Additional details are to be found in other parts of Laso de la Vega's book, and still more would be added by other authors.

The Structure of the Account

Though the foundational account is written in Nahuatl, the story itself is European in form and substance. It follows closely the standard genre of miraculous appearances: the relationship between the apparition and the shrine, the initial skepticism, the fearfulness of the visionary, the need for Mary to identify herself and make an effort to be of service, miraculous signs (including a cure), and a happy ending that culminates in the building of a shrine. It also reflects some other characteristics that were sometimes found in such accounts, such as the supernatural lighting, the blooming of flowers out of season, and the fact that the Virgin appears without the Christ child. As in similar accounts Mary shows herself to be compassionate and affectionate toward the poor and oppressed, in this case the Indians. In keeping with the standard form of apparition accounts, God the Father and Christ play no roles in the story of the Guadalupe apparitions. In addition, there are Nahua elements in the descriptions of the apparition, especially the flowers, turquoise, and beautiful music.[7] There are two important variations from the standard genre. The first is that the image is not found or discovered but is divinely imprinted, a fact that would assume great importance for the criollos. The second is that the Virgin's message is not eschatological or a call to repentance but rather one of compassion and comfort.

From the point of view of structure, the story of Juan Bernardino seems to stand apart from the main story. The introductory sentence of the *Nican mopohua* states that it is an account of the Virgin's apparition to Juan Diego and the appearance of the image to Zumárraga but says nothing about the uncle. The Virgin's appearance to Juan Bernardino is narrated briefly and indirectly and lacks both the dialogue and details of her appearances to Juan Diego. It parallels the cure of the son in the story of the Extremaduran Guadalupe and compensates for a lack in the Juan Diego account, that is, the naming of the image as Saint Mary of Guadalupe. The cure of Juan Bernardino is an extra, almost superfluous sign that lacks the social dimension of the miracle of the roses and image. If the story of Juan Bernardino is removed from the account and the Virgin's gift of the flowers is united to the events of Sunday, what remains is an entirely logical and comprehensible story in the standard apparition genre, even without the naming of the shrine. Some early traditions associated Tepeyac with a cure of Juan de Tovar, the discoverer of the image of Remedios. It is possible, therefore, that the *Nican mopohua* was a conflation of various traditions, one of which was originally a variation of the story of Remedios, that were somewhat awkwardly combined. This, of course, is speculation, and it will probably be impossible ever to prove it conclusively.

As in other apparition stories, the visionary is a rather undefined figure. Few details are given about Juan Diego, though it would be reasonable to think that he would be the object of much interest and attention. Additional information about Juan Diego's life before and after the apparitions comes from many sources and survives in varying traditions. One was that Juan Diego was born in Cuauhtitlan around 1474 and that his native name was Quauhtlatoatzin (The Eagle Speaks).[8] He and his wife, María Lucía, were baptized in 1524. After hearing a particularly effective sermon by Motolinía they decided to live together in celibacy, though the biographical data given in the *Huey tlamahui-çoltica* states that Juan Diego was a lifelong virgin. According to this tradition María Lucía died some time prior to the apparitions, and Juan Diego was an elderly man of fifty-seven when these occurred. After the construction of the chapel at Tepeyac, he lived there as custodian.

Another tradition, found in the so-called will of Gregoria María (to be considered in chapter 11), says that Juan Diego's wife was named Malintzin and that she died very soon after the wedding. In this tradition Juan Diego was a young man at the time of the apparitions, which took place a few days after his wife's death.

A third version was given by Luis Becerra Tanco, who wrote that Juan Diego's wife was alive at the time of the apparitions and died two years after them, rather than two years before. Francisco Javier Clavigero repeated this, saying that she died in 1534.[9]

No cult grew up around Juan Diego, except for some hints of one in the 1665 to 1666 investigation (which will be treated in chapter 8) and some references by Cayetano de Cabrera y Quintero in his book *Escudo de armas de Mexico*.[10] His burial place, which today is unknown, did not become a place of devotion or pilgrimage, and no serious attempt was made to find it until the eighteenth century.[11] Even more shadowy is Juan Bernardino, his uncle, to whom the account says that the Virgin also appeared.

Internal Difficulties of the Account

Critics of the story have pointed to a number of elements that seem anachronistic or inconsistent with known facts. The earliest account presumes that Zumárraga was already a bishop, though he was only bishop-elect. On the other hand a bishop-elect who had already begun administering the diocese was often referred to as the bishop of his diocese. Another criticism is that some of the assertions made about Zumárraga do not fit what is known about him; for example, that his servants hindered Juan Diego from seeing the bishop-elect, whereas in reality he was very available to the natives, and that he immediately accepted the image as miraculous and put it in his oratory (he had been an inquisitor and would probably have investigated the apparitions, although such investigations were not officially demanded before the Council of Trent).[12] Existing evidence indicates that Zumárraga was not credulous, for example, in such matters as witchcraft or astrology.[13] On the whole these do not seem to be strong arguments against the veracity of the account. While Zumárraga was personally available to the Indians, his servants might well have acted otherwise on occasions. It can also be argued that the extraordinary nature of the event would have overwhelmed any initial skepticism he might have felt.

García Icazbalceta asserted that the reference to Juan Diego's seeking a priest for his uncle was anachronistic. Extreme unction (as it was then called) was not administered to Indians at that time because of doubts about their capacity and because of a shortage of oils in New Spain.[14] The oils had to be imported from Spain since the oil-producing plants, such as olives, were not yet grown locally. The *Nican mopohua*, however, does not say that Juan Diego's uncle wanted the priest to administer extreme unction but only "to go hear his confession and go prepare him" [quimoyolcuitilitiuh ihuan quimocencahuilitiuh]. Confession was customarily administered to Indians, especially during illness. The term *extreme unction* was first used by Becerra Tanco in a work published posthumously in 1675. This also does not seem to be a valid objection.

A somewhat more substantial problem is that of the double Spanish names of the principal characters in the account. In 1531 native commoners (*macehualtin*) ordinarily kept at least one of their Nahuatl names, usually as a surname after their newly received Christian name. It is not impossible that Juan Diego, Juan Bernardino, and María Lucía all had two Christian names, but it would have been unusual.[15]

There are, in addition, two other considerations that pose serious difficulties for the account. First, it is related that Juan Diego went from his hometown of Cuauhtitlan to Tlatelolco to attend mass and on another occasion to get a priest for his uncle, whereas current research indicates that by 1531 the Franciscans had done mission work in Cuauhtitlan but not in Tlatelolco. The Franciscans had a friary in Cuauhtitlan, which was about four leagues from Tlatelolco, as early as 1525.[16] On 17 November 1532 ten Franciscans, including Martín de Valencia and Motolinía, wrote a letter to Charles I from Cuauhtitlan, which they had apparently used as their meeting place.[17] The letter shows clearly that within less than a year after the date assigned to the apparitions the town had a special importance for the Franciscans. It seems highly unlikely that so many of them would have met there if there had not been a Franciscan house still functioning.

The date of the first presence of the Franciscans in Tlatelolco is more difficult to establish with precision. A *cédula* of Charles I to Viceroy Antonio de Mendoza (1 May 1543) stated that the king had been told by fray Jacobo de Testera that the Franciscans had always had charge of the Indians of Tlatelolco. The cédula also mentioned that there had been two Franciscans there since 1535 who were living in cells next to the church. They were engaged both in parochial and educational work, and their church was already named Santiago. This is the earliest sure date for their establishment in Tlatelolco. The Franciscan *colegio* of Santa Cruz de Tlatelolco was not formally opened until 1536.[18] The *Nican mopohua* emphasized the importance of Tlatelolco, an emphasis that probably originated with the later importance of the colegio. Even if there had been Franciscans in Tlatelolco in 1531, Cuauhtitlan would still have been the more important center for evangelization. All this points to a later origin for the account at a time when Tlatelolco had emerged, in reality and memory, as the preeminent Christian center for the Indians.

The other problem is to be found in the very name of the devotion, Guadalupe. Why were the image and the shrine given a Spanish name of Arabic origin? The word was difficult for the Nahuas to pronounce because there is no *g* or *d* in Nahuatl.[19] Attempts have been made to find a Nahuatl substratum for it on the grounds that Juan Bernardino used a native word that Zumárraga heard as Guadalupe. Why the archbishop or those who were in his entourage could not have learned the correct Nahuatl term from the two Indians or why the latter would have permitted an incorrect name to be given to the chapel is not explained. Why, too, did the archbishop, who was so obedient to the Virgin's command to build a chapel, fail to obey her command to give it a specific name? In the seventeenth century Luis Becerra Tanco, an advocate of the apparitions, confessed himself baffled by this. "The motive that the Virgin had for naming her image Guadalupe, she did not say, and so it is not known, until God will be pleased to clarify this mystery."[20] He went on, however, to suggest two hypotheses: Tecuatlanopeuh (she who had origin on the rocky peak) or Tecuantlaxopeuh (she who drove away those who were eating us). Though Becerra Tanco was an accomplished linguist, there is room for reservations about his formulations. The first appears to be a combination of *te* (from *tetl*, stone), *cuaitl* (peak or extremity), and *opeuh* (preterit of *pehua*, to begin), with the literal meaning "she had a beginning on the rocky peak." The second seems to combine *tecuani* (literally, people eater, that is, cannibal or wild beast) with *tlaxo* (alternate nonactive form of *tlaza*, to throw out) and *opeuh* (preterit of *pehua*, to conquer or overcome), giving the literal meaning of "she drove away and overcame the people eaters."[21] In addition to the grammatical problems, the theological significance of these terms is rather arcane, and they are not in any way relevant to the Virgin's message. In the seventeenth century Florencia cited some unnamed interpreters who believed the original term was Quauhtlalapan, "the trees on the land of water," which some hypothesized to have been the original name of Tepeyacac.[22] Weckmann cites Mariano Jacobo Rojas and Ignacio Dávila Garibi as suggesting Cuatlaxopeuti or Cutlalopeuh, "she who drives away the serpent."[23] Both these constructions have *coatl* (serpent) as the first part of the compound, but the other parts are not clear. Either Weckmann's transcriptions are faulty or the reconstructions are erroneous.

The fallacy in this form of argument is that in other instances of the transfer of a word from one language to a similar-sounding word in another (for example, *ahuacatl* to avocado, *estanque* to tank, *rato* to rat hole), the original is known. The solutions described above require hypothesizing or inventing an original for which the sources offer no evidence whatever. Also, in the *Nican mopohua*, the Virgin specifically commands that the shrine be given the name "Saint Mary of Guadalupe." All other documents on Guadalupe in the Nahuatl language, with two exceptions in an eighteenth-century account and an eighteenth-century drama, both to be discussed in chapter 10, use the Spanish name, leading to the inescapable conclusion that the shrine, with its Spanish name, antedated the formation of the account of the apparitions. The apparitions, then, did not bring about the founding of the shrine but were a postfactum explanation for it.[24]

What may be called the "standard" account of the appearances of Our Lady of Guadalupe varies greatly in details. What was related above is probably the most commonly accepted version. It is not free of internal problems, although in themselves these may not be enough to undermine the veracity of the account. There is, however, a major problem that casts substantial doubt on the apparition tradition, specifically, the lack of any written, incontrovertible, supporting evidence in the sixteenth century. In a special way this means the silence of the man to whom the message of Tepeyac was supposedly directed, Juan de Zumárraga, first bishop and archbishop of Mexico.

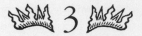

Zumárraga and His Contemporaries

The missionary enterprise in the Indies was the first one of such magnitude since the conversion of the Slavs some four hundred years earlier. In the first decades of the sixteenth century the missionary friars sought to work out a program of evangelization. With little or no experience to fall back on, they improvised, adapting the structures and methods of the Old World to the challenges of the New. Faced with a people, society, and outlook that were so alien to their own, they attempted to bridge the gap and find approaches suitable for a new and daunting task. If they were not always successful in their quest, they still showed great ingenuity and tenacity. The structuring of the Mexican Church took a major step forward when in 1532 Juan de Zumárraga went to Spain and on 27 April 1533 was consecrated the bishop of Mexico in Valladolid. In October of the following year he returned to New Spain. In 1536 a cathedral chapter was established. In 1547 the diocese of Mexico was detached from its dependence on that of Seville and raised to the rank of an archdiocesan or metropolitan see, with two suffragan dioceses, Chiapas and Nueva Galicia (Guadalajara). Zumárraga did not long enjoy his new rank, for he died in 1548, the same year that tradition assigns for the death of Juan Diego. In this pioneering period the historical record is totally silent about the Guadalupe apparitions and makes only two passing references to the existence of a chapel at Tepeyac.

The Silence of Archbishop Zumárraga

Little is known of the early life of fray Juan de Zumárraga, the first bishop and archbishop of Mexico. He was born in Durango in the Basque country around the year 1468 and entered the Franciscan order at a young age, probably in the province of Concepción. From 1520 to 1523 he was the provincial minister of his province, and in 1527 he was guardian (the Franciscan term for superior) of the friary of Abrojo. In that year, in an almost accidental way, he came to the attention of Charles I, who was attending a *cortes*, or Castilian assembly, at Valladolid. Impressed by the Franciscan's qualities, the king appointed him ad hoc inquisitor to investigate cases of suspected witchcraft. The results of the investigation are not known. On 12 December 1527, the king nominated him to be bishop of the newly created diocese of Mexico, with the additional title of protector of the Indians.[1] At the king's direction and without waiting to be consecrated bishop, he left Spain together with the four judges of the first audiencia and arrived in New Spain on 6 December 1528. Zumárraga quickly became involved in a stormy dispute with Nuño de Guzmán and the first audiencia. He finally succeeded in smuggling a letter of denunciation, carried by a Basque sailor, to the king. The result was the deposition of the first audiencia in favor of the second (1530), which stabilized civil government and laid the foundations of effective administration.

Zumárraga is justly famous for his solicitude toward the Indians, but it was a solicitude like that of many Spanish churchmen then and later, that is, paternalistic and sometimes authoritarian. In his capacity as apostolic inquisitor (1535–1543) he was responsible for the execution of the native ruler, don Carlos of Texcoco, on the charge of heresy in 1539. For this he was rebuked by the crown and lost his position as inquisitor.[2] Although he strenuously defended the natives against Spanish mistreatment, he also believed in some sort of compulsory labor system, specifically the encomienda that was so vigorously denounced by the pro-Indian faction. Zumárraga belonged to the "realist" or middle of the road school of Indian defenders. For that reason he found himself at odds with the more extreme positions of men like the fiery Dominican Bartolomé de las Casas.

In 1547 Zumárraga sponsored the publication of the *Regla cristiana breve*, of which he was probably the author. It contains the following significant statement: "You ought not, brethren, give way to the thoughts and blasphemies of the world, which tempts souls with the desire to see by marvels and miracles what they believe by faith. . . . That is a lack of faith and arises from great pride. That is how they receive their reward, by falling miserably into great errors. The redeemer of the world no longer wants miracles to be worked because they are not necessary, because our holy faith is so well established by so many thousands of miracles as we have in the Old and New Testaments."[3] If that statement reflected Zumárraga's own attitude, as it seemingly did, it was a remarkable one to be made within sixteen years of the apparitions, for it would indicate an antecedent skepticism of any such miraculous story.

Even more important is the fact that there is no mention of the apparitions, the devotion, or the shrine in any of Zumárraga's surviving writings. The absence of references in his correspondence may be attributable, as is often asserted, to the fact that not all of it has survived.[4] On the other hand, his failure to mention it in his will is significant. A Spaniard of the sixteenth century who founded a chapel or had a special devotion to it would ordinarily leave a legacy or set up a foundation of masses. The two principal institutions that benefited from Zumárraga's charity were the friary of San Francisco and the Hospital del Amor de Dios, both in Mexico City. Prior to his death he gave money to establish a Franciscan hospice in his native city of Durango. In his will he also left personal items to the metropolitan cathedral and some convents. Never, however, did he mention Guadalupe nor did he ask to be buried there.[5] Though the chapel, according to a report made in 1570 by Antonio Freire, the chapel's chaplain (see chapter 4), was supported by a combination of alms and endowment, there is no evidence of this in Zumárraga's will and no indication of the right of appointment for the chaplain. All this does not accord with the tradition that he received and obeyed the Virgin's command to build the first chapel.

Did Zumárraga write an account of the apparitions? If, indeed, he played the prominent role in the events of Tepeyac that tradition has assigned to him, it would be reasonable to presume that he did so. Some traditions reflect this presumption, though no written account has survived to this day. One tradition states that around the years 1602 to 1604 a priest named Alonso Muñoz went to visit the archbishop of Mexico, fray García de Mendoza, and found him reading the original acts and processes of the apparitions "with singular tenderness." This, however, is based entirely on an unreliable, thirdhand oral tradition related in 1666 by Miguel Sánchez, who claimed to have heard it from Bartolomé García, the vicar of the chapel at Guadalupe.[6] In 1740 Cayetano de Cabrera y Quintero, in his book, *Escudo de armas de Mexico*, told the story of the Franciscan friar Pedro de Mezquía, who claimed to have read an account of the apparitions written by Zumárraga for the Franciscan friary of Vitoria, where the archbishop took the habit. Mezquía promised to bring the document to Mexico but later claimed that it had disappeared in a fire that destroyed the archive of the friary.[7] While the precise place where Zumárraga took the Franciscan habit is not clear, it seems evident that it was not Vitoria. García Icazbalceta also claimed that Zumárraga was never in Vitoria and that there was no evidence of a fire in the friary archives. This story also relies on a questionable oral tradition.

Zumárraga's silence was not unique to him. It was shared by his fellow bishops of New Spain.

The Bishops of New Spain

The Juntas Apostólicas

Between 1524 and 1546 the leaders of the nascent Mexican Church held a series of informal and semiformal meetings at which they discussed issues and problems facing the missionary enterprise and worked toward formulating Church

policies. Because of the scant documentation and casual nature of these meetings, it is difficult to determine just how many took place. Recent studies put
the number between nine and twelve, all before or during the episcopate of
Zumárraga.[8] Sebastián Ramírez de Fuenleal, president of the second audiencia,
called two such meetings in 1532, one at the beginning of the year and another
in May. Zumárraga was present at both. Also present was Alonso de Herrera,
the guardian or superior of the Franciscan friary at Cuauhtitlan. The purpose of
the meetings was to deliberate on means of expediting the conversion of the
Indians. There is also evidence for at least two other meetings in that same
year.[9] There were three juntas in 1536 that dealt with Indian baptism and tribute and ordinances for the good treatment of the natives. The single junta of
1537 dealt with the proposed general council that would open at Trent six years
later. In April 1539 Zumárraga, bishops Vasco de Quiroga of Michoacan and
Juan López de Zárate of Oaxaca, together with the provincials of the religious
orders, met to consider ways of organizing the life of the Church in New Spain
and dealing with certain pastoral problems, such as the persistence of idolatry,
the teaching of doctrine, and the administration of the sacraments.[10] In 1544,
in the aftermath of the New Laws, the *visitador* Francisco Tello de Sandoval
called a junta. In attendance were Zumárraga, López de Zárate, and the leaders
of the various orders, including Martín de Hojacastro, Domingo de Betanzos,
and Alonso de la Veracruz. The purpose of the meeting was to register opposition to the New Laws.[11] Tello de Sandoval was also responsible for calling the
junta of 1546, about which little is known. Present were bishops Zumárraga,
Zárate, Francisco de Marroquín of Guatemala, and Bartolomé de las Casas of
Chiapas. Their primary consideration was the religious instruction of the Indians, as a result of which the *Regla cristiana breve* was published.[12]

These meetings dealt with the immediate problems of the fledgling Church:
the gathering of geographical and ethnographic information, the regulation of
the use of native carriers, the justice of the encomienda, methods of instructing
the natives, the rites of baptism, problems involved in marriage cases, and the
growing conflict between bishops and religious.[13] Such agendas did not lend
themselves to a consideration of individual devotions, such as Guadalupe. The
bishops, religious provincials, and civil leaders who attended them were more
concerned about the immediate problems of the day. Consequently, undue importance should not be attached to their failure to mention the apparitions at
Tepeyac.

The same is true of the joint letter sent by the three bishops of New Spain
to Charles I, 30 November 1537.[14] Zumárraga, López de Zárate, and Marroquín
were in Mexico City for the latter's consecration as bishop and took advantage
of the opportunity to seek answers to pressing problems, both from the king
and the pope. They covered a wide variety of problems, including the qualifi-
cations of churchmen seeking positions, the payment of tithes by the Indians,

Indian marriages (with the attendant problem of polygamy), the support of the Franciscan colegio at Tlatelolco, differences of opinion on the administration of baptism to the Indians, and the persistence of idolatry. While it would be logical that the three bishops would have informed the king of the great event at Guadalupe, still the letter was concerned with problems and questions. The bishops were seeking answers and help, not making a status report. Again, the absence of any reference to the apparition account should not be given undue importance.

The Letter of Bishop Garcés

In 1536 Las Casas was summoned to a conference with Zumárraga and Garcés, probably in Oaxaca, where they drew up a number of petitions, apparently modeled on Las Casas's treatise on peaceful conversion, *De Unico Vocationis Modo*, for forwarding to Pope Paul III. The petitions were accompanied by letters of endorsement from a number of people, including the empress Isabel, wife of Charles I. The result was the papal bull *Sublimis Deus* (1537), which emphatically asserted the humanity and rationality of the Indians, their natural rights, and their capacity for Christianity. The supporting letter that Garcés sent to the pope has often been credited as the one most responsible for the bull.[15] Although García Icazbalceta claimed that Garcés narrated heavenly favors to the Indians, the bishop actually emphasized the Indians' capability for Christianity, their desire for it, and their natural morality.[16] A great deal of attention was devoted to their manner of making confession, about which he related several anecdotes. One of these dealt with a vision seen by two Indians named Pedro and Diego, who were early converts. After going to confession they had a vision of two roads, one of which was foul and stinking, the other sweet smelling and full of roses. They saw Saint Mary Magdalene and Saint Catherine (whose likenesses they knew from holy pictures), who told them that the foul road was the one they had formerly taken, whereas the one scented with roses was the one they were following after baptism. The two neophytes told this story in the presence of 10,000 natives ("in conspectu decem milium animarum"), many of whom then sought baptism. That same night many heard the angelic Christmas hymn, "Glory to God in the Highest," sung in their own language, even though it had not yet been translated. This was regarded as a miracle. Garcés, however, made no reference to Guadalupe or any apparition at Tepeyac.

The Franciscans

The Franciscans of Cuauhtitlan

As was mentioned above, the Franciscans meeting at Cuauhtitlan wrote to Charles I on 17 November 1532. The ten friars, coming together in Juan

Diego's hometown less than a year after the traditional date of the apparitions, described their missionary and educational efforts among the Indians. They also mounted a strong defense of Zumárraga against his detractors, with special praise for his defense of the Indians against the abuses of the Spanish colonials. The letter, however, did not contain any reference to Guadalupe, Tepeyac, or the apparition account. In view of their location in Juan Diego's hometown and the date at which they were writing, this silence on the part of the Franciscans is particularly significant. It would have been an ideal opportunity for them to show heaven's solicitude for the natives.

Toribio de Motolinía

In 1541 appeared Toribio de Motolinía's major work, *Historia de los indios de la Nueva España*. Motolinía had arrived in New Spain with "The Twelve," the second group of Franciscans who had captured the imagination of subsequent generations. Motolinía was a zealous and dedicated missionary who was also a strong defender of the Indians against Spanish mistreatment. He belonged, however, to the moderate school of reform. He was opposed to the more extreme positions of Las Casas, which he considered exaggerated and unrealistic, and in 1555 wrote a scathing denunciation of that Dominican that would have done credit to any Spanish colonial.

Motolinía closely studied both Indian languages and Indian history. In addition to the *Historia*, he wrote a series of *Memoriales*, which were not published in his lifetime. Both works show him to be a pioneer ethnologist, although his own attitude toward the Indian of both the pre- and postconquest periods wavered.[17] From 1555 on, though his sympathy for contemporary Indians continued, his view of pre-Hispanic civilization had grown more negative. In the *Memoriales*, he related two stories of divine revelations made to dying Indian youths.[18] Motolinía had personally assisted one of the young men, who told him of a vision he had during his final illness. The other account was of a dying Indian youth who had been a catechist for Indian children and who had a vision of being taken along a dark and dangerous road by some blacks. He was saved by calling to the Virgin Mary. Motolinía observed that there were many such accounts, some of which were true while others were not. In neither the *Historia* nor the *Memoriales*, however, did he make mention of the apparitions at Tepeyac.

Cuevas claimed that Motolinía was saving the account for the unwritten fourth part of his work or that his silence was caused by the Montúfar-Bustamante controversy, to be described in the next chapter.[19] There is no evidence for the first assertion, since he had numerous opportunities to mention it earlier. The second assertion is not plausible since Motolinía was writing fifteen years before that dispute.

As will be seen later, this silence on the part of the Franciscans was not the result of indifference but was rather a positive hostility to the shrine and devotion at Guadalupe as they existed in the first half of the sixteenth century.

Native Sources

Inin huey tlamahuiçoltzin

During one of his exiles in the United States as a result of the religious conflict in Mexico in the 1920s, the Jesuit historian Mariano Cuevas visited the New York Public Library. There he came upon a manuscript containing a brief account of the Guadalupe tradition that had originally been in the library of José Fernando Ramírez.[20] The manuscript was a translation of a Nahuatl original into Spanish made by Ramírez's secretary, Faustino Chimalpopoca Galicia. The Nahuatl version had belonged to the Jesuits, and after the expulsion of the society from New Spain in 1767 it had passed to Ramírez, who in turn donated it to the Biblioteca Nacional de México. On his return to Mexico Cuevas found the original in the Biblioteca in a volume of sermons for saints' days called *Santoral en mexicano*.[21] This account is called *Inin huey tlamahuiçoltzin* (This is the great miracle) from its opening words and sometimes, less accurately, the *Relación primitiva*. It is given here in a translation from the original Nahuatl.[22]

> This is the great marvel. It was our Lord God who worked it on behalf of the ever Virgin Saint Mary. This is it, so that you will grasp and hear how by a miracle she wished that her house be built, that her home be established that they call the Lady Saint Mary in Tepeyac.
>
> This is how it happened. A lowly man, a commoner[23]—was he not a man of great devotion, this humble digging stick, humble tumpline[24] who was walking at the hillock of Tepeyac? Was he not perhaps scraping for a small root, where the precious Mother of God showed herself to him? She summoned him and she said to him, "My youngest son, go into the great altepetl[25] of Mexico, tell him who has charge of spiritual matters, the archbishop, that I want, that it is by my will that here at Tepeyac they build me a home and that they erect my house for me in order that believing souls, the Christians,[26] may come there to know me well and to pray to me in the very place where it will come about when they take me for their advocate."
>
> Thereupon this poor humble man went to appear before the great priestly ruler archbishop. He said to him, "O lord, may I not bother you. The heavenly lady has sent me. She told me to come to tell you how she desires that there in Tepeyac there be built and erected a house for her in order that Christians may pray to her there. She definitely told me in private [huel iyoca] that it will come about there when they pray to her there." The archbishop did not believe him. He just said to him, "What are you saying, my son? Perhaps you have dreamed it or perhaps you were drunk. If what she says is true and is the truth, tell that lady what I have told you: that she give you some sign in order that we may believe that what you say is true and that it is the truth."[27]

Our man returned again.[28] He came away sad, and the sovereign Lady appeared to him again. And when our man saw her he said to her, "Lady, I went to where you sent me, but the ruler did not believe me. He just said to me that perhaps I dreamed it or perhaps I was drunk and he told me that for him to believe it, you should give me some sign to take back to him." And the sovereign Lady, the precious Mother of God, then said to him, "Do not be sad, my youngster. Collect and cut the flowers where they have bloomed." It was only by a miracle that these flowers bloomed there. When it is dry on the ground, flowers did not bloom anywhere.

When our man cut them, he put them in the fold of his cloak. He went to Mexico. He went to say to the priestly ruler, "O lord, here I bring the flowers that the heavenly Lady gave me in order that you may believe that what I come to tell you is the truth and that it is her word and her wish. In truth, she has said it to me herself." And when he extended his cloak in order to show the flowers to the archbishop, he saw there on our man's cloak, there by a miracle the sovereign Lady was painted, was copied, and was expressed in order that the archbishop would now believe. They knelt down and wondered at it.

And it is the very same image of the sovereign Lady which was painted as a portrait on the lowly person's cloak only by a miracle, which today is placed as luster for all the world [cemanahuàcatocatl].[29] They come there to know her and pray to her here. And it is she, who in her great compassionate motherhood helps them there. She gives them whatever they ask for. And in truth whoever fully accepts her as his advocate and totally gives himself to her, the precious Mother of God by her love will make herself his intercessor. In truth she will help him very much and she will show him that she loves him who goes to place himself under her shadow, under her shade.[30]

Aside from the brevity of the narration, there are notable differences between this and the standard tradition of the apparitions. The protagonists have no names, and the Indian is an even more vague figure than in the *Nican mopohua*. There is no information about him or where he lived. Emphasis is laid on his poverty. The prelate is always referred to as the archbishop, a title Zumárraga did not receive until 1547. No date is given for the apparitions. The favorable references to Tlatelolco and the Franciscans are lacking. There are only two interviews with the archbishop. The servants play no role. The archbishop's initial rejection of the message is stronger than in the *Nican mopohua*. Juan Bernardino, his cure, and his vision of the Virgin are not mentioned. The name Guadalupe does not appear except in the title. The text is hortatory in form and strongly emphasizes the Virgin's motherly love for the Indians.

Cuevas believed that the account dated from the late sixteenth century, a belief that was strengthened by the American historian Herbert Eugene Bolton.[31] On the basis of its Jesuit origins, Cuevas dated it as far back as 1574. Ramírez, on the other hand, gave more latitude, from the end of the sixteenth to the middle of the seventeenth centuries. The process for the beatification of Juan Diego gave it the earliest date of all, 1541 to 1545. According to Roberto Moreno, however, all the sermons in the first volume of the *Santoral* appear to be in an eighteenth-century hand.[32] Because Ramírez identified the document as coming from the Jesuit colegio of San Gregorio, Cuevas concluded that it was a sermon written by a Jesuit missionary for use outside Mexico City in areas not yet reached by news of the apparitions.[33] Because of similarity of style with some Nahuatl sermons attributed to the Jesuit Juan de Tovar (not to be confused with the Indian cacique of Remedios), Cuevas, who did not know Nahuatl, named him the author. This attribution rests on conjecture and need not be taken seriously. Cuevas made a further and totally arbitrary assumption about this document: that it was a copy or redaction of an earlier work that went back to the very time of the apparitions. There is, however, no reason or documentary basis for making such an assertion.

A different authorship was conjectured by Garibay. He claimed that the author was the priest Juan González, who in 1531 was supposedly acting as Zumárraga's interpreter with the Indians. In this hypothesis it was not a sermon but a brief account drawn up by a person who was present at the conversations between Zumárraga and Juan Diego.[34] Consequently he dated it before the *Nican mopohua*. Garibay carried his thesis still further by attempting to show a connection between González and the Jesuit Tovar (both had been members of the cathedral chapter of Mexico), thus establishing the provenance of the manuscript from González to the Jesuits. Garibay's theory has been accepted, in whole or in part, by a large number of historians.[35]

The original identification of González as the archbishop's interpreter comes from a portrait, dated 1716, that is now in the basilica museum at Guadalupe. The inscription on the picture says that González acted as interpreter between the two men. O'Gorman, however, has shown convincingly that any relationship between them, especially in the chapter, was chronologically impossible. González was not a member of Zumárraga's household in 1531 nor was he his interpreter at that time.[36] O'Gorman also makes a strong case for the fact that the portrait of González dates not from the eighteenth but from the late nineteenth century.[37] Though O'Gorman correctly asserts that nothing was said about González's role as interpreter when the cause of his canonization was introduced in 1718, it was mentioned two years later. In the autos submitted to Archbishop José de Lanciego in 1720 there is the statement that González was "chaplain and confessor of the Most Illustrious and Venerable señor don Fray Juan de Zumárraga, first archbishop of Mexico, in whose palace he was master of the Mexican [Nahuatl] language and Juan Diego's interpreter the times that he spoke of the apparitions of Our Lady of Guadalupe."[38] While this dates the first identification of González as interpreter to the early eighteenth century, it was still almost two hundred years after the traditional date of the apparitions. It seems probable that the identification grew up in the course of time as a means of improving González's chances for canonization.

O'Gorman also states that it was not until García Icazbalceta published two of Zumárraga's letters in 1881, in which the archbishop confessed his ignorance of the native languages, that it became known that he did not speak Nahuatl. Prior to that time it had been assumed that he and Juan Diego spoke the same language.[39] O'Gorman's thesis is that the portrait and the identification of González as the interpreter was a deliberate effort to counteract the negative effects of the publication of the Montúfar-Bustamante interrogatory in 1888 and García Icazbalceta's letter to the archbishop of Mexico.[40] It should also be noted that Archbishop Pedro Moya de Contreras, in his report to Philip II on the clergy of Mexico, 24 March 1575, gave data on the life of González, including his relationship with Zumárraga. He said nothing, however, about his having been an interpreter or about any connection with Guadalupe. Similarly, fray Alonso Franco, who included a brief biography of González in a history of the Dominicans of New Spain published in 1645, made no reference to Guadalupe or to his having been the bishop's interpreter.[41] Finally, aside from the fact that the style of the document is clearly not stenographic, it seems improbable that a verbatim or shorthand account of the apparitions should omit so much important material, including the person of Juan Bernardino.

What, then, is to be said about the *Inin huey tlamahuiçoltzin?* (1) It is clearly some form of instructional or hortatory material for the Indians and in all probability is a model or sample sermon, like others in the *Santoral*. (2) There is no evidence to support Cuevas's assertion that it is a copy of an earlier, more contemporaneous document. (3) There is no basis to Garibay's claim that it was Juan González's transcription of Juan Diego's original account, a claim that cannot be reconciled with the omissions in the account. (4) It is impossible to identify the author with any certainty, but if the original did come from San Gregorio, he may have been a Jesuit. (5) It dates from some time in the eighteenth century. (6) It opens up the possibility, as do some other sermons of the eighteenth century, that the apparition tradition had not yet become fixed. This invites the interesting speculation that the Jesuits, who had a great devotion to Guadalupe, may have had their own tradition of the apparitions. In summary, this document tells us relatively little about the Guadalupe tradition, in its favor or otherwise.[42]

The sermon, however, is instructive for what it does not say. It seeks to enhance the Indians' devotion to Guadalupe but contains no references to special election or divine favoritism toward them. This makes it radically different from criollo sermons of the same period.

The Cantares Mexicanos

Among the Nahuas, traditions and history were often preserved in songs, or *cantares*. The composers of these songs held official positions in preconquest native society, though their names are unknown today.[43] Durán wrote of Mexico and Texcoco that "they all had their singers, who composed for them songs about the greatness of their ancestors and their own greatness, especially Montezuma, who is the lord who receives the most attention, and Nezahualpiltzintli of Texcoco. They had composed for them in their kingdoms songs of their greatness and of their victories and conquests and lineage and their singular riches."[44] The songs, however, were not always clear. Their language was refined and artificial. The native composers used figures of speech, metaphors, and circumlocutions that made and continue to make the cantares inaccessible to any who do not know the language or style thoroughly. The majority of extant songs are now generally considered to be of preconquest origin, with adaptations to changed circumstances.

In the manuscript division of the Biblioteca Nacional de México in Mexico City there is a volume called *Cantares Mexicanos*, containing a number of songs, usually sung to the accompaniment of a drum.[45] The songs have been studied and published by Brinton, Peñafiel, Garibay, and most recently by Bierhorst,[46] who views the cantares as ghost songs that hark back to preconquest times and invoke the spirits of the past in a dispirited present.[47]

From the point of view of this study, the important question is whether the cantares contain any references to Guadalupe and, especially, the story of the apparitions. Bierhorst sees similarities in vocabulary and expressions between the first few cantares and the *Nican mopohua*. These will be considered in chapter 7, when the *Nican mopohua* is discussed in more detail. It has been claimed that at least one cantar contains an early, almost contemporaneous allusion to the apparitions: folio 27v of the original volume, number 44 in Bierhorst's enumeration. Garibay says that it is the second part of a three-part poem, titled *teponazcuicatl*, or "log drum song," beginning on folio 26v.[48] It is sometimes known by the Spanish name *Pregón del atabal*. Garibay made a literal translation of the poem into Spanish, whereas Bierhorst gave a much freer English translation. To give some idea of the complexity of the question, the two versions are here given together.[49]

Garibay	Bierhorst
The red-striped ear of corn I was born,	"As a varicolored ear of corn I come to life."
the varied flower of our sustenance was blended,	A multitude of maize flowers, spilling forth,
there it rose to open its grain	come blooming: they arrive

before the god who shines sun [*sic*]
  Santa María
In the region of the waters and
  clouds only
precious water flowers are going to
  be thick with buds
I am the creation of God the only
  God
only in pictures was your heart
  walking
on a mat of paper you were singing
you were causing the princes to
  dance
the bishop only our father
you were shouting there in
  Atlitempan
God created you
abundant flowers he caused you to
  be born
a song he painted you Santa María
  the bishop
The Toltecs were painting, ay!,
finished are the books
your whole heart came to be perfect
Oh, with the Toltec art I will live
  here.[50]

before the face of our mother,
  Santa Maria
Plume-water turquoise gems are
  singing in these
waters: they're sprouting.
"I am a creature of the Only
  Spirit, God. I am his
creation." They've arrived.
Your hearts are alive in this place
  of paintings.
Upon this mat of pictures You are
  singing,
that the lords may dance
O Bishop, Our Father,
You warble yonder at the Shore.
God has formed you,
has given you birth as a flower.
He paints you as a song. O Santa
  Maria, O Bishop,
You warble yonder at the Shore.
Painted are the Toltecs,
completed are the pictures:
All Your hearts are arriving.
"Here, through art, I'll live."
Who'll take them from me?
Who'll go with me
  and be arisen, O younger
  brothers? Singers and
  weighty ones, are these, my
  flowers, song plumes
that I pick before this company.[51]

Even a cursory reading makes clear the obscure nature of the cantar, a quality that it shares with others of the genre, and the difficulty of arriving at an accurate translation. More important, it shows how difficult it is to find support for the apparition account in this poem. Some, however, see a reference to the apparitions in the lines which in literal translation read, "Your heart lives only on the picture, you sing there on your mat of paper [or book mat], you cause the rulers to dance, the bishop, only our father, you speak there on the edge of the water. God himself created you as a flower, he causes you to be born as a song, he paints you, Santa María, the bishop, etc." The original Nahuatl, without the vocables, reads, "Çan ca tlacuilolpa[n] nemi moyollo amoxpetlatl ypan toncuica tiquimonitotia teteuctin in obispo ça ca[n] totatzin onca[n] titlatoa atl itempa[n]. Yehuan Dios mitzyocox xochitl mitztlacatili yan cuicatl mitzicuiloa Santa Maria in obispo." For Cuevas, the reference to painting and to the bishop rather than archbishop (which for him proved that the reference is to Zumárraga, the only bishop that Mexico City ever had) was sufficient to establish the cantar as a witness to the apparitions. He gave the following translation of the second line, "God created you, O Santa María, among abundant flowers; recently he begets you, painting you in the bishopric."[52] To obtain the translation "bishopric," he left the vocable on *obispo* and added the preposition -*c*, giving *obispoyac*. Chauvet also uses the cantar as proof of the apparition and gives the following translation: "Your soul, O Santa María, is as if living in the picture. We rulers were singing to it from behind the large book and we were dancing to it with perfection, and you, O bishop, our father, were preaching there on the shore of the lake."[53] He assigns it a date prior to 1548 and says that it refers to the procession of 26 December 1531.

Obviously, differing translations are possible. The significant thing for this study is that there is no mention of Juan Diego, the image on the cloak, Zumárraga by name, the appearance of the Virgin, the miracle of the flowers, the cure of Juan Bernardino, or even the shrine itself. The context of the cantares is entirely different. Garibay, an apparitionist, gave the cantar a close and detailed study. His conclusion was that it "is not a Christian song; much less, dedicated to Saint Mary; much, much less, the song of Francisco Plácido" (an Indian poet whose supposed authorship of the cantar is discussed below).[54] Far too much importance has been attached to this cantar. To find any reference to the Guadalupe apparitions in it is to stretch its meaning beyond credibility. As Bierhorst has pointed out with great accuracy, the cantares and the Guadalupe devotion (though not the apparitions) are "parallel, not integrated phenomena."[55]

It is not certain if this is the same cantar of which Florencia spoke. According to him, the Indian poet Francisco Plácido wrote a cantar on the occasion of the transfer of the image to the newly built chapel of Guadalupe on 26 December 1531.[56] Florencia, who said that he had received the poem from Mexican savant Carlos de Sigüenza y Góngora, promised that he would include it in his book, *Estrella del norte*, but never did so. Sigüenza y Góngora was supposed to have found it among the papers of the Indian historian Domingo Francisco de San Antón Muñón Chimalpahin, an assertion that led Bierhorst to conclude that Chimalpahin was responsible for the association of Plácido with a Guadalupan cantar.[57] In the volume of the cantares in the Biblioteca Nacional de México, an anonymous glossarist has attributed some to don Francisco Plácido, all of which are dated from the middle of the sixteenth century. Little is known about

Plácido, other than that he was a descendant of the lords of Azcapotzalco and that he was the author of some cantares.[58]

It can be safely asserted that the existing cantares say nothing about Guadalupe, either in terms of the apparitions or the devotion. Similarly, aside from a vague tradition handed on by Sigüenza y Góngora and those who follow him, there is no evidence that Francisco Plácido, whose existing cantares date from 1551 to 1565, was the author of any Guadalupan songs.

Other Sources

Francisco Cervantes de Salazar

Another witness notable for his silence was Francisco Cervantes de Salazar, perhaps the most famous scholar in New Spain in the sixteenth century. He was born in the province of Toledo in Spain and was a student of the humanist Juan Luis Vives. After an academic career in Spain that also saw the publication of some philosophical works, he came to New Spain in 1550 or 1551.[59] At first he taught Latin in a private school and then assumed a position as professor of rhetoric at the Royal and Pontifical University (1553). In 1567 he was named rector of the university. His reputation, which was high in his lifetime, declined in subsequent centuries. Recent scholarship has seen him as a pedant, an academic opportunist, and a plagiarizer.[60] His archbishop, Pedro Moya de Contreras, did not hold him in high esteem. "He likes people to listen to him and praise him and flattery is agreeable to him; he is flighty and changeable and does not have a good reputation for being upright or chaste and is ambitious for honor and believes he should be a bishop. . . . He is not in any way an ecclesiastic or a man to be trusted with business."[61] His account of the Spanish conquest, *Crónica de la Nueva España*, is marred not only by literary dependence on the work of Francisco López de Gómara but also by a strong anti-Indian prejudice. In 1554 he published his famous dialogues in praise of the great city of Mexico. In describing the environs of Mexico City, Cervantes de Salazar included Tepeaquilla among the larger Indian towns and added, "belonging to those [towns] are those white churches that lie towards the city of Mexico."[62] Some have interpreted this statement as referring to a church or chapel at Tepeyac, but it is too vague to be of any use.

The Map of Uppsala

The earliest depiction of the *ermita* at Guadalupe is in a map that has often been attributed to cartographer Alonso de Santa Cruz and that is now at the University of Uppsala, Sweden.[63] The map is an artistic depiction of the city of Mexico and its environs around the years 1556 to 1562. Manuel Toussaint has argued persuasively that it was not the work of Santa Cruz but of local Indian artists.[64]

It was sent to Spain and through some unknown process went to Sweden. The map shows a small and simple church building at Tepeyac.[65]

Prior to 1555 there was a total silence in the written sources about any apparitions at Tepeyac or even the existence of a chapel there. Both the *Inin huey tlamahuiçoltzin* and the cantar analyzed above are useless as testimonies. The silence of Zumárraga, Motolinía, Garcés, and the Franciscans of Cuauhtitlan is strong evidence that they did not know the apparition tradition. As will now be seen, even stronger evidence would be forthcoming in the years between 1555 and 1570.

4

Testimonies to 1570

In the mid–sixteenth century the Spanish imperial system became entrenched in New Spain. As early as 1528 the crown had decided that New Spain should be ruled by a viceroy, but it was not until 1535 that the first of these, Antonio de Mendoza, arrived. Below the viceroy and the audiencia, a combination of appellate court and viceregal council, flourished a bureaucracy dominated by *letrados*, professional civil servants trained in law at the great universities such as Salamanca and Valladolid. This organizational framework, hierarchical and as centralized as communications permitted, served the Spanish empire effectively until the coming of the national period. In the 1560s the so-called Avila-Cortés conspiracy, led by a youthful criollo and involving the sole legitimate son of the great conquistador, was the last attempt in the sixteenth century by the *encomenderos* and burgeoning criollo class to achieve independence from the crown. After its suppression there was no serious challenge to royal authority by white colonials until just before the wars of independence. The encomienda diminished in importance until by the end of the century the crown no longer feared the growth of the encomenderos as an independent power bloc. Since the Spanish presence in New Spain depended ultimately on the labor of the Indian, a new system of conscript labor, the *repartimiento*, was developed. It too came under fire by humanitarians for its abuses.

New Spain consisted of two "republics," that of the Spaniards and that of the Indians. As a matter of royal policy they lived apart from each other, yet there was inevitably some mutual influence. Local government and society in the towns and villages began to grow more Spanish in character. The native languages, especially Nahuatl, assumed written form with the adoption of the Latin alphabet and also increased their borrowings from Castilian. With the help of the friars, especially the Franciscans, the Nahuas took to the new mode of expression with vigor. In the outpouring of documents and writings that ensued, legal papers, such as wills or land claims, predominated, but there were also chronicles, sermons, catechisms, and even edifying stage plays. In 1565

Alonso de Molina published his classic Nahuatl/Castilian dictionary, and Bernardino de Sahagún was deep into his researches into the pre-Hispanic past.

At the same time the Church was moving into a period of institutional consolidation. The more improvised—some would say more creative—missionary methods of the first generation of mendicant friars began to feel pressure from an increasingly powerful and organized diocesan structure. Buoyed by the decrees of the Council of Trent and the often inconsistent support of the crown, the bishops of New Spain sought to assert their authority over the missions, especially in areas where these had evolved into stable Indian parishes (*doctrinas*). Even when the bishops were themselves members of the orders, they championed the primacy of the diocesan organization over that of the friars. The resulting conflicts between mendicants and bishops, sometimes venomous in intensity, were never fully resolved and hindered the overall effectiveness of evangelization. By midcentury this hostility was at full heat, and the chapel at Tepeyac and the devotion to Guadalupe became part of the conflict. Partly for this reason, the silence that had shrouded Guadalupe in the earlier part of the century changed markedly. From 1556 on there were numerous references to the chapel at Tepeyac, though not to the tradition of the apparitions. The chapel, or ermita, emerged from the mists of history but without the story that allegedly gave rise to its existence. By the 1570s Guadalupe had become the principal point of entrance into Mexico City, and it was customary for important figures, such as arriving viceroys and archbishops, to tarry there while being met by reception committees from the city.

The Native Annalists

An important source of factual information on New Spain, both before and after the conquest, is the Indian chroniclers or authors/compilers of annals. In preconquest times Nahua annalists (*tlacuilohque*, painters) kept records of the important social events of their times, including the genealogies of kings, births and deaths of rulers, wars, natural disasters, and dedications of temples. These were painted in glyphs on skins or paper made of fiber.[1] Though anonymous, annalists performed an important function in Nahua societies, a function that continued well into the period of Spanish rule. They were often encouraged in this by the friars, though the annals then took on a different form and emphasis. While glyphs were still used in some documents, the annals came to be written in Nahuatl in the Latin alphabet, European paper was substituted for vegetable fiber, and dates were correlated with the European calendar, often being given in both native and European forms. The authors were no longer anonymous, at least in some cases, and the subject matter covered new areas, such as the activities of the religious.

The annals, then, were chronological records of the principal events of the land, written in Nahuatl from the point of view of the writer's *altepetl*. The entries dealing with events prior to the annalist's life were usually brief, whereas contemporary events were treated in much greater detail. Though most of the chroniclers to be considered below worked and published much later than the events at Tepeyac, they are often cited in support of the apparition tradition. For that reason they need to be considered in detail.

Juan Bautista

All that is known about Juan Bautista is that he was an Indian official in charge of collecting tribute from the natives. This information is found at the beginning of a notebook dated 1574 that was intended to be a ledger for tribute collections.[2] It was never used as such, however, and instead contained a chronicle that was close to being a diary. Garibay believed that the author was an Indian who was closely associated with the Franciscans. The work covers the years 1555, 1564 to 1569, and 1582.[3] It contains the following statement: "In the year 1555: at that time Saint Mary of Guadalupe appeared there on Tepeyacac" [Yn ipan xihuitl mill e qui.os 55 a.os iquac monexititzino in Santa Maria de Guatalupe yn ompa Tepeyacac]. It also contains a description of the festivities that accompanied Archbishop Alonso de Montúfar's visit to the shrine on 15 September 1566, when together with the principal civil authorities of Mexico City he led a procession to Tepeyac to celebrate the octave of the Nativity of the Blessed Virgin, and don Alonso de Villaseca showed the people a Guadalupan image made entirely of silver (or covered with silver).[4]

As is immediately apparent, these statements are fraught with difficulties. If the first one does refer to an apparition of the Virgin Mary, the date places it almost a quarter of a century after that given in the standard accounts. The second statement corroborates the fact that in the sixteenth century, the patronal feast of the church at Guadalupe was that of the Nativity of the Blessed Virgin Mary, 8 September (which was also the feast of the Extremaduran Guadalupe), not 12 December. Garibay claimed that Marian feasts that did not have a proper mass or office were celebrated with that of 8 September.[5] There is the fact, however, that the annals specifically mention the nativity of the Virgin, "nativitas Maria [*sic* for Mariae]."

The reference to the procession is notable because it opens up the possibility that Montúfar solemnly installed a statue that came to rival in popularity whatever image may already have been in the chapel. The annals of Juan Bautista make reference to the procession of 15 September 1566, "on which day, the octave of the Nativity of Mary, Our Mother, everyone went to Tepeyac to celebrate the feast of Saint Mary of Guadalupe. Villaseca made a gift of a statue that he made of pure silver; and he built some dwellings where the sick slept. There was a procession, in which all the *oidores* and the archbishop went, together with us Indians. Villaseca fed the gentlemen in order to make it known that he looked on the church of Tepeyac as his own."[6] According to Velázquez, the inventories made of the ermita's possessions in 1698 included "an image of Our Lady, silver, reinforced with copper plate and bolts, which weighed forty and three quarters *marcos* [somewhat more than twenty pounds]."[7] Florencia also listed the ermita's treasures and referred to "an image cast in silver, with its pedestal, a little more than a *vara* [about three feet] high, which Alonso de Villaseca gave; it weighed thirty nine *marcos* and two ounces."[8]

The reference to an image covered with silver, together with similar statements made later by Miles Philips and Martín Enríquez, has led to speculation that the original image in the ermita was a statue, not a painting. This probably arises from the presence of Villaseca's statue. As will be seen, Miles Philips's testimony later in the century indicated that this statue was the chief object of veneration in the chapel. Toward the beginning of the eighteenth century it was melted down to make candlesticks, an act that is credible only if it had come to be considered a rival to the present image.

Chimalpahin

Some time in the first quarter of the seventeenth century don Domingo Francisco de San Antón Muñón Chimalpahin Quauhtlehuanitzin wrote his *Historia*. He was a remote descendant of the kings of Chalco and had received an excellent humanistic education.[9] His most productive years were spent in association with the church of San Antón in Mexico City, from which he derived one of his surnames. His work was written in annals style, that is, by years, which were given in both their Nahuatl and Spanish forms. It contained two references to Guadalupe. One was in a description of the departure of the viceroy Gastón de Peralta, the marquess of Falces, on 4 March 1568.[10] The other is: "12 Flint the year 1556. And likewise in this year was when our precious mother Saint Mary of Guadalupe appeared at Tepeyacac" [12 tecpatl xihuitl 1556 años. Auh çano ypan in yhcuac monextitzino yn totlaçonantzin Sancta Maria Guadalope yn Tepeyacac].[11] The date of the apparition, about which no further information is given, is twenty-three years before Chimalpahin's birth. The entry is brief, especially in comparison with others that were less wondrous, for example, the birth of a child to a local Indian lord. Again there is evidence for a tradition of an apparition to an Indian some time in the mid-1550s.

The Anales antiguos de Mexico y sus contornos

This is not, as the title might suggest, a single work; rather, it is a collection of many different annals of varying quality that were gathered together in the first half of the nineteenth century by José Fernando Ramírez. They were copied into two large volumes, with the original Nahuatl and a Spanish translation by Faustino Chimalpopoca Galicia in parallel columns. At the present time they are in the Biblioteca Nacional de Antropología e Historia in Mexico City.[12]

Cuevas, who seems to have regarded them as a single work, believed that they belonged entirely to Ramírez, though some of the individual annals clearly came from other collections.[13] Cuevas also stated that the volumes had been sold in London in 1880 and published by J. M. A. Aubin in Paris in the nineteenth century, though he gave no bibliographical data. An incomplete and inadequate version was published in Mexico City in 1946.[14] Medina Ascensio says that knowledge of the document comes from an entry in García Icazbalceta's *Apuntes para un catálogo de escritores en lenguas indígenas de América*.[15] He also says that the annals were written in Nahuatl between 1589 and 1596 and, like Cuevas, that the originals are in the library of the Instituto Nacional de Antropología e Historia. Garibay gave the annals the name of Anónimo A.[16]

Of the annals in the two volumes, only one has a reference to Tepeyac, the *Anales de Mexico y sus alderredores* [*sic*] in the second volume. Ramírez's introductory note states that Chimalpopoca Galicia made the copy and translation from among some papers that he owned. The annals begin in 1546 and end in 1625. Ramírez denied any firsthand knowledge of these annals because he had been in Europe while Chimalpopoca Galicia was working on them. It is important to note that although some authors refer to the original of the annals as being in the Biblioteca, that is misleading. They are apparently referring to copies of the original Nahuatl, not autograph manuscripts.

The statement that is cited in support of the apparition tradition is found on page 668 (old pagination). "1556: 12 flint. The Virgin came down here to Tepeyac, likewise at the same time the star smoked [that is, there was a comet]" [1556: 12 tecpatl. Hual temohui cihuapilli tepeyacac, ça ye no yquac popocac citlallin].[17] Cuevas was the first to use this text as a proof for the apparitions. He cited the Nahuatl with two errors (*ca* for *ça*, *popoca* for *popocac*) and tried to relate the smoking star to a solar eclipse of 1531, when the mountain Citlaltepec, or Citlaltepetl, appeared to issue smoke.[18] A *popoca citlalin*, or "smoking star," however, was a comet.

These annals assign the same date, 1556, to the apparitions that Chimalpahin does. Again, this is evidence of a midcentury tradition for the apparitions. They do not, however, offer any clear evidence of the apparition tradition as it is commonly known. At best they may refer to the placing of the image in the chapel by Archbishop Montúfar.

Códice Gómez de Orozco

This name was given to a volume of annals by Cuevas, who said that he called it by the name of its owner.[19] Garibay called it Anónimo B (Gómez de Orozco). It is a copy of a Nahuatl original that covers the years 1524 to 1691 and that Garibay associated with Puebla.[20] Velázquez published a quotation that seems to be from the same document but that does not indicate either a name or a source.[21] Medina Ascensio, however, calls it the *Anales de Tlaxcala* and says that the original was in the possession of the heirs of Federico Gómez de Orozco.[22] It related information about the early missionaries and, with some gaps, covered the years 1524 to 1691. It contained the following statement: "In that year the president came here, the first who came to rule Mexico. In that same year the priestly lord bishop named Juan de Zumárraga, a friar of Saint Francis, first came at the very time when our precious mother of Guadalupe appeared" [Nican ypan xihuitl huala presidente yancuican tlatocatico Mexico sanno ypan xihuitl yn huel yancuican hualmohuicac teopixcatlatoani obispo ytocatzin frai Juan de Zumarraga San Francisco teopixqui yn huel ycuac monextitzino yn totlazonantzin de Guadalupe].[23] Cuevas claimed hyperbolically that "these words of the authentic and contemporary document seem to be the voice of the Mexican people."[24] The difficulty, of course, is in the date of the passage, since the antecedent for "in that year" is 1530. Cuevas himself admitted that the manuscript was written in the same hand for the years 1525 to 1609, which opens up the possibility that a copyist inserted the comment about Guadalupe. Garibay, on the basis of a picture of flint next to the entry, identified the year as 1531. He said that the date was written below the glyph and had been corrected from 1510.[25]

The Spanish translation of these annals in the Biblioteca Nacional de Antropología e Historia carries the introduction, "This manuscript, written in the Nahuatl or Mexican language, deals with historic events that occurred in the same places [Tlaxcala and Puebla] and also in the city of Mexico. These annals began with the year 1524 and end with the year 1691. This manuscript is mutilated in part, at the beginning and end." If the format of the translation is accurate, the annals themselves are quite spotty. Some years are not in chronological order and others are omitted. Zumárraga is mentioned only once and Montúfar not at all. The entry for 1548 contains nothing about the death of Juan Diego. In contrast, the closer the annalist comes to the seventeenth century, the more detailed his account becomes. For example, many details are given about the arrival of Bishop Palafox y Mendoza in Puebla in 1640 and the pilgrimage of Viceroy Francisco Fernández, the duke of Alburquerque, to Guadalupe in 1653.[26] For the later years the annalist even includes direct quotations. It seems clear that he obtained his sixteenth-century material from another source. These annals need further study.

Anónimo C

Garibay cited other annals that he called Anónimo C (Gómez de Orozco).[27] Written in Tlaxcala, they cover the years 1519 to 1720 and contain this important statement: "1510. Flint year. It was when the president came again to govern in Mexico; it was also in this year that Our Beloved Mother of Hualalope deigned to appear; she deigned to appear to a humble Indian named Juan Diego" [1510. decpa [sic for tecpatl] xihuitli [sic for xihuitl] ycquac huala precidente yecuican tlatocatico mexico zanno ypan xihuitli monextitzino totla-çonantzin de hualolope quimonextili macehualtzintli ytoca Juo. Diego].[28] The year corresponds to the one originally found in the Códice Gómez de Orozco and, as in Anónimo B, opens up the possibility of a scribal insertion.

None of these annals gives 1531 as the date for the appearance of the Virgin at Tepeyac. The year 1556 is given by Chimalpahin and Anónimo A, 1555 by Juan Bautista. Cuevas, following Ramírez, claimed that the Indian chroniclers were inexact about dates and had difficulty coordinating the native calendar with the European. On that basis and what he considered to be internal evidence, he dated three of the annals, that is, Juan Bautista, the *Anales de Mexico*, and Chimalpahin, to 1531.[29] The hypothesis that all three could have been mistaken in almost exactly the same way stretches credibility. Nor is there any evidence that they copied from one another. As Garibay pointed out, the annalists represented different geographical areas of New Spain: Mexico City, Puebla, and Tlaxcala. Garibay also presented a number of hypotheses based on the same premise of a confusion between the two calendars.[30] He synchronized the two by stating that the years 1531 to 1532 were the year 1 flint (1 tecpatl) in the native reckoning and 1556 to 1557 were 12 flint (12 tecpatl) and that the confusion arose from the similarity of numbers.[31] A likelier explanation is the existence in the late sixteenth and early seventeenth centuries of a tradition about an apparition at Tepeyac around the years 1555 to 1556.

The Annals of Bartolache

In the eighteenth century physician and scientist José Ignacio Bartolache said that he had found annals in Nahuatl in the library of the Royal and Pontifical University that referred to Guadalupe "and I believe with reason that I have made a great find."[32] The title page on the document was signed by a certain Marcelo de Salazar. It covered the years 1454 to 1737, with each year indicated by its appropriate sign in the margin. The writing, drawing, and orthography, according to Bartolache, were poor. It contained two references to Guadalupe. The first is "13 reed year 1531. The Spaniards leveled the ground of Cuitlaxcuapa, city of Los Angeles [Puebla]; and Juan Diego made known the precious noble lady of Guadalupe of Mexico; it was called Tepeyacac" [Acaxiuitl 1531. Otlalmanque in caxtilteca in cuitlaxcuapa Ciudad de los Angeles, ihuan in Juan Diego oquimotenextilli in tlazocihuapilli de Guadalupe Mexico motocayotia Tepeyacac].[33] The second is "8 flint 1548: Juan Diego, to whom the precious noble lady of Guadalupe of Mexico appeared, died; and a hailstorm fell on the white hill" [Tecxia 1548. Omomiquili Juan Diego, yn oquimonextilli, yn Tlazocihuapilli Guadalupe Mexico. Otecihuilo nistac (*sic* for iztac) tepetl]. The second date may be a mistake because 1548 was 4 flint, according to García Icazbalceta.[34] The annals end with the year of the epidemic and the oath of the *patronato* of Guadalupe in 1737. There is no evidence of an earlier original of these annals. The two entries are undoubtedly a projection back to 1531 and 1548 of the viewpoint of 1737, which, as will be seen in chapter 10, was a significant year in the history of Guadalupe.

The Annals of the Cathedral of Mexico City

On the verbal authority of Agustín de la Rosa, Velázquez stated that there was once in the cathedral of Mexico City a copy of annals that had texts somewhat similar to those of Bartolache.[35] "1531. The Christians [that is, Spaniards] leveled the ground of Cuetlaxcoapan City of the Angels. In this same year Juan Diego made known the precious mother noble lady of Guadalupe in Mexico. 1548. Juan Diego died, to whom this Precious noble lady of Guadalupe in Mexico appeared" [1531. Otlalmanque in quixtianotzin Cuetlaxcoapan Ciudad de los Angeles. Zano ipan inin xihuitl in Juan Diego oquimotenextili in tlazonantzin Çihuapilli Guadalupe Mexico. 1548. Omomiquili in Juan Diego oquimonextililitzino inin TlazoÇihuapilli Guadalupe de Mexico]. Velázquez concluded that this was not the same as Bartolache's because of the difference in wording and in the dates covered by the two annals. Until such time as the original can be discovered and studied, nothing certain can be said about this document.

The Annals of Tlaxcala

"Likewise I have had before me a manuscript of ten folios which, as it says, contains 'Curious news copied exactly from a small notebook in 8mo written in Mexican, without an author's name, bound in parchment, the title folio has a picture of the sun, the moon, and a star and two crossed shanks in the upper part of the folio; and in the lower part two figures that represent Indians looking at the sky. It consists of twenty-eight marked folios and seems very similar to the annals mentioned by Doctor don José Ignacio Bartolache in his *Manifiesto satisfactorio*, printed in Mexico in the year 1790, folio 37. At the foot of these figures are written these words *Yxtlamatque tlaxcaltecac.*'"[36] That is the identification of annals that Velázquez claimed to have seen and which he said covered the years 1519 to 1738. Parts were written in two columns, Nahuatl on the left, Spanish on the right, and narrated the history of the rulers of the Mexica from Acamapichtli (1383–1396) to Cuauhtemoc (1520–1521). Later entries were written exclusively in Spanish. Velázquez said that they were clearly from Tlaxcala. He quoted the following references to Guadalupe: "In the year 1531 the Spaniards leveled the ground for the City of Puebla or Cuitlaxcoapan and in the same year our precious noble lady of Guadalupe of Mexico appeared to Juan Diego. In the year 1548 Juan Diego died, to whom our precious noble lady of Guadalupe appeared" [De 1531 as. otlalmanque in quichtianome Cuitlachquapam (*sic* for cuitlaxcuapa) Ciudad de los Angeles, sanno ipan inin xihuilt (*sic* for xihuitl) in Juan Diego oquimotenextili in totlaçoCihuapili Guadalupe

Mexico. Año de 1548 omomiquili in Juan Diego in oquimotenechtzino in tlaço Cihuapili Guadalupe Mexico].³⁷ Again, for lack of identification and location, it is impossible to evaluate this document other than to note that the quotation is very similar to that from Bartolache's annals and may have come from a common source.

The Codex Sutro

Medina Ascensio cites another source from the sixteenth century, the Codex Sutro in the Sutro Library at the California State University, San Francisco. He writes that "it makes mention that Our Lady of Guadalupe appeared in 1531."³⁸ The codex, which I have been able to examine only in photographic reproduction, has on one unnumbered folio what appears to be a picture of a church that somewhat resembles early representations of the ermita. On the left a bearded man is kneeling. Above the facade of the church there is writing in Nahuatl that is very difficult to read. The last two words appear to be "ilhuicac cihuapilli" (heavenly Lady), but the rest is illegible. The codex probably dates from 1530 to 1540, perhaps from the school of Pedro de Gante in Mexico. It contains references to caciques and to Cuauhtitlan and may well deal with land titles in that area. It cannot be cited as any clear proof of the Guadalupe apparitions.

Other Annals

The annals of Tlatelolco, the Códice de Tlatelolco, and the annals of Cuauhtitlan, valuable as they are, deal with preconquest and conquest materials and so are not pertinent to the Guadalupe question.³⁹ In addition to these annals, the *Positio* for Juan Diego's beatification cites four others: the Codex Tetlapalco (also called the Codex Brooklyn or the Seville Codex), the Codex Aztactepetl Citlaltepetl, the Tira de Tepechpan, and the Lienzo de Cuauhquechollan.⁴⁰ The Codex Tetlapalco, which is in the Heye collection of the National Museum of the American Indian in New York City, is a record of the most important events in Mexica history from their arrival in the valley of Mexico until the Spanish conquest. One page, in rather tattered condition, shows a cross, a saint, a madonna, and a bell opposite the symbols for the years 1531 to 1535. Edwin Sylvest writes, "[The madonna] almost certainly represents Nuestra Señora de Guadalupe of Tepeyac; it is the earliest depiction of her other than that on the tilma."⁴¹ The identification of this image with Guadalupe comes from Cuevas, who reproduces it and calls it the "protohistoria de México."⁴² Aside from the inexactness of the dating, it should be noted that the picture is that of the Immaculate Conception. It lacks not only many features of the image but more important the figure of Juan Diego. Glass and Robertson call Cuevas's interpretation "controversial."⁴³ The contents of all these annals are so obscure as to be useless in determining the history of the apparitions.

The theory is sometimes advanced that the terms "appear," "manifest," and "come down" that are used in the annals may refer to the discovery or appearance of the image, not to an apparition or revelation by the Virgin. This is plausible, for it fits in with the manner of speech of the sixteenth and seventeenth centuries. When an image was moved into a shrine, the Virgin was said to be entering her home. The identification of the image and the person it represented was very strong.

From all the above it is clear that the annals offer many difficulties in approaching the apparition question. One is the lack of fixed nomenclature for the individual annals. Another is that of finding and consulting the originals. The data given by those historians who refer to or quote the annals are sometimes vague or misleading. It is clear, however, that these annals do not refer in detail to the traditional account of the Guadalupe apparitions. The laconic nature of these references indicates that the events were distant from the annalists' time and personal experience. The evidence that they give, for example, for the use of the term "appear," is ambiguous at best, and the dates they give are confusing and contradictory. In general, however, they seem to agree in assigning some sort of apparition, or positioning of the image in the chapel, to the years 1555 to 1556. This midcentury date receives added support from the anti-Guadalupan polemic of fray Francisco de Bustamante.

The Sermon of Francisco de Bustamante

After the death of Zumárraga in 1548 there was a period of three years when the archdiocese of Mexico was without an archbishop. Finally, Alonso de Montúfar, a Dominican, was appointed in 1551 but did not take possession of his see until three years later. Montúfar was born at Loja, in the archdiocese of Granada, in 1489.[44] At the age of fifteen he entered the Dominican order and was professed in 1514. In 1524 he began his theological studies at the Dominican friary of Santa Cruz in Granada, the same one in which he had entered the order, and received the degree of master. He later became a theological consultant to the Inquisition. He was sixty-one years of age when he was nominated to the see of Mexico, probably through the influence of the marquess of Mondéjar, president of the Council of the Indies, whose confessor he was. He was consecrated in Granada in 1553, but it was not until 23 June of the following year that he entered Mexico City together with his friend and fellow Dominican, Bartolomé de Ledesma, the future bishop of Oaxaca. The latter became the vicar general of the archdiocese and administered it during Montúfar's prolonged illness. The archbishop died on 7 March 1572.

Montúfar had a great devotion to the chapel at Guadalupe, though there is no mention of the apparitions in any of his extant writings. In 1555 he appointed a resident priest there, the first one for whom there is any record. In

1561 the cathedral chapter, which was hostile to Montúfar, wrote to the king to complain, among other things, that the archbishop had diverted alms from other places to Guadalupe because of his devotion to it.[45] In 1555 he convoked and presided over the First Mexican Provincial Council, which took the initial steps toward consolidating ecclesiastical organization in New Spain. There is, however, no mention of the Guadalupe apparitions in any of its decrees or published records.[46] Though a friar himself, the archbishop was hostile to the work of the mendicants, especially the Franciscans, and tried to assert the primacy of the Church's episcopal structure. Specifically this meant the removal of the religious from the parishes of recently converted Indians, which were known as doctrinas. He also differed with them over the question of whether the Indians should pay tithes.[47] Montúfar's reputation has suffered through comparison with his illustrious predecessor, and he has been called a mediocrity.[48] Allowance should be made, however, for the fact that he received the see at a late age and that he suffered from ill health.

Montúfar was at the center of a controversy that erupted over the devotion to Guadalupe in 1556. The occasion was a sermon preached by the Franciscan provincial, Francisco de Bustamante. A native of the province of Toledo, he came to New Spain in 1542, in company with two other friars, Jacobo de Testera and Martín de Hojacastro.[49] He soon achieved a notable reputation as a Latinist and preacher. Cervantes de Salazar wrote of him, "this man is listened to with great acclaim by the Mexicans [Indians]. . . . He teaches clearly, delights greatly, and moves profoundly."[50] He was appointed commissary general, a type of overall superior who acted as intermediary with the civil authorities, in 1547. In 1555 he was elected provincial but had served only two years when he was reappointed commissary general. He was reelected provincial in 1560. At some point in his career he went to the Franciscan house in Cuernavaca to learn Nahuatl. He returned to Spain in 1561, together with the Dominican and Franciscan provincials, in order to defend the mendicants' doctrinas against the inroads of the bishops. His mission failed and he died in Spain in 1562.

Bustamante's sermon was in reaction to one that Montúfar had given on 6 September 1556. Insofar as it is possible to reconstruct the archbishop's sermon, he apparently praised the devotion to the Virgin of Guadalupe and made favorable mention of miracles that had been reported at the shrine. He attempted to link the devotion to the Mexican Guadalupe to other major Marian devotions in both Europe and New Spain, such as Remedios, and thus put it in the mainstream of Catholic devotional life. He claimed that the Indians had no devotion to the Virgin Mary. In referring to the miracles, he was careful to cite one of the Lateran Councils, which had established penalties for the propagation of false miracles.[51]

Bustamante responded on 8 September, the feast of the Nativity of the Blessed Virgin Mary, the feast of Our Lady of Guadalupe of Extremadura, and a holy day of obligation for the Indians. This date, and not 12 December, was at this time the feast day of the ermita. The sermon was delivered in the chapel of San José de los Naturales in the convent of San Francisco with some of the civil officials, including the audiencia, present.[52]

The original of Bustamante's sermon has not survived. Its main points, however, can be reconstructed from the investigation that Montúfar ordered on the following day.[53] This investigation was concerned primarily with how Bustamante's comments reflected on the archbishop rather than with the shrine or the devotion as such. Eight persons gave depositions, three of them clerics. According to the witnesses, most of the sermon concerned the feast day, and it was only toward the end that the Franciscan began an emotional condemnation of the devotion. The testimonies agreed that Bustamante mentioned or touched on the following points: (1) the devotion "at the chapel . . . to which they have given the name Guadalupe" was prejudicial to the Indians because they believed that the image itself worked miracles, contrary to what the missionary friars had been teaching them, and because many were disappointed when it did not; (2) the devotion was new and lacked a basis ("sin fundamento"); this apparently was a reply to Montúfar's attempt to put Guadalupe in the mainstream of Marian devotions; (3) if the devotion continued, he would no longer preach to the Indians because the devotion would undo everything he preached; (4) the money donated to the chapel would be better used for the poor and sick, for no one knew what was presently done with the donations;[54] (5) the so-called miracles should be investigated to see if they were real or not; (6) the individual who invented the devotion or propagated false miracles should be given one hundred lashes and whoever continued to propagate it, two hundred; (7) he appealed to the civil authorities to put a stop to this; (8) he accused the archbishop of encouraging the devotion and said that the archbishop was mistaken in thinking that the Indians had no devotion to the Virgin, since many considered her a goddess; (9) he claimed the image was painted by an Indian.

Bustamante was held in high esteem in New Spain. He was hostile to Montúfar, partly because of the conflict between the mendicants and the bishops over doctrinas and tithes, which the Guadalupe devotion gave him an opportunity to voice.[55] His criticisms applied only to the devotion's impact on the Indians, not the Spaniards. Nevertheless, the sermon created a stir, and most of the witnesses testified to the scandal it caused.

The investigation was intended to be secret.[56] The information provided by the witnesses offers intriguing insight into the devotion and the chapel as they were in 1556. The testimony of the cleric Juan de Mesa reflected Bustamante's accusation that the devotion was new and quoted the Franciscan as saying, "If, when this devotion was first publicized, care had been taken to find out its author, and whether the miracles that were reported were true, and if it was discovered that they were not true," then the culprit should be punished, and that "if His Excellency knew the condition of these natives as they [the friars] did, he would have taken another way or procedure at the beginning of this devotion at this ermita."[57] This was also reflected in the testimony of Francisco de Salazar, who spoke of the excesses such as picnicking and gambling in the groves committed by Spaniards who went to Guadalupe. He said that "after the devotion of Our Lady of Guadalupe spread here, much of what he related has ended."[58] After describing the popularity of the devotion, he added, "According to this witness's understanding, the fact that the devotion to Our Lady of Guadalupe has begun has been very advantageous to souls."[59]

Three witnesses, Juan de Salazar, Francisco de Salazar, and Alvar Gómez de León, testified to the strength of the devotion among the Spaniards; for example, the large crowds who frequented the shrine, the upper-class women who walked barefoot, carrying their pilgrim's staffs, and people walking the length of the chapel on their knees. They thus testified to the positive effect of the devotion, though it should be noted that all three were partisans of Montúfar.[60]

Juan de Salazar specifically called the image the "image of Our Lady of Guadalupe," which tallies with later assertions that it resembled that of the Extremaduran Guadalupe. He also testified that the religious of the city were opposed to the devotion.[61] This testimony was corroborated by others. Gonzalo de Alarcón reported that on the same day as Montúfar's sermon he accompanied the *bachiller* (holder of a bachelor's degree) Carriazo to the Franciscan friary of San Francisco to talk to fray Antonio de Huete (or Güete), where they were joined by fray Alonso de Santiago and others, including Alonso Sánchez de Cisneros.[62] Alarcón and his companions were possibly sent there to sound out the friars' attitude and to obtain evidence favorable to the archbishop. Alonso de Santiago said that he did not think that the archbishop should encourage the devotion, because there was danger that the natives "would think that [the image] was really Our Lady and that they would adore it because in former times they used to adore idols."[63] The friar added that "since the Most Illustrious Señor Archbishop would wish that people go to that ermita out of devotion, he should order that it not be called Our Lady of Guadalupe but Tepeaca or Tepeaquilla, because if in Spain Our Lady of Guadalupe had that name, it was because the town itself was called that, Guadalupe."[64] Alonso Sánchez de Cisneros testified that the other friars agreed with Bustamante. He quoted both Santiago and Huete as saying that the ermita should be called Tepeaquilla. Santiago also hinted that large processions of Indians to Tepeyac could lead to native rebellions. Juan de Maseguer quoted a Franciscan, fray Luis (no last name was given), as discouraging him from going to Guadalupe to seek a cure for his sick daughter, saying, "Give up this drunkenness because that is a devotion that none of us likes." Maseguer asked the friar if he was trying to do away with all Maseguer's Marian devotion. "No, but in truth I tell you that rather it is my belief that you offend God, that you earn no merit, because you give bad example to these natives, and if His Excellency the archbishop says what he says, it is because he is seeking his own interests and is over sixty years of age and is now senile."[65] This conversation took place on 20 September, and Maseguer gave his testimony four days later. Maseguer also testified that the Indians had grown lukewarm in their devotion to the image because the friars had so ordered.

Four witnesses testified to Bustamante's claim that the image was painted by an Indian: Marcial de Contreras (who said that he walked out on the sermon because he thought it was given in anger), Francisco de Salazar, Juan de Maseguer (who quoted Bustamante as saying it was painted "yesterday"), and Alonso Sánchez de Cisneros, the only witness who said that Bustamante identified the artist as the Indian Marcos.[66] Another witness, Alvar Gómez de León, said that Bustamante had asserted that there were similar images in the cathedral and the monasteries.[67] Francisco de Salazar testified that it was his understanding that from the beginning the ermita had had the title of Mother of God.[68]

All the witnesses in this inquiry appear to have been favorable to Montúfar. No religious or mendicants were interviewed directly. None of the witnesses mentioned the accusation about the possible misuse of the alms donated to the ermita. It is clear that the mendicants, especially the Franciscans, were hostile to the devotion because they considered it to be pagan or false. The name of Guadalupe had no special significance for them, for some believed that it should be abandoned in favor of a place-name. Bustamante had definitely asserted that the image was painted by an Indian. The witnesses, however, merely expressed what they heard, not whether they agreed with the assertions or not.

What is particularly significant, however, is that there was absolutely no reference to the story of the apparitions. It is as if they had never occurred. No one, neither archbishop nor witnesses, contradicted Bustamante's assertions about the origin of the picture nor did anyone use the apparition story to refute the Franciscan's claims. Bustamante, Huete, and Santiago all arrived in New Spain in 1542. It is inconceivable that Bustamante, named commissary general the year before Zumárraga died, did not know the archbishop. This makes both his silence and his hostility all the more remarkable. His statement that the picture was painted by an Indian artist named Marcos is the only known time that this assertion was made. Again, however, no one denied it or attempted to refute it. This perhaps can be explained by the fact that the witnesses were merely stating what they heard, not their agreement or disagreement with it. On the other hand, it is clear that Montúfar, in his original sermon, did not attribute a miraculous origin to the image.

Who was this Marcos? In all probability he was the Marcos de Aquino mentioned by Bernal Díaz del Castillo. When describing the glories of Moteucçoma's palace, Díaz del Castillo compared the present with the past: "There are three Indians in Mexico, named Marcos de Aquino and Juan de la Cruz and El Crespillo, so advanced in their office of carvers and painters that, if they lived in the time of that ancient and famed Apelles and in our own time of Michelangelo and Berruguete, they would be placed among their number." Later, when narrating the glories of Christian New Spain, he made a similar comment concerning artists on grinding wheels and shrines (*relicarios*), "which three Indians do, great masters of their craft, Mexicans, who are named Andrés [*sic*] de Aquino and Juan de la Cruz and El Crespillo."[69] In the first quotation Bernal Díaz was clearly referring to painters. In the second he did not identify the craft of each person named, and his memory of Aquino's given name failed him. Antiapparitionists have readily, even unquestioningly, accepted Marcos de Aquino as the painter of the image of Our Lady of Guadalupe. While this is not implausible, it should still be remembered that the identification of Marcos, or an anonymous Indian, as the painter of the image ultimately depends solely on a claim by one person, Bustamante. Although his assertion was not challenged (none of his assertions was, since the witnesses related only facts), the attribution is never again found in any Guadalupan document. It may reflect the true origin of the image, but in the present state of knowledge it must be treated with great caution.[70]

It is important to note that the testimonies agreed in referring to the image as a picture (*pintura*), not a statue. Statements made later in the century by Viceroy Martín Enríquez and English sailor Miles Philips have led some to assert that the image in the ermita in 1556 was a statue. They were undoubtedly referring to Villaseca's gift. Bustamante's claim that the devotion was new, a view shared by other Franciscans, bolsters the tradition of an apparition or miracle around 1555 to 1556. Bustamante made no reference to a supposed divine origin of the image, and, in fact, at no time prior to 1634 was the image ever described as being miraculous in origin.

In summary, what do the inquiry and its testimonies say about Guadalupe in 1556? There seems to be sufficient basis for several points:

(1) The story of the apparitions was unknown among the Spaniards of Mexico City in 1556. Whatever the image may have been, it was regarded as miraculous in the sense that it worked miracles, not that it was miraculous in origin.

(2) The devotion and the shrine were recent in origin. They appeared abruptly, together with claims of miracles. The name Guadalupe had no special significance.

(3) The devotion was favored by the archbishop and the diocesan Church structure but strongly opposed by the Franciscans.

(4) It was more a Spanish than an Indian devotion in 1556. There was some fear about its impact, both religious and political, on the native population.

(5) The image was of human manufacture but was still believed by some to work miracles.

It is important to note that while Bustamante condemned the devotion to Guadalupe as a revival of idolatry, he did not associate Tepeyac with any pre-Hispanic deity or devotion.

Nothing came of Montúfar's investigation, the results of which do not seem to have been sent to Spain. In light of the scandal and notoriety that Busta-mante's sermon and the subsequent inquiry occasioned, it is remarkable that it left no trace in contemporary or later chronicles. The Franciscan chroniclers such as Mendieta who gave information on Bustamante did not mention the incident. A note on the original manuscript indicates that the investigation was suspended because of Bustamante's death, though this did not happen until six years after the inquiry. The testimonies went into the archdiocesan archive and remained unknown until they were rediscovered in 1846.

A Bishop and Two Conquistadores

Bartolomé de las Casas

In 1564 Bartolomé de las Casas, the fiery and often intemperate defender of the Indians, died at Valladolid, Spain.[71] He was born in Seville in 1484 and received his early education in his home city. In 1501 his father, in an attempt to better his financial situation, migrated with his son to Española. Prior to leaving, Bartolomé received tonsure and thus became a *clérigo*, or member of the clerical state. In 1507 he journeyed to Rome, where he was ordained to the priesthood. In 1508 he was granted an encomienda on Española and became moderately prosperous. He served as chaplain to the expedition that conquered Cuba (1513), during which he witnessed at first hand the atrocities committed by the Spaniards and tried to prevent or moderate them. He was given a large encomienda on Cuba and settled down to the comfortable life of a gentleman farmer and landowning cleric. In the years between 1508 and 1515, on both Española and Cuba, Las Casas saw little contradiction between his life as an encomendero and his commitment as a Christian and priest. In 1514, however, he underwent a total conversion, divested himself of his encomienda, and began a life of advocacy on behalf of the oppressed Indians. Eight years later he joined the Dominican order.

During his long life Las Casas produced an immense body of writings. In addition to his extensive correspondence, there were his histories, including the *History of the Indies*, the *Apologetic History*, and the controversial *Very Brief Account of the Destruction of the Indies*. There were treatises, such as *The Only Way of Attracting All Unbelievers to the True Religion*, and his *Apologia* against Sepúlveda. The latter is especially important because it resulted from his famous dispute with Juan Ginés de Sepúlveda at Valladolid in 1551 concerning the humanity and rationality of the Indians. In this voluminous outpouring, but especially in the *Apologia*, Las Casas used every weapon in his arsenal—history, Roman and canon law, Scripture, the fathers of the Church, scholastic theology—to defend the Indians and portray them as a great people. He described in detail their culture, religious practices, government, and almost every aspect of their lives. Not once, however, in all his discussions of heavenly favors to the natives did the great Dominican, who was in New Spain eight years after the traditional date of the Guadalupe apparitions, ever mention them.

Bernal Díaz del Castillo

The shrine was mentioned, however, four years after Las Casas's death by the chronicler Bernal Díaz del Castillo in his classic work *La verdadera historia de la conquista de la Nueva España* (The true history of the conquest of New Spain). At the conclusion of chapter 150 he wrote, "Thereupon Cortés ordered Gonzalo de Sandoval to leave the area of Iztapalapa and go overland to lay siege to another causeway that goes from Mexico [City] to a town called Tepeaquilla, which they now call Our Lady of Guadalupe, where she works and has worked many and wonderful miracles."[72] In chapter 210 he strove to prove that the conquest of New Spain was greater and more beneficial than that of Peru, and so he challenged his readers, "Let them look to the holy house of Our Lady of Guadalupe, which is there in Tepeaquilla, where Gonzalo de Sandoval's camp used to be when we won Mexico; and let them look at the holy miracles that she has performed and performs daily and let us give many thanks for it to God and his blessed mother, Our Lady, who gave us favor and help to win these lands where there is so much Christianity."[73]

What is clear from this quotation is that Bernal Díaz mentioned nothing about the apparitions, the image, or any miracles worked by the image. He affirmed only that Guadalupe, or Tepeaquilla as he still called it, was a place of devotion where miracles occurred and where the Spaniards camped during their conquest of Mexico. His testimony shows that miracles were early associated with the shrine but not necessarily the image.[74]

Andrés de Tapia

The *Positio*, or papers for the process of Juan Diego's beatification, cites the testimony of the conquistador Andrés de Tapia, a soldier who was with Fernando Cortés throughout the conquest of Mexico, as contemporary evidence for the apparitions. According to the *Positio*, the key statement was to be found in an account that was intended to keep alive the memory of the events and also to secure a grant of money from the crown: "For the first bishop of Tenochtitlan, Mexico, the Most Illustrious Señor don fray Juan de Zumárraga, to whom in the year of the Lord 1531 the most holy Virgin of Guadalupe appeared, imprinting herself on the *ayate* of Juan Diego, an Indian of the town of San Juanico, a *sujeto* of Tlatelolco, on the twelfth of December of that same year."[75] This statement varies from the standard account in some details. The most important thing, however, is that it is not taken from any sixteenth-century account but from a *relación de servicios y méritos* submitted by one of Tapia's descendants on 2 March 1667.[76] It is not Tapia's own words but those of his descendants, written at a time when the standard account had already become widely known.

Montúfar: The Founder of the Ermita

There are two testimonies, both dating from after the middle of the century, that support the probability that Archbishop Montúfar, not Zumárraga, was the true founder of the ermita at Tepeyac.

The Censo of Martín de Aranguren

Aranguren was married to Zumárraga's niece and for many years was majordomo of tithes for the cathedral chapter. He played a major role in handling the bequests of the archbishop's will. On 1 July 1562, in return for 1,000 pesos from Archbishop Montúfar, he established a *censo* (mortgage) on some houses he owned in Mexico City, with the interest of 100 pesos to be paid annually to the ermita at Guadalupe as a form of annuity.[77] In the course of this document Aranguren described Montúfar as "the patron and founder of the said building [the ermita]." Though it can be argued that this was an honorific title, the weight of the evidence points to Montúfar as the man to first set up a chapel at Tepeyac dedicated to the nativity of the Virgin Mary and popularly called Guadalupe.

Descripción del arzobispado de México

In 1569, when Juan de Ovando, the president of the Council of the Indies, asked for a comprehensive description of the archdiocese of Mexico, either Archbishop Montúfar or his vicar general, Bartolomé de Ledesma, sent a questionnaire to archdiocesan parishes and ermitas and also gathered information from the friars. The result was a document that came to be known as the *Descripción del arzobispado de México*. In 1883 the original or a contemporary copy was in the possession of Joaquín García Icazbalceta, who in his letter to Archbishop Labastida y Dávalos wrote that it contained no mention of Guadalupe.[78] In 1897 the *Descripción* was edited and published by his son, Luis García Pimentel. It also contained no mention of Guadalupe, though in another document published in the same volume, dated 7 January 1570, there was information about Antonio Freire, the chaplain of the ermita. The *Descripción* was republished in 1905 in the third volume of the *Papeles de Nueva España*, edited by Francisco del Paso y Troncoso. This version of the *Descripción* did contain a report on the ermita and its finances written by the same Antonio Freire.[79]

The question, of course, is, Why did García Icazbalceta deny that the *Descripción* contained any reference to Guadalupe? There are three possible answers: his copy may not have contained this information; he was guilty of carelessness or lack of scholarship; or for some reason he deliberately stated a falsehood. The last is highly improbable, if only because the contents of Freire's report supported García Icazbalceta's antiapparitionist arguments. Why did his son not publish it? Again, there is the possibility that the manuscript lacked this information or that it may have been too controversial in the wake of his father's letter to Archbishop Labastida y Dávalos of fourteen years before. At the present time it is impossible to answer these questions with any finality.

Freire, a Portuguese born near Lisbon, identified himself as the chaplain (*capellán*) of the ermita.[80] His report was dated 10 January 1570. He wrote that there were 150 married Indians and 100 unmarried ones, from the age of twelve or fourteen on up, living there. In addition there were six sheep ranches belonging to Spaniards in the area and thirty or forty slaves. According to Freire, Montúfar founded and built the ermita about fifteen years before, that is, circa 1555, with alms donated by the Christian faithful.[81] It had an annual income of 7,000 to 8,000 pesos, and the accounts were kept by two majordomos. The ermita was supported by alms and by the income from the endowment, which was used for the upkeep of the buildings, sacramental wine, oil, and the salaries of the priest and sacristan. The priest's income was 150 pesos de minas a year and the sacristan's eighty-four. The priest's salary was not high; the holder of a chaplaincy in the church of Vera Cruz in Mexico City made twice as much. Freire said that the terms of the endowment required him to say mass there on Saturday and Sunday. There were no chaplaincies (*capellanías*) attached to the ermita. At the time of writing, the ermita was adequately (*medianamente*) provided with ornaments and vestments. The archbishop was the patron of the shrine. Freire made no mention of the image or miracles or any widespread devotion to the shrine, and his testimony supports the thesis that the ermita at Tepeyac dated from midcentury, about the years 1555 to 1556. Given his position and the circumstances of the report, it is astounding that he made no mention of the image or the tradition of the apparitions. The only explanation is that he was unaware of the tradition and the supposedly miraculous origin of the image.

Freire's account of the foundation of the ermita received support from the *cosmógrafo-cronista*, Juan López de Velasco, who drew up a detailed report on the Indies between 1571 and 1574. In reference to Guadalupe, he wrote, "And in the same way an ermita called Our Lady of Guadalupe, half a league from the city, which the archbishop, fray Alonso de Montúfar, founded about fourteen years ago, and a good part of the income that it has comes from alms."[82] Given the closeness in time to the Montúfar-Ledesma *Descripción*, it is quite possible that López de Velasco obtained his information from Freire's report.[83]

The Epidemic of 1576

In the mid-1570s a devastating epidemic, called the *matlazahuatl*, swept through New Spain.[84] For the most part it struck only the Indians, of whom it was said that at least a third or perhaps half died of it. Though the history of the colony is filled with accounts of similar scourges, this seems to have been one of the worst. Its progress and mortality rate, the steps taken by Church and civil officials, and its eventual passing were carefully chronicled by the archbishop, viceroy, and religious. Nowhere, however, was there any mention of an invocation of the Virgin of Guadalupe, such as was later claimed about the epidemic of 1544. In contrast, Remedios was invoked and would continue to be so until the end of the seventeenth century.

The conclusion to be drawn from the data given in this chapter is that by the second half of the sixteenth century there was no unequivocal, written evidence of the Guadalupe apparitions. Such references as are found are ambiguous at best. On the other hand, there is evidence of an ongoing Franciscan hostility to the devotion and shrine on the grounds that they encouraged relapses into idolatry. This hostility would be incomprehensible if the ermita had been built by Zumárraga at the express command of the Virgin Mary. From the beginning miraculous cures were associated with it or may well have led to its foundation, miracles that some considered to be fraudulent. The preponderance of evidence also points to the conclusion that the chapel was built by Montúfar, who was an enthusiastic supporter of the chapel and the devotion. The name of Guadalupe may have been given to it by Montúfar, but it seems more likely that it was a popular designation, a topic that will be treated in the next chapter. There is some plausibility, however, to the theory advanced by some antiapparitionists, such as O'Gorman, that it was Montúfar who installed the original image in the ermita. Precisely what that image was is discussed in the next chapter. In the 1570s the picture grows even clearer as one finds references to and detailed descriptions of the shrine and its devotion.

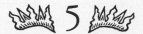

The Corsair, the Viceroy, and the Friar

The most detailed descriptions of the chapel and devotion at Tepeyac in the sixteenth century come from three widely disparate sources: an English Protestant corsair under arrest by the Inquisition, a strong-willed Spanish Catholic viceroy, and a humble Franciscan friar who was a pioneer historian and ethnologist. All three descriptions were written within a short space of time, 1571 to 1576, all three went into some detail about Guadalupe, two mentioned the images, and none referred to the apparition account.

The Corsair

Miles Philips was a survivor of an ill-fated expedition by John Hawkins that put to port at San Juan de Ulúa in 1568, supposedly under a safe conduct. The Spanish viceroy, Martín Enríquez de Almansa, then attacked it, either as a preemptive strike or out of treachery. At first, the English survivors were allowed to stay in New Spain in comparative freedom, but that situation changed with the establishment of the Inquisition in 1571 under Pedro Moya de Contreras, later the archbishop of Mexico. The presence of English Protestants was considered dangerous, and so they were rounded up and brought to Mexico for trial in 1573. Philips later returned to England, where he wrote an account of his experiences.[1]

As Philips and others were en route to Mexico City, they passed by the shrine of Guadalupe, of which he left the following description.

> The next morning we departed from thence on our journey towards Mexico, and so travelled till we came within two leagues of it, where there was built by the Spaniards a very fair Church, called our Lady's Church, in which there is an image of our Lady of silver and gilt, being as high and as large as a tall woman, in which Church, and before this image, there are as many lamps of silver as there be days in the year, which upon high days are all lighted. Whensoever any Spaniards pass by this Church, although they be on horse back, they will alight,

and come into the Church, and kneel before the image, and pray to our Lady to defend them from all evil, so that whether he be horseman or footman he will not pass by, but first go into the Church, and pray as aforesaid, which if they do not, they think and believe that they shall never prosper; which image they call in the Spanish tongue, Nuestra Senora de Guadalupe. At this place there are certain cold baths, which arise, springing up as though the water did seethe; the water whereof is somewhat brackish in taste, but very good for any that have any sore or wound, to wash themselves therewith, for as they say, it healeth many. And every year once, upon our Lady Day [25 March, the feast of the Annunciation] the people use to repair thither to offer, and to pray in that Church before the image; and they say that Our Lady of Guadalupe doth work a number of miracles. About this Church there is not any town of Spaniards that is inhabited, but certain Indians do dwell there in houses of their own country building.[2]

This description presents both problems and tantalizing clues.

First of all, Philips's description of the image as being of silver and gold when taken together with Juan Bautista's reference to Alonso Villaseca's silver image and Martín Enríquez's statement, to be cited below, that the image at Tepeyac resembled the Iberian Guadalupe, has led some to conclude that the image in the ermita in the sixteenth century was a statue. This, however, would directly contradict the statement in the Montúfar-Bustamante interrogatory that it was a pintura. It seems clear that Philips was referring to the Villaseca statue, the copper plating of which could easily have been mistaken for gold. What is surprising in his description is that it was this statue, not a painting, that was venerated and invoked by the Spaniards. Philips also seemed clearly to attribute miraculous powers to it. In the late seventeenth or early eighteenth century, when the apparition account was fully developed, the statue was melted down to make candlesticks, probably because it was seen as a rival to the present image.

His description of the spring at Tepeyac, the first known written one, agrees with later descriptions of the area. In fact, there was a spring on the hill which was thought to have healing powers, though these were not necessarily considered miraculous. Its waters gushed forth very strongly and were generally described as brackish or sulfurous. An enclosure was put over it in the seventeenth century by Luis Laso de la Vega, then vicar of the ermita. At the present time there is a voluminous discharge of water into the park that now occupies the east side of the hill. Its waters, however, do not appear to be either brackish or sulfurous.

Philips's statement about the number of lamps before the image may be hyperbole, unless he was referring to small votive lamps. The earliest descriptions of the chapel, however, make it unlikely that it was large enough to hold so many, no matter how small they may have been. His reference to a "very fair" church, however, when taken together with other indications of its wealth, may well be accurate.

Philips's account described the devotion as being a Spanish rather than an Indian one. Most significant is the fact that he said nothing about the origin of the image, the shrine, or the devotion. In view of the fact that he seemed to have been well informed about the chapel, this silence takes on added meaning. There was no reason for him to have omitted the story of the apparitions, if he knew it, since it would have been further evidence to his readers of popish superstition.

The Viceroy

Even more important is the description given by the Spanish viceroy Martín Enríquez de Almansa, lord of Valderrábano. A gruff but enlightened and astute administrator, he did not inherit a noble title, though he was related to the first families of Castile, including royalty. He assumed the office of viceroy of Mexico in 1568 at the age of sixty and held it until 1580. Enríquez was a staunch, if somewhat anticlerical, Catholic and a humanitarian. He was given to fits of temper and seemingly did not suffer fools gladly. He is generally credited with having raised the standards and prestige of the viceregal office and with firmly implanting royal authority in the wake of the Avila-Cortés conspiracy. In 1580 he was appointed viceroy of Peru and died in that office in 1583.[3]

Enríquez's account of the origin and status of the chapel at Guadalupe was in response to an attempt by the Hieronymite friars, who had charge of the shrine of Our Lady of Guadalupe in Extremadura, to claim alms of which they believed the peninsular shrine was being defrauded. The peninsular Guadalupe was one of the richest and most popular shrines in Castile. Like other major shrines it had spawned "satellite" shrines over which it tried to maintain a close control.[4] When the Hieronymite authorities heard of Guadalupe shrines in the New World, they commissioned two friars, Diego de Ocaña and Diego de Santa María, to go to Peru and New Spain, respectively, to investigate the situation. On 12 December 1574, Santa María wrote to Philip II from New Spain.

> I found in this city an ermita under the invocation of Our Lady of Guadalupe, half a league from here, where large numbers of people gather. It originated when a man came to this province twelve years ago with forged papers from our monastery of Our Lady of Guadalupe [in Extremadura]. He collected a large quantity of alms and, once the falsity of his authorization became known, he fled. A certain amount of the money that the majordomos of this ermita had collected remained. At that time it was called by another name. Seeing the devotion with which Christians would come to Our Lady of Guadalupe, they changed the name and gave it the name of Our Lady of Guadalupe, as nowadays it is said to be called, and they appointed alms seekers to solicit for Our Lady of

Guadalupe. In that way they have defrauded the alms that used to go regularly to Our Lady of Guadalupe [in Extremadura], and they have weakened the devotion that the inhabitants of this province used to have toward that establishment. This ermita today has 2,000 pesos of income and they collect almost another 2,000 in alms. I do not see what that can be spent on, because it is not decorated and the building is very poor.[5]

The good friar is the only known source for the story of the confidence man, though this assertion is in accord with Bustamante's choleric denunciation of the inventor and propagator of false miracles. It is possible that there was an oral tradition of a swindle in connection with the shrine. Santa María was clearly in error when he spoke of the change of name, at least in terms of a deliberate effort to obtain money that should have gone to Extremadura, or that the ermita had a different name twelve years before, that is, 1562. Although the early history of the ermita is obscure, the name Guadalupe is found in the very first references to it. Perhaps one source of this claim could be the possibility that since it was also dedicated to the Nativity of the Blessed Virgin, there may have been a shift in names, from an official one to a popular one, a not uncommon occurrence with some churches. Santa María was engaged in special pleading. Still, it is remarkable that he felt free to make such charges.

The friar asked the king to arrange for a taking of the accounts of the ermita, at least since the time that it had the name of Guadalupe. He went on to point out that "the location where the ermita is established is very bad, salty, and next to the lake, unhealthy, and without water. For that and many other reasons, although the income increases, divine worship and the service of God cannot increase."[6] He asked the king either to change the name of the ermita or remove it to a different place, where it could be put under the charge of the Hieronymites. He suggested Chapultepec as a suitable new location.

After receiving and considering the letter, the Council of the Indies sent a cédula to Enríquez, telling him to have Archbishop Moya de Contreras make a visitation of the ermita and audit its accounts. It also sent a similar cédula to the archbishop and asked him to send an account of the ermita.

On 24 March 1575 Santa María sent another letter in response to a prompt reply that he had received from Juan de Ovando, the president of the Council of the Indies.[7] He claimed that the ermita had been known as Guadalupe only since 1560, a statement that is clearly as erroneous as his previous one that it had another name in 1562. He said again that the Guadalupe of Tepeyac was making people forget the Guadalupe of Extremadura and that many who contributed to the ermita believed that their money was going to Spain, or at least that the two devotions were the same. He recommended that the Hieronymites of Extremadura be given charge of the ermita and establish a monastery in connection with it. He also suggested securing a papal grant or brief to that effect, since he feared that the archbishop might be opposed to his idea. Santa María's purpose was to turn the ermita into a satellite of Extremadura. Failing that, he wanted to undo the identification of the two shrines. His motivation was clearly financial, and the implication was that the ermita made money.

On 23 September 1575 the viceroy gave the following detailed reply to Philip II, in which his account differed substantially from that of the Hieronymite.

> Another [cédula] dated at San Lorenzo el Real, 15 May 1575, about what concerns the foundation of the ermita of Our Lady of Guadalupe and that I should arrange with the archbishop that he make the visitations of it. Visiting it and taking its accounts have always been done by the bishops.[8] With regard to the foundation of the church that has now been erected, the common understanding is that in the year 1555 or 1556 there was a small ermita there, in which was the image that is now in the church, and that a herdsman, who used to wander about the area, proclaimed that he had recovered his health by going to that ermita. The people's devotion began to grow and they named the image Our Lady of Guadalupe because it was said that it resembled that of Guadalupe in Spain. And from that time a confraternity was established, in which they say that there are probably 400 members. The church was built from alms and the entire building is complete. It has a fixed income and as for the income that it now seems to have and that which is drawn from alms, there is a record, taken from the majordomos' book, of the latest accountings that have been made of them. A more detailed account will be sent to Your Majesty. As for establishing a monastery, there is no suitable location, by reason of the locale, and there are so many in the neighborhood that it does not seem necessary; even less the establishment of a parish, either for Spaniards or Indians, as the prelate [Moya de Contreras] would like. I have begun to negotiate with him that it would be enough there if there were one secular priest of the appropriate age and of good life, so that if some of the people who go there out of devotion wish to go to confession, they can do so; and that the alms and whatever else might be there should be spent on the poor at the hospital of the Indians, which is what has the greater need. Since it has the name of a royal hospital, they think that that is enough for it to be in Your Majesty's care, and that if you do not think so, it should be applied to dowries for orphan girls. The archbishop has already put two secular priests there and if the income should increase, they will want to put another, with the result that everything will come down to the fact that two or three secular priests may eat.[9]

This testimony, as is immediately evident, is of the greatest value. Much of it is based on hearsay or common opinion, but in the context of the apparition accounts this becomes very important. It reflected what people believed about the shrine. The following specifics should be noted.

First is the viceroy's description of the origins of the chapel, which he dates to about 1555 or 1556, almost a quarter of a century after the date assigned by the traditional account, but in the years recorded by the native annalists,

Bustamante, and Freire. The popularity of the devotion is credited to a cure claimed by a herdsman who traveled in the area, though Enríquez related the cure to the shrine, not the image. Like Bustamante, the viceroy implied that the name of Guadalupe was given to the shrine after its foundation and that it was a popular rather than official title. Enríquez's testimony, like Bustamante's, lends weight to the idea that there was a tradition of a miracle at midcentury that popularized both the shrine and the devotion centered in it. It also supports Bustamante's claim that the devotion was new in 1556.

Enríquez linked the name of the church to the Extremaduran Guadalupe. His statement about the naming of the shrine, taken together with Bustamante's claim "to which they have given the name Guadalupe [han intitulado]" and that of Moya de Contreras cited below that Guadalupe was a popular name ("as it is commonly called"), confirms that it was an unofficial name for an ermita originally dedicated to the Nativity of the Virgin. How, then, did it acquire the name of Guadalupe? Enríquez's explanation about the resemblance to the Extremaduran Guadalupe seems implausible. No one familiar with the images of Guadalupe of Extremadura and that of Tepeyac could have confused the two or seen any resemblance between them. The former is a small, dark wooden statue, about eighteen inches high, covered with cloth robes and holding a child. Enríquez must have had firsthand knowledge of the image at Tepeyac, but it is not certain that he had ever seen that of Extremadura. This has led some to assert that the original image was different from the present one or that it was a statue. The viceroy could not have been referring to the Villaseca statue, since that was not placed in the shrine until some ten years after it received the name Guadalupe.

The likeliest explanation is that Enríquez was not referring to the primary image in Extremadura but to another, well-known one situated in the choir stalls near the prior's throne. This wooden statue bears a striking resemblance to that of Tepeyac, the most notable difference being that the Extremaduran holds a child. To my knowledge the only author within the time period of this study who made reference to this resemblance was the Hieronymite friar Francisco de San José, who published a history of the Extremaduran shrine in 1743. After noting that there was no resemblance between the Mexican Guadalupe and the primary image in Extremadura, he wrote:

> In front of the most ancient image of Our Lady of Guapalupe [sic] there is another wooden one in the choir, located in an arch that rises over the prior's chair, when [the prior] of this monastery was the Most Reverend Father fray Pedro de Vidania, in the year 1499, thirty-two years before the appearance of the one in Mexico. And it is so similar to the latter that it seems that the Virgin took it as the pattern for making a perfect copy in the Mexican one. In celebration of this resemblance, and it is the most ancient in our choir . . . a poet of these times sang the following sweet epigram:

Illa Novae Hesperiae Urbs, illius quae est Caput Orbis,
Guadalupanae Almam continet effigiem.
Archetypon quoeris, vivumve Exemplar in illa?
Haec tibi demonstrat sculpta Tabella suum.

[That city of the new western land, the capital of that world,
holds the fair image of the Guadalupan.
Do you seek the archetype and living model in that [city]?
This one shows its [archetype] to you in the carved picture.

For this reason if some of those who come from New Spain enter our choir, immediately without hesitation they say "Virgin of Guadalupe of Mexico." They call her that in joy and wonder, because her devotees recognize her as such.[10]

In addition to the presence of the child, the other differences are that the Extremaduran image's head is not turned to the right as is that of Tepeyac and the clothing is different. The statue is surrounded by a sunburst of thirty-three rays with clouds as a background. Like the Mexican Virgin, it stands on an upturned moon, the classic symbol of the woman of Revelation 12. The moon is upheld by a small angel, almost identical to the one at Tepeyac. Since the sunburst, the moon, and the angel were later additions to the Mexican image, there appears to have been a deliberate effort to adapt the latter to that of Extremadura. It would also be evidence that the present image was in the shrine from midcentury and that the retouchings date to almost the same period. It should be emphasized, however, that the image was not important in Enríquez's account. It was not associated with the cure of the herdsman nor was it described as miraculous.

The differences between the viceroy's account and Santa María's are notable. There is no way of reconciling them, although it appears that Santa María's is marred by his special pleading in favor of his order. What is most noteworthy is the general vagueness about the origins of the chapel. No one seemed to have a clear idea of how and when it began. What was known about it was based on hearsay. If the foremost religious event of Mexican history had indeed led to the construction of the chapel, there would surely have been some lingering evidence of this.

On 25 September Archbishop Moya de Contreras, who had succeeded Montúfar in 1572, wrote to the king that Enríquez had showed him the cédula of 15 May, which the archbishop had not yet received. "It appears that someone has given Your Majesty a misleading [siniestra] report of the establishment, income, expenditures, and alms of that building."[11] After a visitation, made personally or through another, Moya had his *provisor* (chief ecclesiastical judge), draw up a true account "in order that there the matter may be clear and that false opinions be stopped."[12] The viceroy had suggested that the surplus funds from the shrine be used for dowries for orphan girls or some other pious work so that people would be edified and their devotion to the chapel increased. Moya apparently agreed. According to a statement by Mariano Fernández de Echeverría y Veytia, the archbishop issued an *auto* (constitution) in 1576 that since Montúfar's motive in establishing the chapel was that the surplus from the income and alms be used for the dowries of orphan girls, henceforth each year the funds were to be applied to six dowries of 300 pesos each. Echeverría y Veytia commented how wealthy the chapel must have been in those days.[13] After that no more is heard about the matter.

Neither Enríquez nor Moya de Contreras nor Santa María made any reference, not even by the slightest hint, to the apparition accounts or the miraculous origin of the image or shrine. The claim that they did not do so because this was no concern to the Council of the Indies cannot be accepted, because the viceroy had no hesitation about including a reference to the cure of a herdsman. That council, under Ovando, sought all possible information on Spain's New World possessions. In addition, an event as extraordinary as the apparitions, which would have contributed greatly to the Indians' self-esteem and identity, would not have been considered insignificant. At the very time that the viceroy was writing, the Spanish crown was worrying about a rise in Indian self-awareness, a concern that led to the confiscation of Bernardino de Sahagún's classic history of the preconquest Nahuas. An attempt by the Hieronymites to assume control of and found a monastery at the site or change the name or the location of a church founded at the command of the Virgin Mary would certainly have aroused the most intense opposition.

Moya de Contreras had a special concern for the chapel at Guadalupe and helped to secure some indulgences for it. At some time before 1576 the members of the cofradía at Guadalupe asked him to secure the extension of some indulgences that had been granted in 1573 during a jubilee.[14] These included a plenary indulgence for those who visited the chapel on the feasts of the Nativity of the Virgin Mary and the Assumption (15 August), though not on 12 December. There was, however, a time limit of ten years for the indulgence, after which it was reduced. Moya enlisted the help of the Jesuit superior general, Everard Mercurian, to secure this, together with some relics for the cathedral, from the papacy. On 12 March 1576 Mercurian wrote to the archbishop that he had secured "the prorogation [extension] of the indulgence granted to the ermita of Our Lady of Guadalupe and the commutation of the day, as was asked, and the brief is included with this letter."[15] On 28 March Pope Gregory XIII issued the brief *Ut Deiparae semper virginis,* which renewed the plenary indulgence for an additional ten years and extended it to the cathedral so that the latter would not suffer from the competition.[16] On 17 December of that same year Moya wrote to the pope to acknowledge the receipt of the brief with effusive thanks. "We all most openly acknowledge that you have granted the relics of the saints and also the holy indulgences taken from the treasury of Christ, given in part to the cathedral church of Mexico and in part to the chapel of Saint Mary of Guadalupe (as it is commonly called), and from the same letter we have all experienced your fatherly benevolence and humanity toward us."[17] The archbishop's parenthetical comment implies that Guadalupe was not the official name of the chapel.

Apologists of the apparition tradition have viewed these actions by the archbishop as proofs of his devotion to the shrine and hence the divine nature of its origin. Even if they do demonstrate a special devotion, that in itself says nothing about the apparition account. Nowhere in any part of his meticulous reports to the king and the Council of the Indies is there any reference to the tradition of an apparition at Tepeyac. Nor is there any reference to it in the decrees and papers of the Third Mexican Provincial Council (1585), which he convoked and over which he presided. The papal brief made no mention of the apparition tradition, giving only the good of the newly converted Indians as a reason for the indulgence. The grant did not in any way constitute a special or unique recognition of the ermita. In 1576, at the request of the people and city council of Mexico, the pope granted indulgences to the church of Remedios because of that Virgin's role in the conquest.[18]

In view of the involvement of the Jesuit superior general in this grant, it is noteworthy that the earliest accounts of the foundation of the Society of Jesus in New Spain made no mention of Guadalupe or the apparition tradition.[19] This stands in stark contrast to the period from 1660 to 1767, when the Jesuits were in the forefront of popularizing the apparition devotion.

The Friar

Bernardino de Sahagún (ca. 1499–1590) was one of the foundational figures in the history of colonial Mexico, even though relatively little is known about him.[20] His original surname is believed to have been Ribeira, which would imply a Portuguese or Galician ancestry, but like other Franciscans of that time, he replaced it with the name of his native city on entering the seraphic order. Nothing is known of his life prior to his arrival in New Spain in 1529. He was one of the founders of the Franciscan school of Santa Cruz de Tlatelolco, which was dedicated to giving upper-class Indian boys a European humanistic education. Throughout his life he dedicated himself to linguistic studies, specifically Nahuatl, in which he became proficient. After being directed by his provincial superior to gather information on preconquest history and culture to help the missionaries in their work, he dedicated his whole life to this task. Working with a group of older Indians and sifting through their recollections, he sought to reconstruct the pre-Hispanic history of the Nahuas. The information he gathered was incorporated into the *Florentine Codex,* a Nahuatl/Spanish work done under his supervision by Nahua aides. Sahagún translated the Nahuatl into Spanish with the title of *Historia general de las cosas de Nueva España* (General history of the things of New Spain). Though no one single version or manuscript source exists for this landmark work, it is still one of the most valuable sources available to the modern scholar. Sahagún's last years were troubled by strife between the criollo and peninsular factions among the Franciscans and by the crown's concern about the possible threat posed by the revival of past Nahua glories. This royal concern led to the confiscation of his manuscripts.

In view of Sahagún's high opinion of the Indians and his interest in everything Nahua, an interest that went beyond mere pragmatism for the ministry, his comments on the shrine and devotion at Guadalupe are particularly valuable. About the year 1576 he wrote a Spanish appendix on superstitions for his *Historia general* in which he described three devotions that he considered to smack of renascent idolatry: Santa Ana in Tlaxcala, San Juan Bautista in Tianquizmanalco, and Guadalupe.

> Near the mountains are three or four places where they used to offer very solemn sacrifices, and they would come to them from very distant lands. One of these is here in Mexico [City], where there is a hill that is called Tepeyacac and the Spaniards call Tepeaquilla and is now called Our Lady of Guadalupe. In this place they used to have a temple dedicated to the mother of the gods, whom they called Tonantzin, which means "our mother." . . . The gathering of people in those days was great and everyone would say "let us go to the feast of Tonantzin." Now that the church of Our Lady of Guadalupe has been built there, they also call her [or it] Tonantzin, taking their cue from the preachers who call Our Lady, the Mother of God, Tonantzin. What may be the basis for this use of Tonantzin is not clear. However, we know for certain that the original use of the word means that ancient Tonantzin. It is something that should be remedied because the proper name for the Mother of God, Our Lady, is not Tonantzin but Dios inantzin. This appears to be an invention of the devil to cover over idolatry under the ambiguity of this name Tonantzin. They now come to visit this Tonantzin from far away, as far as in former times. The devotion itself is suspect because everywhere there are many churches to Our Lady and they do not go to them. They come from distant lands to this Tonantzin, as they did in former times.[21]

Sahagún was the first to identify Tepeyac as a place of pre-Hispanic pagan worship. Not much is known about Tonantzin, whose name is the reverential form of "our mother." She was sometimes identified with two other mother deities, Coatlicue (serpent skirt) and Cihuacoatl (woman serpent). Sahagún also identified Tonantzin with Cihuacoatl (which he translated as "mother of the serpent") and Clavigero with the maize goddess Centeotl.[22] Schendel says that Tonantzin was the goddess of herb medicines and hence associated with healing.[23] Coatlicue was sometimes identified as the mother of Coyolxauhqui and her four hundred brothers, and some traditions, which may have been influenced by postconquest Christian thought, identified her as a virgin.[24] Native traditions concerning the gods were often varied and contradictory, in part because of variations from one locale to another, in part because of the Mexicas' custom of adopting deities from subject peoples.

Sahagún was not only the first to make the identification of Tonantzin with the Virgin of Guadalupe, he is also the principal source for it. His assertion about the pagan antecedent of Guadalupe has been widely accepted and is frequently cited even today. It has also been the basis for the claim of a conscious substitution of the Christian devotion for the pagan one. Louise Burkhart, however, questions Sahagún's statement.[25] She bases this in part on the fact that Tonantzin was not a proper name but rather a respectful form of address that was generally used in the sixteenth century not only for the Virgin Mary but also for the Church. Sahagún himself had used the term for the Virgin in some sermons he wrote in the 1540s. She also points out that Sahagún's native informants never mentioned a preconquest shrine at Tepeyac. "The Indians were not perpetuating memories of precolumbian goddesses but were projecting elements of their Christian worship into their pre-Christian past, conceptualizing their ancient worship in terms of Mary. . . . There is no evidence that Tepeyacac held any special meaning for sixteenth-century Indians."[26] Her assertion is all the more plausible in view of the fact that Bustamante, who would have been expected to denounce any such neo-idolatry in the strongest terms, made no mention of pagan religious association at Tepeyac. On the other hand, the use of a respectful form of address rather than a proper name for a goddess was not unknown, as Toci (our grandmother) indicates. Lockhart has pointed out that the standard term was *totlaçonantzin*, "our precious mother," rather than the simple *tonantzin*. "Possibly because of this convergence [of pagan and Christian elements], but more likely because *tlaço*, 'precious, dear,' was routinely added to the description of almost any benevolent Christian supernatural, the simple form 'tonantzin' was avoided; I have yet to see it in any Nahuatl document in reference to the Virgin."[27]

De la Maza, Bravo Ugarte, Velázquez, and O'Gorman say that Sahagún's words "what may be the basis for this use of Tonantzin is not clear," of which a literal translation is "whence may have been born this foundation of this Tonantzin is not known for sure" [de donde haya nacido esta fundacion de esta Tonantzin no se sabe de cierto] should be taken to mean that no one knew the origin of the ermita.[28] O'Gorman quotes the original Spanish in altered form: "no se sabía de cierto el origen de aquella fundación." De la Maza sees Sahagún's reference to "this Tonantzin" as referring to the image; that is, the friar considered the image to be the new Tonantzin, even though Sahagún never mentioned the image. I incline toward the translation given above because the context of this and the previous and following sentences is clearly linguistic: Sahagún was saying that no one knew how or on what basis the preachers began using the term Tonantzin in reference to the Virgin Mary. While the term was appropriate in a literal sense, Sahagún objected to it on the grounds that it was the proper name of a pagan deity and was so understood by the Indians. Hence to use it was to encourage a confusion between the Virgin Mary and the mother goddess of the Aztecs, something that in Sahagún's mind laid the way open for a revival of idolatry. The proper Nahuatl term for the Christian Virgin was *Dios inantzin,* "Mother of God." As was mentioned above, the term Tonantzin does not seem to have been widely used.

Beyond that Sahagún considered the devotion itself to smack of neo-paganism. There were ample places and opportunities for the Indians to show their devotion to the Virgin Mary. The fact that so many repaired to Guadalupe, just as they had done in pagan times, and under the name Tonantzin, was for him proof that the natives were thinking in pre-Christian terms. He believed that the Indians' devotion was to the ancient goddess, not the Christian Virgin.

Again, there is total silence about the apparitions or any cures or miracles, and there is no reference to the existence of the image, even to show hostility or skepticism. Had he known of the apparition tradition, it hardly seems likely that he would have accused the devotion of being pagan. Like his fellow Franciscans two decades before, Sahagún was hostile to the devotion at Guadalupe, as it existed in the sixteenth century.

This hostility has posed a problem for those who seek to associate the Guadalupe tradition with the Franciscans, the Colegio de Santa Cruz, or even Sahagún himself. This has led to some convoluted explanations, of which Bravo Ugarte's may be considered typical. Referring to Sahagún's professed ignorance of the origin of the devotion, he wrote, "The very character of the event, which occurred among the Indians without the intervention of the Franciscans, in a place famous for the idolatrous cult of the goddess Tonantzin or Cihuacoatl and where the Indians spoke of the latter's appearances, as Sahagún himself notes in another passage . . . all this undoubtedly made him consider uncertain what was said of the miraculous origin of the image, which he must have known, as his disciple and collaborator [Antonio] Valeriano knew."[29] Other explanations base the friar's silence on his respect for Bustamante or his unwillingness to run contrary to the strong feelings among the Franciscans. Garibay, who claimed that the Guadalupe account came from Sahagún's Indian collaborators, believed that it was an "affected" or deliberate silence about what they were writing. He gave no reason for this, saying rather cryptically, "Mysterious as his behavior is, it totally explains his silence."[30] In light of all this it is impossible to accept the assertion that the Virgin of Guadalupe was a deliberate substitution for the pre-Hispanic mother goddess as a means of weaning the Indians from their old religion by giving them a Christian replacement. The Franciscan attitude went beyond the *silencio franciscano* mentioned by some historians. It was an overt, active hostility.[31]

There are a number of conclusions to be drawn from all the above. The testimony of Santa María is suspect and should be approached with great caution. Those of Philips, Enríquez, and Sahagún, however, are of the greatest importance. Enríquez corroborated the midcentury origin of the ermita. Only he and Philips mentioned the image and only Philips attributed miracles to it. Sahagún believed that the devotion was neo-idolatry. His assertion, however, that it was associated with or located at the site of a pre-Christian devotion is open to question. Most striking, of course, is the total silence by all three concerning any aspect of the apparitions or miraculous origins of the image. There is no reasonable explanation for this silence except that they were unaware of the apparition story.

6

A Confusion of Tongues:
Testimonies from 1572 to 1648

The late sixteenth and early seventeenth centuries saw a proliferation of chronicles and religious writings in New Spain. A new generation of friars arose, many of them criollos. At a time when the missionary enterprise had lost much of its original fervor and become more institutionalized and when its difficulties and limited success had become more apparent, the friars looked back to the early days as a golden age. Their accounts were often nostalgic and triumphalistic, an exaltation of a glorious past in a pedestrian present. At the same time, as the diocesan clergy displaced the mendicants in the colonial Church, the ecclesiastical hierarchy became more sympathetic to the criollos, a sympathy based in large part on its need of them. A rapidly accelerating criollo consciousness and pride gave the Spaniards born in the Indies, or those who identified with them, a strong sense of identity and self-esteem. This esteem coexisted with a sense of insecurity and a low self-image, the result in part of their second-class status. Increasingly, however, the criollos came to regard themselves as a special people, as God's own elect. Bernardo de Balbuena's extravagant work, *Grandeza mexicana* (1604), gave expression to this criollo messianism. The first publication of the Guadalupe tradition in 1648 would carry the process even further by imbuing it with a sense of divine election, an election that belonged to the criollos, not the Indians.

Hence at this point consideration must be given to the chroniclers, the majority of them mendicants, who wrote from 1572 until the appearance of the first published account of the apparitions in 1648. Though this necessarily involves a tedious survey of writers and their works, it is necessary in order to have a clear view of the state of the question. It will soon become apparent that there is no consistent pattern to these testimonies other than an absence of any references to the apparitions.

Further Silences

In the period from 1572 to 1648 there was a continued lack of references to the apparitions in written documents. In some cases this was clearly because the writers had no occasion or reason for referring to the account. Typical of this was the Jesuit historian José de Acosta, born at Medina del Campo in 1540.[1] After joining the Society of Jesus at an early age in 1552, he studied in his hometown until 1557. From 1559 until 1567 he studied at Alcalá de Henares and traveled widely throughout the Iberian peninsula. He was ordained to the priesthood in 1566 and four years later went to Peru as one of the founders of the Jesuit mission there. Forced to return to Spain because of ill health, Acosta traveled by way of New Spain, where he stayed from June 1586 until March 1587. He died at Salamanca in 1600. A member of the moderate pro-Indian school, Acosta wrote two major works. The first was the *Historia natural y moral de las Indias,* published at Seville in 1590, which included a great deal of information on Indian religious and social institutions. The other was *De promulgatione evangelii apud barbaros seu de procuranda indorum salute,* which was written in 1575 to 1576 and published at Salamanca in 1588. It is not surprising that neither work dealt with Guadalupe, even though Acosta, who spent a little less than a year in New Spain, would have had the opportunity to learn about it. The *Historia* dealt with preconquest history, and the *De promulgatione* was a rather legal work that dealt more with rights and juridical procedures than with popular devotion.

Similarly, one finds no reference to the apparitions in the works of Fernando Alvarado Tezozomoc, a grandson of Moteuccoma II. He was born about 1525/1530 of pure Indian stock.[2] As a chronicler, he published two important works. The *Crónica mexicana,* a major contribution to pre-Hispanic history, was written in Spanish, probably in 1598. The other, *Cronica mexicayotl,* was written in Nahuatl and published in a revised version in 1609. Again the limits imposed by subject matter precluded any reference to Guadalupe.

In contrast it would be expected that Pedro de Gante would have said something about Guadalupe. The great Franciscan lay brother had been in New Spain since 1523 and had been deeply involved in efforts to provide education, especially in crafts, to the Indians. Today he is fondly remembered for his concern for the natives and his work in their behalf. In none of his correspondence, however, is there any reference to the apparition account.

Antonio Valeriano

In August 1605 came the death of a figure who today is of surpassing importance in the history of the Guadalupe account, the Indian governor and Latinist, don Antonio Valeriano. He was a native of Azcapotzalco, was said to have been related to Moteucçoma II, and had been one of the first students at the Franciscan college of Santa Cruz de Tlatelolco, where he later taught.[3] He was also a student and confidant of Sahagún. In 1554, when describing the colegio at Tlatelolco, Cervantes de Salazar wrote that the Indians "have a teacher of their own nationality, Antonio Valeriano, who is in no respect inferior to our grammarians. He is well trained in the observance of Christian law and is an ardent student of oratory."[4] From 1573 until the 1590s he was governor of the Nahua barrios in Mexico City and had a widespread reputation as a Latinist and scholar.[5] Even in his old age he could speak Latin extemporaneously. He instructed some of the early missionaries, including Sahagún, Juan Bautista, and Torquemada, in Nahuatl.[6] Valeriano was one of the first Indian informants mentioned by name by the pioneer Franciscan historians and ethnologists and the only one mentioned by Cervantes de Salazar. As an early alumnus of Santa Cruz de Tlatelolco, he was clearly a source of pride to the Franciscans.

Valeriano was reputed to have been the author of a "Relación," an account of the Guadalupe apparitions, usually dated either 1540 to 1545 or 1558 to 1572. If the former date is accepted, it would mean that Valeriano was very young at the time of the composition. There is no extant copy of this "Relación." This and the related question of whether Valeriano's supposed "Relación" was the basis of or the same as the *Nican mopohua* will be discussed in chapters 9 and 11. Here it should be noted that the association of Valeriano with a Nahuatl account of the apparitions began with Sigüenza y Góngora some eighty-five years after Valeriano's death. The few biographical data on Valeriano list his accomplishments as a Latinist, including translating Nahuatl to Latin in the style of Cato, and as Nahua governor of Mexico City, but say nothing about him as the author of the earliest account of the Guadalupe apparitions.[7] It seems strange that something as arcane as translating Nahuatl into the Latin of Cato should be noted but not an account of the most important religious event of the time.

There are other references from this time period that are ambiguous and pose problems of interpretation.

Juan Suárez de Peralta

One of the more interesting personalities of sixteenth-century New Spain was Juan Suárez de Peralta. Related by marriage to Cortés, he spent most of his life in various schemes to better his position. Finally, in 1579, he abandoned the New World for Spain. In the following year he began writing a history of his colonial homeland, the *Noticias históricas de Nueva España*. Although it was concerned primarily with the Cortés-Avila conspiracy, it also contained descriptions of the natives and their land. In 1589 he completed his *Tratado de descubrimiento de las Indias*. He described the arrival of the new viceroy, Martín Enríquez, at Guadalupe in May 1568 and added, "It is an image of great

devotion which is about two leagues from Mexico. It has worked many miracles. It [she] appeared among some rocks and the whole land flocks to this
devotion."[8] It is impossible to say for sure just what he meant or how his
account is related to any of the other Guadalupe stories. It is unclear if the
subject of "appeared" (*apareciose*) is the image or the Virgin. Some have claimed
that the subject was the Virgin Mary and that this was a clear reference to an
apparition at Guadalupe. From the immediate context, however, it seems that
the reference was to the image.[9] This would fit in with the standard genre of
apparition stories in which the image is found or discovered. His description
also lacked the adjectives such as "portentosa" and "milagrosa" which were usually attached to accounts of the apparitions and it did not mention any circumstance of the appearance. It is a stark reference and ambiguous at best.

Fernando de Alva Ixtlilxochitl

The great mestizo historian, don Fernando de Alva Ixtlilxochitl, was a descendant of Nezahualpilli, the last king of Texcoco.[10] He was probably born about
1570 and may have studied at the Franciscan college of Santa Cruz de Tlatelolco. Despite his learning and the important positions he held in local government, he and his family suffered economic hardship. He complained bitterly
about this, though perhaps with an element of exaggeration.[11] As a historian
he followed the best European norms, such as they were, for his research and
writing.

Alva Ixtlilxochitl's major works were his *Relaciones* and the *Historia chichimeca,* both of which were written in Spanish and dealt with pre-Hispanic
history from the Texcocan point of view. The *Historia* was written at the direction of the viceroy don Luis de Velasco II. Of the *Relaciones,* only the thirteenth,
the *Relación de la venida de los españoles y principio de la ley evangélica,* narrated
events after the conquest. It also contained a denunciation of Spanish mistreatment of the Indians.[12] Because of the time span covered by these works, there
was no reference to the postconquest apparition story.

Cuevas quoted an account of a favor done to the rulers and people of Teotihuacan through the intercession of the Virgin of Guadalupe that he attributed
to Alva Ixtlilxochitl. He said that it existed in a copy made by Alva's son don
Juan de Alva y Cortés. Cuevas did not give any source for the story or state
where it could be found. The following is a translation of the Spanish as given
by Cuevas, who said mistakenly that it was translated from the original Nahuatl by the Mexican priest-historian Fortino Hipólito Vera.

> On taking their seat and the first place,[13] when the beautiful image of the per-
> fect Virgin, our beloved mother, appeared, the people, the lords, the nobles, in-
> voked her from that time on in order that she might help and defend them in
> their labors and in the hour of death, all of them putting themselves into her
> hands. Don Francisco Quetzalmamalitzin occupied the lordship of Teotihuacan

when the people of the town disbanded, having agreed to give up their homes
and to leave violently, without anyone's remaining, in order that the religious
of Saint Francis would not give up their doctrinas since the viceroy, don Luis de
Velasco, wished the religious of Saint Augustine to take them over. As a conse-
quence of this the people of the town underwent much hardship, since their
lord and the principal men were in hiding because they were being looked for
everywhere. But, finally, [their lord] having gone secretly to Azcatpotzalco [sic],
he begged the heavenly lady of Guadalupe that she would inspire her beloved
son, the viceroy, and the judges of the royal audiencia to pardon the people of
the town in order that they might return to their homes and that they again
be given the religious of Saint Francis. And so it happened, because the lord,
the principal men, and the people of the town were pardoned, and they again
ordered the religious of Saint Francis to have charge of them. And they all
returned to their homes without further difficulty. This happened in the year
1558. It is also certain that don Francisco at the time of his death commended
himself to the Queen of Heaven, our adored Mother of Guadalupe, in order that
she might intercede for his life and for his soul. And he left her an offering, as
appears in the first clause or bequest of the will made by him on 2 March
1563.[14]

The story of the resistance of the Indians of Teotihuacan to the change of
religious in the doctrinas is well documented, particularly by Mendieta. According to him, the Augustinians sought to build a house in Teotihuacan, beginning in 1557. Although the Franciscans had previously evangelized the
town, they did not have a foundation there. The Indians unsuccessfully peti-
tioned the Franciscan chapter and the provincial, Bustamante, to send their
friars to the town.[15] The chief of the town was Francisco Verdugo Quetzalmamalitzin, who led the opposition to the Augustinians. When a group of the
latter, who had tried to establish a residence in Teotihuacan, grew weary of the
hostility and went en masse to see their provincial, the Indians stripped their
house of all its possessions. The Indians, in turn, fled from the town, which was
depopulated for almost a year. Eventually, a reconciliation was arranged, and
the rebellious Indians were pardoned by Viceroy Velasco. Neither Mendieta nor
any contemporary source, however, mentioned recourse to Guadalupe or to any
divine help.

On what basis, then, did Cuevas attribute this story to Alva Ixtlilxochitl and
associate it with Guadalupe? Though he gave no source for the account, he did
say that the translation was by Vera. The latter included the account both in
Nahuatl and in a Spanish translation, which is the same as Cuevas's, in his *Tesoro
guadalupano.*[16] The Spanish translation was actually by Francisco del Paso y
Troncoso. Vera also cited a map that Botturini Benaduci claimed to possess that
gave the original Nahuatl. Vera noted the similarity of the Nahuatl account
with that given by Luis Laso de la Vega in the collection of miracle stories,
called the *Nican motecpana,* included in the *Huey tlamahuiçoltica* (1649).[17] In fact

they are the same. Cuevas, then, took the account from Vera, who got it from Laso de la Vega and published it together with a Spanish translation by Paso y Troncoso. On the basis of a statement by Sigüenza y Góngora these miracle stories were later attributed to Alva Ixtlilxochitl (see chapter 9). The attribution to Alva Ixtlilxochitl is erroneous, as is the insertion of Guadalupe into the Teotihuacan story.

As was mentioned in the above account, don Francisco Verdugo Quetzalmamalitzin, the lord of Teotihuacan, in his last will, dated 2 April 1563, among other bequests made the following to the shrine at Guadalupe: "I order that if God should take me from this life, four pesos of alms should immediately be given to Our Lady of Guadalupe in order that the priest who resides in the said church may say masses for me."[18] This obviously reflects a devotion to the Virgin of Guadalupe or the shrine but proves nothing about the apparitions. Don Francisco's bequest was only one of many that he made in his will to religious houses and causes. A similar situation is found with the will of Esteban Tomelín or Lomelín, which is often cited by apparitionists. He was the father of the Venerable María de Jesús, a nun of La Concepción, Puebla, whose cause of canonization had been introduced. He also left a sum of money to Guadalupe, but it was only one among many bequests to religious causes that he made.[19]

Mendicant Chroniclers

Diego de Valadés

Diego de Valadés was a mestizo, the son of a conquistador and a Tlaxcalan noblewoman.[20] He was born in 1533 and at an early age entered the Franciscan order, where he was strongly influenced by Pedro de Gante. After missionary work among the Chichimeca Indians to the north of Mexico City, he went to Rome in 1570 to act as his order's procurator before the Holy See. In 1579 he published in Italy his *Rhetorica Christiana,* a work on Christian eloquence. Valadés was an excellent Latinist and had imbibed the Christian humanism that characterized many Franciscans. Though devoted to the art of eloquence, his book contained many digressions on the Indians and their culture. Chapter 25, in particular, was devoted to a description of how the Indians celebrated Christian feasts, especially in their music. There was, however, no mention of the apparition tradition.

Diego Durán

One of the most pro-Indian of sixteenth-century writers was the Dominican Diego Durán. Born in Spain, he came to New Spain as a young child and grew up in Texcoco. In 1556 he entered the Dominican order and dedicated the rest of his life to missionary work and a study of the Nahuatl language and Nahua antiquities. In 1580 he published his major work *Historia de las Indias de Nueva*

España e islas de tierra firme. Like other friars of that century, one of his principal purposes was to help missionaries in their work, especially by showing them how to detect cryptopaganism. Durán's extensive and careful research places his *Historia* in the same category as Sahagún's. Because it dealt exclusively with the preconquest and conquest periods, there was no reference to Guadalupe.

Alonso Ponce

In the 1570s and 1580s Alonso Ponce, the commissary general of the Franciscans, conducted a visitation of his order's houses in New Spain. At that time the Franciscans were deeply divided by conflict between the criollo and peninsular factions. The experience was an unhappy one for Ponce, and it cost him dearly in both mental and physical health. Two of his companions later published an account of his visitation, known as the *Relación.* On 23 July 1585 they passed near Guadalupe, "a small town of Mexican [Nahua] Indians and in it, situated on a hill, an ermita or church of Our Lady of Guadalupe, where the Spaniards of Mexico [City] go to keep vigil and to have novenas, and there is a resident secular priest there who says mass for them. In that town the Indians in the time of their paganism used to have an idol called Ixpuchtli, which means virgin or maiden, and they would come there as to a sanctuary from all over that land with their gifts and offerings. The father commissary passed by there at a distance."[21]

It is immediately evident that the author has confused at least one fact. He identified Tonantzin as *Ixpuchtli* (more correctly, *ichpochtli*), which is the Nahuatl word for a young unmarried girl, but which in postconquest times could also be used for virgin. It is remotely possible that the reference was to Coatlicue, who was sometimes identified as a virgin. It is also possible that there was more than one legend about the religious significance of Tepeyac. Some have concluded that it was another name for Tonantzin, but it seems more likely that the author simply made a mistake. He also emphasized that the devotion at Guadalupe was a Spanish, not an Indian, one. Again, there was no reference to the apparition or to an image of miraculous origin.

Gerónimo de Mendieta

One friar whose witness is of special value is Gerónimo de Mendieta. He was born in Spain and entered the Franciscan order at an early age. In 1554 he came to New Spain, which was the scene of his ministry for the next fifty years. As a member of the Franciscan house of Xochimilco, he studied Nahuatl under the famed Andrés de Olmos and achieved such fluency that he was said to have spoken it better than Castilian. In 1573, at the direction of his superiors in Spain, he undertook his classic work, *Historia eclesiástica indiana.* It was completed in 1596 but not published until 1870, undoubtedly because of its fierce denunciations of the encomenderos and outspoken criticisms of Indian policy under Philip II (1556–1598). Mendieta was in the extreme pro-Indian camp and viewed them, and the Spanish conquest, in apocalyptic and millenarian terms. In the *Historia* he devoted three chapters to the life of Zumárraga but made no mention of Guadalupe.[22] The *Historia* contains numerous references to Tepeaca, but they are to the town of that name in Tlaxcala.

More significant is the fact that Mendieta devoted five chapters of his history to the visions, revelations, and special heavenly favors granted to the Indians.[23] One was an account of a vision received by an elderly Indian, Miguel de San Jerónimo. On Friday, 12 October, during the great epidemic of 1576, as he was rowing his canoe across lake Xochimilco, Miguel saw an Indian woman who told him that sinners should repent in order to stop the epidemic. He informed Mendieta of the vision. After initial skepticism the friar accepted it as authentic and decided that the woman was either the Virgin or an angel. "She appeared in the form of an Indian woman in order not to frighten that poor old man in another shape."[24] There is no evidence of a recourse to Guadalupe during that epidemic.

In another chapter Mendieta related revelations given to Indian children.[25] He observed that, as Motolinía had said in his *De Moribus Indorum,* visions, such as seeing Christ in the elevated host during mass, were more common in the past than in his days.[26] He related two cases of Indians who had received communion directly from the Virgin or the saints, one at Huexotzingo in December 1591, another at Tepeaca in Tlaxcala. There was also a story of how the Virgin Mary had appeared to the Indian wife of the Spaniard Hernando Alonso, of the town of Xuchipila, during her final illness. Mary told her that she had one month to live, a prophecy that was fulfilled to the day. A chapter was devoted to accounts of souls that had returned to dead bodies and individuals who were given out-of-body experiences for their correction. An Indian of Tlaxcala was rescued from demons by Saint James and another cured of illness by Saint Peter. Mendieta's account of Juan, an Indian youth of Santa Ana in Tlaxcala, who in his final illness was rescued from black demons by his invocation of the Virgin Mary, was a verbatim retelling of a story previously related by Motolinía. The final of the five chapters told of the dead who appeared to the living in order to seek help.[27]

The accounts given by Mendieta were those he heard or experienced in the areas where he served. This means that the majority came from Tlaxcala rather than from the environs of Mexico City. Two of them, however, were situated in Xochimilco and Tlatelolco, in both of which places Mendieta had been stationed. The accounts of Motolinía and Mendieta clearly demonstrate that there were myriad stories of miracles, visions, apparitions, and divine favors to Indians in circulation in the later sixteenth and early seventeenth centuries. They were sufficiently numerous that Mendieta could catalog them by genre. They also show that the friars tended to be initially skeptical of such stories but eventually came to believe most of them. What is particularly striking, of course, is the absence of any mention of Guadalupe.

Juan de Grijalva

The year 1611 saw the appearance of four works of importance. One was the history of the Augustinians in New Spain written by Juan de Grijalva, *Cronica de la orden de N. P. S. Augustin en las prouincias de la Nueua España.* Grijalva was credulous with regard to omens and miracles, but he never mentioned Guadalupe. He did, however, include a lengthy treatment of the Virgin of Remedios, though his account had its own variations. He wrote that the Virgin had appeared on the causeway on the Noche Triste and by her warlike appearance had forced the Aztecs to retreat and thus saved the Spaniards. Don Juan, the discoverer of Remedios, was in the native forces at that time. Many years after the conquest he had several visions of the Virgin along a roadway. He told the local Franciscans of this, but they were skeptical. Later, when hunting, he found the image, and he took it to his home and kept it there for ten years. Then the image began returning to its original place, thus indicating the Virgin's will that a chapel be built on that spot. It was don Juan, the cacique, who built the church and tended it. In Grijalva's account, it was not an illness that brought the Indian close to death but an accident, and he was healed not at Guadalupe but by means of a leather belt, a supposed relic of Saint Augustine, that was with the image. Undoubtedly it was this relic of his order's putative founder that caused Grijalva to be so interested in Remedios. The story, of course, followed the classic lines of the apparition genre.[28]

According to Grijalva, the statue of Remedios was brought to Mexico City three times. The first was in 1567 under Viceroy Martín Enríquez to help stop the great matlazahuatl. This date is an obvious error and is nothing more than an accidental inversion of the last two numbers. The other two occasions that Grijalva cited were droughts in 1597 and 1616. Grijalva also devoted a full chapter to the reasons why so few miracles accompanied the conversion of the Indians.[29]

Antonio Daza

The Franciscan Antonio Daza's *Chronica general de S. Francisco y su apostolica orden,* which was also published in 1611, contained an extended treatment of Zumárraga but made no mention of Guadalupe. It is possible that Daza may never have been in New Spain.

Alonso Fernández

In the same year Alonso Fernández published his *Historia eclesiastica.* Fernández lived an extraordinarily long time (1572–1687) and had been master general of the Dominican order. He apparently never visited the New World. His book was intended to be edifying and was based on published accounts. It described the great achievements of the religious of all orders in the Indies, with special emphasis on the holiness of some individuals and the miracles they wrought. He included a comprehensive and accurate biography of Zumárraga that repeated some of the better-known anecdotes of the bishop's life.[30] No mention, however, was made of Guadalupe.

Martín de León

The fourth work to appear in 1611 did contain a reference to Guadalupe. It was the *Camino del cielo* of the Dominican Martín de León. Written in both Nahuatl and Spanish, it was a general reference for priests working among the natives and contained a catechism, prayers, two directories for confessors (*confesionarios*), as well as other pastoral aids. León had occasion to speak of the difficulties in converting or serving the Indians, difficulties that he had experienced at first hand. Historically, he wrote, the Nahuas had freely accepted other gods into their pantheon, where they were worshiped together with the ancestral gods. Initially, they had intended to accept the Christian God in the same way and were baffled by attempts to exclude the old deities. Hence, León asserted, the devil had led them to hide or dissimulate their idolatry. He delineated three kinds of dissimulation. The first was that on feast days the Indians honored the saint of the day externally but "many of them honor the idol that the ancestors honored in the days of their paganism." The second dissimulation was to hide pagan idols inside Christian statues.

> The third is taken from the very names of the idols that were venerated in those towns, for the names with which they are signified in Latin or Spanish are the same in meaning that the names of these idols signified. For example, in the city of Mexico, on the hill where Our Lady of Guadalupe is, they used to adore an idol of a goddess whom they called Tonantzin, that is, "our mother," and this same name they give to Our Lady, and they always say that they are going to Tonantzin, or that they are celebrating a feast to Tonantzin, and many of them understand it in reference to the ancient one, not the modern one of today. That is like what I said about the one in Tlaxcala, the church of Saint Ann, in place of a goddess they used to call Tocitzin, our grandmother, and nowadays they say that they are celebrating a feast to Toci, or they are going to the temple of Toci.[31]

The other suspect devotion was that of San Juan Tianquizmanalco, "the most superstitious that there has been in all New Spain."[32]

What is immediately apparent is how closely León's argument parallels that of Sahagún, from whom he probably borrowed it. This is evidence of the continued hostility of the mendicants toward the devotion of Guadalupe on the grounds that it was neopagan. Like Sahagún, León believed that the Indians were going to Guadalupe because of its pre-Christian associations and the confusion of names. Also, like Sahagún, he omitted any reference to the image. He followed Sahagún in naming Santa Ana of Tlaxcala and San Juan Bautista of Tianquizmanalco as among the cryptoidolatries of New Spain.

León went on to warn priests about the months of the Aztec calendar when the Indians were liable to worship their pagan deities. In the eleventh month, which began on 24 August, "they used to celebrate the feast of the mother of the gods, called Toci, meaning 'our grandmother.'"[33] What is interesting is that this feast was celebrated so closely to the twin feasts of the Nativity of the Virgin Mary and the Extremaduran Guadalupe, both of which were closely associated with the shrine at Tepeyac.

Juan de Torquemada

A testimony similar to those of Sahagún and León was given by Juan de Torquemada. Born in Spain around the year 1557, he came to New Spain as a child. He joined the Franciscan order and studied under Antonio Valeriano, Bernardino de Sahagún, and Juan Bautista. He became deeply interested in Indian studies and in 1603 was named guardian, or superior, of the Franciscan house of Santiago de Tlatelolco, a center of Franciscan scholarship on Indian language and antiquities. He was a friend and admirer of Gerónimo de Mendieta. From 1614 to 1617 he was provincial of his order in New Spain. At the request of his superiors he began writing a history of the Franciscan missionary effort in that kingdom, in part because Mendieta's work had never been published. The result was the *Monarquía indiana,* published at Seville in 1615. The work had three principal themes: preconquest history together with the first century of colonial life, pre-Hispanic culture, and the conversion of the Indians by Franciscan missionaries. It also incorporated large sections of Mendieta's *Historica eclesiástica,* a fact that caused Torquemada to be accused of plagiarism.[34]

Torquemada wrote that there were three places where the pagan Indians once worshiped three different gods. After describing the first two at Tlaxcala and Tianquizmanalco, he continued:

> And in the other, which is one league from this city of Mexico, to the north, they held celebrations for another goddess, called Tonan, which means "our mother." This devotion to the gods was prevalent when our friars came to this land. Large crowds of people gathered from many leagues roundabout, especially to that of Tianquizmanalco. They came to it on pilgrimage from Guatemala, which is three hundred leagues away, and from even farther, to offer gifts and presents. And so, wishing to remedy this great harm, our first religious, who were those who came before the others to cultivate this unkempt vineyard in order to renew the field . . . and in it they set up the Most Glorious Saint Ann, grandmother of Our Lord, in order that it might coincide with the ancient festivity, so far as the glorious saint is concerned, and the celebration of

her day, although without any abuse or idolatrous intention. In Tianhuizma-
nalco [*sic*] they established a church to Saint John the Baptist and on Tonantzin, near Mexico [City], a church to the most holy Virgin, who is our lady and
mother. And in these three places these three festivals are celebrated, to which
the people come, especially to that of Saint John. There are very great offerings,
although greater devotion has been lacking, probably because there are other devotions nearer their towns and territories.[35]

It is immediately clear that there is a sequential literary dependence, starting
with Sahagún and copied, with varying degrees of fidelity, by the *Santoral en
mexicano,* Martín de León, and Torquemada. Sahagún made the original assertion, and the others simply copied from him.

On the face of it Torquemada was saying that the first Franciscans built the
shrine at Guadalupe in order to erase the memory of the pagan gods that had
been worshiped there. He was the first person to make this assertion and the
only one within the time limits of this study. His writing, however, is confusing. He mistakenly called the hill Tonantzin instead of Tepeyac. Why did he
give credit to the Franciscans when they had earlier opposed the devotion? One
possible explanation, given by Lafaye, is that the Franciscans of New Spain were
by then almost totally criollo and so favored the devotion.[36] On the other hand,
the peninsulars still maintained a slim control in the early seventeenth century
and there is no evidence of a Franciscan house or presence at Tepeyac at any
date. Another, and more probable explanation, is that Torquemada made a mistake. As has been said previously, the idea that the friars originated the Guadalupe devotion and apparition account in order to win the Indians to Christianity does not fit the known facts. Like Sahagún and León, Torquemada made no
reference to the image or to any miracles.

Agustín Dávila Padilla

In 1596 Agustín Dávila Padilla published a history of the Dominican order in
New Spain, *Historia de la fundacion y discurso de la provincia de Santiago de Mexico,
de la Orden de Predicadores.* Again there was no mention of Guadalupe.

Gabriel de Talavera

In the following year, however, there was a mention, this time in a history of
Our Lady of Guadalupe of Extremadura.' This work was *Historia de Nvestra Señora de Gvadalvpe* by the Hieronymite Gabriel de Talavera, prior of the Extremaduran monastery. In it he made the following observation: "the devotion and
respect for the sanctuary took such deep root in those inhabitants that they
immediately began to show signs of the good spirit with which they had received [Christian] doctrine, raising churches and sanctuaries with much devotion with the title of Our Lady of Guadalupe, especially in the city of Mexico
in New Spain."[37]

Talavera was a Spaniard who had never seen the New World. His purpose was to glorify the devotion to the patroness of Extremadura and so he related the Mexican Guadalupe to the Iberian one. His statement cannot be cited either for or against the apparitions.

Antonio de Remesal

Antonio de Remesal, a Dominican, was a follower of Torquemada and with the latter's encouragement published in 1620 a combined religious and political history of the Indies, *Historia general de las Indias occidentales.* This work devoted much space to both Zumárraga and Las Casas, but there was no reference to Guadalupe.

Luis de Cisneros

There was, however, a mention of Guadalupe in the following year. In 1619 Luis de Cisneros, a Mercedarian friar and professor of theology at the Royal and Pontifical University, died, leaving for the press his history of the shrine of Remedios. "The oldest [sanctuary] is that of Guadalupe, which is one league from this toward the north. It is an image of great devotion and crowds, almost since the day the land was won. It has worked and does work many miracles. They are building a notable church to it which by the order and care of the archbishop is in a very good state."[38]

Cisneros dated the foundation of the sanctuary almost to the time of the conquest, perhaps an indication that there was more than one tradition about its origin. It is equally probable that he may simply have been in error. One tradition traced it to the very time of the conquest, the other (such as that narrated by Martín Enríquez) put it at midcentury. Again, there is no mention of the apparitions nor is there any indication of antagonism between Remedios and Guadalupe.

Thomas Gage

In 1625, Thomas Gage, at that time a Dominican priest, made two references to Guadalupe in his account of his travels in New Spain. In one he described it as a town of five thousand inhabitants, in the other he referred to passing through it. He said nothing, however, about the religious significance of the place.[39]

Juan de Cepeda

In 1622 Archbishop Juan de la Serna consecrated the new church of Our Lady of Guadalupe. In that same year an Augustinian friar, Juan de Cepeda, published a sermon that he had given there on 8 September. Cepeda had preached at Guadalupe on this feast for ten successive years, but it was only in 1622 that he finally published one of his sermons. The reason for preaching on 8 September, according to Cepeda, was that it was the "patronal day [*vocación*] of the ermita of Guadalupe."[40] The association, again, was clearly with the Nativity of the Virgin and the feast of the Extremaduran Guadalupe. Although the sermon was dedicated to the feast of the chapel, it made no mention of any apparitions. The image on the cover of the published sermon was that of Our Lady of Grace, not the present image in the basilica. It has been argued that the mass of 8 September was used for all Marian devotions and chapels that did not have a proper one. Cepeda's testimony goes beyond that to indicate that it was a true patronage.

The association with the nativity is shown by the fact that on 29 August 1600 the cathedral chapter of Mexico decided that the feast of the Nativity of the Blessed Virgin should be celebrated at Guadalupe on Sunday, 10 September, rather than 8 September, because it was the titular feast of the chapel and the cornerstone of a new church would be laid on that day. Again, it is clear that the church was originally dedicated to the Nativity of the Blessed Virgin and that 12 December was not yet its feast day. The chapter also deliberated about changing the site of the church. It finally delegated the choice of the location to two of its members and the superintendent of construction. No consideration was given to situating it on the hill of Tepeyac, the actual site of the apparitions.

Poetic Allusions

Angel Betancurt

De la Maza wrote of a certain Captain Angel Betancurt, who came to New Spain in 1608 and who wrote a poem, *Historia de la Milagrosa Imagen de Nuestra Señora de los Remedios,* that also contained a reference to Guadalupe.[41] Almost nothing is known about Betancurt. Botturini Benaduci said that he belonged to the Third Order of Saint Francis and that he wrote his verse history of Remedios before the publication of those by Luis de Cisneros and Francisco de Florencia.[42] It contains several hundred stanzas, some of which refer specifically to Guadalupe. In the poem a bird addresses Juan Diego.

"Look at the blood of those sacrificed
which in this idolatry is hot;
it will come to be purified of vices
the Christianity of my rose-colored east;
and in order that you may have clues of your glory,
go down diligently to Tepeaquilla,
and among the hewed [sharp?] and round stones
you will see my image next to the waves.

Not like here [Remedios?], not of sculpture [*bulto*], of paint brushes
that on the empty canvas the great Apelles applies [*tupe*],
because God, the true Praxiteles,
will there give me the name of Guadalupe.
You will build me a temple there when the faithful
raise the cross and it will fill this hemisphere,
after the conquest of this land,
for nothing good comes from war."

It spoke and the commanding heron went away
and the devout cacique went down to the valley;
he found the precious painting of the rose
and he was to keep it, together with the first
[Remedios?],
until the majestic city
was clothed by Spain to our measure,
and to the one of Guadalupe, blessed flower,
don Juan built an ermita of pines.[43]

The poem, to all appearances, is wretchedly written and at times unintelligible. It has, however, been cited as evidence for a belief in the miraculous origin of the image of Guadalupe. What witness it gives, however, is unclear and useless. Some important points, however, should be noted. The poet confuses Juan Diego of Guadalupe and don Juan de Tovar of Remedios; the Juan in the poem is called a cacique, or chief, and is given the honorific "don." The image is found among the rocks and by the waters, a classic example of what happens in traditional apparition stories. Both Remedios and Guadalupe are described as painted by God, and it is God, not the Virgin, who through the agency of a bird commands the building of an ermita at Guadalupe. The visionary keeps the image with himself for a period of time, as happened in the story of Remedios. It is the visionary, not the bishop, who builds the first ermita, something also found in most versions of the Remedios story. The account in general has no similarities with the Guadalupe tradition.

De la Maza, Velázquez, and others have attached great importance to the poem as the first witness to the divine origin of the image at Guadalupe. In view of Betancurt's great poetic license (or confusion) and the fact that his account has nothing in common with the standard Guadalupe tradition, they have given this poem an importance that it does not deserve. On the other hand, it may well be evidence that the tradition had not yet become fixed by the early seventeenth century and that there was an early confusion of Guadalupe with Remedios—or at least that somehow the two accounts had become intertwined. Beyond that speculation nothing can be said with certainty.

The Flood of 1629 to 1634

Two other poetic allusions resulted from one of the worst natural disasters in the history of Mexico City, the great flood of 1629. As the successor to the Mexica capital of Tenochtitlan, the city inherited the perils that came with a location on a sandy island surrounded by lakes. Flooding had been a constant danger in Mexica times and was still so in the seventeenth century. The drainage system (*desagüe*) that had been inaugurated in 1607 had been allowed to deteriorate in subsequent years.

In February 1629 the city of Mexico celebrated the canonization of Felipe de Jesús, the first and only canonized saint in Mexican history. As Alegre remarked, "The happy beginning of the year was followed, as usually happens according to the law of human affairs, by a most sad end."[44] The sad end was the flood that began in September 1629. Within a short time it was impossible to travel in or about the city except by canoe. Pestilence accompanied the flood, and Archbishop Francisco Manso y Zúñiga, a Castilian with marked procriollo sympathies, together with some local citizens seriously suggested abandoning the site altogether and rebuilding the city elsewhere.[45] At the archbishop's direction, the image of Our Lady of Guadalupe was brought to Mexico City by canoe and, after a night in the archbishop's palace, was placed in the cathedral, where it remained throughout the entire period of the flood.[46] Alegre commented on the novelty of this move: "There had been nothing like that action up to that time." A novena was held, concluding with solemn vespers and a mass at the main altar before the image.[47] According to the Dominican chronicler Baltasar de Medina, the Virgin of Guadalupe stopped the flood, though the waters subsided "little by little."[48] Alegre, writing in 1630, said that the waters had not yet subsided. It seems most likely that the flood lasted until 1634.[49] Guadalupe was credited with the fact that the flood did not become worse.

Whatever the case, the image was not returned to Tepeyac until 1634, at which time there was a solemn procession. On that occasion, at least two different poetic compositions were written by anonymous authors. The first was a sonnet on "the miracle that Our Lady of Guadalupe worked in the flood in Mexico." It was she "who freed us from the wretched deluge, being our guest in Mexico for four years."[50] The other composition was *Coplas a la partida, qve la Soberana Virgen de Guadalupe, hizo de esta Ciudad de Mexico, para su hermita.* Though the *coplas* (couplets) make no reference to the standard apparition account, one of them did imply that the image was of divine origin. "But here they are painted by diverse human hands with blends of color that human hands invent. You, O Virgin, are painted by him who made heaven and earth."[51] This copla said very little about Guadalupe, other than that the Virgin was responsible for stopping the flood, that her image had been in the city for four years, and that it was not painted by human hands. This is the first sure instance in which the image was described as having any sort of miraculous origin.

Not all were in agreement that the Virgin of Guadalupe deserved credit for ending the flood, if only because of the fact that it took four years. Dávila Padilla divided the credit between Guadalupe and Saint Dominic.[52] Saint Gregory the Wonder Worker (San Gregorio Taumaturgo), a patron against flood, was invoked even after Guadalupe came to the city. The most striking variation was that of the Jesuit Francisco de Florencia. He stated that the inundation lasted four years and was stopped by the prayers of a nun who had a vision of the Virgin Mary (but not Our Lady of Guadalupe), who then interceded with her wrathful son.[53] This will be described in more detail in chapter 9.

In subsequent years the Virgin of Guadalupe continued to be invoked against flood, just as the Virgin of Remedios was invoked against drought. Significantly, however, there is no evidence that the image of Guadalupe was ever again brought to the city. Remedios, on the other hand, was brought to the city numerous times: 1576, during the epidemic of matlazahuatl when it remained for nine days and was given credit for stopping the epidemic; 1597, because of drought, which ended immediately; 1616, at the initiative of Archbishop Pérez de la Serna, because of drought; 1639, because of both drought and a threat to the flota by the Dutch; 1641, because of drought, which was quickly ended; 1642, at the initiative of Bishop Palafox y Mendoza, probably for drought; 1653, because of drought, which quickly ended; 1656, for the safety of the flota from a Cromwellian fleet; 1663, reason unknown; 1667, reason unknown; 1668, reason unknown; 1678, reason unknown; 1685, because of drought.[54]

Some authors have attached great significance to Guadalupe's role in the 1629 flood. In 1794 Juan Bautista Muñoz, the first person publicly to impugn the apparitions, said that the apparition account originated between 1629 and 1634 as a result of the image's stay in the city.[55] A few years later Servando Teresa de Mier denied Guadalupe any role in alleviating the flood and used it to discredit the apparition account.[56] More recently Lafaye has claimed that the successful intervention of the Virgin of Guadalupe on this occasion marked her triumph over the other protective images in the city.[57] Aside from the dubious nature of her "success" on this occasion, there is the additional consideration that the image was never again brought to the city and that Remedios was more frequently invoked. All these assertions stand on a questionable historical basis.

Despite the confusion to be found in the testimonies cited in this chapter, the continued silence of all chroniclers and writers about any apparitions at Guadalupe is striking. It would be only natural to expect that Mendieta, when describing visions and heavenly favors to the Indians, or the biographers of Valeriano, when listing his accomplishments, would say something about the miraculous events associated with the shrine. Alonso Ponce's companions appear to have been unaware of the story, while León testified to the lingering hostility of the mendicants. Betancurt's poem, on the other hand, is a model of confusion and gives evidence mostly of a mingling of the Guadalupe and Remedios traditions. Whether that mingling was his doing or a popular belief is now impossible to ascertain. The references in the coplas may point to the years 1629 to 1634 as the beginning of a tradition of a heavenly origin of the image.

In the period from 1531 to 1648 there is no clear evidence for the story of Juan Diego and the apparitions at Tepeyac. There is no clear evidence of a strong Indian devotion, at least not after 1556. Still less is there any association of the chapel and devotion at Tepeyac with criollismo or an inchoate sense of Mexican self-identity. In 1648 an Oratorian priest in Mexico City would not only popularize the story of the apparitions but would also give the criollos a powerful new symbol of their status as a great and chosen people.

7

The Woman of the Apocalypse

In 1648 and 1649 the silence that shrouded the apparitions changed dramatically with the publication of the first accounts of them. These were the work of two criollo priests, Miguel Sánchez and Luis Laso de la Vega, who together opened up an abrupt new chapter in the history of Our Lady of Guadalupe. Sánchez, in particular, was responsible not just for first making the story known but also for bonding it to criollo identity.

The appearance of the apparition story coincided with the flowering of criollismo. By the early seventeenth century the growing numbers of the criollos made them a force to be reckoned with. That and the failure of the dismal prophecies about their eventual physical and mental deterioration meant that they could no longer be disregarded. Though peninsular-criollo antagonisms still existed and broke out in open hostility, the snobbery and prejudice of the previous century generally assumed subtler forms. The criollos had come to dominate the ranks of the diocesan clergy, for the diocesan priesthood was more open to them than other avenues of social mobility, and the peninsular bishops, who needed the diocesans in their conflicts with the orders, were generally favorable to them. The Jesuits, whose educational work was primarily among the criollos, also tended to be sympathetic.

The eagerness and rapidity with which the criollos, especially the clergy, embraced the new devotion and used it as the basis for a myth of uniqueness and distinct identity show that criollismo had reached a critical mass by the mid-seventeenth century. It needed only the opportunity to express itself, and that opportunity was provided in a special way by Miguel Sánchez. New Spain was not just the homeland of the criollos, it was also the new homeland of the Virgin Mary, who, through the miracle of the image, had her second birth there. Though initially centered in Mexico City, the new devotion quickly spread outward. For half a century, the image/apparition devotion, which logically should have appealed to the Indians, was exclusively criollo. The fusion of Guadalupe and Mexican identity began not at Tepeyac in 1531 but in Mexico

City in 1648. In the story of the apparitions criollismo found its legitimacy.

This period also saw a flourishing of Nahuatl language studies. Whereas in the sixteenth century these studies had been mostly in the hands of the Franciscans, in the seventeenth century they came to be the domain of the Jesuits. Of these Horacio Carochi, the author of a Nahuatl grammar, *Arte de la lengua mexicana,* is probably the most famous. In addition to grammars and dictionaries, the Franciscans of the sixteenth century had produced numerous *sermonarios* and *confesionarios.* In contrast, works in Nahuatl in the following century began to include those of a more secular culture, such as translations of Spanish plays. There also seems to have been a conscious attempt to revive the classical Nahuatl of pre-Hispanic and early postconquest times.

Miguel Sánchez

Miguel Sánchez was a learned and highly respected priest of the archdiocese of Mexico who in later life joined the Oratory.[1] He was born in Mexico City in 1594 and studied at the Royal and Pontifical University, where he received the degree of *licenciado* (licentiate, a degree intermediate between bachelor and doctor). As a young man he unsuccessfully sought a teaching position at the university. He was considered a great authority on the writings of Saint Augustine, although the claim that he knew them all by heart is implausible.[2] His reputation as a preacher was high, though on the basis of his extant writings his style must be judged baroque, meandering, and highly metaphorical. At unknown dates he was chaplain to the nuns of San Jerónimo and later of the Hospital Real. At the time of his entry into the Oratory in 1662, he was the chaplain of the ermita of Remedios. He was noted for the simplicity and voluntary poverty of his life. In 1640 he published a sermon on San Felipe de Jesús in which he said, "I remain hopeful of another major writing: the second Eve in our sanctuary of Guadalupe."[3] At an unknown date he resigned his chaplaincy and retired to Guadalupe, where he died on 22 March 1674.

Sánchez was the author of the first published account of the appearance of the Virgin of Guadalupe to Juan Diego, the earliest one to which an indisputable date can be attached. This work was titled *Imagen de la Virgen Maria, Madre de Dios de Guadalupe, Milagrosamente aparecida en la ciudad de Mexico* and was published in 1648.[4] In format the book begins with the approval of the censors and then Sánchez's introduction. This is followed by a brief exegesis of the principal verses of Revelation 12, then a second exegesis applying these verses to the Virgin Mary, and then a narration of the apparitions. After this account there is a third exegesis of Revelation 12, a word-by-word application to the Virgin of Guadalupe. There follow descriptions of the procession of 26 December 1531 and the sanctuary and a series of miracle stories. The book concludes with laudatory letters by Francisco de Siles and Luis Laso de la Vega.

Approval for the work was given by two censors.[5] The first was Juan de Poblete, the *chantre* (choirmaster) of the cathedral chapter. He spoke of the carelessness that had prevented the publication of the apparition account until such a late period after the events. "With special attention and more than human disposition, the great enterprise has been reserved after 116 [*sic*] years to the superior genius, sharp intelligence, eloquent speech, and delicate pen of the author."[6] The other approbation was by fray Pedro de Rozas, professor of theology at the Augustinian convent in Mexico City. "Should this prodigy remain in silence? No, for such a singular favor was reserved to a careful preacher, the licenciado Miguel Sánchez, whose rare devotion has raised him up to understand the miracle and, profiting from it, to declare it to us to our profit. Let all New Spain thank him that after 116 [*sic*] years he took up his pen in order that what we knew only by tradition, we may understand without distinction, in its details and defined with authority and foundation."[7] Again, there is a reference to the lack of written sources.

Sánchez himself claimed to have studied the matter for more than half a century. In a sworn declaration before representatives of the cathedral chapter in 1666 he stated that "for more than fifty years in these parts he has had individual notices, both remote and proximate, of the tradition and apparition of the most holy Virgin of Guadalupe."[8] Yet in an introduction to his book entitled the "foundation of the history" [fundamento de la historia], he admitted that there were no authentic written records.

> With determination, eagerness, and diligence I looked for documents and writings that dealt with the holy image and its miracle. I did not find them, although I went through the archives where they could have been kept. I learned that through the accident of time and events those that there were had been lost. I appealed to the providential curiosity of the elderly, in which I found some sufficient for the truth. Not content I examined them in all their circumstances, now confronting the chronicles of the conquest, now gathering information from the oldest and most trustworthy persons of the city, now looking for those who were said to have been the original owners of these papers. And I admit that even if everything would have been lacking to me, I would not have desisted from my purpose, when I had on my side the common, grave, and venerated law of tradition, ancient, uniform, and general about that miracle.[9]

Sánchez is maddeningly vague when referring to his sources. The phrase "some" (*unos*) may refer to the elderly, but more probably to documents. All Spanish language authorities who have written on this point agree that he was referring to some sort of native documents. What were these? He did not say or even hint. He was clear about the fact that he was unable to find official records of the apparitions, but he also implied that his primary source was an oral tradition among the Indians. Significantly, however, he never named or specified any of his sources, other than what he called a reliable tradition.

The lack of documentary evidence would be noted by others and would present a difficulty even for the earliest proponents of the apparitions. In 1666 Sánchez gave the following explanation for this lack that he said he had heard from a rector of the sanctuary of Guadalupe. "The reason for not finding the original papers of this miraculous apparition that were written on that occasion had been and was because many papers were missing from the archbishop's archive of the administration of this archdiocese by reason of their being in the shops where every kind of spice was sold, a theft that originated and was caused by the shortage of paper in this kingdom in that year."[10] Aside from the fact that the assertion is secondhand and seems rather bizarre, it presents other difficulties. There was, indeed, a paper shortage in New Spain about the year 1621, but there is no record of the extremities that Sánchez mentioned.[11] Although many papers have been lost from Spanish and Mexican archives, as any researcher can attest with deep frustration, there was also a tendency for administrators and archivists to make multiple copies of significant documents. It seems improbable that a paper shortage would have led to the wholesale looting of all testimonies to the Guadalupe apparitions. Sánchez's explanation is too pat for a major problem: the total absence of corroborating documentation prior to 1648.

In his account of the apparitions Sánchez followed what has become the standard chronology, though his wording was not always clear. The first apparition occurred on Saturday, followed by the first interview with Zumárraga and then the second apparition. On Sunday (though it was not specified as such), Juan Diego went to mass and instruction at Tlatelolco and after ten o'clock in the morning went to see Zumárraga. Sánchez did not describe that interview; rather, he had Juan Diego describe it to the Virgin in the third interview, when he also told her of the bishop-elect's request for a sign. Monday (which was referred to only as "the following day") was spent in trying to find medicine or a doctor for Juan Bernardino. The attempt to avoid the Virgin and the fourth apparition took place on "the third day, in reference to the one on which he was with the Virgin Mary,"[12] as did the gathering of the flowers and the fifth apparition, that to Juan Bernardino. Sánchez did not, however, assign any dates to these days.

Sánchez was the first person to describe the translation of the image from the cathedral, where Zumárraga had taken it from his home, to the new chapel at Tepeyac. He wrote that after the bishop-elect had consulted both cabildos, that is, the city council and the cathedral chapter, Zumárraga set Tuesday, 26 December 1531, as the date for the procession, which Sánchez described in exuberant detail. He referred to the dances by the Indians, although Zumárraga was known to be opposed to these. Once arrived at the shrine, Zumárraga blessed it and celebrated a pontifical mass.[13] In the account of the transferal of the image to Guadalupe, he added that both Juan Diego and his uncle lived out their lives at the sanctuary. This, too, has become a constant tradition.

With regard to the ermita Sánchez stated that "the principal [invocation] and title of the ermita is that of her [the Virgin's] nativity."[14] In his description of the sanctuary he addressed the question of why it was built at the foot of the hill, not on the top, on the actual site of the apparitions.

> The wish to obey the mandate of the Virgin Mary and the experience of the favor that had been received, impelled the Most Illustrious Bishop don Juan de Zumárraga and the citizens of Mexico to build the first ermita in a short space of time. It was constructed at the base of the hill in order to protect it from the north winds, which blow strongly at that spot. It was established in sight of and along the royal highway, which, where the causeway ends on the bridge, divides into different highways for all New Spain. And since the first apparition of the Virgin was on the summit of the hill and in the sprouting of miraculous flowers, it was a grave matter that she permitted them to build her ermita at the base and on a site so frequently traveled. Perhaps the mystery of that permission is that of Genesis 31.[15]

He went on to draw a parallel from that biblical passage, actually Genesis 35:19–20, which describes how Jacob buried his wife, Rachel, by the roadside rather than in a nearby city, so that future generations would pass by her tomb.

In the interior of the sanctuary, according to Sánchez, there were more than sixty silver lamps hanging from the ceiling. The number is different from that given by Miles Philips, but the essential idea is the same. The description of the image states that it had a crown. Like Philips he described the curative spring, which was at the base of the hill, on the side looking east. According to Sánchez, it was the spot where the Virgin stopped Juan Diego when he was trying to avoid her. He described the waters as being heavy and miraculously healing.

As was standard practice in hagiographical accounts, Sánchez related the various miracles that had occurred through the intercession of the Virgin of Guadalupe. These will be considered in detail in the next section, where they will be compared with similar accounts by Laso de la Vega. The greatest miracle, according to Sánchez, was the preservation of the image, on its fragile base, for so long. This, too, was to be a standard argument of other writers throughout that century in response to the lack of documentary sources.

The account was followed by two laudatory letters. The first was by Francisco de Siles, a member of the cathedral chapter, professor of theology at the university, a friend of Sánchez, and later an enthusiastic champion of Guadalupe. It reflected a strong criollo consciousness. The Virgin of Guadalupe was called "our criolla sovereign" and the image "the criolla image of Guadalupe, so that she may always intercede for her homeland," and at another point, "I speak and I write for the whole homeland, which receives this history, the letters patent of its greatness." He commended Sánchez for writing a book "for those born in this land."[16]

The second introductory letter, by Luis Laso de la Vega, the vicar of the ermita at Guadalupe, had no such criollo emphasis. It has, however, been the subject of some dispute. For a clear understanding of the nature of this dispute, it will be necessary to quote the letter at length in all its baroque complexity.

> And although I have always venerated, admired, and praised it [the image] as much as my thoughts have been capable of, after I read the history of her miracle, which with such living emotion you have written and published, I confess that there have grown in my heart the desire to be totally hers and the glory of having her as mine with the title of her priest-minister. I think that what happened to our father Adam has happened to me. God favored him by putting him in paradise, in the freshness of its woodland and its fertile plain by the river, where the trunks and branches were the bonds that embraced it. He slept in sweet abandon. God took one of his ribs, from which he formed Eve, that miraculous creation. He placed her before the eyes of Adam, who woke up. And seeing her, he first claims her as his own and then declares her to be his love in tender expressions. Hoc nunc os ex ossibus meis, et caro de carne mea: haec vocabitur virago . . . quamobrem relinquet homo patrem et matrem et adhaerebit uxori suae.[17] Now Eve is flesh of my flesh and bone of my bone. Let her be called virile[18] and for her sake let father and mother be forgotten, preferring her love to all love. Here Adam was being notably mysterious because Eve had always been his; he had her as his own, as he declared. It seems that when he looks at her from a distance, well formed and distinct in parts and the perfection of beauty through God's care, then he says that she is his: hoc nunc. And because his heart could not endure that he merely proclaim it, it moves him to praise her sweetly, protesting in his love everlasting support. It was something great. If Adam was aware of it through contemplation, now that he is awake it is stated openly and in his very own pledge he shows special appreciation that she is his, dedicating his whole will to her.
>
> I and all my predecessors have been sleeping Adams, possessing this second Eve in the paradise of her Mexican Guadalupe among the miraculous flowers that painted her, and amid their fragrance we were contemplating her in wonder. But now it falls to me to be the Adam who has awakened in order that he might see in print the account of her history: well formed, composed, and shared, in the prodigious fact of the miracle, in the event of her apparition, in the mysteries which her picture signifies, and in the brief map of her sanctuary, which now speaks, having decoded what previously it kept silent for so many years. I can say what Adam said, Hoc nunc os ex ossibus meis, because, although she was already mine by my title as her vicar, I now proclaim myself to be her glorious possessor.[19]

There is disagreement as to whether Laso de la Vega was speaking with baroque hyperbole, as Lafaye suggests, or whether he was stating categorically that the account of the apparitions was entirely new to him.[20] His words "we were contemplating her in wonder" can be taken to mean that he and his predecessors were aware of the marvel prior to Sánchez's book. On the other hand, the entire letter and its context clearly expresses wonderment and surprise—like Adam, he realized that he possessed the wonder only after he awoke. In addition, the comments made by Antonio de Lara, Francisco de Siles, and Antonio de Robles, which will be discussed below, reinforce the conclusion that the story of the apparitions was unknown to the Spaniards and criollos of Mexico City in 1648.

Sánchez's work contained some obvious historical errors, such as referring to Zumárraga as the consecrated bishop of Mexico or to the cathedral chapter as existing in 1531, five years before its establishment. These errors may reflect Sánchez's own views rather than his sources. They are not strong arguments against the veracity of his account. On the other hand, because Sánchez is so vague about his sources, it is impossible to say to what extent he embellished the story.

Sánchez's book is baroque in character, its style ornate and repetitious. Writing as a hagiographer, not a historian, he sought to link the Virgin of Guadalupe with the woman of the Apocalypse (Revelation 12). "[And] a great sign appeared in heaven, a woman clothed with the sun, and the moon under her feet, and on her head a crown of twelve stars. . . . She cried out in childbirth and was in pain until she gave birth. . . . There was a great battle. . . . The woman fled into the wilderness. . . . Two wings were given to the woman . . . and the serpent sent [a torrent] from his mouth. . . . The dragon was angered against the woman."[21] Consequently his account of the apparitions was interrupted by lengthy commentaries, digressions, exegetical tangents, and theological excursuses. The narration itself seems like a paraphrase of the standard account as found later in the *Nican mopohua,* though he omits the doublets, terms of endearment, and poetry of the Nahuatl version.

Criollismo is the central theme of the book. His reason for writing it was that he was moved by "the homeland, my people, companions, citizens, those of this new world; I thought it better to reveal myself to be presumptuously ignorant for such an undertaking than to give a motive for presuming such a guilty ignorance on the part of all."[22] The story of the apparitions is little more than a framework on which Sánchez can build his criollo interpretations. He had a messianic view of Mexico City, which he sought to put on a par with the great religious centers of the Catholic world. He compared Zumárraga to Saint John the Evangelist and Mexico to Patmos (the island where the evangelist was exiled), and he interpreted Revelation 12 in terms of Mexico and the Spanish empire. The woman clothed with the sun was the city of Mexico. Mary, he asserted, had aided the Spanish conquest, she was the "assistant conquistador."[23] New Spain was her homeland. His emphasis, which took up most of the first part of the work, was that Revelation 12 prefigured Mexico, Guadalupe, and the destiny of the sons of the land. Guadalupe was for him primarily a devotion for those "born in this land." They had an "intimate and special brotherhood of relationship with Mary in this her image, since she is reborn miraculously in the land where they are born."[24] His reasoning was often contrived, for example, when he pointed out that Juan Diego was called by Mary, and he was named for John and James, whose mother was named Mary, or when he formulated elaborate relationships based on the name John between Juan Diego, Zumárraga, and Saint John the Evangelist. The eagle whose wings were given to the woman fleeing the dragon was the eagle on the escutcheon of Mexico. The eagle in flight formed a cross and so the eagle that symbolized pre-Christian New Spain was to be Christianized by Mary, giving the gift of the cross. He blamed the periodic floods in the city on the influence of the moon and made a bizarre observation about the climate, when discussing the fact that the woman of Revelation 12 was clothed with the sun: "We have learned, as something evident, that by nature this land and new world were a torrid zone and a region burned by the sun and presumed to be uninhabitable. Most holy Mary took control of the sun, moderated its rigors, reduced its heat, calmed its fire, tempered its rays, served as a cloud."[25]

What must strike the modern reader as strange is that the traditional account as given by Sánchez offers no objective basis for his unrestrained criollo interpretations. In itself the story is directed toward the Indians, not the Europeans, though it is cast in the classic European apparition genre. Although at times Sánchez included the Indians in the devotion and spoke of the apparitions as a special blessing to them, it is difficult to say what place he intended to give them. He did remark, however, on the strength of their devotion. In a very real sense Sánchez took a cult story that should have been exclusively Indian and appropriated it for the criollos. In this he was followed by the preachers and writers of the seventeenth and eighteenth centuries, especially the diocesan clergy and the Jesuits. It is impossible to trace the subsequent history of the Guadalupe devotion without the awareness that it was a criollo devotion, in which the sons of the land saw their own special election. If the Indians had any share in it, it was apart from the criollos. This meant in turn that the Indian aspects of the story would have to be devalued or diluted.

The emphasis on criollismo and the downplaying of the Indian aspect of the story are clear in the differences between the dialogues in the *Imagen* and those in the *Nican mopohua,* which appeared six months later. As they are quoted by Sánchez, the native element is definitely attenuated. In the *Nican mopohua* the Virgin reveals to Juan Diego her wish for a church in tender words: "I ardently wish and I greatly desire that they build my temple for me here, where I will reveal, I will make known, and I will give to people all my love, my compassion, my aid, and my protection, for I am your compassionate mother. . . .

There I will hear their weeping and their sorrows in order to remedy and to heal all their various afflictions, their miseries, and their torments." In Sánchez's wording the message is brief and generic. "I want a house and ermita built for me here, a temple in which to show myself a compassionate mother with you, with yours, with my devotees, with those who seek me in order to remedy their needs." Her words on Tuesday morning are even more tender and poignant in the *Nican mopohua*. "Know, rest very much assured, my youngest child, let nothing whatever frighten you or worry you. Do not be concerned. Do not fear [your uncle's] illness nor any illness or affliction. Am I, your mother, not here? Are you not under my shade and my shadow? Am I not your happiness? Are you not in my lap and in my carrying gear? Is there anything more you need? Do not let anything worry you further or upset you. Do not let your uncle's illness worry you. He will not die of what is now upon him. Rest assured, for he is already well." Sánchez's wording is in the third person and has all the poignancy of a government report. "He was [not] to fear dangers, fear illnesses, nor be afflicted in his tasks, taking her for his mother, for his health and protection, that the illness of his uncle, who was not to be in danger of death, would not hinder him, and she assured him that from that moment he was completely well."

Although Sánchez's book was printed in only a limited number of copies, it was quite influential. At the time of his death on 22 March 1674, his obituary, written by Antonio de Robles, testified both to the impact of his work and to the fact that the apparition account was new to the people of Mexico.

> [He lived retired] for some time in the sanctuary of Our Lady of Guadalupe, to whom he was very devoted. He wrote a learned book about her apparition, which seemingly has been the means by which devotion to this holy image has spread throughout all Christendom. It had been forgotten, even by the citizens of Mexico [City], until this venerable priest made it known, since there was in all Mexico [City] only one image of this sovereign lady, in the convent of Santo Domingo, and today there is not a convent or church where it is not venerated, and rare indeed is the religious house or cell where there is not a copy of it, universally in all New Spain, the kingdoms of Peru, and in almost all Europe.[26]

Robles may have been exaggerating, or speaking from limited knowledge, when he said that there was only one picture of Our Lady of Guadalupe in Mexico City. As will be mentioned in chapter 12, the Basque artist Baltasar Echave Orio made a copy in 1606, and Archbishop Juan Pérez de la Serna commissioned an engraving in 1615 which was put on sale to help fund the construction of a new chapel at Tepeyac. Stephanie Wood has found at least one example in the Toluca region of a household image of Guadalupe bequeathed in a will in 1632.[27] More important, it is antecedently improbable that a religious event as transcendently important as the Guadalupe apparitions could have been forgotten or lost, even in the course of a century.

In 1653 Sánchez published a sermon that he preached at the University of Mexico in honor of the Immaculate Conception. Although he made one reference to Revelation 12, there was no mention of Guadalupe.[28] In 1665 he published a devotional book called *Novenas de la Virgen Maria, Madre de Dios, para sus devotisimos Santuarios de los Remedios y Guadalupe*. The censor for the book was Doctor Antonio de Lara Mogrovejo, who wrote in his letter of approval, "Having brought to light the rare and mysterious apparition . . . it was a pledge of his obligation to arouse new fervor with this book in the devotion of the faithful, when he introduced it to their notice. . . . The history of the apparition of Guadalupe cost him much hard work. Traditions and fragments weakened by the forgetfulness of time and the scant curiosity of the ancients always put the truth at risk, even though his learning made it so clear that he achieved his purpose easily."[29] The fact that the apparitions were unknown in 1648 is confirmed by a second approbation by the same Francisco de Siles who had written one of the introductory letters to Sánchez's *Imagen*. The author, he wrote, "made known the apparition, forgotten in the course of more than a century and rescued by his effort from the lack of care within a brief time; a book so profitable that I do not know if before he gave it to the press this miracle was well known, even in our America."[30] These statements show again that the tradition was unknown and that there was little or no evidence for it. It also opens up the possibility that Sánchez may have embellished the original account from which he worked. The exact extent to which the standard apparition account is an Indian tradition or the work of the Oratorian's imagination will never be known for sure.

Although Sánchez's work was influential in encouraging the Guadalupan devotion, its overall impact seems to have been blunted by the small number of volumes printed and his ornate, gongoristic style. It has rarely been reprinted.[31] In 1660, at a time when the devotion was beginning to spread, the Jesuit Mateo de la Cruz published anonymously an abbreviated and vastly improved version of Sánchez's work.[32] It enjoyed a great popularity and probably did as much to spread the devotion as Sánchez's original. Florencia, writing in 1688, considered it the best account. De la Cruz excised the long digressions and scriptural exegeses of Sánchez's work and reduced it to a summary of the apparitions themselves. In fact, his work is more rewrite than abridgement. It was the first published account to give dates for the apparitions, specifically 9 to 12 December. It follows Sánchez's chronology of the apparitions rather than that of Laso de la Vega.

De la Cruz omitted almost all the extravagant criollismo of Sánchez's account. He was, however, one of the first authors to note the growing rivalry between Guadalupe and Remedios and the first, so far as I can determine, to refer to them in print as La Criolla and La Conquistadora/La Gachupina. He also cited their different invocations: Guadalupe against floods, Remedios against drought. He went to some pains to demonstrate that the image of Guadalupe was that of the Immaculate Conception. In one of his few nods to criollismo, he contrasted the Extremaduran Guadalupe with the Mexican.

> The former image was made by Saint Luke, the latter was painted either by God or the Virgin herself or at least by angels. Over there they sent it from Rome to an archbishop of Seville, over here from heaven to an archbishop of Mexico. Over there it was buried 600 years, like a seed, in order to come to its invocation 200 years after being discovered over there, to bloom as if born over here, more than 3,040 leagues away. In both places it is called Guadalupe which . . . means "River of Wolves" . . . wolves being symbols of the demons . . . and she wanted this place to be called Guadalupe in order to show that by her presence she put to flight the hellish demons of this place . . . there, where they used to worship the demons in the idol Theotenantzin, with the title of the Mother of the gods.[33]

In 1662 this version was reprinted in Spain under the patronage of Pedro de Gálvez, former *visitador* of New Spain, a member of the Council of the Indies (1657–1662), and later bishop of Zamora, who was an ardent devotee of Guadalupe.[34]

Although Sánchez's work was the first published account of the apparitions, it has not become the standard account. That was to come from the vicar of Guadalupe.

Luis Laso de la Vega

In 1649 Luis Laso de la Vega, the vicar of the ermita of Guadalupe, published the *Huey tlamahuiçoltica*, to which reference has already been made. Almost nothing is known about his life except that he was vicar of the ermita in 1648 and received the post of *medio racionero* of the cathedral chapter nine years later.[35] The publication of the new work followed very closely on that of Sánchez. Laso de la Vega's introduction to Sánchez's work was dated 2 July 1648, and Baltasar González's approbation of the *Huey tlamahuiçoltica* carried the date 9 January 1649, a time span of approximately six months. The book was poorly printed and contained a number of typographical errors, perhaps a sign of haste in preparation. It is also full of orthographic inconsistencies, especially in the use of diacritical marks. It is Laso de la Vega's only known publication.

The approval for the book was given by the Jesuit censor, Baltasar González, who wrote, "I find that it is in agreement with what is known of the event by tradition and annals."[36] Almost immediately, however, he seems to bear testimony to a degree of ignorance and disinterest, "because it will be very useful and profitable to enliven devotion in the lukewarm and engender it anew in those who live in ignorance of the mysterious origin of this heavenly portrait of the Queen of Heaven."[37] Again, there is a frustrating lack of precision about what the "tradition and annals" are.

Laso de la Vega's authorship of all parts of the *Huey tlamahuiçoltica* is open to question. The book is clearly a compilation of diverse elements, dating from different periods and written in varying styles. Both Stage 1 and Stage 2 Nahuatl are to be found in it. Hence authorship in this context may be taken in the sense of compilation or perhaps sponsorship and supervision.[38] Even if he was the author in a more substantial sense, like many Spanish clerics of the day he undoubtedly gave it to native assistants for final polishing.

The *Huey tlamahuiçoltica* is divided into six distinct parts: (1) Laso de la Vega's introduction; (2) the account of the apparitions (the *Nican mopohua*); (3) a brief description of the image; (4) an account of the miracles worked at Guadalupe (the *Nican motecpana*); (5) a life of Juan Diego; and (6) an exhortation and prayer.

The Introduction

Laso de la Vega's introduction is phrased as a prayer to the Virgin. The introduction appears to have been written specifically for the book or close to its publication. The language is complex and seems almost consciously archaic. Garibay praised its "perfect Nahuatl," whereas Lockhart sees it as having the flavor of a translation from Spanish.[39] The introduction implies that not all Indians were aware of the miracle and needed instruction about it in order to make it known to others. "That fact has enticed and encouraged me to write in the Nahuatl language the very great miracle by which you revealed yourself to people and you have given them your image [which] is here in your precious home in Tepeyacac. May the Indians see there and know in their language all that you have done on their behalf and your love for people" [Ca ye yèhuatl in onechyoleuh, in onechyolchicauh inic nahuatlàtolcopa onoconìcuilo in çenca huei motlamahuiçoltzin inic otimoteittitìtzino, ihuan inic oticmotemaquilìtia in mixiptlatzin in nican motlaçòchantzinco Tepeyacac ma oncā quittacan in maçehualtzitzintin, ma intlàtoltica quimatican in ixquich in impanpa oticmochihuili motetlaçòtlaliztzin]. "Therefore, may it be written in different languages in order that many people may be called in different languages to see and to know your wonder and your very great miracle that you have worked on their behalf" [Ipampa ma nepapan tlàtoltica mìcuilo inic mochintin in nepapan tlàtolica monotza quittazque, quimatizquè in momahuizçotzin, ihuan in çenca huey motlamahuiçoltzin in inpampa oticmochihuili].[40]

The Nican mopohua

Following the introduction is the most important part of the book, the actual account of the apparitions, called the *Nican mopohua* (Here is recounted), written in a smooth, standard Church Nahuatl that shows minimal Spanish influence. Because of its status in the history of Guadalupe it requires a detailed study.

The *Nican mopohua* does not appear to be directly dependent on Sánchez's book. It parallels Sánchez's in many ways, but it is not a translation or even a paraphrase of the earlier work. In fact, Laso de la Vega made no reference to Sánchez at all. The approach and style of the two accounts are strikingly different. The *Nican mopohua* follows a chronology of the apparitions that differs in details from that of Miguel Sánchez, specifically by omitting the third apparition, in which Juan Diego told the Virgin about his interview with Zumárraga.[41] Laso de la Vega, or his native aides, may have adapted Sánchez's account and given it the Nahuatl style that characterizes it. An equally likely hypothesis is that they both used an unwritten common source, perhaps a story in circulation among some local Nahuas.

Did Laso de la Vega write the *Nican mopohua*? He clearly stated four times in his introduction that he was the author of the apparition account and made no reference to either written documents or published works. "I who have traced and written your miracle in Nahuatl" [In onocontlilan onoconnìcuilo nahuatlàtolcopa in motlahuiçoltzin]. "That fact has enticed and encouraged me to write in the Nahuatl language the very great miracle by which you revealed hourself to people" [Ca ye yèhuatl in onechyoleuh, in onechyolchicauh inic nahuatlàtolcopa onoconìcuilo in cenca huei motlamahuiçoltzin inic otimoteittitzino]. "There is also one other item by which I took heart and was encouraged to write your miracle in the Nahuatl language" [Auh ca ocno centlamantli inic oniyoleuh inic oniyolchicauh nahuatlàtolcopa noconcuìloz in motlamahuiçoltzin]. "In order that I may trace in the Nahuatl language your altogether great miracle by which that you revealed yourself to the humble Indians" [Inic nocontlilanaz nahuatlàtolcopa in cenca huei in motlamahuiçoltzin inic otiquinmottititzino icnomacehualtzitzintin].[42] Despite these claims, Laso de la Vega's authorship of the *Nican mopohua* is questionable. Velázquez believed that the great difference in style between Laso de la Vega's gongoristic letter of introduction to Sánchez's book and the unadorned narration of the *Nican mopohua* made Laso de la Vega's authorship suspect. The same can be said about his rather florid introduction to the *Huey tlamahuiçoltica*. Lockhart also believes that "the story proper is in such fluent and idiomatic Nahuatl that Laso de la Vega would have had to possess very unusual language gifts to have written it himself unless he was guided by an already existing model; indeed, the tale itself is so smooth that it gives the impression of having been through the polishing process of frequent telling by various narrators." Lockhart adds, however, "since Spanish ecclesiastics had long been wont to ignore the fact that their indigenous aides actually put the texts they published into Nahuatl, there is nothing to prevent us from assuming the existence of a Nahua ghostwriter who could have had much latitude."[43] It can safely be presumed that Laso de la Vega entrusted his manuscript to native writers for final embellishment. The claim that the native scholar and governor, Antonio Valeriano, was the author of the *Nican mopohua* will be discussed in chapters 9 and 11.

Laso de la Vega made no reference to sources for his account. He did mention that much had been lost during the passage of time and also testified to a lack of written sources. "Very much has been abandoned, which time has erased and which no one remembers any longer, because the ancients did not take care to have it written down at the time it happened" [Auh ca çenca miec in omocauh, in oquipolò in cahuitl, in aoc mà aca quilnamiqui inic àmo oquimocuitlahuiq̃ in huehuetq̃ in ma quimìcuilhuiani niman in ìquac mochiuh].[44] People, he complained, tended to forget heavenly favors very quickly. In order that everything should not be forgotten or blotted out with time, he wrote, the Queen of Heaven wanted it written and published, "although it has been brought about with difficulty, because it happens that there is still need for other [sources] here and there" [maçihui ohuìtica in omoneltili, inic çen nohuian tepan àçitiuh motemachiltitiuh].[45]

Almost all commentators have praised the quality of the Nahuatl in the *Nican mopohua*. In his letter of approval Baltasar González, a *nahuatlahto* (speaker or student of Nahuatl), spoke of the "correct and elegant Mexican language" of the account.[46] Andrews thinks that the author's use of directionals lies somewhat between that of Tezozomoc (which he considers quite skillful) and that of the *Historia Tolteca Chichimeca* (which, he says, "demonstrates a less felicitous use").[47] Ascención H. de León-Portilla speaks of its "elegant language and full of metaphors in the style of classic Nahuatl literature, as it was transcribed in the alphabet of the sixteenth century."[48] Burkhart considers it "standard church Nahuatl, a linguistic variety developed by priests and literate Indians early in the colonial epoch and maintained with few changes throughout the colonial era. It is formal and archaizing, with a syntax simplified so that nonnative speakers could more easily understand it, and with relatively few Spanish loanwords."[49] Lockhart judges the entire work to be in excellent Nahuatl that could have been written at any time from 1550 or 1560 onward, "with overwhelmingly indigenous and traditional vocabulary and idiom, no obvious calques, and a few Spanish loan nouns."[50] Siller, who considers the account to be very ancient, calls the language classical Nahuatl, which he extravagantly describes as "a plain, direct, smooth, precise, elegant, sonorous, beautiful, profound, highly meaningful, and even sublime language."[51] Its style may also reflect the cultural and linguistic renaissance of the mid–seventeenth century, one aspect of which was a move to restore a pristine, classical form of Nahuatl.

From style and language alone, however, it is impossible to date the *Nican mopohua* with exactitude. There are some expressions, such as *notecuiyoè* (O my lady, the female equivalent of lord), *tlacatlè* (O personage), *cihuapillè* (O no-blewoman), *noxocoyohuè* (O my youngest child), and *nochpochtzinè* (O my daughter), that were typical of preconquest polite speech: the first three as terms of inferior to superior, the last two as polite inversions. On the other hand, the use of the Spanish rather than Nahuatl numbering system and the use of *omocac misa* (mass was heard) instead of the more common sixteenth-century *omottac misa* (mass was seen) argue for a provenance from the late sixteenth or early seventeenth century.

Bierhorst has pointed out similarities in vocabulary between Laso de la Vega's account and the *Cantares mexicanos*. The uses he specifies are *tzinitzcan* (the Mexican trogon, a species of bird), *manoce* (a common conjunction, nor, although), *nocuexanco nictemaz* (I will fill my lapfolds with them, for which Laso de la Vega has *quicuixanten*, "he filled his lapfolds with them"), *iuqui{n} tepetl quinnahnanquilia* (for which Laso de la Vega has *iuhquin quinananquilia Tepetl,* "as if the hill answers them"), *coyoltototl* (the bellbird), *in xochitlalpan in tonacatlalpan* (in the land of flowers, in the land of abundance), *xixochitetequi* (for which Laso de la Vega has *xochitl xictetequi,* "cut the flowers"). His conclusion is that "one suspects that Lasso [*sic*] de la Vega had access to our manuscript."[52] Granted that this is a possibility, still the differences between the two are so stark that, as has been mentioned before, it is impossible to consider any of the cantares as a source for the *Nican mopohua*. On the other hand, many idioms and phrases used in it can also be found in the *Bancroft Dialogues* published by Karttunen and Lockhart. Thus both the *Dialogues* and the *Nican mopohua* use the identical phrase *nictequipachoz in mixtzin in moyollotzin* (I will disturb your spirit, an apology for importunity, often used at the beginning or end of a speech). Both use *mati* in the sense of to feel and *huelmati,* to feel well, in an inquiry. In the *Dialogues* the question is *quen ticmomachiltia in moteopixcanacayotzin* (literally, How do you feel your priestly flesh? or Father, how is your bodily health?), while the *Nican mopohua* has *cuix ticmohuelmachitia in motlaçònacayotzin.* Similarly, both use the preconquest descriptive terms for God, *ipalnemohuani, in tloque in nahuaque, ilhuicahua tlalticpaque,* and *teyocoyani* (the *Dialogues* twice use *ipalnemohuani teotl dios,* the same form used by the *Nican mopohua*), both use *-macehual* as a possessed noun meaning "deserve," both use *-col, -achton* to mean "ancestors" and *coco teopouhqui* for "affliction." All these terms, however, were common in standard Church Nahuatl of the time. If, as is probable, Laso de la Vega entrusted his manuscript to Indian secretaries for final polishing, it is quite possible that they were responsible for the verbal similarities.

Because the *Nican mopohua* appeared in its first and final form in a printed work, it has no manuscript history as such. There are, however, handwritten copies in the New York Public Library and the Bibliothèque Nationale de France, Paris, that must be considered, though ultimately they provide no useful information.

There is a partial manuscript of the *Nican mopohua* in the New York Public Library, Monumentos Guadalupanos, series 1, volume 1, number 12.[53] It is written on European paper and consists of eight folios, torn at the edges and sometimes difficult to read. It goes only as far as Juan Diego's encounter with the Virgin after he has attempted to avoid her on Tuesday. The hand is semicursive, and the scribe was clearly copying from another document. Letters that were left out were inserted between the lines, incorrect copyings were smudged out, and there are occasional repeated words or phrases and in one instance an entire sentence.

On the basis of the hand and the use of *h* to indicate glottal stops, Burkhart dates it from the late sixteenth or very early seventeenth century.[54] While it is true that this manuscript frequently uses *h* to mark glottal stops, the usage is inconsistent. Sometimes the accent grave (ˋ) is employed, sometimes the two together. There are other distinctive features. One is the carrying over of a final letter of one word to the beginning of the following one. Generally this occurs with *n* (*in nocan, in noc, in noquicac*), but it also occurs twice with *c* (*ic comonehlchiuh, oc quipan*). Such carryovers, which seemingly reflected speech patterns, were not unusual in early Nahuatl documents. There is a frequent doubling of letters, especially the *l* of the applicative but also in such forms as *innic, nopiltzinne, noxxocoyouh, oquimahuizzo, moquetztzinohtica.* The letter *z* replaces *s* in some Spanish loan words, while the reverse occurs in many Nahuatl words (*Dioz, obizpo, quinientoz, quesqui, metstli, yas*). On occasions the hard *k* sound is reduplicated (*monecqui*). There are also some simple orthographic errors, such as *moçuep.* Burrus believed that the manuscript dated from the mid–sixteenth century and that if not the original, it was at least a copy of it, thus making it the oldest existing copy of the *Nican mopohua.*

> The paper, the watermarks, the spelling of the words, the form of the individual letters, the expressions and the language—all are characteristic of mid-sixteenth-century Spanish American documents, as anyone can ascertain from a careful comparison with dated writings of the same period and in the same area. . . . Deserving particular notice are the letters "b," "h," "ç" (before "e" and "i") and the initial "rr" as in "rreal/religiose" [*sic*]. Father Mario Rojas . . . called my attention to the fact that not only are the spelling and writing characteristic of the mid–sixteenth century, but also the vocabulary and language, sentence structure, idioms and style, etc. He observed a marked difference between the two oldest copies. The first, a mid-sixteenth-century production written in a much more popular style, reflects the way the Indians spoke at the time. The second copy, made about forty years after the first, toward the end of the sixteenth century, was written in a far more careful and literary style.[55]

These assertions are confusing. Burrus seems to be referring to the Spanish rather than the Nahuatl document. The letter *b,* which does not exist in Nahuatl, occurs in the manuscript only in Spanish loan words, and there is nothing distinctively old in the way it is written. The same is true of the letter *r*, which also does not occur in Nahuatl, and *rr* never appears in the document at all. Similarly, there is no notable difference in wording between this document and the second copy, which is considered in the next paragraph. Attempts to date this document prior to Laso de la Vega's publication rest on frail evidence and are impossible to reconcile with the total silence of authors and commentators prior to 1648.

In that same collection, series, and volume there is a manuscript of the *Nican mopohua* and the *Nican motecpana,* the latter including the exhortation and prayer. It is the "second copy" mentioned by Burrus and consists of twenty-one folios. Though this copy of the *Nican mopohua* is sometimes cited as having a sixteenth-century provenance (Burrus dated it at the close of the century), the hand is clearly later.[56] Stylistically, in contrast with Laso de la Vega's version, it consistently uses the *o-* prefix for the preterit and modal suffixes for verbs (especially *-catca*) and frequently uses the verbal reverential (*-tzino*). The version from which this copy was made contained several major omissions, all of them noted by the copyist. The narrative is first interrupted when Juan Diego informs the Virgin that he is going for a priest for his sick uncle and resumes with her assurance that he will recover. The poignant questions the Virgin asks on Tuesday concerning her protection of Juan Diego are omitted. The text is interrupted again at the point at which the Virgin commands Juan Diego to go cut the flowers and resumes with her command to take them to the bishop. It omits the attempts by the bishop's servants to look at the flowers in Juan Diego's tilma. It also omits much of Juan Diego's final dialogue with Zumárraga. Most remarkably, it omits the entire narrative of the delivery of the roses and the appearance of the image. In the light of all this, no special importance can be attached to this copy. Sánchez Rojas's claim that it was written in a more literary and less popular style than the partial manuscript discussed in the previous paragraph is impossible to accept.

In the Bibliothèque Nationale de France, Mexicains, 302, there is the "Fragment d'une histoire de N. D. de Guadalupe écrite en langage nahuatl par le Br. Luis Lazo de la Vega en 1649." It corresponds with Laso de la Vega's version of the *Nican mopohua* from folio 1v to folio 23r and with the *Nican motecpana* from folio 28v to folio 33r. The *Nican mopohua* lacks Laso de la Vega's introduction and ends with the words "ca onicneltilito in miîyotzin, in motlatoltzin" [I go to carry out your message]. It resumes on folio 28v with the words "ihuan in ixquich tlamahuiçolli ye quimochihuilia" [and all the miracles that she works]. The copy was made by the criollo priest José Pichardo (1748–1812) some time in the late eighteenth or early nineteenth century.[57] Folio 24r and v contains a written note, unsigned and undated, on the documentary history of the *Nican mopohua*. It specifically states that the first publication in 1648, that is, Miguel

Sánchez's book, was not based on any Nahuatl sources. The note also surveys the copies of the *Nican mopohua* in Botturini's *museo,* none of which appears to have any special significance in the history of the account. An entirely distinct Nahuatl account of the apparitions, the *Relación mercurina,* will be discussed in chapter 10.

De la Maza and Garibay mentioned a manuscript that they said had once belonged to the collection of the English engineer and amateur historian G. R. G. Conway.[58] This document was supposedly the handwritten original of the *Huey tlamahuiçoltica,* possibly a printer's copy, signed and dated 1646. Garibay claimed that he had seen it at the publishing house of Porrúa in Mexico City. After Conway's death his collection was broken up and sold. At the present time the Archivo General de la Nación has photocopies of seventeen volumes of the collection, of which only the first seven have been inventoried. Much of Conway's collection covered the colonial period, but it is not clear whether it contained any Nahuatl manuscripts. Garibay's claim for the manuscript's authenticity is impossible to accept. Working copies of manuscripts used by printers were not usually saved or rarely survived. That a document of such surpassing importance should suddenly appear and then fade again into the unknown or that Garibay made no effort to secure a copy, if only to compare it with the standard version, goes beyond all credibility. This, however, conforms to a consistent pattern in Guadalupan history: authors, such as Becerra Tanco, Florencia, Sigüenza y Góngora, and Garibay, claim to have seen or used an authentic, corroborating document but without publishing it or, in most cases, even citing it.

In the twentieth century the *Nican mopohua* has been widely accepted as the foundational account of the apparitions because of the claim that in its original form it was almost contemporaneous with the events. Yet it appears to have had little or no impact on the Spanish or criollo population of New Spain. Botturini Benaduci commissioned a translation in the early eighteenth century. This translation, which is very literal, was published in 1895 by the Mexican scholar Fortino Hipólito Vera from an incomplete copy made by José Pichardo sometime in the late eighteenth or early nineteenth century.[59] Archbishop Francisco Antonio Lorenzana, who was very interested in everything that concerned Guadalupe, commissioned Carlos Tapia y Centeno to translate the *Nican mopohua* into Spanish from a "maguey document written in Mexican [Nahuatl], in the handwriting that the Indians used at the beginning of their conversion" that had been found in the museo of Botturini Benaduci at the Royal and Pontifical University.[60] The copy of Tapia y Centeno's translation that is presently in the Bibliothèque Nationale de France is more a paraphrase than a translation. It ends with Juan Diego's greeting to the Virgin on Tuesday after he tried to avoid her, suggesting that it may have been translated from document 1 in the

New York Public Library mentioned above. The paraphrase was never published. The *Nican mopohua* was not cited by preachers in Spanish in the seventeenth or eighteenth century and, as will be seen, seems to have influenced only one Nahuatl sermon. It was not translated in full until 1926, when Primo Feliciano Velázquez published a photographic reproduction of the entire *Huey tlamahuiçoltica,* together with his translation of it. Only in this century, and specifically after the publication of Cuevas's *Historia* in 1921 to 1924, did the *Nican mopohua* become the *textus receptus.* This will be treated in detail in chapters 9 and 11.

The documentary sources for the seventeenth century tell us nothing about the impact of the *Nican mopohua* on the Indians' devotion. There are no known Nahuatl sermons on Guadalupe for that century, as there are for the eighteenth century. On the other hand, there is evidence that the Indian devotion to the Dark Virgin, as it exists today, dates from the eighteenth century.

The Tilma Description

After the account of the apparitions comes a paragraph that describes the tilma and the image. This is written in a different, later style, with several Spanish loan words (*cruz, corona, ángel*) and the consistent use of the -*ticac* modal. It is clearly of a later date, for it presupposes that its readers were not familiar with Mexica dress in the pre- and immediate postconquest periods. "The cloak on which the image of the heavenly Lady appeared was the garment of Juan Diego. The maguey cloak was rather stiff and well woven because at that time the maguey cloak was the clothing and the covering of all the common people. Only those who were nobles, leaders, and valiant warriors adorned and dressed themselves with soft cotton thread cloaks" [In tilmàtzintli in colol (*sic* for eolol) catca in Iuan Diego in itech tlamahuiçoltica monexiti in ixiptlatzin ilhuicac çihuapilli ca Ayatzintli achi tilactic catca, ihuan tlayec ìquitilli yèica ca in iquac in, in maçehualtzitzintin mochtin ayatl in intlaquen in inNeololtzin catca, çan yèhuantin in Pipiltin in Teteuctin, yhuan in yaotiàcahuan in yamanqui in ichca tilmàtli ic mochìchihuaya, ic mololoaya].[61] Certainly, in the thirty or forty years after 1531 such an explanation would have been unnecessary. This description was clearly written for natives who had no recollection of preconquest society. It appears to belong to Stage 2 Nahuatl.

The Miracle Stories

The tilma description is followed by an account of miracles that were worked through the intercession of the Virgin of Guadalupe. Miracles were an integral part of apparition stories. They were a divine seal of approval on the validity of an apparition, a devotion, or the sanctity of a person's life. Even today they are a standard element in the procedure for the canonization of saints. Sánchez and Laso de la Vega included miracle accounts to show both the authenticity of the apparition account and the devotion based on it and also to encourage fervor in those who were not yet devotees of the shrine. Hence the miracles centered on dramatic rescues from danger and cures from life-threatening illnesses.

Laso de la Vega's collection of miracle stories, known from its opening words as the *Nican motecpana,* is often attributed to the native historian Fernando de Alva Ixtlilxochitl, thus dating it toward the beginning of the seventeenth century. The style of this section is so different from that of the *Nican mopohua* that it can safely be said that they are the works of different authors. Velázquez considered the *Nican motecpana* to be both later than and stylistically inferior to the *Nican mopohua.*[62] In support of this he cited the large number of Hispanicisms (*testamento, ánima, aceite, candela, sacristán, altar, misa, lámpara, freno, caballo*) and various ungrammatical expressions. His arguments are persuasive but raise the troubling question of whether Alva Ixtlilxochitl would have written in such highly Hispanicized Nahuatl. The most likely hypothesis is that the *Nican motecpana* is a compilation of miracle stories associated with the shrine but with diverse origins. Sánchez and Laso de la Vega joined them to the *Nican mopohua* and edited some of them to give them a Guadalupan significance.

There are similarities and differences in the stories given by Sánchez and Laso de la Vega. The former has seven miracles, while the latter has fourteen. In general Laso de la Vega gives more details than Sánchez, and his accounts tend to be more vivid. Sánchez concluded the narration of each miracle with a complex and often esoteric biblical parallel, relating each one to some event in Scripture and then drawing conclusions for the edification of his readers. Laso de la Vega's few commentaries tended to stress the Virgin Mary's love and concern for the Indians.

The following are the miracles related, with an indication of the differences between the two authors.

The first one given by Sánchez involved an Indian accidentally killed by an arrow in the neck during a mock skirmish that was part of the celebration of the dedication of the first ermita at Tepeyac on 26 December 1531. His body was carried before the image, and when the arrow was removed, the Indian was immediately restored to full health. Laso de la Vega added some details, including the fact that the resurrected Indian remained at Tepeyac as a custodian for the shrine. Both Sánchez and Laso de la Vega saw this as a sign of the Virgin's special care for the Indians.

The second occurred during the epidemic of 1544, one of the worst to strike the Indians of New Spain in the sixteenth century. Because of the vagueness of symptomatic descriptions, it is impossible to identify the sickness with any certainty. It was characterized by bleeding from the nose and high fever and, according to Sánchez, was killing a hundred Indians each day.[63] Mendieta wrote that 150,000 Indians died in Tlaxcala and another 100,000 in Cholula.[64] According to tradition, Juan Bernardino died during this epidemic. Sánchez wrote that the Franciscans organized a procession of boys and girls, age six to seven, from Santiago Tlatelolco to Guadalupe to pray for its end. According to Sánchez, the epidemic began to abate the next day. Laso de la Vega gives a longer description and adds that the children took the discipline (*momacahuitectaque*) during the course of the procession. These two are the only sources for the story of the procession.[65]

The third concerned don Juan Tovar, the Indian who was credited with finding the image of the Virgin of Remedios. Laso de la Vega, whose account is much more detailed than that of Sánchez, emphasizes the priority of Guadalupe. He says that don Juan found the image of Remedios on the hill called Totoltepec and took it to his home, where he kept it for some years. Later he built a small chapel in front of his home and placed the image within it. Both Sánchez and Laso de la Vega say that some time after that Tovar fell ill during an epidemic. Seeing himself very ill and remembering how the Virgin had cured Juan Bernardino, he begged his neighbors to take him to Guadalupe. There the Virgin smiled at him and cured him. She also directed him to build a chapel on the summit of Totoltepec for her image. More so than Sánchez, Laso de la Vega sought to subordinate Remedios (which later became the peninsular devotion) to Guadalupe (the criollo and Indian devotion). On the other hand, Sánchez preached both devotions, and in the mid–seventeenth century there were few signs of the rivalry that would emerge later.

On another occasion a gentleman named Antonio de Carvajal left Mexico City for Tulancingo on horseback, accompanied by a young relative. On the way out of the city the party stopped and prayed at Guadalupe in the manner described by Miles Philips. Having resumed their journey they discussed the wondrous image and the miracles it had wrought. The young relative's horse bolted and carried him precipitously through ravines and rocky territory. His companions followed after him, expecting to find him dead. Instead he was alive and unharmed, with the horse in a bowed and reverential position. He explained that during his danger he had invoked the Virgin of Guadalupe. The Virgin, exactly as painted on the image, appeared and grabbed the horse's reins. The horse stopped and knelt before her. Again, Laso de la Vega's account is more detailed. This became one of the most popular miracle stories associated with Guadalupe.

Sánchez tells of a man who was praying before the image of the Virgin when a cord supporting a ceiling lamp broke and it fell on his head. Neither the man nor the lamp was harmed in any way. The glass was not broken, the oil was not spilled, and the flame continued to burn. Laso de la Vega's account is almost the same, except that he identifies the man as a Spaniard.

Once, when the licenciado Juan Vázquez de Acuña, at that time the vicar of Guadalupe, went to the main altar to say mass, all the candles had been blown out by the strong winds prevalent in the area. As his acolyte went out to relight them, the priest and others in the chapel saw two rays of light that miraculously lighted the candles. Laso de la Vega's version is almost exactly the same.

In relating the miracles worked at the shrine or by the image, Sánchez includes the flood of 1629 to 1634, of which he was an eyewitness. He writes that the flood began on Tuesday, 25 September (he does not mention the year). At the direction of Archbishop Francisco Manso y Zúñiga, the image was brought to Mexico City and kept for the night in the archbishop's palace. The next morning it was taken to the cathedral, where it remained through the entire period of the flood. The flood subsided little by little, and the credit was given to the Virgin. After the flood had subsided, the archbishop returned the image to Guadalupe. The procession took place on Sunday, 14 May 1634. Laso de la Vega does not give this story, which is the last of the miracles related by Sánchez.

Laso de la Vega added seven other miracles, six of them accounts of cures.

A Spanish woman suffered from distension of the stomach because of dropsy. The physician's effort to help her only made matters worse. After ten months of suffering she had herself brought to Guadalupe. After she had drunk some water from the spring her body felt better, and she fell asleep. An Indian saw a large, frightful snake emerge from under her, and his cries for help awakened her. Both their cries brought help, the snake was killed, and the woman's swelling disappeared.

A Spanish nobleman suffered severe headaches and earaches. On the way to Guadalupe, he made a vow that if he was cured he would make an offering of a head made of silver. He was cured as soon as he arrived.

A young woman named Catalina suffered from dropsy and asked to be taken to Guadalupe. On drinking water from the spring she was instantly healed. This appears to be a doublet of the first miracle.

A Discalced Franciscan named Pedro de Valderrama had cancer of the toe and was instantly cured when he showed it to the Virgin of Guadalupe.[66]

A Spanish nobleman named Luis de Castilla suffered from a swollen foot, which turned gangrenous. Valderrama, it was said, recommended that he go to Guadalupe. He had a silver foot made, the same size as his, which he sent ahead of him to the ermita. When the delivery was made, the nobleman was cured.[67]

The son of the sacristan Juan Pavón had a swelling in the neck that threatened to kill him. He was taken to Guadalupe, where he was anointed with oil from one of the lamps. He was immediately cured.

The seventh miracle was not a cure but the Blessed Virgin's intervention to bring religious peace to Teotihuacan at the time that the Augustinians were attempting to establish a house there. Laso de la Vega's account is an almost verbatim version of the one attributed by Cuevas to Alva Ixtlilxochitl and is probably the source of the one published by Vera and quoted by Cuevas.

These miracle accounts obviously belong to a more credulous age. Viewed from today's standpoint, they are fanciful, legendary, and even frivolous or grotesque. No serious credence can be given to any of them. They are, however, significant for other reasons. The majority of the miracles narrated by Sánchez and Laso de la Vega involve Spaniards, not Indians. This lack of Indian emphasis or orientation is a clear difference between the *Nican mopohua* and the *Nican motecpana*. In addition, five of the six cures in the *Nican motecpana* were brought about by actions that were associated with the shrine and its spring rather than with the image as such. The two cures of dropsical women were brought about by drinking water from the spring at Guadalupe. The son of Juan Pavón was healed by anointing with oil from one of the lamps. Two Spaniards were healed because of their ex-voto offerings, a common occurrence in the genre of miracle stories. Only Pedro de Valderrama made a direct appeal to the image.

The language and style of the miracle stories in the *Nican motecpana* indicate that they did not have a common origin. Of the fourteen miracles only three benefit natives; the rest are worked on behalf of Spaniards. Most of the latter appear to have a later origin than the former. The story of the Indian miraculously restored to life at the time of the dedication parade contains no Spanish loan words and uses the older term *nican tlaca* for natives. The account of Juan de Tovar, the Indian discoverer of Remedios, has only one Spanish loan word (*leguas*). The story of the governors of Teotihuacan has Spanish loan words only for technical terms and refers to the viceroy Luis de Velasco as the Virgin's "beloved son." It also uses the older form *yolia anima* for soul. As has been noted earlier this event dates back to the time of its actual occurrence in the sixteenth century, though without the intercession of Guadalupe. It would not be rash to say that in its original form it may date from the sixteenth century and may be Stage 1 Nahuatl.

In general, with certain exceptions, such as the story of the rescue of Antonio de Carvajal's young relative, the narration of the miracles performed for Spaniards is less rhetorical, ornate, and elaborate. They are brief, simple, and at times almost stark, perhaps because they were translated from Spanish originals. This, too, permits us to surmise an earlier origin for the Indian stories. The briefer stories, such as the cure of the son of the sacristan Juan Pavón, also contain the largest number of Spanish loan words and seem to belong to Stage 2.

Important testimony concerning these miracles is found in one of the earliest known reproductions of the image of Our Lady of Guadalupe in its present form, an engraving by the Flemish artist Samuel Stradanus that probably dates from 1615.[68] Stradanus (the Latinized form of van der Straet) was a native of Antwerp who came to New Spain early in the seventeenth century. The engraving was commissioned by Archbishop de la Serna, who intended to sell copies to raise funds for the new chapel at Tepeyac. The copy consulted for this study belonged to the collection of H. H. Behrens, who donated it to the Metropolitan

Museum of Art in New York City in 1948.[69] In the center is the image as it is known today, except that it has a crown and is surrounded by the cherubim mentioned at a later date by Florencia. Above the image are some miscellaneous ex-votos, and on each side are two lamps. On the right and left sides of the engraving are eight panels depicting various miracles worked at the shrine with captions that narrate the miracles. Because of the deteriorated condition of the original copper plate, the captions are difficult or even impossible to read. Viewed clockwise from the top right-hand side these include (1) Antonio de Carvajal's relative's horse accident; the young man is shown dangling from the stirrup; at the very top is a view of Tulancingo (of which the caption says that the elder Carvajal was mayor) and in the upper left-hand corner is the image of Guadalupe; (2) the fall of the lamp on a Spaniard while he was praying in the shrine; the lamp is shown striking his head; the image of Guadalupe is above and behind the altar; another Spaniard and a nun witness the accident; the caption says that the lamp was heavy and that no oil was spilled and the glass was not broken; (3) the cure of the son of the sacristan Juan Pavón, who is shown being presented to the image, which is behind the altar, by his father, while a woman, perhaps the boy's mother, kneels before the altar; the caption says that the child was cured as soon as he was anointed with oil from the lamp; outside the church is a group of buildings labeled "the great city of Mexico"; (4) the miraculous lighting of the candles when Vázquez de Acuña was preparing to say mass; a man in Spanish dress and a woman (perhaps a nun) are in the foreground, while another man in Spanish dress is kneeling at the communion rail; the image is above and behind the altar; the caption says that "the candles were miraculously lighted by Our Lady"; (5) the cure of Luis de Castilla, who is shown lying in bed with one bare leg outside the covers; a friar (Valderrama?) holds the silver foot that Castilla offered; in the foreground a woman, perhaps a nun or Castilla's wife, kneels before a table that holds a crucifix and an ink-stand; in the upper left-hand corner is a church labeled Guadalupe; there is no image in this picture; the caption states that as soon as the silver head was hung in the church Castilla was cured; (6) Pedro de Valderrama, the Discalced Franciscan cured of a tumorous toe, who is shown displaying it to the image, which is above and behind the altar; Valderrama is sitting and praying with the foot exposed; another friar is kneeling and praying; on the ground are a friar's hat and walking staff; a man in Spanish dress is walking through the door, through which can be seen a group of buildings labeled Pachuca; the caption is one of the most difficult to read but appears to say that after the cure Valderrama walked to Pachuca from Guadalupe; (7) the cure of Catarina de Monta, who was suffering from incurable hydropsy and was cured by drinking water from the spring; she is shown lying before the image and also lying outside the door of the shrine, where the spring is also clearly visible and identified; the image is above and behind the altar; a man in Spanish dress with arms extended is in the foreground with his back to the viewer, apparently pointing to the image; in the upper right-hand corner can be seen a group of buildings labeled Mexico-Tenochtitlan; this panel is significant because it makes a clear allusion to the spring as the place where the Virgin appeared ("Mexico-Tenochtitlan: Catarina de Monta . . . hydropic for eleven years, without hope of health, attended novenas and drank from the water of the spring where Our Lady of Guadalupe appeared and she was immediately cured"); (8) the Spaniard cured of headaches when he offered a silver head; he sits on the edge of his bed fully clothed with his left hand to his head; a man in Spanish dress, apparently a servant, stands holding the silver head; through the door a friar or nun can be seen kneeling in prayer; there is no image; the caption gives the sick man's name as Bartholomé Grandía (the last name is almost illegible) and says that he was cured as soon as the head was hung in the church.[70]

The Stradanus engraving shows that by 1615 at least eight of the miracle stories had reached a stage close to their final form and were well known. This does not mean, however, that they had yet been gathered together in the *Nican motecpana*. The miracle panels offer some tantalizing insights into the development of the Guadalupe tradition. There are variations from the accounts given by Sánchez, Laso de la Vega, and later Francisco de Florencia. Five of them were used by Laso de la Vega but not by Sánchez. The engraving gives the full names, not always intelligible, of the Spaniard cured of headaches and the young lady cured of hydropsy. Two sets of miracles appear to be developments of a common source: the cures of the two hydropsical women and the cures of the two Spaniards, one of a disease of the foot, the other of headaches. Though six of the eight panels show the image, not all the miracles were directly attributed to it. One was the result of drinking water from the spring, one from anointing with oil from the sanctuary lamp, and two to the presentation of ex-voto offerings. All the persons involved were Spaniards; no miracle benefits an Indian. Two of the most important of those related by Sánchez and Laso de la Vega which dealt with natives, the cure of the wounded Indian in the mock battle and the apparition to Juan de Tovar, are absent from this engraving. It is particularly interesting that the cure of the young hydropsical woman, Catarina, refers to the Virgin's having appeared at the spring. This may well represent an early stage in the development of the apparition story. Most significant of all, of course, is that the greatest miracles of all—the apparition to Juan Diego and the cure of Juan Bernardino—are not shown. There is nothing in the engraving that refers in any way to the traditional apparition account.

The Life of Juan Diego

After relating the miracle accounts, Laso de la Vega added information about the later life of Juan Diego. This included his moving to Guadalupe, where he lived a life of work and penance. "He was a widower. Two years before the ever

Virgin appeared to him, his wife died. She was named María Lucía. They both lived chastely, they kept themselves [chaste]. She died a virgin. He also lived as a virgin. He never knew a woman" [Icnoquichtli catca, oc yuh òxihuitl qui-mottititzinoz iz çenquizca Ichpochtzintli in omomiquilì in içihuahuàtzin catca itoca Maria Lucia; auh in ehuan chipahuaca nenque, mopixque mochpochmi-quilì in içihuah, no yèhuatl telpochnen, aic quixtimà Çihuatl].[71] The reason given for this was the sermon by Motolinía that caused the couple to resolve to live in celibacy, though this is inconsistent with the assertion of lifelong celibacy.

The story of the celibate marriage has become an accepted part of the tradition, although it involves chronological difficulties. If, as this account asserts, Juan Diego died in 1548 at the age of seventy-four, he would have been born about the year 1474 and would have been approximately fifty at the time of Motolinía's arrival in 1524 and approximately fifty-seven at the time of the apparitions. The marriage, then, would clearly have been preconquest, a time when the concept of a celibate marriage, or celibacy itself outside the Mexica priesthood, would have been all but incomprehensible. If María Lucía died in 1529, there would have been five years of celibacy at the most. Becerra Tanco, writing in 1666, and Francisco Javier Clavigero, writing in 1782, seem to have been the only writers of the colonial period to have noticed the discrepancies, for they wrote that the couple refrained from the use of marriage after the sermon.[72] In the seventeenth century virginity and celibacy were viewed as a primary sign of virtue that also validated the seer's message. Combining as it did asceticism with renunciation of one of life's strongest forces, it added credibility to the visionary's message. Clearly this is the intrusion of a postconquest Catholic outlook into the story of Juan Diego.

This brief biography belongs to the category of European hagiography, especially in its emphasis on the celibacy of Juan Diego. It also shows signs of Spanish borrowings, such as the calque "he never knew a woman" (*aic quixtimà Çihuatl*), which is ultimately derived from biblical Hebrew. Significantly, it is totally separate from the *Nican mopohua* and shows signs of later composition. In all probability it had a later and distinct origin from the apparition account.

The Conclusion

The book concludes with an exhortation to devotion to Guadalupe and a prayer. Like the introduction, these were probably written by Laso de la Vega or his native assistants in a complex and archaic style at some time close to the publication of the book. The exhortation contrasts Guadalupe, which is seen primarily as an Indian devotion, and Remedios, which belongs to the Castilians. It also strongly implies that the account had fallen into oblivion and was now being revived.

And that is what the people of the world were like formerly. Only at that very moment did they wonder at and give thanks for the favor of the heavenly sovereign noble lady. If they have obtained what they want, from that time onward they go casting it into their forgetfulness, so that those who come here afterward will no longer have the good fortune of obtaining the light, the sun of Our Lord. And that is how it is, because of this the favor of the heavenly noble lady by which she appeared very miraculously here in her home of Tepeyacac has perished somewhat and has been abandoned, because not to the extent that was necessary did her commoners [Indians] make it known nor did they have it acknowledged, that she built her house there for their sakes in order that there she might hear their affliction, their grief, their tears, and their entreaties, and she might give them and bestow on them the favor of her help.[73]

Unlike Sánchez, Laso de la Vega did not identify the Virgin of Guadalupe with criollismo; rather, he pictured her as the mother and protectress of the Indians, toward whom she shows a special love. As a result, he claimed, the Indians turned away from idolatry and destroyed the images they had hidden in their homes. This claim later became part of the Guadalupe tradition, that is, that the apparitions were followed by a mass conversion of the Indians to Christianity. Laso de la Vega also saw the apparition and image as the crowning work of the Virgin in New Spain, together with Remedios and other devotions.

The years 1648 and 1649 are the crucial ones in the history of the Guadalupe apparitions. Miguel Sánchez made known to the criollos of New Spain a story that until that time was unknown or forgotten. Suddenly, as if out of nowhere, he gave them a story that he and they appropriated as divine witness to the legitimacy of criollismo. In the years that followed the predominantly criollo secular clergy would embrace the story wholeheartedly and spread it among the criollos. With Sánchez began the long process whereby Guadalupe was fused with Mexican identity. Laso de la Vega, in contrast, sought to bring the message of compassion and consolation to the Indians. If he had any success, it was limited, because it was not until the eighteenth century that the Indians began to seek refuge under the shadow of the Virgin of Tepeyac.

 **8**

"It Is a Tradition. Seek No Further."

The rapid spread of devotion to Our Lady of Guadalupe among the criollos of New Spain in the aftermath of Sánchez's book is well attested. Evidence can be found in the foundation of churches and chapels dedicated to Guadalupe outside the archdiocese of Mexico and in the appearance of sermons that for the first time glorified the image and referred to the apparitions. The problem posed by the lack of written sources accompanied this popularization. Within eighteen years of Sánchez's book, the governing body of the archdiocese of Mexico conducted an investigation designed to establish the existence of a constant and uniform tradition. After that three major writers attempted to establish a documentary basis for the tradition.

Other Silences

In the same year that Laso de la Vega's work appeared, Gil González Dávila published *Teatro eclesiástico*, which contained short biographies of Zumárraga and Montúfar. Though he spoke of Montúfar's refurbishing of the ermita, he made no mention of the apparitions.[1] More significant was the lack of any mention by the canon Gregorio Martín de Guijo, who kept a diary of gossip and events, notable and otherwise, from 1648 to 1664. He mentioned Miguel Sánchez twice in connection with sermons the latter delivered, one for the Virgin of Remedios, the other for Corpus Christi. Laso de la Vega was mentioned only once, under the year 1657, when he received the position of *medio racionero* on the cathedral chapter. Guijo also made six references to Guadalupe but only in connection with other events that took place there, such as the arrival and departure of dignitaries. Although he devoted much space to describing processions, novenas, and various devotions in Mexico City, there was no mention of the apparitions or of the books by Sánchez and Laso de la Vega.[2]

Juan de Correa

This silence, however, was not total. Within a few months of Sánchez's work, Juan de Correa, a criollo surgeon and teacher of anatomy at the Royal and Pontifical University, published a work on the qualities of mercury, *Tratado de la qualidad manifiesta, qve el Mercurio tiene*, which he dedicated to the Virgin of Guadalupe. The letter of approbation was written by Francisco de Siles at the direction of Pedro de Barrientos Lomelín, the treasurer of the cathedral chapter and vicar general of the archdiocese, who had also given permission for the publication of the *Huey tlamahuiçoltica*. "From the first page I was assured of the author's astuteness in dedicating it and the success of his work in composing it. The former because it was to the sovereign Virgin Mary, Our Lady, the miraculous prodigy in her most holy image of Guadalupe." Even if by an impossible hypothesis, Siles wrote, the book did not deserve approbation because of its contents, "it would deserve to have it because of the devotion with which he offers this work to the protection of our Most Holy Criolla, the Most Holy Virgin of Guadalupe." The work was also prefaced by a sonnet written by Miguel Sánchez in honor of the Virgin of Guadalupe. "You offer unction by the hand of Mary, of our Guadalupe among her flowers, ingenious Juan, profound craftsman." The same thing was done in another sonnet by Juan Rivero. "Mary offers flowers that burst forth from her miracle and having handed them over to an Indian Juan, she sends them to another Juan." The frontispiece of the work is an engraving of the image as it is now, except that it has a crown and both crown and head are surrounded by a large nimbus. The sunburst also has wavy rays as well as straight ones. In his introduction Correa testified to a generic or vague tradition. "To your miracle, which you conserve within yourself, as one devoted I dedicated myself since the first studies of my craft, having experienced your mercy, to which I owe my understanding and my work."[3]

The Capitular Inquiry of 1665 to 1666

The next major step was involvement by the cathedral chapter of Mexico City. There can be no doubt that three of its members, Miguel Sánchez, Juan de Poblete, and Francisco de Siles, were ardent champions of this involvement. In 1662, when the see of Mexico was vacant, Siles, who was the *canónigo magistral*, or canon preacher, contacted Diego Osorio de Escobar y Llamas, the bishop of Puebla and administrator pro tempore of the archdiocese, a Galician of pronounced criollo sympathies, as well as the viceroy Juan de Leyva y de la Cerda and the cathedral chapter.[4] The purpose was to send a petition to Pope Alexander VII asking that 12 December, "the day on which is observed the annual memorial of the apparition of the holy image," be made a feast day for all of New Spain and that it have a proper office.[5] This is the first evidence of that date's being used in connection with Guadalupe, and the change probably reflected the popularity of Mateo de la Cruz's version of the traditional account published two years earlier, the first one to give specific dates for the apparitions. If Rome granted the request, it would be regarded as an endorsement of the devotion and at least indirectly of the truth of the apparition tradition. It would also provide the criollos with a major feast that was uniquely theirs. It is unclear how much supporting documentation accompanied the petition to Rome, though there was definitely a Latin account of the apparitions together with a number of other requests.[6] The petition was not according to the form and procedure required by the Congregation of Rites, and so Rome demanded a canonical investigation.[7] The response said that a questionnaire was being prepared for the examination of witnesses and the procedure for naming the examiners. It was only after this investigation had been made that the congregation would examine the petition.

In 1665 to 1666, after the brief interregnum of Alonso de Cuevas Dávalos, the first criollo archbishop of Mexico, the chapter carried on its own investigation at the instigation of Siles, out of fear that the Roman rescript would be long in coming or that the aged witnesses would soon die off.[8] The ultimate purpose of the investigation was to secure the desired feast and proper mass and office. More immediately, the investigation sought to demonstrate the existence and continuity of a tradition, a strong argument in canonical procedures, and to enliven devotion to the Virgin of Guadalupe. The judges were named between 11 and 19 December 1665: the dean, Juan de Poblete; the chantre, Juan de la Cámara; and two canons, Juan Díez de la Barrera (treasurer of the chapter) and Nicolás del Puerto. The formal decree of the inquiry was issued on 22 December. On the same day the three judges appointed a cleric, Antonio de Gama, to take the testimonies outside the city, specifically from Cuauhtitlan, from the "oldest persons to be found and who may know and have news" of the apparition.[9] Siles also sought the assistance of the city council of Mexico City on 14 December. In order that "the cult and veneration of a prodigy so rare and the like of which was never granted to any other city or republic in the world, and with which this [city of] Mexico was enriched should be increased," the council appointed Siles and Captain Francisco García Guerrero, a *familiar* (deputy or police agent) of the Inquisition, as its representatives to take the autos to Rome.[10] Andrés García Guerrero, the captain's nephew, and Captain Miguel de Benavides were chosen as alternates. On 3 January 1666 the interpreters were appointed, two of them being citizens of Cuauhtitlan. Though Florencia claimed that the questionnaire used in the inquiry came from Rome, it clearly owes its origin to the cabildo, probably to Siles, as Medina Ascensio states.[11]

The questionnaire was quite detailed.[12] The witnesses were asked first if they knew Siles, who apparently selected and presented them, and about their personal knowledge of the tradition. The second and third questions were the most important, for they contained a synopsis of the entire apparition account. The second asked "Whether they know, by sight, hearsay, or certain knowledge how on 12 December of the past year 1531, when the Most Illustrious and Most Reverend Señor don fray Juan de Zumárraga of happy memory was prelate of this archdiocese, there came to his house and archiepiscopal palace Juan Diego, a native Indian and a citizen at that time of the pueblo of Cuauhtitlan, and had His Excellency advised that he wanted to speak to him on behalf of the Lady, for whom he had previously brought other messages."[13] The question went on to describe the flowers in great detail and the miraculous appearance of the image. "Let them say in particular, and give an account, etc., how it is also the tradition that there has been in this matter among common people or whether among those of higher rank and importance in this aforesaid city and kingdoms of New Spain, whether common knowledge has also been dominant, without there having been anything said, heard, or understood to the contrary."[14] As will be seen, this last part was essential to the concept of tradition. The third question dealt with the building of the ermita and the placing of the image. Questions four, six, and seven dealt with the image itself, that is, whether it was considered miraculous or beyond the powers of human artists and whether the tilma had been sized. The fifth asked about the life and virtues of Juan Diego, though surprisingly it made no reference to the celibate marriage. The eighth question dealt with the image's survival in the humid and salty climate of Tepeyac, and the ninth recapitulated the idea of a tradition as being something well known and uncontradicted.

Testimonies were taken from January to April 1666. The investigators ultimately questioned twenty witnesses: one mestizo, seven Indians, ten Spanish clerics or religious, and two laypersons. Written testimony was also submitted by Luis Becerra Tanco. Miguel Sánchez was one of the witnesses (and the only diocesan priest), but not Laso de la Vega. In fact, no witness was called from Guadalupe itself, for the investigation was confined to Cuauhtitlan (for indigenous witnesses) and Mexico City (for criollo and peninsular witnesses). The first witnesses were a mestizo and seven Indians from Cuauhtitlan.

Marcos Pacheco, a mestizo more than eighty years of age, gave testimony on 7 January 1666, the only witness from Cuauhtitlan who did not use an interpreter.[15] He had been raised in Cuauhtitlan and held civil offices there. He spoke of a picture that used to be on the wall of a room of the old church of Cuauhtitlan, showing Juan Diego and Juan Bernardino with a Franciscan lay brother, "fray someone de Gante."[16] He recalled hearing his aunt, who died at the age of seventy or eighty, say to him and his brother that "God would do to you as he did to Juan Diego, an Indian native of this town, who lived in the barrio of Tlayac, because she knew him and dealt with the aforesaid and María Lucía, his wife, and Juan Bernardino, uncle of the aforesaid, because she treated all of them as relatives of the mother-in-law of his said aunt."[17] He said that his aunt had heard the story of the apparitions from Juan Diego himself, and she told them how the Virgin gave him a message for the *guey teopisque* (*huey teopix-qui*, or great priest) to build a chapel at Tepeyac. The story of the apparition, preceded by trumpets, *chirimías* (a flute of Moorish origin), and drums, was published in the marketplace before a large crowd, "among whom was the aunt of this witness."[18] The aunt also made a somewhat baffling assertion that she had seen the roses stamped on the tilma.

The aunt's account followed the traditional one rather closely. Like the *Nican mopohua*, it omitted the third appearance of the Virgin after the second interview with the bishop. She was said to have remembered the dedication of the ermita and the placing of the image. Pacheco said that Juan Diego was fifty-five or fifty-six at the time of the apparitions. He also spoke of the devotion of the people and the miracles worked through the intercession of the Virgin, especially by drinking and bathing in the waters of the spring. He testified that the Indians of Cuauhtitlan had built an adobe hut for Juan Diego next to the ermita and that Juan Diego had been a good and holy man. "This witness said that everything that he had said and declared is public and well known, common knowledge and report in this kingdom of New Spain."[19] The formula of public knowledge is found at the end of most of the testimonies and was a standard way of testifying to the existence of a tradition. Similarly, all the witnesses testified to the fact that the image that appeared on Juan Diego's tilma was the same as the one that in 1666 was venerated at Tepeyac, again a sign of continuity.

On the following day, Gabriel Suárez, a native, made his statement in Nahuatl through interpreters.[20] He declared that he could not state his age exactly, but Gama estimated that it was more than 110 years because he looked old and could remember ancient events. He was a native of Cuauhtitlan, born in the barrio of San José Tequixquiagua, which adjoined that of Tlayacac. He recalled that at the age of nine he had seen the viceroy, Luis de Velasco, "who was blind in one eye" and who at that time went to Peru. He also claimed to have met Pedro de Gante (who died in 1572) and fray "someone" de Escalona.[21] At the age of six or seven, he testified, his father had taken him to the ermita at Tepeyac, "which at that time was of adobe, without any kind of stone or mortar," and which had been built on the spot where the Virgin appeared.[22]

The witness stated that he had heard the story of the apparition from his father, who had known Juan Diego well, a "native and citizen of this said town, in the barrio of Tlayacac."[23] He testified that when he was a youth of fifteen or twenty, he heard of the events from other Indians who had been alive when they occurred. He said that he saw the image at that time and it appeared the same as when he saw it just two years before his testimony. He could not remember how many times the Virgin appeared. His father told him that the apparition had been proclaimed in the marketplace with many trumpets and drums. All this had been common knowledge in Cuauhtitlan for ninety years. The Indians of Cuauhtitlan called Juan Diego "the pilgrim" because he always walked alone and went alone to instructions at Tlatelolco. After the apparition he left his home and land to Juan Bernardino and went to live at Tepeyac, where the Indians, who regarded him as a holy man, came to ask his prayers for good harvests.[24]

Andrés Juan, a native and a citizen of the barrio of Teacoac in Cuauhtitlan who did not know his age, testified on 9 January through interpreters.[25] The questioners estimated that he was 112 to 115 years old because he said that he had known Luis de Velasco (which one was not stated) when he was ten years old, that he was over ten when the great epidemic (*cocoliztli*) of *tabardillo* (fever, probably typhus) broke out, that he was fifteen when the drainage of Mexico City began (1607), and that he remembered the first governor of Cuauhtitlan, Francisco Sánchez. Andrés Juan testified that his parents had told him that he was born a few years after the apparitions and the public proclamation of them. His parents knew Juan Diego well, and when the event occurred, it was publicized with trumpets and chirimías in the marketplace. Most of the villagers went to the site to bring flowers and have dances because Juan Diego was a fellow villager from the barrio of Tlayacac. His parents told him that the Mother of God had appeared to Juan Diego three times and that he had two interviews with the bishop or archbishop, whose name he could not remember being told. More than a hundred years before, his parents had taken him to the old ermita, which had just been completed and was made of adobe. He saw the image there, the same one that was currently in the ermita. The Indians of Cuauhtitlan used to go to the ermita to clean and repair it, a laudable practice he claimed to remember after a century. In language very similar to that of Gabriel Suárez, he told how Juan Diego was so solitary that he seemed like a pilgrim and how the Indians regarded him as a holy person whose intercession they sought for good harvests. He also described the spring and its miraculous powers and ended with the customary formula of tradition.

Juana de la Concepción, an Indian who believed that she was about eighty-five years of age, gave testimony through interpreters on 10 January 1666.[26] She testified to having been married by Rodrigo de Santillán, a Franciscan who had been guardian of the convent of Cuauhtitlan. The registers of the cofradía showed him to have been there in 1609.[27] She recalled that as a young child she met the viceroy Luis de Velasco, who lodged with her parents when hunting near her village of San Miguel. Her father, don Lorenzo de San Francisco Tlaxtlazontli, the cacique of San Miguel who died fifty years before, was the first person in Cuauhtitlan to hear of the apparitions.[28] He was fond of making picture records of notable events. "If she remembers correctly" [si mal no se acuerda], he included a picture of the apparition and he knew Juan Diego well.[29] Thieves had twice robbed her father's house and so the maps were lost.

In his capacity as a *principal* (Indian noble) and cacique her father had been in the procession that accompanied the placing of the image. She stated that Juan Diego was a native of the barrio of Tlayacac in Cuauhtitlan. When she was fifteen or twenty her father told her about the apparitions. Her account, which was very detailed, followed the *Nican mopohua* rather closely, although like others she could not remember if she had been told the name of the bishop, only that he was a Franciscan. She herself had never been to the ermita nor seen the original of the image.

Pablo Suárez, seventy-eight years of age and successor to his father as native governor of Cuauhtitlan, gave his testimony on 10 January.[30] His father had been governor for thirty years. His parents, both of whom lived beyond age one hundred, had spent their entire lives in Cuauhtitlan and had died seven or eight years before. He testified that his maternal grandmother, who died forty years before at the age of 110, knew Juan Diego, María Lucía, and Juan Bernardino, all of whom were natives of the barrio of Tlayacac. She told her grandson and his mother how the Virgin had appeared to Juan Diego when he was going to Tlatelolco, where the grandmother herself was accustomed to go "with all the other people and that on some Sundays of the year a religious of the said church of Tlatelolco would come to this one to say mass for them."[31] The Virgin appeared three times and had Juan Diego take flowers to the archbishop. The archbishop had wept a great deal and immediately tried to build the chapel. The image was taken in a great procession from Mexico City, with the archbishop walking barefoot and bare-legged ("descalzo de pie y pierna") with many people from the city. They danced on the way and played musical instruments, all of which the grandmother saw. She also said that all this was so public that even Indian children recounted and sang the procession. She had also visited Juan Diego at Tepeyac, where the Indians asked him to pray for good harvests.

Martín de San Luis, a former *alcalde ordinario* (judge and administrative official) of Cuauhtitlan, was an Indian of eighty years of age when he gave testimony through interpreters on 11 January.[32] He said that when he was between the ages of ten and twelve, Diego Torres de Bullón, a native who was for many years the master of the chapel, told him the account. Torres at the time was more than eighty or ninety years old, an Indian who knew how to read and write and who had known Juan Diego, a native of Tlayacac. Torres de Bullón recounted the story and said that he had been in the procession to Tepeyac and had seen the archbishop barefoot. He repeated the story of the publication of the miracle in the marketplace with music and dance. He testified that in 1531 he and all the Indians of Cuauhtitlan went to Tlatelolco for mass and instruction. He also stated that he had visited Juan Diego at the ermita, where he went with other Indians to sweep and care for it.

Juan Suárez, a native from the barrio of San Sebastián Xala who believed he was one hundred years old or more, was a former city councilman of Cuauhti-tlan and claimed also to have seen Luis de Velasco I.[33] He gave testimony through interpreters on 19 January and said that when the great eclipse took place on the vespers of Saint Barnabas he was already old enough to shave ("hombre que tenía barbas") and that he was a grown man when the drainage began (1607).[34] He had heard his father say that in 1531 the archbishop was "don fray someone Zumárraga," the only witness who actually named the bishop. He said that Tlatelolco was "at that time the doctrina of the natives of this said town."[35] He gave the accepted account of the apparitions, saying that there were two of them. He testified that at the time of Juan Diego's first two interviews with the bishop, the latter and his servants had mocked Juan Diego. According to Suárez, his father had been present at the public proclamation of the celebration and that he had heard many persons in the village, including relatives of Juan Diego, speak of it. He said that Juan Diego lived in the barrio of Tlayacac and described the publication of the miracle with musical instru-ments and the procession to Tepeyac. He was the first of the witnesses to re-count the appearance of the Virgin to Juan Bernardino, and he, too, recalled the mural of Juan Bernardino with Pedro de Gante. He described Juan Diego as being so solitary that he was like a hermit.

Catarina Mónica, an Indian from the barrio of Carnicería who testified through interpreters, said that she was more than one hundred years old ("ma-cuilpuali xiguil," *sic* for "macuilpohualli xihuitl").[36] The investigator accepted this because she could remember the ermita at Guadalupe when there was no stone bridge but only planks whereby people came to it. Though she herself had not seen the picture of Juan Diego and Juan Bernardino with Pedro de Gante, she had heard about it from others. However, she referred to the Virgin as "the Most Holy Virgin of the Rosary." Her account of the apparitions was detailed. She testified that her parents, who had died more than seventy years before, and an aunt had said that the Mother of God of Guadalupe had appeared to an Indian, a native of the barrio of Tlayacac in Cuauhtitlan. The parents and aunt said that the archbishop immediately set about building the chapel and that there was a great procession, preceded by public proclamations and music. Catarina also mentioned the appearance to Juan Bernardino and said that the Indians were accustomed to go to the ermita on the day after the celebration of the Virgin's feast.

The inquiry then turned to peninsular and criollo witnesses, all of whom were in Mexico City.[37] These were also presented by Siles but testified only before a notary, not a *juez de comisión* (judge appointed for a specific inquiry).

Miguel Sánchez, age sixty, gave his testimony, some of which has been noted previously, on 18 February.[38] In keeping with the proofs for a tradition, he said that he had heard the account "from many persons of quality, nobility, and learning in times past and since fifty years before."[39] He did not, however, name any of those persons. He specified 12 December as the day on which the miracle occurred, something that was not to be found in his book. He recounted the story of the paper shortage as a reason for the lack of a written account and the story of Doctor Alonso Muñoz's finding the archbishop of Mexico reading an account of the apparitions with singular tenderness. He said that he had learned from elderly persons that Zumárraga had placed the image in the cathedral and then taken it to Tepeyac in a great procession on 26 December 1531, accompanied by both cabildos and the viceroy. "And this witness with all diligence undertook to look for the surest notices of this tradition and apparition" in writing his book.[40]

Fray Pedro Oyanguren, who said he was more than eighty-five years of age, was a Dominican priest who had been born and raised in Mexico City.[41] In his testimony of 22 January he said that he had heard the account from numerous people of all conditions since as long as he could remember, specifically from his parents and others. His testimony followed the standard account closely, saying that there were three interviews with Zumárraga. He called the Virgin of Guadalupe La Criolla. He also told the story of the procession to Tepeyac on the day after Christmas, including the presence of the viceroy, Zumárraga's having gone in pontifical robes, and the revival of the dead Indian. According to him the original autos of the miracle, which must have existed, probably perished, as so often happened over a long period of time and changes of administration. He also said that the image had been in the ermita for at least sixty years. Like Sánchez, Oyanguren was conscious of the fact that he was testifying to a tradition, saying that "his parents, grandparents, and ancestors and other innumerable persons had told him about it, of the greatest importance, position, and dignities in this said city, without there having been in any way any contradiction of one or another of the said notices."[42]

On 25 January fray Bartolomé de Tapia, a former Franciscan provincial who said he was more than fifty-five years of age, a criollo, and a native of Puebla, deposed that he had heard the account from his ancestors.[43] He cited only one interview with Zumárraga. He also testified in terms of a tradition: "until the present day it is common knowledge in all New Spain . . . without there having been anything to the contrary."[44] He made the interesting statement that he did not know, nor had he ever heard, that the image had been retouched by any human painter.

In a somewhat rambling deposition given on 27 February, fray Antonio de Mendoza, an Augustinian and member of their provincial council (*definidor*), sixty-six years of age, a criollo born in Mexico City, referred to his parents and grandparents, who had lived to be very old.[45] These included his grandfather Antonio Maldonado, former *oidor* (judge) of the royal chancellery of Mexico City, and his father, Alonso de Mendoza, former captain of the guard for the viceroy, the count of Coruña (1566–1568).[46] His father died at the age of ninety. They had told him the traditional account, though he spoke of only one interview with Zumárraga. Mendoza said that he knew from personal experience that the viceroys of Mexico had great devotion to Mary, Queen of Heaven. He stated that as a person who "has on different occasions seen [the image of] this most sacred Lady, who is so beautiful and perfect that there has not been nor has there been found a master or craftsman of the art of painting who has been able to paint or copy her in the many and numberless [copies] with such accuracy, perfection, color, and beauty, as His Divine Majesty shows in his original."[47] Mendoza mentioned how popular and widespread the devotion had become, so that there was hardly a house that did not have a copy of the image. He was the source of the quaint story about how the image was permitted to choose which church it would reside in. According to him, when the new church had been completed in 1622, the people prepared to move the image from the old one to the new one. They worried, however, that in so doing they were acting contrary to the wishes of the Virgin, who had ordered the first ermita built on a specific site. In order to give her an opportunity to express her preference, the image was placed in a shelter midway between the two buildings. After eight days the Virgin had not returned to the ermita, a sign to the people that she could be safely moved into the new building.

Fray Juan de Herrera, seventy-one years of age, a Mercedarian and a criollo born in Mexico City, three times provincial of his order in New Spain, and *catedrático* of theology at the university, gave the standard account on 28 February.[48] He claimed that since childhood he had heard the story from his parents and grandparents and persons of every status. He also testified to the great devotion of the archbishops and viceroys.

Fray Pedro de San Simón, Discalced Carmelite, member of the provincial council and former provincial, a peninsular who had been in New Spain for thirty-two years, said that he was over sixty-five years of age.[49] He gave his testimony on 28 February. He had heard many persons of quality and trust speak of the apparition of the "Queen of Angels." He also testified to the viceroys' devotion to this Virgin, including the current one, the marquess of Mancera, who went to the church and sanctuary of Guadalupe every Saturday of the year. San Simón also concluded his testimony by stating that he had never seen, heard, or known of anything to the contrary.

Diego de Monroy, a Jesuit of sixty-five years of age who said he had heard the tradition for more than forty years, recounted it in his testimony of 2 March but also with only one interview between Zumárraga and Juan Diego.[50] He described Guadalupe's role in the flood of 1629. Monroy, with typical Jesuit precision, described the maguey fiber on which the image was impressed. He said that the material was such that it could not be sized. Like most of the non-Indian witnesses, he testified to the great devotion that the viceroys of New

Spain had to Guadalupe, especially the marquess of Mancera, who went to Guadalupe every Saturday.

Fray Juan de San José, Discalced Franciscan, former provincial, and at the time of the interview an official of the Inquisition, was seventy-six years of age and gave his testimony on 5 March. He had heard the story of the apparition for more than fifty-four years from older and trustworthy persons.[51] His recounting of the tradition was essentially the same as the standard one. He said that he had seen the flood of 1629, when the people of Mexico City brought the image in a canoe to stop it. Looking back from a distance of more than thirty years he incorrectly declared that the city became dry by a miracle. Like the other non-Indian witnesses he emphasized the devotion of the archbishops and viceroys, especially Mancera.

Pedro de San Nicolás was a priest of the order of Saint John of God and a former provincial who testified on 5 March.[52] He was seventy-one years of age and said that he had heard the story since he reached the use of reason. He too cited the devotion of the archbishops and viceroys, especially Mancera. He described the image's role in the flood of 1629 in wording that was almost identical to that of Juan de San José.

On 11 March fray Nicolás Cerdán, of the order of San Hipólito, sixty-one years of age, testified that he had heard the story from trustworthy persons from the time he reached the use of reason. Like the others, he cited the flood of 1629, the miraculous dryness of the city, and the devotion of the viceroys, especially Mancera.[53]

The last two witnesses were laypersons.

Miguel de Cuevas Dávalos, former alcalde ordinario of Mexico City, eighty-one years of age, said in testimony given on 11 March that he had heard the story since he reached the use of reason.[54] It was the accepted account but with only one interview. He testified to the devotion of archbishops and viceroys, especially the current one, the marquess of Mancera. He also said that he had been an eyewitness to the flood of 1629, which according to him lasted three years, when the image was brought to the city by canoe to stop it. It had done so by a miracle. In these assertions his wording is almost identical to that of the previous witnesses. He described the image in detail, saying that it was made of maguey, roughly woven, and impossible to size.

On 11 March Diego Cano Moctezuma, knight of the order of Santiago and twice alcalde ordinario of Mexico City, sixty-one years of age, said that he was a grandson of the Emperor Moteucçoma.[55] He said that he had heard the story of the apparitions, which he gave in the standard form, since childhood from his parents and ancestors. He also testified to the devotion of the viceroys, including Mancera, who was accustomed to visit the shrine every Saturday.

On 22 March Luis Becerra Tanco presented his testimony in writing.[56] This will be dealt with below.

Since the investigation is of prime importance in Guadalupan studies, some observations should be made about it.

The first is that the only copy of the inquiry, now in the archive of the basilica of Guadalupe, dates from 1737, a critical year in the history of the Guadalupan devotion. Florencia, who gave an extensive summary of the testimonies, used a copy that was paginated differently from that of 1737. The variation in details between Florencia's citations and the later version opens up the possibility that some errors crept into the copy.

Those who spearheaded the inquiry were enthusiastic advocates of the devotion. Siles was a close friend of Sánchez. He wrote an introductory letter to Sánchez's *Imagen*, a letter of approval for his *Novenas*, and an introductory letter to Juan de Correa's book and was deeply involved in the foundation of a Guadalupan congregation of diocesan priests in Querétaro—again, a sign of the story's rapid spread among the predominantly criollo clergy.[57] It was he who selected the witnesses and presented them to Gama or the notary. Juan de Poblete was one of the two censors for the *Imagen*. Antonio de Gama was a friend of Becerra Tanco and was responsible for the posthumous publication of the latter's Guadalupan book, *Felicidad de Mexico*. He also wrote a letter of approbation for Florencia's *Estrella del norte*. Nicolás del Puerto, later bishop of Oaxaca, was a devotee of miracle stories. One of the witnesses, Jesuit Diego de Monroy, was a partisan of Guadalupe who later told Florencia about a copy of the image that had supposedly belonged to Juan Diego. He was also a grandson of Alonso de Villaseca, a great devotee of Guadalupe and donor of a silver statue of the Virgin to the ermita (1566).

The ultimate intent of the inquiry was to secure from Rome a grant of a special feast, mass, and office. The means to this end was to prove the existence of a tradition that reached back to the events themselves. Hence the inquiry was not an objective or dispassionate search for the truth about the apparition account. It was not concerned with the evidence pro and con but with establishing the existence and continuity of a tradition, which for the investigators would have been sufficient evidence of the truth of the account. In canon law an established tradition was a potent weapon. It could preserve ancient customs and exempt communities from laws. "Traditio est, nihil amplius quaeras." A tradition was its own motive of credibility, as Florencia wrote: "It needs no more support than that of itself."[58]

In Catholic theology the classic definition of tradition was formulated in the fifth century by Vincent of Lérins in a work called the *Commonitoria*. "In the Catholic Church special care should be taken that we hold to what has been believed everywhere, always, by everyone."[59] Thus tradition had to be universal, immemorial, and uncontested. The first element, "everywhere," would in practice be limited to the locale for which the tradition was being established, in this case Mexico City and its environs. "Always" refers to an uninterrupted acceptance dating back to the event itself. "Everyone" means that the tradition had never been effectively challenged. These three elements were clearly the thrust of the capitular inquiry. They are apparent in the ending formulas in which the witnesses testify to the public knowledge of the event and the lack of contradiction. They are also found in the insistence on a continuum between the image that was given to Zumárraga and that which was venerated in the ermita.

The investigation was made 134 years after the date traditionally given for the apparitions and 117 years after the date traditionally given for the death of Juan Diego. This long lapse obviously put the investigators and witnesses at a great distance from the events of 1531. Again, however, their purpose was not to obtain eyewitness testimony but to demonstrate a continuum from 1531 to 1666.

While at first reading these testimonies seem to have great force, they cannot be accepted uncritically. The questions asked were very leading and contained a synopsis of the entire apparition account, which the witnesses were asked to verify. Their responses generally followed the interrogatory closely, almost verbatim, though with variations in detail, more so among the Indians than among the Spaniards. The accounts of a public proclamation with drums and trumpets that were given by the natives, though not by the Spaniards, are not found in other Guadalupan sources. The immense time gulf that separated the witnesses from the events they were recalling casts doubt on the reliability of their testimony, even as far as the existence of a tradition was concerned. To this must be added the general tendency to tell those in authority what they wanted to hear, and the testimony becomes even less convincing.[60]

All the indigenous witnesses claimed to have heard stories of the apparitions from parents, grandparents, aunts, or uncles. Four Indians claimed to be one hundred years old or more or had that age assigned to them by their questioners, and another claimed to have had a mother who died at 110. This was a large number of centenarians for a small village like Cuauhtitlan, especially in an age when common people often did not know their precise ages. They agreed that Juan Diego came from a barrio called Tlayac or Tlayacac, which cannot now be identified with certainty.[61] Some testified that a proverb among the Indians was "may God be as good to you as he was to Juan Diego." All the Indians stressed the holiness of Juan Diego, and there is even indication of a cult directed toward him, almost the only such evidence until recent times. The natives were asked to testify to highly technical matters, such as the impossibility of an artist painting on the tilma, the supernatural character of the image, and its survival in the salty, humid climate of Tepeyac. Though the Indians' responses show more variation than do those of the Spaniards, especially in the apparition accounts, they still follow the questionnaire closely, almost slavishly. As a result the answers of both natives and Spaniards tended to be consistently similar in wording. Despite the somewhat inaccurate citation of four indigenous words, such as *teopisque* for *teopixqui*, the indigenous testimonies show no sign of a Nahuatl substratum or of direct translation from that language. Rather, they are in legal Spanish that is simply a repetition of the questionnaire. If they were direct translations, they were smoothed out to conform to the questionnaire.

There are problems with the dates given by the witnesses. The claim of Diego Cano Moctezuma, sixty-one years of age in 1666, to have been a grandson of the emperor entails insuperable problems of chronology—eighty-three years would have separated his birthdate from the death of Moteucçoma II.[62] Marcos Pacheco would have been born about the year 1585. He said that his aunt, who was his informant, died at the age of seventy or eighty. For her to have known Juan Diego and Juan Bernardino, she would have had to be in her sixties or seventies at the time of Marcos's birth. Actually, if she had known María Lucía as she claimed, she would have had to be much older, since Juan Diego's wife died in 1529 or 1533, depending on the tradition. Similarly, if Gabriel Suárez heard about the tradition in 1575 to 1585, his informants would also have had to be very old. Juana de la Concepción's father could not possibly have participated in the procession of 12 December 1531 as a principal or cacique, unless he was an old man at the time of her birth. Juan Suárez claimed to have remembered Luis de Velasco I (viceroy, 1550–1564), a practical impossibility even if he were one hundred years old as he claimed. Oyanguren's parents would have had to have been in their fifties or sixties at the time of his birth for them to have been alive in 1531. Mendoza spoke of his grandfather as having been one of the first oidores, but the only Antonio Maldonado on record for that office lived long after the apparitions.

The testimony of Andrés Juan was especially confused. He said that his parents had told him he was born soon after the apparitions. If he was 112 to 115 years old, as his questioners guessed, he would have been born some twenty years after the apparitions. On the hypothesis that he was truly that old, it would have been possible for him to meet Luis de Velasco I at the age of ten, but he would have been a middle-aged man, not a boy of fifteen, when the drainage of Mexico City began. His statement about a recently completed ermita of adobe to which he was taken in 1566 would reflect the great procession organized by Archbishop Montúfar, not that traditionally ascribed to Zumárraga. If the witnesses were indeed reflecting an oral tradition, then their data would point more toward the tradition of a midcentury cure or apparition, that is, about 1555 or 1556. In that case the procession they described would have been that organized by Montúfar for 15 September 1566, a hypothesis that would explain the publication of the event with music and heralds in Cuauhtitlan.

All the Indian witnesses agreed in saying that Juan Diego went to Tlatelolco for mass and instruction. Martín de San Luis testified that all the people went there for mass and instruction, and Juan Suárez said that it was the doctrina for the Indians of Cuauhtitlan. Pablo Suárez said that a priest would come occasionally from Tlatelolco to Cuauhtitlan to say mass for the Indians. All this, of course, is inconsistent with what is known today about the Franciscan presence in both towns. Similarly, the testimony of the Spaniards that the viceroy, together with the ecclesiastical and civil cabildos, participated in the procession of 26 December 1531 is anachronistic. There can be little doubt that the entire capitular inquiry was carefully rehearsed and stage-managed but not kept free of errors resulting from a faulty knowledge of the early history of New Spain.

The testimonies given by Spaniards are of interest for a number of reasons. One is the high percentage of religious and criollos (five are clearly identified as such). The two who are clearly identified as peninsulars had been in New Spain for a long period. Several of the testimonies are very general, being little more than assertions that a tradition existed. Thus, for example, they make no mention of Juan Bernardino. The frequently verbatim similarity of the responses is even more apparent than in those given by the Indians. There is room to suspect that Siles elicited an affirmative response and the notary did the rest. Also significant is the identification, made by two of the witnesses, of the Virgin of Guadalupe with Mary, Queen of Angels (San Simón) or Queen of Heaven (Mendoza), rather than with the woman of Revelation 12 or the Immaculate Conception. The association of this devotion with the archbishops and viceroys seems to have given it a special authenticity in the eyes of the Spaniards. In general the Spaniards' testimony is more generic than that of the Indians, emphasizing mostly the fact of a tradition having been in existence, at least since the beginning of the seventeenth century. They use the stock formula of "many persons of quality, nobility, and learning," numerous people of all conditions, "ancestors," without further identification. Generic attributions of that sort, it should be noted, were common among hagiographers and religious writers of that century.

It is impossible to reconcile these testimonies with the statements by Laso de la Vega, Siles, Lara Mogrovejo, and Robles cited in chapter 7. The historian is faced with a clear contradiction. On the one hand, there are the declarations under oath that the tradition was continuous and unchallenged, passed on from father to son, "until the present day it is common knowledge in all New Spain." On the other hand, there is Laso de la Vega's assertion that the account had been consigned to oblivion by persons who quickly forgot divine favors, Siles's statement that it had been "forgotten in the course of more than a century," Lara Mogrovejo's that the truth had been put at risk, and Robles's that "it had been forgotten, even by the citizens of Mexico [City]." This contradiction cannot now be resolved with any finality. The second group of statements is more credible in that it reflects a more contemporaneous and spontaneous reaction. The Spanish/criollo declarations are vague and generic and probably the result

of some eighteen years of mental evolution following the publication of Sánchez's book in 1648. García Icazbalceta was deeply disturbed by these testimonies. "When I see grave priests and illustrious gentleman *affirm the same falsehood*, I cannot but be confused, considering how far moral contagion and the
straying of religious feeling can go. There is no room for saying that these witnesses knowingly came close to perjury, but it is evident that they affirmed
under oath what was not true."[63]

There is no testimony that any of this tradition was written down prior to
the publication of Sánchez's book, except for the maps, long disappeared, of the
father of Juana de la Concepción. This and the emphasis on the continuity of
the tradition again reinforce the fact that there was no written source. What
the testimonies point to is the possibility of an oral tradition in the first half of
the seventeenth century, a tradition that differed in details and probably received reinforcement and refinement from the books of Sánchez and Laso de la
Vega. There is no reason to doubt that the testimonies were heavily influenced
by both those works.[64] They do not, therefore, provide incontrovertible evidence of the truth of the apparition account.

These testimonies were the major part of the interrogatory but not the only
one. Another element was an investigation of the image by experts, specifically
in the art of painting. At an unknown date Siles asked Escobar y Llamas to
appoint a panel to examine the image. The bishop did so on 11 March, and on
13 March the viceroy, Poblete, and assorted clerics and artists met at Guadalupe. After the celebration of mass the image was removed from its place in the
church and examined front and back. Their unanimous conclusion was that it
was impossible for any human artist to paint so well on such a rough surface
and that the image was of miraculous origin.[65]

On 28 March there was another inspection and declaration, this time by
the *protomedicato* of New Spain, the supervisory body for medical and scientific
endeavors.[66] In a long, pedantic report that quoted extensively from Hippocra-
tes and Galen, the experts concluded that the survival of the image in the warm,
humid, and salty climate was in itself a miracle. The elements had not affected
the luster and sharpness of the colors, except for the fact that some eager devotee had sought to enhance the image by adding gold to the sunburst and silver
to the moon, with the result that the moon turned black and the sunburst
faded. Along with all these reports the chapter sent some sections from a book
on Guadalupe called *Opera parthenica*, by Juan Eusebio Nieremberg, a Spanish
Jesuit of German parentage.

Florencia, whose account is no model of clarity, is the only source for the
subsequent history of the interrogatory.[67] Rome was reluctant to give approval
for the capitular requests, and it seems to have employed tactics of delay. According to Florencia, Siles sent the results to Mateo de Bicunia, a canon of the
cathedral of Seville and a representative to the Roman Curia, whom he asked

to make further efforts to secure Roman approval for the feast and proper office. There is evidence of the documentation's having been received in Seville on 4 March 1667.[68] On 2 November 1666, Cardinal Giulio Rospigliosi wrote to Antonio de Peralta y Castañeda, the canónigo magistral of Puebla and friend of Siles who was deeply involved in the matter, pointing out the difficulty of securing a proper office. Even the Jesuits at the celebrated shrine of the Holy House of Loretto had failed to do so. The cardinal promised to keep working on behalf of the request. Peralta y Castañeda replied in May 1667, but by the time his letter reached Rome, Rospigliosi had been elected Pope Clement IX on 20 June 1667. The new pope wrote to Peralta y Castañeda through his nephew, also called Cardinal Rospigliosi, that since the image was that of the Immaculate Conception and 12 December fell within the octave of that feast, it would be inappropriate to give it a special office (*rezo*). Instead the pope granted a full jubilee (*jubileo plenisimo*) for that day. When the papal brief arrived, however, it mistakenly contained the date 12 September. Siles and Peralta y Castañeda returned it to Rome for correction, but the pope died on 9 December 1669 before this could be done. He, Siles, and Peralta all died within a year of one another. A curial official later told Florencia that Rome's reluctance to grant that request, and others like it, was based on the fear of setting a precedent. It would mean intervention by monarchs and the approbation of innumerable images and devotions. Hence there is reason to doubt that the substitution of dates was a true error rather than a time-honored curial means of refusing a request without appearing to do so.

Bicunia's agent in Rome, to whom the papers had been sent, fell ill and returned to Spain to recuperate. In 1670 Florencia himself went to Rome to help with the negotiations, and only on his arrival did he hear about the fate of the inquiry. After Bicunia's death in 1684 the papers came into the possession of Captain Andrés García Guerrero, the nephew of the Mexico City council's representative. How they eventually returned to New Spain is not known. The request to Rome had not been granted, and the entire inquiry fell into oblivion until the following century.

Despite this failure the capitular inquiry marked the formal acceptance of Guadalupe as its preeminent patron by the institutional Church of the archdiocese of Mexico, whose clergy were predominantly criollo. All that Sánchez had written would now become an integral part of Mexican religious life. By the end of the century the devotion would spread even farther, beginning in Querétaro. La Criolla was on her way to total triumph.

Luis Becerra Tanco

Luis Becerra Tanco was born in Taxco in 1603. He grew up among the natives and spoke Nahuatl from his youth. He earned a bachelor's degree in arts and canon law and served as pastor in various churches in Mexico City. He was multilingual, being conversant with Hebrew, Greek, Latin, Italian, French, Portuguese, Nahuatl, and Otomí. At one time he taught Nahuatl at the University of Mexico and was the synodal examiner who certified the Nahuatl competence of candidates for pastorates. Francisco de Siles called him a "Demosthenes of the Mexican language."[69] Like Miguel Sánchez he was a member of the Oratory and at the time of his death in 1672 was professor of mathematics at the Royal and Pontifical University of Mexico.

As has been mentioned above, Becerra Tanco submitted his testimony in writing to the capitular inquiry in 1666. Later that year he published it in pamphlet form in Mexico City with the title *Origen milagroso del santuario de Nuestra Señora de Guadalupe*.[70] Shortly thereafter he revised the work but could not publish it for lack of money.[71] Through the agency of his friend Antonio de Gama it was printed posthumously in 1675 with a new title, *Felicidad de Mexico*.[72] As will be noted later, there were some important differences in regard to Guadalupe between the two editions. Although Becerra Tanco was a fervent believer in the apparitions and devotion, he was not credulous. He was careful to reject what he considered to be hearsay or unreliable evidence, and he was the first to use a certain level of sophistication in dealing with the question.

In approaching Becerra Tanco's Guadalupan writings, I will deal first with his testimony before the capitular inquiry, at the same time indicating some of the differences between it and the 1675 edition of the *Felicidad de Mexico*.

He began by reaffirming the lack of official or authentic sources, which were "not found in the archives of this ecclesiastical court and government." Among the possible reasons he gave were that the event took place in the Indies, where it was natural for people to discount things and remedies were late, and "because the criollo nation has been so newly born in this world, the testimonies have grown old."[73] The very fact that it took place in the Indies was enough to arouse prejudice in some quarters: "it is no wonder that simply for being *indiana* it is discredited."[74] He also attributed the lack of official documents to the fact that at the time of the apparitions there was no archdiocesan archive.

For Becerra Tanco the most important testimony to Guadalupe was to be found in the constant tradition from father to son, as Miguel Sánchez indicated in his book and Laso de la Vega in his work, "as it is preserved in the memory of the natives." Significantly, he added that "neither one explained the way in which it was ascertained or how this information came down to us."[75] Because he was familiar with Indian pictures and documents from his youth and "because today there is no eyewitness who can verify it from knowledge of the persons involved in the event," he felt himself obliged to submit his testimony.[76] This testimony, it should be noted, followed the general outline of the capitular questionnaire, though it was really an independent treatise.

In this testimony Becerra Tanco gave a brief summary of the traditional apparition account. The wording seems to be a paraphrase or shortened version of the *Nican mopohua*, although he included the third apparition, which it lacks. Concluding the account, he wrote, "This is the entire tradition, simple and without embellishment of words."[77] In the 1675 edition, he added the words, "and this account is in such a high degree certain that any circumstance that may be added to it, if it were not absolutely false, then will at least be apocryphal."[78] This is a remarkable statement in view of the fact that some of what he related did not become part of the accepted Guadalupe tradition.

In 1675, however, he did add much detail to his account, bringing it closer in wording to the *Nican mopohua*. The former contained elements that were substantially different from the traditional account and from Becerra Tanco's own testimony of 1666.[79] Thus he added that while Juan Diego was a native of Cuauhtitlan, he resided in Tolpetlac.[80] He specified Juan Diego's destination as the church of Santiago el mayor in Tlatelolco. The testimony of 1666 did not contain Juan Diego's exclamation about the paradise of his forefathers, whereas the 1675 version did. The same is true of the description of the rainbow and the splendor of the locale where the Virgin appeared. The dialogues between the Virgin and Juan Diego were also longer and more detailed than in the 1666 testimony. He wrote that when Juan Diego ascended the hill of Tepeyac he saw a white cloud and a splendid rainbow. In relating the second apparition, he indicated that Juan Diego's wife was still alive: "it is not known if he told his wife or any other person what had happened." At a later point he said clearly that she died two years after the apparition.[81] In the third apparition, he stated that Juan Diego was seeking a priest to give extreme unction to his uncle, whereas in 1666 he said only "the holy sacraments."[82] He was the first to use the specific term "extreme unction," and it seems clearly to have been his own interpretation, not part of an earlier tradition. He said that at the time of the fourth apparition the Virgin met Juan Diego by the spring that issued from the hill. In 1675, but not in 1666, Becerra Tanco wrote that while Juan Diego was collecting the flowers on the hilltop, the Virgin remained "at the foot of a tree that the Indians call Quauzahuatl," which he went on to describe in detail.[83] It should be noted again that Becerra Tanco claimed very strongly that his account was totally in accord with the way indigenous historians wrote in the sixteenth century and that any variation from it was apocryphal at best.

Both versions, however, were quite similar in their descriptions of the way in which the natives preserved the memory of past events and Becerra Tanco's use of these records. He testified to the strength of tradition among the natives. "These notices, and thus the preservation in their writings and papers and among the traditions of their ancestors as a memorable event, remained more vividly imprinted in the minds of the natives, because those to whom the Virgin, the Most Holy Mary, Our Lady, appeared were Indians; so it is necessary first to establish the faith and credit that ought to be given to their writings and memoirs."[84] In order to show that these early histories were reliable, he entered into a long treatment of how history was kept among the natives. There were two kinds, picture writing and cantares, and both kept alive the early traditions. Both forms were also used after the conquest. With regard to pictographic or alphabetic writings Becerra Tanco made this declaration in his testimony of 1666:

> Having established this, I say and affirm that among the memorable events that the skilled and accomplished natives of the said college [Santiago de Tlatelolco], who for the most part were from the nobility of this kingdom, sons of princes and lords of vassals, painted for those who did not know how to read our letters, with their ancient figures and characters according to their usage, and with the letters of our alphabet for those who did know how to read them, the miraculous apparition of Our Lady of Guadalupe and her blessed image. In these writings and pictures the tradition was transcribed and copied, which the licenciado Miguel Sánchez, a person of well-known gifts, wrote and which was published in 1648. It is not cited here because it can be consulted in the original, to which total belief and credit are due.[85]

In 1675, however, Becerra Tanco omitted the reference to Sánchez's work, apparently having reached the conclusion that it was not based on any of the figure writings or cantares to which he was referring.[86]

In his testimony of 1666 he made two other references to documents.

> I certify that I have seen and read a map of notable antiquity written in ancient figures and characters, in which were painted the events of more than 300 years before the Spaniards came to this kingdom and many years after, with additions made afterward in our letters in order to understand it better, in the possession of don Fernando de Alva [Ixtlilxochitl], formerly an interpreter of the Indian Court in this city, a very capable, older man who both understood and spoke his Mexican language with great skill and who had a complete knowledge of the characters and figures of the natives, since he was a noble and descended on his mother's side from the kings of Texcoco. He possessed and inherited from his ancestors many papers, in which were narrated the successions of the ancient kings and lords and among other events that occurred after the pacification [of this city] and the kingdom of Mexico, was painted the miraculous apparition of our blessed image.[87]

He followed this statement with an assertion that he had seen a Nahuatl account of the apparition. Becerra Tanco was the first to claim the existence of such a written account, but there were two notable variations between what he wrote about it in his testimony of 1666 and the *Felicidad de Mexico* of 1675. In the former he wrote that he had seen "a notebook written in the letters of our alphabet in the hand of an Indian, in which were described the four apparitions of the Most Holy Virgin to the Indian Juan Diego and the fifth to his uncle Juan Bernardino. It was the one that was published in the Mexican language in 1649 by order of licenciado Luis Laso de la Vega, vicar of the sanctuary of Our Lady of Guadalupe."[88] In the 1675 edition, however, he wrote that Alva Ixtlilxochitl "had in his possession a notebook written in the letters of our alphabet in the Mexican language, in the hand of an Indian who was one of the earliest graduates of the Colegio de Santa Cruz, which was mentioned above, in which reference is made to the four apparitions of the Holy Virgin to the Indian Juan Diego and the fifth to his uncle Juan Bernardino."[89] The differences are clear. Becerra Tanco added the identification of the Indian as a graduate of Santa Cruz and suppressed the identification of his Nahuatl "Relación" with the *Nican mopohua*. Why? There is no way of knowing for sure. De la Maza conjectures that Laso de la Vega, who was still alive, complained about the implied plagiarism.[90] But was Laso de la Vega still alive in 1666? Very little is known about his life and nothing about the dates of his birth or death. He was not a witness in the capitular inquiry of 1666. A more likely explanation is that Becerra Tanco, a nahuatlahto, was aware of the differences between this "Relación" and the *Nican mopohua*. Whatever the reason, Becerra Tanco was clearly being more cautious in his attribution and may not even have known the "Relación" firsthand. Neither Miguel Sánchez nor Laso de la Vega is mentioned in the *Felicidad de Mexico*, and Becerra Tanco avoided identifying either of their accounts as being based on an indigenous source.

Becerra Tanco's description of this "Relación" is the first reference to any specific document and the first that relates any account to an Indian scribe— he says only that it was in the hand of an Indian, not that the Indian was the author. Four points should be noted: (1) Becerra Tanco did not give the name of the author of this account in either version of his book and, specifically, he did not mention Antonio Valeriano; (2) he moved away from identifying it with Miguel Sánchez's account or the *Nican mopohua*; (3) he gave the document a Franciscan provenance; (4) he did not identify it as the one that he used in his own narration of the apparitions. Later, he stated that his uncle, the diocesan priest Gabriel de Prábez, had heard an oral account from Valeriano, but for Becerra Tanco these were two different things. Becerra Tanco's testimony, however, runs counter to the assertions made by Sánchez and Florencia that there was no authentic written source for the tradition and is also at variance with the known hostility of the Franciscans toward Guadalupe, especially in the sixteenth century.

In the *Felicidad de Mexico*, Becerra Tanco was at pains to emphasize his own interest in the traditional account and his special competence for writing the history. The latter included his knowledge of Nahuatl and his acquaintance with the native histories. "So I wrote a summary of what I could remember at that time, because I learned that some notebooks in my handwriting, in which

I copied this and that ancient event in this kingdom, had been lost while in the possession of a person of authority, who had asked me for them and was now dead."[91] It must be admitted that this Delphic statement sheds little light on his sources. He was equally vague when he stated, after his description of the second apparition, "this conversation in the form in which it has been given was contained in the historical writing of the natives, and it contains nothing of my own, but is the translation from the Mexican language into our Castilian tongue, sentence by sentence."[92] His translation was not a literal one from the *Nican mopohua*, though the substance is the same. On the basis of Becerra Tanco's own words, it is impossible to arrive at any firm conclusion about the sources he used for his version of the Guadalupan tradition.

As for the cantares, Becerra Tanco testified that prior to the flood of 1629 he had seen and heard them sung by the Indians during their dances at the shrine of Guadalupe. In them, he wrote, the Indians sang of the apparitions and the miracles that occurred when the image was moved from Mexico City to the ermita.

With regard to anything else that the Indians of his time might say about the past, Becerra Tanco was skeptical. He asserted that those who knew Spanish could not read the ancient texts or remember the Nahua reckoning of dates. "And because what the Indians today affirm about their ancient days contains many errors and is confused and disordered and only those ministers of the gospel who applied themselves to scrutinizing those maps and pictures were able to make them understood. And it cost me much lack of sleep to adjust their reckoning to ours and to separate the superstitious from the real."[93] If what he said was true, it would certainly cast doubt on the testimony of the native witnesses in 1666 or any native tradition concerning Guadalupe.

He went on to cite a list of reliable witnesses, all but one of them diocesan priests, who testified to the existence of the tradition. The first of these was the licenciado Pedro Ruiz de Alarcón, a diocesan priest who died in 1659 at the age of eighty-six. The second was Becerra Tanco's uncle, Gaspar de Prábez, the grandson of a conquistador, who had spent many years ministering to the Indians and who said that he had heard the account from a don "Juan" Valeriano, who, from the subsequent description, was Antonio Valeriano. Significantly, however, Becerra Tanco did not attribute any written account to Valeriano. A close friend of Prábez was the priest licenciado Pedro Ponce de León, who died in 1626 at more than eighty years of age. Becerra Tanco said that he also heard Ponce de León refer to the tradition, as he had from Gerónimo de León, who died around the year 1631 at the age of eighty-five. The last witness, who apparently was not a priest, was Francisco de Mercado, an interpreter for the general Indian court who had taught Becerra Tanco some of the finer points of Nahuatl.[94]

As was mentioned above, Becerra Tanco was not credulous. "I pass over many others, to whom as much credit should not be given as to those mentioned, because they did not have a fundamental knowledge of the things of the native Mexicans, insofar as the tradition, which is written here, remained more vividly imprinted on the memory of the Indians of this city and because it was they to whom the Virgin, Our Lady, appeared and spoke: a sufficient reason why the Spaniards of that era did not hold the miracle in high regard, since they considered the Indians as beasts and incapable of reason, as our historians affirm."[95]

In the *Felicidad de Mexico*, though not in his 1666 testimony, Becerra Tanco was the first to address the problem created by the use of the name Guadalupe, a problem to which he gave an answer that has become standard.

> The motive that the Virgin had for naming her image Guadalupe, she did
> not say, and so it is not known, until God will be pleased to clarify this mystery. . . . Some clever persons have wearied themselves in searching out the origin of the name Guadalupe, which this holy image has at the present time, thinking that it holds some mystery. Tradition says only that this name was not heard by anyone except the Indian Juan Bernardino, who could not pronounce it correctly or have any knowledge of the image of Our Lady of Guadalupe in the kingdom of Castile. Add to this the scant similarity between the two images (except that both are of the same Lady and this is common to all of them), and the fact that the land was recently conquered and for many years after there was no Indian who succeeded in pronouncing our Castilian tongue correctly . . . . So, in my opinion, this is what happened: the Indian said the name that was to be given in his own language and our people, simply because of the sameness of the vowels, gave it the name of Guadalupe.[96]

After giving some examples of other Indian words that were corrupted into Spanish ones, he hypothesized the Nahuatl words given in chapter 2, that is, Tecuatlanopeuh (she who had her origin on the rocky peak) or Tecuantlaxopeuh (she who drove away those who were eating us, that is, demons). He correctly pointed out that the Indians would have pronounced the name as Tecuatalope, which is the Nahuatl form of "de Guadalupe."

Becerra Tanco stated that the celibate marriage of Juan Diego and his wife was a well-known fact, though, unlike other sources such as the *Nican motecpana*, he did not claim that it had been so from the beginning. "The tradition also affirms that the Indian Juan Diego and his wife, María Lucía, observed chastity after they received the water of holy baptism . . . and this reputation was constant among those who knew them and had frequent contact with the married couple."[97] "And this renown for continence was very public, and all those who had familiar contact with this married couple affirmed it."[98] Neither Becerra Tanco nor any other author in the history of the Guadalupe tradition ever explained how such a private and intimate fact became "very public."

In conclusion, Becerra Tanco asserted that while there were numerous devotions to the Virgin Mary, none was comparable to Guadalupe. In part this was because she had appeared in Mexico City, "the head and metropolis of this North America of the Indies."[99] Just as the preconquest monarchy had sacrificed innumerable souls to false gods, so now the postconquest rule, through the intercession and devotion of Guadalupe, would offer even more souls to God.

Becerra Tanco's testimony is supremely important. His arguments about the original form of the name Guadalupe and its erroneous application are used to the present day. The *Felicidad de Mexico* has been reprinted at least sixteen times.[100] He was the first to state that there were indigenous written sources for the apparition account and to relate the written account to the Franciscan Colegio of Santa Cruz de Tlatelolco, though not to Antonio Valeriano. He laid the groundwork for much of the apologetics used by later historians for the authenticity of the Guadalupe event, yet he gave tantalizingly few details about the "Relación" and, more important, did not publish it.

His testimony is not without difficulties. It does not tally with the known silence of the chroniclers of the sixteenth and early seventeenth centuries. His assertion that the Spaniards ignored the miracle because of their disdain for the Indians is also difficult to accept. It contradicts the known popularity of the shrine among Spaniards in the sixteenth century, though this was a different devotion from the native one, and it certainly was not true of Spaniards like Sahagún, Motolinía, Las Casas, and Mendieta. It also ignores the great criollo emphasis that the apparition devotion had. In view of the continued hostility of the Franciscans toward Guadalupe in the sixteenth century, the idea that the account came out of Santa Cruz is highly improbable. The account which he claimed to have translated clearly differed in important details from the *Nican mopohua*. The "Relación" of which he spoke has not survived, either in the original or in copies.

What emerges from both Becerra Tanco and the interrogatory of 1665 to 1666 is the possibility of an unwritten native tradition of an apparition that may originally have been associated with the events of 1555 to 1556. This tradition would have varied in details, such as the date of the apparitions or the date of María Lucía's death, though the core material would have been the same. In all probability the works of Sánchez and Laso de la Vega popularized one version of the native tradition and, after the passage of some eighteen years, undoubtedly influenced the witnesses both in the capitular investigation and in Becerra Tanco's book. This tradition, if indeed it existed, had little or no widespread impact before 1648 (in fact, there is no evidence that it was known at all), and it appears in no written source before that year. Because the tradition belongs to a classic European genre, though with Indian protagonists and told for their benefit, it would seem to have been a later development.

Clearly Becerra Tanco felt the need to find a secure foundation for the apparition account. This, in turn, would imply that the problem posed by the lack of
documentation had arisen early in the history of the tradition. Hence the need
to fall back on tradition and on the preservation of the image as prima facie
evidence of its supernatural origin. This same defensiveness will be seen again
in the writers who dealt with the subject later in the century.

Guadalupan Sermons, 1660 to 1697

The popularity of the shrine and devotion in the aftermath of Sánchez's publication of the account of the apparitions and its acceptance by the criollo clergy in
the archdiocese of Mexico is seen in the sudden appearance of sermons with
Guadalupan themes. Obviously, the only known sermons are those that were
published, but it should be noted that in the seventeenth century this happened
with great frequency. Sermons were intensely popular in Europe and America
among both Catholics and Protestants. In Spain and Spanish America the
printed text was not necessarily the same as the spoken one, although reading
the text from a manuscript was regarded as bad form. In all likelihood there
were additions and changes prior to publication. Scriptural quotations were
given in the Latin of the Vulgate followed by a translation or paraphrase. The
cost of publication was usually borne by the preacher, his religious order, or
patrons or sponsoring organizations. The printed sermon was regarded as devotional reading, which was very popular in the seventeenth century, and as a
continuation of the preacher's mission. All the Guadalupan sermons consulted
for this study fall into the category of *sueltos*, printed records of what was
preached, published shortly after the event, with the date and place of preaching part of the title. Some were also *panegyricos*, preached about saints on their
feast days.[101]

There is no known sermon prior to 1660 that dealt specifically with the
apparitions or miraculous origin of the image. Beginning in that year, however,
and with accelerating frequency, the topic claimed the attention of preachers.
For the period from 1651 to 1699 there are at least seventy-six known published sermons on Guadalupe.[102] There is no way of knowing what proportion
of published sermons dealt with Guadalupe. What is significant is the pattern:
nothing before Sánchez's book and then a rapid crescendo that reached its peak
in the mid–eighteenth century.

On 12 December 1660 José Vidal de Figueroa, pastor of an Indian parish in
Texopilco in the archdiocese of Mexico, delivered a sermon that was published
in the following year with the title *Theorica de la prodigiosa Imagen de la Virgen
Santa Maria de Gvadalvpe*. One letter of approval for the publication was by
Francisco de Siles, who was already closely involved in spreading the Guadalupe

devotion. The work was dedicated to Pedro de Gálvez of the Council of the Indies, a devotee who had donated a copy of the image to the Colegio de San Agustín in Madrid and in 1662 subsidized the publication of Mateo de la Cruz's version of the story in Spain. Although the title indicated that it would deal with Guadalupe, it was in fact an extended and pedantic excursus on Saint Augustine, filled with mythological, biblical, and patristic allusions. Hence it is of little value in the history of the tradition, though like Juan de Correa's introduction it is indicative not only of the spread of the devotion in the aftermath of Sánchez's book but also of an increased interest on the part of the diocesan church structure, with its criollo sympathies.

The published sermons from the rest of the century showed a marked similarity in their approach to Guadalupe. There were certain themes that were dominant and that betrayed the interests and prejudices of the preachers and their audiences. The most prominent theme is that of rampant criollismo. The image of Guadalupe was viewed as a divine gift to the criollos of Mexico City, who regarded themselves as a chosen people. This emphasis necessarily involved a corresponding deemphasis of the Indian aspect of the tradition and devotion. In contrast with the sermons of the eighteenth century, to be discussed later, those of the late seventeenth century paid scant attention to the Indian message of Guadalupe and in general concentrated on the importance of the image rather than the apparition account itself. Juan Diego was rarely mentioned. It can be argued that knowledge of the story was presupposed, but that fact rarely stopped preachers from narrating it again, as the sermons of the following century showed. The sermons of this period definitely show an appropriation of Guadalupe by the criollos, with particularistic claims that were in no way justified by the traditional apparition account itself.

In 1681 Juan de Robles, a Jesuit theologian, preached on Guadalupe on the anniversary of the apparitions. The locale was his native city of Querétaro, where the devotion had early become popular and where there was a church, completed the year before, dedicated to the Virgin of Tepeyac. In his introduction Robles spoke of 12 December as "the day on which our New Spain was blessed, among all the nations of the world, with that hitherto never seen nor heard benefit, when she wanted to remain with us in her image imprinted on the rough mantle of a poor Indian."[103] Also typical was the sermon of the Carmelite Manuel de San José, who preached on the feast of Guadalupe in 1686 or 1687 in the Colegio of San Angel in Mexico City. He quoted Psalm 147, "Non fecit taliter omni nationi" [He has not done the like for any other nation], and asserted, "There is no brush, there is no finery or beauty like that of our criollo kingdom in all the kingdoms of the world."[104] The Jesuit Juan de San Miguel, in a sermon given on the feast of the Nativity of the Virgin, 8 September 1671, made several references to the "miraculous image" that came from heaven. He also mentioned the tilma at least once, but he related the image of Guadalupe to the feast of the Nativity of the Virgin Mary. He gave a brief description of the presentation of the roses to Zumárraga but never mentioned Juan Diego by name.[105] On 12 December of the following year the Franciscan Juan de Mendoza preached a sermon at the Franciscan house in Mexico City. Mendoza's sermon exalted the image but had only one sentence that referred to the "image that appeared to a fortunate Indian named Juan."[106] Again, there was no Indian orientation to the sermon and little about the standard tradition. A similar situation is to be found in a sermon preached by the diocesan priest Antonio Delgado y Buenrostro as part of a thanksgiving service for the safe arrival of Juan García de Palacios, a Mexican criollo who had been named bishop of Santiago, Cuba, in his see.[107] Much was said about the image but nothing about the apparitions or their tradition.

In 1683 the Augustinian José de Olivares preached on the occasion of a transfer of the miraculous image of Christ crucified from the sanctuary of San Miguel de Chalma to the new chapel of Guadalupe. Olivares referred to the fact that Tepeyac had once been dedicated to the mother goddess of the Aztecs, but he never mentioned Juan Diego or the image.[108] More space was given to Juan Diego in a sermon given in Querétaro by the Discalced Carmelite Luis de Santa Teresa in 1682. He gave a lengthier description of the tradition than did the others and also mentioned both Zumárraga and Juan Diego by name. He said that the first apparition had taken place on 8 December, the feast of the Immaculate Conception.[109] In 1684 the Franciscan Lorenzo Benítez sounded a similar note. In his salutation to his readers he drew a complex, punning comparison: "our hill of Guadalupe awakens to feel again in the apparition of Mary what so many years before the world [orbe] felt: the ancient Horeb [oreb] is renewed on our hill."[110] Juan Diego was mentioned only once in a chapter heading. The Dominican Bartolomé Navarro, in a sermon preached at the dedication of a chapel to Guadalupe in the church of Santángel de Guarda in Puebla in 1685, named Juan Diego only once. The increasing popularity of the devotion was shown in 1690 when a new church was built to replace the older one of San Bernardo in Mexico City. The name of the new church was then changed to that of Guadalupe. Pedro Manso, professor of theology at the university, preached at its dedication and made only one reference to the apparition story without naming Juan Diego or identifying him as a native. The same was true of other sermons given during the octave.[111]

An indication of this criollo emphasis is found in the sources that the preachers used. Never once were Laso de la Vega or the *Nican mopohua* mentioned. Few of the preachers explicitly mentioned the sources from which they obtained the story, but when they did these were Miguel Sánchez, Becerra Tanco, and Florencia.

Almost all the preachers associated Guadalupe with the Immaculate Conception or the Nativity of Mary. It has been argued that the latter association arose from the fact that Marian devotions that lacked a proper mass and office used those of the feast of the Virgin's Nativity. This may well be so, but it should not be forgotten that Cepeda called the feast the *vocación* of the ermita. From Cepeda onward the sermons overwhelmingly used as the introductory text the genealogy of Christ as given in the first chapter of Matthew's Gospel, concluding with the words "Maria, de qua natus est Iesus qui vocatur Christus" [Mary, of whom was born Jesus, called the Christ]. This text was taken from the Gospel for the feast of the Nativity of the Virgin. The association of Guadalupe with those two mysteries led the preachers to make elaborate comparisons involving the two appearances of Mary: on the one hand, her conception and birth; on the other, her appearance on the miraculous image. The sermon of the Jesuit Juan de San Miguel blended the two traditions of the Nativity and Guadalupe. The theme of the two apparitions was stated specifically by Luis de Santa Teresa. Beginning with the standard genealogy of Christ taken from Matthew 1, he related Guadalupe to the Immaculate Conception, the day on which, he said, the first apparition had taken place.

The Virgin Mary, he asserted, had appeared the first time in her conception, the second time in the portrait that she imprinted on the mantle. A similar note was sounded by the Dominican José de Herrera in 1672 in a sermon sponsored by the *consulado*, or merchant guild, of Mexico City. The sermon was concerned primarily with the Immaculate Conception but drew a comparison between the conception of Mary in December and her miraculous appearance at Tepeyac in that same month. It also laid a great emphasis on the roses, both as miracle and symbol, more so than on the image. Herrera also made an interesting observation on Guadalupe and Remedios. "The event that we all know through repeated hearing is pertinent. The first building, which was supposed to be a church suitable to the devout image of los Remedios, was being raised. The craftsman fell from the scaffold, pinned down by a very heavy column. That lady lifted it with a belt, but because the effects of the blow lasted for some time, she compelled him to be freed from the danger over there, by taking him to Guadalupe to visit this holy image."[112] This appears to be a variation on the story of the cure of Juan de Tovar and another testimony to the somewhat confused relationship between the two devotions. Lorenzo Benítez made the same comparison between the conception and the apparition in 1684, as did the Dominican Bartolomé Navarro in the following year. Manuel de San José referred to the image of Guadalupe as the second nativity of Mary.

One of the strangest writings on Guadalupe was not a sermon but a Latin poem published in 1680. It was composed by Bernardo de Riofrío, a criollo and a canon of the cathedral chapter of Michoacan, and was a lengthy poem in dactylic hexameter based on Vergil, especially the *Aeneid*, the *Georgics*, and the *Eclogues*. It was not an original work but was an adaptation of lines and sections from these works to the Virgin of Guadalupe. The sources were cited in left-hand marginal notes. The story of the apparitions was related in a Latin introduction. Not surprisingly, it was full of classical and mythological allusions. In fact, it was almost entirely pagan and mythological in content, with the Christian and Guadalupan interpretations given in the right-hand marginal notes.[113]

There are other Guadalupan references that do not fit into the category of sermons. In 1691 José Varón de Berieza defended a number of propositions concerning the Virgin of Guadalupe in a scholastic disputation at the academy of San Carlos in Guatemala City. In 1694 the Inquisition had an edict of faith read publicly at the church at Guadalupe. This edict is known only from the sermon given on the occasion by Luis de Rivera. In the introduction he said that "Mary had promised to be the benefactress of this kingdom."[114] In his *parecer* (theological evaluation) Juan Millan de Poblete, former pastor of the cathedral of Mexico City, declared that inquisitors had been chosen by God to work hard so that "no remnant of heresy or error should remain in the land . . . not even superstition of the former heathenism that had its adoration on the hill of Guadalupe."[115] The sermon made many references to abuses and superstitions and even to new dogmas and propositions, but nothing further was specified. This matter deserves further research.

Unfortunately, there is insufficient evidence with which to make generalizations concerning the impact or extent of the devotion among the Indians for this period.[116] It is clear, however, that the criollo preachers, probably taking their cue from the unrestrained criollismo of Miguel Sánchez, saw the image and devotion in terms of the special position and election of the sons of the land. The criollo Church was lining up fully behind the Virgin of Tepeyac. Still, she had not eliminated all rivals. In 1680 a copy of the image of the Extremaduran Guadalupe arrived in Mexico and was enshrined with much solemnity in the Augustinian chapel on 12 January. On that occasion the Augustinian theologian Nicolás de Fuenlabrada delivered a panegyric in honor of the peninsular devotion in which he also made room for the Mexican Guadalupe. He apparently saw no competition between the two but rather viewed them as two manifestations of the same devotion. He also made a favorable reference to Miguel Sánchez.

One result of the renewed interest in Guadalupe was a greater interest in and care for the image. On 16 January 1667 the archbishop of Mexico ordered that the glass case enclosing the image should no longer be opened for devotional purposes, such as kissing it or pressing medals and rosaries against it. The devotion to the image apparently had become popular enough to constitute a threat to it.

 *9*

The Need for Documentation:
Francisco de Florencia and Carlos de Sigüenza
y Góngora

As important as the apparition account was for criollo self-esteem, it was open to rebuttal if there was no solid historical basis for it. Almost from the beginning there was a defensiveness on the part of many proponents of the apparition devotion concerning the lack of documentation to support it. By the 1680s the news of the apparitions had reached Spain, where there was at least one effort to demean their importance and to appropriate them for Spain itself. Perhaps even at that early stage there was concern about the political potential of the Dark Virgin.

In the years 1688 to 1689 the apparition tradition was stabilized more or less in the form that is known today. After that time most authors and preachers were content to repeat what came to be the accepted account as found in Sánchez, Becerra Tanco, and Florencia, although variations in details were to be found well into the following century. These same years also witnessed a clear attempt to establish documentation for the account, especially in Nahuatl. This, in turn, laid the groundwork for a thesis that would be completed in the following century and that has endured to this day: that a Nahuatl account of the apparitions, later identified with the *Nican mopohua*, was written by Antonio Valeriano and was nearly contemporaneous with the events it narrated.

Francisco de Florencia

In 1688 the Jesuit Francisco de Florencia published his work *Estrella del norte*, to which references have already been made. This was the most detailed account of the apparitions and devotion up to that time, and it has been one of the most influential works in the history of the tradition.

Little is known about Florencia's life.[1] He was born in Florida in the present-day United States in 1619 or 1620. After having studied at the Colegio Real de San Ildefonso in Mexico City, he entered the Society of Jesus in 1641, 1642, or 1643, depending on the source. Before and after his ordination to the priesthood around 1654, he taught philosophy at his alma mater. In 1668 he went to Madrid and Rome as representative of his province. After his visit to Rome in 1670, he returned to Seville, where he spent the next five years acting as representative of the Jesuit provinces in the Indies. In 1680 he was named rector of the Colegio del Espíritu Santo in Puebla. He died in Mexico City in 1695. Florencia was a prolific author who wrote about the history of the Jesuits in New Spain, the lives of famous Jesuits, and the origins of shrines and churches. He was a determined apologist for these topics, as well as a criollo patriot, but he was credulous and uncritical. His primary purpose was to encourage Marian devotion and criollo awareness. His role in the inquiry of 1665 to 1666 has already been mentioned.

One occasion for writing *Estrella del norte* was a sermon delivered on 13 December 1683 in Madrid by an unidentified Spanish priest who made several astonishing claims about Guadalupe. One was that though the image of Guadalupe was born in Mexico, it appeared in Madrid and hence belonged more to Spain than to the Indies. Another was that Mexico had furnished the material (*içotl*) of the image, but Spain had given the roses. A third was that the Indies gave the image due veneration only after Madrid had done so. Another was that the Spanish devotion was more meritorious because it was free rather than obligatory. One wonders why a peninsular priest would feel the need to appropriate the image and devotion for the homeland. Perhaps the self-esteem and self-identity the image gave the criollos was already seen as a threat to the empire or as presumption on the part of an inferior people. Florencia rebutted each point because he wanted Spain to have no role in the miracle.

Jerónimo de Valladolid, the majordomo of the ermita, wrote an introductory letter to *Estrella del norte* that strongly reflected both criollismo and the influence of Miguel Sánchez. In it he admitted the lack of official documentation and sought to explain it. "No authentic document on this holy image is to be found among the official papers of this holy church [the cathedral] of Mexico. The reason is that the former [the woman of Revelation 12] needed to endure in writings because she was not to remain alive in colors; the latter [Guadalupe], who is speaking on her own behalf and testifying to her miraculous origin, enduring after more than a century and a half in the brightness of her hues and in the representation of her marvelous colors, does not seem to need writings nor does she lack pens."[2] In doing this, he added, she was following the Indian custom of writing in hieroglyphics. Because of the lack of written sources he emphasized that the existence and preservation of the image were testimony enough. What need of documents, he asked, when the image was document enough?

Far more than other writers of the seventeenth century, Valladolid emphasized the importance of Guadalupe for the natives. The Virgin taught "how much the prelates of Mexico ought to love and esteem the natives, poor and disdained, of their bishopric, when the sovereign empress of heaven chose them as the instrument of his most wonderful works."[3] She wished to oblige Zumárraga and his successors to regard, in the person of one Indian, all Indians as their children.

The first censor of the book was Antonio de Gama, whose advocacy of the apparition devotion has already been mentioned. He, too, discussed the lack of documentation while emphasizing the existence of a tradition. "For our ancestors evidence was the clearest testimony of these signs, just as tradition is for us. And so it seems that it was not just human carelessness, but also the foresight of divine providence that for us the only proof of those signs should be tradition, which, supported by the fragility of our memory, should serve continually to awaken our distrust of its forgetfulness."[4]

The second censor of the book was Carlos de Sigüenza y Góngora, who also testified to the lack of documentary evidence and to the mystery of where the account came from. "The fact that we do not know juridically how we possess such a sovereign wonder is the result of our innate carelessness . . . and after so many years what by the lack of individual notices is made known to the world with such clarity that only among the pusillanimous may it be considered doubtful."[5] It should be noted that he did not say just that there were no official documents but that no one knew how the account had originated. His approval was dated 11 January 1687. This testimony is important in view of the fact that he would radically change his position two years later.

In dealing with the question of the lack of written sources, Florencia stated categorically that Miguel Sánchez had obtained his account from an oral tradition. After noting that there were differences in Sánchez's account and those given by other authors, especially Becerra Tanco in his testimony of 1666, Florencia explained, "The reason for this difference originated in the fact that the licenciado Miguel Sánchez, and those who followed him, took the history of the tradition from fathers to sons, and in unwritten traditions there is always a difference in the words; in some there are more conciseness and brevity than in others, according to the talents and skills that write them. That does not matter, if the substance of the truth is kept."[6] Clearly he was talking about the total lack of written accounts prior to Sánchez's book. This contradicted what Florencia had to say about the account in the possession of Sigüenza y Góngora that will be mentioned in the next paragraph. Florencia strongly emphasized the fact of a constant tradition among the Indians and even some Spaniards concerning the apparitions. Beyond doubt the silence of the early chroniclers and the lack of archival material were a problem even in 1688. The constancy of tradition was a strong proof in ecclesiastical thought, a factor that explains why Florencia included so much material on the archdiocesan investigation. Florencia did, however, mention three documents that he believed supported the apparition account.

The first of these was lent to him by Sigüenza y Góngora and was entitled "Relación de Nuestra Señora de Guadalupe, la qual se trasladó de unos papeles muy antiguos, que tenia un indio, con otros curiosos."[7] Florencia believed that it had been translated from Nahuatl by Fernando de Alva Ixtlilxochitl. He also claimed that the translation was in Alva Ixtlilxochitl's own hand, though he did not explain how he knew this. Florencia was convinced of the document's antiquity and offered a number of reasons in support of this. From the condition of the paper and ink, he deduced that the translation was some seventy or eighty years old and the original over a hundred.[8] Because the "Relación" erroneously gave 8 December as the date of the first apparition, Florencia, citing a marginal note by Alva Ixtlilxochitl, dated it prior to the Gregorian calendar and said that the error was due to confusion arising from leap years in the Julian calendar. Florencia also believed that the wording proved its antiquity.

Florencia gave numerous quotations from the "Relación" and cited some of the data given in it, all of which make it abundantly clear that it was not the same as the *Nican mopohua* or any other known Guadalupan document. Regarding the celibate marriage of Juan Diego and María Lucía and his subsequent widowhood, Florencia quoted the author of the document as saying, "he was a widower two years before God and his Most Holy Mother chose him for such a singular task. His wife, whose name was María Luisa [*sic*], had died. He had no children because according to what I learned through many inquiries and investigations, he and his wife always observed chastity."[9] As for the identity of the author, Florencia stated in a marginal note that "it seems from the Relación itself that the author was a contemporary of the time of the apparitions."[10] He then deduced that the author was a Franciscan, quoting lines from the document such as "the very exemplary and seraphic fathers of our glorious seraphic Francis"; "[Motolinía,] a holy religious of our order of Saint Francis"; and "[Zumárraga] belonged to the order of Our Holy Father Saint Francis."[11] By a process of elimination and on the word of Agustín de Vetancurt, a nahuatlahto, he concluded that the author was Gerónimo de Mendieta.[12]

Florencia pointed to numerous elements in this "Relación" which did not appear in any other accounts of the apparitions. When Juan Diego left Zumárraga's house, he was late for mass at Tlatelolco and humbly accepted the blows with a stick that even in Florencia's day were still given to tardy natives. When the bishop-elect asked him for a sign, Juan Diego replied with perfect confidence that "he should ask for any sign whatever, that he would go and ask for it in order that he might see that what he was asking was the truth."[13] Some people went to Tepeyac at a later date after the apparitions in order to find the exact place where the Virgin had appeared in order to pray there. When they approached the spring, which in Florencia's day was called the Pozo de la Virgen, it gushed forth. This was taken as a sign that it was the site of the apparitions. When Juan Diego descended from the mountain with the flowers, these included "white lilies, beautiful irises, roses of Alexandria, purple carnations, Spanish broom, jasmines."[14] The Franciscans carried the image to Tepeyac in the procession of 26 December 1531. Zumárraga, barefoot, accompanied them, together with three Dominicans and a few diocesan clergy. There was an emphasis on the great devotion shown by both Spaniards and Indians after the placing of the image in the first ermita. When Juan Diego retired to Tepeyac, the Indians asked him to pray for them and he promised that he would. When he was alone with the image (but secretly watched by the others), he would talk to it. The Virgin appeared to Juan Bernardino before his death in 1544 and consoled him. He was buried in the first ermita. Juan Diego's death in 1548 was hastened by sorrow over the death of Bishop Zumárraga in that same year.

Florencia said that this "Relación" narrated eleven miracles that took place at Guadalupe through the intercession of the Virgin. The ones that he cited seem to be the same as those related in the *Nican motecpana*. He also stated that the resurrected Indian warrior remained at the shrine to live and work there, "a circumstance that I do not find in other documents."[15] This detail, however, is to be found in the *Nican motecpana*. Florencia related another miracle from the "Relación" which was not given by Sánchez, that is, the story of the woman with the distended abdomen who went to Tepeyac, drank water from the spring, and fell asleep. As she was sleeping a large snake was seen to emerge from under her, and her swelling disappeared. This is also in the *Nican motecpana*. It is clear that Florencia was unaware of the contents of Laso de la Vega's book. Regarding don Juan de Tovar, the Indian connected with Remedios, Florencia said that the "Relación" added something that other accounts did not, that is, that he was also suffering from blindness and recovered his sight at the shrine, a fact not found in the *Nican motecpana*. It is apparent that just as the first part of the "Relación," that is, the part that dealt with the apparitions, is distinct from the *Nican mopohua*, the second part is similar to but not identical with the *Nican motecpana*. In addition, Florencia devoted an entire chapter to listing the Spaniards who wrote about the apparitions. He did not mention Laso de la Vega.

Florencia's description of the "Relación" presents difficulties. He did not work from the original Nahuatl nor does he seem to have known the language. Sigüenza y Góngora later stated that what he gave Florencia was a Spanish paraphrase made by Alva Ixtlilxochitl. It is uncertain that Florencia ever saw the original or how he could have been so certain that the paraphrase was in Alva Ixtlilxochitl's hand. His identification of Mendieta as the author was clearly erroneous, since the document related events that occurred after the great Franciscan's death.

Florencia claimed that this "Relación" was the same one from which Miguel Sánchez and Becerra Tanco got their accounts. Yet from all of Florencia's quotations and references it is abundantly clear that the "Relación" was different not only from the *Nican mopohua* but also from both Sánchez's and Becerra Tanco's works; and it cannot be related to any other known account of the apparitions, past or present. Florencia promised to publish it in *Estrella del norte* but did not do so, claiming that the book was already too lengthy.

Because this "Relación" has not survived, it is impossible to make a definitive judgment about it. Its existence cannot be reconciled with so many clear statements about the lack of a written account, and it is not easy to understand why Becerra Tanco (if indeed he knew of it), Florencia, and Sigüenza y Góngora did not quote it in its entirety or publish it. Becerra Tanco did not cite it as the source of his version of the account. On the basis of the citations by Florencia, it would appear to represent a tradition different from the standard one, such as the date of 8 December, which associates the Virgin of Guadalupe with the Immaculate Conception (Florencia himself stated that the image was that of the Immaculate Conception). The "Relación" also appears to have had a strong Franciscan emphasis, and it may well have dated from the seventeenth century when the Franciscan hostility to Guadalupe may have subsided. When coupled with what was said previously about the *Inin huey tlamahuiçoltzin*, this can lead to the conjecture (and it is no more than that) that the Guadalupe account eventually came to exist in two separate traditions, a Jesuit one and a Franciscan one.

The following conclusions seem clear. Florencia's "Relación" was a later document that represented a variant tradition regarding details of the apparitions. Its provenance was Franciscan, but it was not written by either Mendieta or Antonio Valeriano. It was not the basis for the *Nican mopohua*, and despite Florencia's assertion that it was the source used by Sánchez and Becerra Tanco, it was different from both their versions. It had little or no impact on the formulation or transmission of the Guadalupe tradition. It has not survived to the present and it is not the same as any known Guadalupan document.

The second document mentioned by Florencia was another version of the apparition account which he did identify with the *Nican mopohua*. Like Becerra Tanco, he spoke of a Nahuatl account written in the Latin alphabet by an Indian, a graduate of Santa Cruz de Tlatelolco, that was in a notebook in the possession of Alva Ixtlilxochitl.[16] He evidently considered it to be distinct from the "Relación" mentioned above. Unlike Becerra Tanco, Florencia identified it with that published by Laso de la Vega, that is, the *Nican mopohua*. This statement, however, must be measured against the obvious fact that Florencia was not acquainted with the contents of Laso de la Vega's book. He may well have borrowed his information from Becerra Tanco, but it is too vague to be of any help.

The third account, in the form of annals, was in the possession of the Jesuit Baltasar González. Apparently Florencia had no direct knowledge of it but had only heard of it.[17] It began with the Toltecs and Culhuas and ended in the year

1642, with the listing of years adjusted to the European style. It contained a reference to the apparitions under the date 1531. This description does not fit any of the surviving annals known today.

At a later point in his book Florencia related more miracles associated with Guadalupe, some of which were the same as those given by Laso de la Vega. These included the cures of Pedro de Valderrama, Luis de Castilla, the son of the sacristan Juan Pavón, and a dropsical woman who was healed by drinking water from the spring.[18] He repeated the story of the Spaniard cured of headaches by making an ex-voto offering and added that his name was Bartolomé Granado.[19] To these he added others, some of which were more contemporary. One that he showed some hesitation about was the widespread claim that the Virgin's protection was the reason why New Spain had not experienced any cases of diabolical possession, a claim that later would be accepted by Clavigero.[20] Others included the rescue of Miguel de Barsena Valmoseda when his coach overturned; the rescue of an Indian run over by a coach carrying eight clerics; the preservation of the family of Pedro Quijada from lightning on 10 June 1667; the cure of the hemorrhage of María Altamirano Villanueva, sister of the vicar of Guadalupe, who drank water from the spring in 1684; the rescue of the vicar himself when his mule fell during his pursuit of a pair of adulterous Indians; and the preservation in a storm of a vessel on its way to Havana in August 1668.[21] As Florencia dealt with events that were closer to him in time, his accounts tended to become more detailed as to names, dates, and places. As in the *Nican motecpana*, most of the beneficiaries are Spaniards, not Indians.

One of his stories is especially significant. During a celebration at Guadalupe in 1643, there was a running of bulls in the square before the church. Francisco de Almazán was in the bleachers, watching "this cruel entertainment in which all the pleasure of the spectators consists in seeing the danger to those who participate, as they risk their lives on the horns of a wild beast."[22] Later, as Almazán walked toward the church, the fiercest of the bulls broke loose, charged him, knocked him down, and then made ready to gore him. Almazán and the spectators all cried out to the Virgin of Guadalupe to save him, and he promised to observe her feast every year, if saved. Thereupon the bull suddenly turned away. Almazán later told a religious that the bull became so tame that children played with it. Florencia said that Almazán fulfilled his vow, made some sizable contributions to the shrine, and was still alive in 1688. What is significant is that this took place on 13 September, "the principal feast day of Our Lady of Guadalupe, which the Spaniards celebrate on the same day as her glorious Nativity [8 September]."[23] The running of the bulls was part of the celebration during the octave of the feast. As late as 1643, then, the Nativity of the Virgin was still considered a feast day at Guadalupe. As will be seen later in reference to the separate feasts kept by Spaniards and Indians, the date of 12 December had not yet totally eclipsed the others.

Florencia also related the story of the flood of 1629 but with a striking variation.[24] He stated clearly that the image of Guadalupe was brought to Mexico City to stop the flood in 1629 but that the inundation continued for four years. He credited the end of the flood to the prayers and visions of a nun, whom he identified as madre Inés de la Cruz (not to be confused with the great poet, sor Juana Inés de la Cruz). She experienced a vision which reflected the religious attitudes of Spaniards at that time. She saw an angry and threatening Christ who was intent on punishing the city for its sins. The Virgin Mary (but not the Virgin of Guadalupe) and Saint Catherine (who had also been invoked against the flood) knelt before him to plead for mercy for the city. Christ relented but made it clear that it was only because of the prayers of his mother. The vision was related to the archbishop of Mexico, who, when the flood subsided soon after, decided that it was authentic. Florencia wrote that the archbishop credited Guadalupe with saving the city.[25]

With regard to the image itself, Florencia related an interesting anecdote that he heard from Francisco de Siles. At the beginning of the devotion some pious persons who took care of the image and shrine thought it would be good to ornament the image with some cherubs around the sunburst. This was done, but the results deteriorated so quickly that they had to be erased, causing the loss of some colors on the surface. The Stradanus engraving of 1615 shows numerous angelic heads around the image but not the sunburst. The infrared photographs taken by Philip Serna Callahan which showed the erasure of the original hands of the Virgin disclosed no remnants of cherubim around the sunburst.[26]

Diego de Monroy, the Jesuit who gave testimony at the capitular inquiry of 1665 to 1666, related a story that Florencia quoted at length.[27] Monroy gave to a friend, Juan Caballero y Ocio (to whom Sigüenza y Góngora dedicated his history of the Guadalupan congregation of Querétaro), a copy of the image of the Virgin of Guadalupe that he said had been given by Juan Diego to his son at the time of the former's death. After that it passed from father to son until it finally came into the Jesuit's possession. Some believed that the copy had been miraculously made by the Virgin herself, a theory that Florencia rejected. The principal difficulty, however, was that of reconciling this story with the tradition of Juan Diego's celibate marriage. Florencia, unwilling to give up Monroy's story, listed a number of possible explanations: that the son came from a previous marriage prior to Juan Diego's conversion to Christianity (which would contradict the assertion that Juan Diego was a lifelong virgin); that the first wife died or had been repudiated at the time of Juan Diego's conversion so that he would not live polygamously (which also contradicts the tradition of lifelong virginity); or that the son was adopted.[28] Florencia did not try to reconcile this with the tradition that when Juan Diego went to live at Tepeyac, he left all his property to his uncle, not to a son. This is another indication of the variety that seems to have surrounded the apparition account. According to Florencia, this copy of the image was later given to the sanctuary of Guadalupe in Querétaro.

Florencia accepted Becerra Tanco's thesis that the apparitions were heaven's way of demonstrating the humanity of the Indians to the Spaniards. His book also shows that the distinction or separation of the devotion to Remedios and that of Guadalupe was then taking place. Despite his own devotion to Remedios he referred to it as La Conquistadora and La Gachupina and to Guadalupe as La Criolla. Remedios was invoked against drought, Guadalupe against floods, though there is only one documented case of the latter up to Florencia's day. This invocation is reflected in the words in the full title of his book, *para serenidad de las tempestuosas inundancias de la Laguna*. Jerónimo de Valladolid had emphasized in his introductory letter that Guadalupe belonged exclusively to the archbishop of Mexico as the successor of Zumárraga, whereas Remedios belonged to the *corregidor* (chief judicial and administrative official of a district) and the civil administration. Florencia accepted the thesis that the image of Guadalupe was that of the Immaculate Conception.[29] He also speculated on the significance of the angel on the image. For Becerra Tanco it had been the guardian angel of Mexico City, for Miguel Sánchez, Saint Michael. Florencia believed that it was the angel Gabriel.[30] The confraternity at Guadalupe, described by Martín Enríquez in 1575, had disappeared but was revived again in 1673 or 1674.

Ultimately, for Florencia, the two most important proofs of the authenticity of Guadalupe were the preservation of the image and the tradition. "If there were not a constant tradition from fathers to sons, one so firm as to be an irrefutable argument, the belief in the truth of this miraculous apparition could be put at risk, at least among the Spaniards. The Indians in this regard showed themselves more careful and more grateful, leaving in writing, as I shall say later, the benefit that they received from the Lady."[31] Unfortunately, as we have seen above, the written accounts are not helpful.

Florencia has been one of the most influential contributors to the Guadalupe tradition. His book is still cited today as authoritative, though it is ill organized and repetitious. Further, all that has been said above shows that it is not reliable. He depended heavily on the unidentified "Relación," which reflected a tradition at variance with the standard one. Florencia had a frustrating propensity for referring to sources, such as the "Relación" or the cantar of Plácido, without giving further identification or details despite his promises that he would include them in his narrative.[32] He was not acquainted with Laso de la Vega's account. One thing that does emerge from a careful reading of his work is that he was defensive about the apparition account. He was dealing with the unspoken or implicit objection that there was no documentary or authoritative source. For that reason he had to appeal to the survival of the image and the miracles it wrought in order to show its authenticity. This was also the reason for his insistence on the constant tradition, as verified by the capitular inquiry of 1665 to 1666.

As a historian Florencia was flawed and credulous. It would be unfair, however, to leave the matter there. His theological insight into the meaning of the two devotions of Remedios and Guadalupe was profound. He predicted a harsh judgment for "those swollen with pride, those who now scorn and mock the poor Indians, humble and downtrodden, when they will then see many of them among the elect, glorious and honored. . . . We considered them incapable, stupid, and simple. We were the stupid ones and the fools in regarding them that way." The lesson taught by Guadalupe was the value of the natives as persons. "And I am convinced that the Mother of God, in favoring these two poor Indians so much, wanted to teach us that just as they deserved her demonstrations of affection, there will be many others also, perhaps among those whom we mistreat in word and deed."[33]

Carlos de Sigüenza y Góngora

One of the glories of colonial Mexico was the scholar, scientist, historian, mathematician, astronomer, and savant, Carlos de Sigüenza y Góngora (1645–1700).[34] A native of Mexico City and born of a distinguished family, he had a strong love for his *patria chica* (native region). At the age of fifteen he joined the Jesuits, with whom he remained for almost eight years. He was expelled from the society's colegio in Puebla because of an unknown disciplinary infraction. Despite his appeals he was never readmitted, but that did not weaken his lifelong devotion to the order, to which he left his extensive library at his death. At the age of twenty-seven he became a professor of mathematics at the Royal and Pontifical University.

Sigüenza y Góngora was an observant priest of unquestioned orthodoxy, but he was also insatiably curious and of a rational turn of mind, a man attuned to the scientific method. A universal genius, he applied himself to almost every available intellectual discipline. He helped with excavations at Indian ruins, observed eclipses, learned Nahuatl, and was deeply interested in Indian antiquities. He engaged in a dispute with Jesuit missionary and cartographer Eusebio Kino over the nature of comets. Kino held that they were omens, Sigüenza viewed them in astronomical terms. Sigüenza y Góngora was an ardent criollo. In 1680 he published a lengthy and elaborate poem, *Primavera indiana*, in praise of the Virgin of Guadalupe and her association with criollismo.[35]

In 1689 appeared his *Piedad heroyca de Don Fernando Cortes*. Although it was intended primarily to be a panegyric of the conquistador, it also contained references to the apparition account. In a lengthy digression Sigüenza y Góngora attempted to establish the definitive location of Zumárraga's residence where the miracle of the image took place and to disprove a differing assertion by Florencia. After describing how Juan Diego had been sent to the bishop's house with the flowers and there revealed the image, he stated: "as uniformly declare all those historical accounts that have been printed up to the present time, and especially a very ancient one of which I still have the manuscript and that I value very much, and it is the same one that I lent to the Reverend Father Florencia to embellish his history."[36] Sigüenza y Góngora also said that when he read Florencia's original manuscript prior to giving his approval, there was no reference to the location of Zumárraga's residence. Similarly, he claimed that the identification of Mendieta as the author of the "Relación" was not in the manuscript he had read and approved.

> Not only is the said ["Relación"] not by Father Mendieta, but it cannot be so because it recounts miracles and events in years after the death of that religious. I state and I swear that I found this account among the papers of don Fernando de Alva [Ixtlilxochitl],[37] all of which I have, and that it is the same one that the licenciado Luis de Becerra in his book (page 30 of the Seville edition)[38] had seen in his possession. The original in Mexican [Nahuatl] is in the handwriting of don Antonio Valeriano, an Indian, who is its true author, and at the end are added some miracles in the handwriting of don Fernando, also in Mexican. What I lent to Father Francisco de Florencia was a paraphrased translation that don Fernando made of each, and it is also in his handwriting.[39]

The elements of his declaration are that (1) the "Relación" referred to was written in Nahuatl in the hand of its author, Antonio Valeriano; (2) it was in the papers of Alva Ixtlilxochitl; (3) it was the same as the "Relación" seen by Becerra Tanco and described by Florencia; (4) this "Relación" related miracles and events that took place after the death of Gerónimo de Mendieta, that is, after 1604; (5) Alva Ixtlilxochitl had made a paraphrased translation of it; and (6) there was added to it a separate account of miracles in the hand of Alva Ixtlilxochitl (and perhaps composed by him).

Although on first reading Sigüenza y Góngora's declaration seems clear and straightforward, it is actually quite confused. In the first quotation he implied that he lent Florencia the original document, whereas in the second he specified that it was a Spanish paraphrase.[40] According to him the "Relación" related miracles and events that happened after 1604, something that is found in no known account of the apparitions. That was the reason why he denied Mendieta's authorship of the "Relación" and attributed it to Valeriano. This statement is the source of subsequent claims that Valeriano was the author of an account of the apparitions that went back almost to the time of the apparitions themselves, despite the fact that Sigüenza y Góngora identified it as after 1604. Yet the reason given by Sigüenza y Góngora for denying Mendieta's authorship is equally valid for denying Valeriano's. Mendieta died in May 1604 and Valeriano in August 1605.[41]

It is difficult to say why Sigüenza y Góngora made such an abrupt about-face on the existence and authorship of the account or how he knew that his document was the original in Valeriano's hand, especially since it seems to have narrated events that took place after Valeriano's death. It is important to note that Sigüenza y Góngora did not identify this account with the *Nican mopohua*. He identified it as the original of the Spanish paraphrase that he lent to Florencia which the latter said had also been used by Becerra Tanco. As has been mentioned, the quotations given by Florencia show that the "Relación" and the *Nican mopohua* were two different accounts and that the "Relación" also differed from Becerra Tanco's account.

How, then, did Valeriano come to be regarded as the author of the *Nican mopohua*? The first indication comes in the early eighteenth century, when Lorenzo Botturini Benaduci speculated that the "Relación" mentioned by Sigüenza y Góngora "is perhaps that which the Bachelor Laso de la Vega printed."[42] The first person to make a clear attribution was Mexican priest José Patricio Fernández de Uribe in a work called *Disertacion historico-critica*, which was written in 1794 but not published until 1801 (it will be discussed in chapter 11). The next was fray Servando Teresa de Mier in his third letter to Juan Bautista Muñoz (1797). In a footnote, he wrote that "Botturini also complained that Father Florencia had not printed it [the "Relación"] as he had promised; I think that he did not do so because he would see that it was the same as that which the licenciado Laso had published."[43] It seems that Mier, who was hostile to Uribe, did not know of the latter's *Disertacion*. Unfortunately, Mier's writing was so overwrought that it is often difficult to understand precisely what he intended to say.

A much clearer identification was given by Mexican priest and patriot José Miguel Guridi y Alcocer in a note to his sermon on Guadalupe (1804). Surveying the different works on the tradition, he wrote, "don Luis Laso de la Vega, chaplain of the sanctuary and later prebendary of Mexico, made known a history of the miracle, written in Mexican, which was published in 1649 in Mexico, and it is a paraphrase of that of don Antonio Valeriano."[44] He expanded on this in a later work, "Apología de la Aparición." "And although the writers disagree about the original—Florencia attributes it to fray Jerónimo Mendieta and Cabrera to fray Francisco Gómez—the most common and probable opinion considers it to be that of Antonio Valeriano, governor of Tlatelolco, followed by Becerra, Sigüenza, Botturini, and Uribe, who establishes it firmly."[45] In fact, as has been shown, the first two did not identify Valeriano as the author of the *Nican mopohua*. Guridi y Alcocer also demonstrated the importance of the identification as a compensation for the lack of documentary evidence when he spoke of how Uribe "shows at length the moral certainty that a very ancient history was written by don Antonio Valeriano, who was a contemporary of the apparition and who was endowed with the talents that guarantee his credit as a historian."[46] This, of course, became the predominant motive for the identification, since it rebutted the accusation that there was no document that verified the miracle.

The identification was carried forward by Mexican journalist and scholar Carlos María de Bustamante (1774–1848). In one of his defenses of the apparition tradition he wrote somewhat tentatively, "But this lack [of documentation] can be supplied by the account of the miracle which, if not as the author, at least as the translator, don Antonio Valeriano did. . . . He wrote many Latin letters, and don Carlos de Sigüenza y Góngora makes him the author of an account in the Mexican [Nahuatl] language of the image of Our Lady of Guadalupe painted miraculously with *flowers* in the presence of the archbishop of Mexico. It begins thus, 'Nican mopohua.'"[47] In 1835, as one of three persons commissioned by the cathedral chapter of Mexico to make a report on a tradition that the tilma had been laid on a table owned by Zumárraga at the time that the image was formed, Bustamante was less hesitant. "Besides, let us reflect that we have an ancient account in Mexican, written in the hand of *don Antonio Valeriano*, which begins, '*Nican mopohua.*' . . . Here is an original document of that period of the apparition."[48]

Despite these testimonies, the identification does not seem to have had widespread impact, and it is rarely found in most authors prior to the twentieth century. The person most responsible for popularizing it was the Mexican Jesuit historian Mariano Cuevas. According to him, Juan Diego, who was illiterate, dictated his account of the apparitions to Valeriano. Valeriano, in turn, gave the original to Alva Ixtlilxochitl, who wrote an additional account, the *Nican motecpana*, or miracle stories, that were joined to Valeriano's account. The Juan Diego/Valeriano account was the basis for those of Sánchez, Laso de la Vega, and Becerra Tanco. After Valeriano's death his family donated these and other documents to Sigüenza y Góngora, who lent a Spanish paraphrase of the two accounts to Florencia for the book *Estrella del norte*. In 1700 Sigüenza y Góngora willed his manuscript collection to the Jesuit college of San Pedro y San Pablo. After the expulsion of the Jesuits in 1767 a major portion of Sigüenza y Góngora's manuscripts went to the library of the University of Mexico, but many others were eventually dispersed. Cuevas claimed that in 1847 all these papers were plundered by American troops and taken to Washington, D. C. According to this theory, the original of the "Relación" attributed to Valeriano is the same as the *Nican mopohua* and now resides somewhere in an American archive.[49]

This story of the theft by American troops has been thoroughly refuted by Ernest Burrus, who did, however, accept Valeriano's authorship of the "Relación"/*Nican mopohua*.[50] The direct linkage of Valeriano to Juan Diego presents a chronological problem, since a period of fifty-seven years separates the death dates traditionally assigned to the two men. Valeriano died in 1605, but the date of his birth is uncertain.[51] He was an early student at Santa Cruz and later one of its teachers. The colegio was opened in 1536, and if Gibson is correct, the sixty boys who entered were age ten to twelve.[52] Hence the year 1524 would be the earliest possible date for his birth, but it was probably later. This would make Valeriano a very young man in the last years of Juan Diego's life. This does not rule out the possibility of a direct relationship, but it does make it more remote.

Another difficulty is that there is no sure evidence that the "Relación" was among the documents willed by Sigüenza y Góngora to the Jesuits for there is no contemporary document that states what was included in the legacy. When Eguiara y Eguren examined the library in 1754 and Clavigero in 1759, neither found any trace of the "Relación." Of writers on Guadalupe in the eighteenth century only Cabrera y Quintero and Botturini Benaduci seemed to have been aware of its existence. Additional difficulties arise from the conclusions reached above, that is, that the "Relación" is not the same as the *Nican mopohua* and in fact is substantially different from it.

Cuevas's fanciful account of the history of the *Nican mopohua* has been very influential, and even antiapparitionists such as O'Gorman have unquestioningly accepted it.[53] This attribution has given the *Nican mopohua* an importance that it did not have before the twentieth century. It is also one of the greatest single errors in the development of the Guadalupe tradition and in its present form owes more to Cuevas's imagination than to history.

Sigüenza y Góngora's testimony has had a strong impact on the Guadalupe tradition, in part because of his own reputation, in part because later writers have used it to link the *Nican mopohua* to a reliable sixteenth-century source. On what basis did he contradict a clear tradition among historians from 1648 to 1688 and, most specifically, his clear statement of only a year before? He did not say. It is also unclear how Sigüenza y Góngora could be so certain that the manuscript that he saw was in the hand of Valeriano, unless it was by second-hand testimony coming from Alva Ixtlilxochitl. He did not, however, credit Alva Ixtlilxochitl with the identification but merely said that it was clearly in Valeriano's hand. In addition, it must be asked why Eguiara y Eguren and Alegre were unable to find the account among Sigüenza y Góngora's papers in the eighteenth century. Finally, in rejecting Mendieta's authorship on chronological grounds, he ought by necessity to have done the same for Valeriano.

As is evident, this whole matter is quite complex. Further confusion arises from the failure of Becerra Tanco, Florencia, and Sigüenza y Góngora to publish, quote in its entirety, or give an accurate description of the "Relación." Their descriptions are inconsistent and contradictory. What they ask of their readers is an act of faith in an unseen and unpublished document. In view of the importance of the Guadalupe tradition, it is incredible that they did not publish the "Relación," whatever it may have been. It was unknown to all but two writers in the eighteenth century, and no trace of it remains today. And why was such a vital document allowed to disappear, without copies or duplicates?

What conclusions, then, can be drawn from all this? (1) Becerra Tanco, Florencia, and Sigüenza y Góngora testified to the existence of a Nahuatl account of the apparitions, but they did not identify it clearly or publish it and, except for Florencia, did not quote any part of it. (2) The "Relación" quoted by Florencia from a paraphrase lent him by Sigüenza y Góngora was not the same as the one used by Becerra Tanco. (3) Neither this "Relación" nor the one mentioned by Becerra Tanco was the same as the *Nican mopohua*. (4) Though Antonio Valeriano may have been responsible for transmitting an oral tradition, as Becerra Tanco asserted, he was not the author of any written "Relación." (5) Valeriano was not the author of the *Nican mopohua*.

Sigüenza y Góngora also claimed to have a copy of the cantar that Francisco Plácido was supposed to have written on the occasion of the transfer of the image in 1531 or 1533. He said that he had found it among the papers of Chimalpahin and that he was guarding it like a treasure.[54] He gave it to Florencia for use in his *Estrella del norte*, but the Jesuit never used it. Like so many of the other documents referred to, it was never published and it has not survived.

Florencia and Sigüenza y Góngora are two of the most influential writers in the history of the Guadalupe tradition. In particular, they laid the foundation for Valeriano's authorship of the *Nican mopohua*, an authorship that is widely accepted today. Yet careful analysis shows that this is not the case. Like Sánchez and others before them they had a maddening propensity for referring to documents that only they had seen and that they did not see fit to describe in detail or reproduce. Their testimonies were not clear and in the long run only added to the confusion that surrounds most Guadalupan documentation.

10

La Criolla Triumphant

The eighteenth century saw momentous changes in the Spanish empire. In 1700 King Charles II died childless. As the result of a protracted diplomatic and dynastic struggle in the last years of his life, the throne was bequeathed to a grandson of Louis XIV of France. The powers of Europe were alarmed at the prospect of the two kingdoms under the same dynasty and feared the power of a comatose Spain revived by Bourbon vigor. The result was the War of the Spanish Succession (1701–1713), which left the Bourbons on the throne of Spain on condition that the two crowns never be united.

The reforms instituted by the Bourbons, especially Charles III (1759–1788), which seemed progressive and rational in the best tradition of the Enlightenment, actually undermined the implicit social contract that the Habsburg sovereigns had had with their peoples in the New World. In New Spain the *visita* (formal investigation of local government) of José de Gálvez, which introduced a standing militia with its dreaded *leva*, or conscription, greater control of tithes paid to the Church, and increased taxation, culminated in the expulsion of the Jesuits in 1767. Resistance to these measures was ruthlessly suppressed. As a result, centrifugal forces that had been successfully contained for centuries began to be unleashed and in the following century would lead to the wars of independence. The latter part of the eighteenth century saw among the criollos a hostility to the changes that they viewed as a threat to their established way of life. It was in that century that Tepeyac became the paramount focus of both criollo and Indian religiosity, though the sources are not so clear on the latter. This did not mean that the two peoples were equal or that social and racial differences were leveled. The two races celebrated Guadalupe on different feast days. Guadalupe was the focus of criollo identity and Indian religiosity but not yet of national independence.

After the publication of Florencia's *Estrella del norte* in 1688, there was half a century or more when no significant writings on Guadalupe were published. In 1698 Agustín Vetancurt briefly recounted the traditional story in his *Teatro mexicano*, but he added nothing new or original.[1] More significant was his treatment of Remedios, for he gave the name Juan Diego to the Indian who discovered the image of Remedios and repeated the story that the command to build that shrine was given at Guadalupe. Vetancurt also mentioned numerous instances when the image of Remedios was invoked against drought, but he never referred to any invocation or procession in regard to Guadalupe. Vetancurt's work cannot be considered a true exception to the fifty-year gap in Guadalupan writings.

The reasons for this hiatus are not immediately evident. When such works finally did appear, however, they moved in a new direction. The influence of the Enlightenment gave impetus to a more scientific approach to history. Though not so exact or meticulous as writers of a later age, those of the eighteenth century showed an increasing sophistication in dealing with their sources and less reticence in voicing skepticism. Ingenuousness and credulity still abounded, but less so than previously. Enlightenment thinkers voiced skepticism about all miracles and popular pious practices, and for the first time negative criticism was directed openly against the apparition tradition. By the end of the eighteenth century objections were voiced in public and in print; they were no longer implicit in the rebuttals of apparitionist authors. Guadalupan writings became even more defensive. Of special importance is the fact that none of the writers on Guadalupe in this period had at hand, or in all but one case did not know about, the Nahuatl "Relación" described by Florencia and Sigüenza y Góngora.

In the middle and late eighteenth century the devotion continued to spread, encouraged in great part by the archbishops of Mexico, the diocesan clergy, and the Jesuits, all criollos by birth or sympathy. It also gained in prestige through the granting of special favors to the devotion, the church, and the municipality of Guadalupe. In that century there appears to have been an increased evangelization of the devotion among the Indians.[2] In the present stage of research it is difficult to tell to what extent this was a conscious program for binding the Indians to the Church and intensifying their Christianity or a natural, unplanned development. The extent and depth of this devotion are still not clear, and most generalizations about it must be tentative.

The *Relación mercurina*

The *Relación mercurina* is a Nahuatl account of the apparitions that was translated into Spanish by José Antonio Pérez de la Fuente, a criollo priest and accomplished nahuatlahto who signed the copy at Amecameca on 6 May 1712.[3] There is no indication as to why the translation was made or what purpose it was meant to serve. Similarly, the significance of the name remains obscure. It stands apart from the development of the apparition tradition that is described in this book, and so it is difficult to place it within any known documentary context. Though it dates from at least 1712, it is not an exception to the hiatus mentioned above, since it was never published.

There are many notable features about this *Relación*. The name Tepeyac is translated more or less literally into Spanish as *cabocerros* (tip of the hill), an indication that the translator may have been unfamiliar with the area, and Mexico City is called Mixiuhco-Tenochtitlan. The introductory section of the *Nican mopohua*, which sets the background, is lacking, and the *Relación* opens with Juan Diego's arrival at Tepeyac. It does, however, include the second dialogue with the Virgin on Sunday. The story of Zumárraga sending his servants to spy on Juan Diego is presented as a borrowing from the Spanish tradition ("Mitohua in tehualilhuitializpan mochiuh ca tlapohualiuhcatl im Castiltecacayotl"), indicating an unfamiliarity with the *Nican mopohua*. It was while Juan Diego was collecting the flowers on top of the hill that the Virgin appeared to Juan Bernardino to heal him. There is insistence throughout on the fact that the Virgin spoke to Juan Diego in Nahuatl ("mexicanahuatlatolcopa," "ipan in Mexicatlatolli," "tocnotlatol"). Juan Diego's name is almost always preceded by an adjective, such as "good" ("bueno de," "qualli tlacacayoca") or "humble" ("humilde," "tlacnomatca"). The account ends abruptly with the cascade of roses and the appearance of the image.[4]

Most striking is the fact that when the Virgin reveals the name of the devotion to Juan Bernardino, she orders "also that the divine image . . . be named *Santa Maria Tequanihtalopan*. The reason for this was not revealed" [no ca in teoyoca tlaixiptlatzintli . . . onmotocayotitzinottini Santa Maria Tequanihtalopan, amo omitalhuitzino in ipampatillotl].[5] This is the first of only two known instances of a Nahuatl name's being applied to the devotion or the shrine. It obviously puzzled the nahuatlahto author, who indicated that he did not understand its significance. Tequanihtalopan bears a superficial resemblance to the name *tequantlaxopeuh* proposed by Becerra Tanco and may perhaps be a corruption of it. It cannot, however, reflect an earlier tradition since no native name was used by anyone who wrote about the apparitions prior to this time.

Much of the language of this *Relación* is obscure, difficult to understand, and difficult to situate in any specific geographical location. Some of the words appear to have been made up or formed arbitrarily. The account may not have been written by a native speaker or may have been tampered with by a non-native.[6] There is a consistent use of *zua-* for *zohuatl*, "woman," which is a feature of the Puebla-Tlaxcala region.[7] There is also an extensive use of the abstract suffix *-yotl* with ordinary nouns. The use of *h* to indicate the glottal stop is frequent, though inconsistent.

There is no overt criollismo in this account, but it does contain one rhapsodic description of New Spain. "The dawn came laughing, it awoke on Tuesday, the twelfth of December of the year 1531. Then it seemed that the weather manifested the joy and blessed prosperity of this crowned kingdom, as if smiling unleashed happiness, because cheer bathed the land. Everything was rejoicing, the different kinds of precious little birds in the sweet noise that they made seemed to have tempered their musical instruments. . . . Then it seemed that the sky in this hemisphere, applauding with pleasure the favor that God's majesty was piously doing, and all creatures aroused men to praise their creator."[8]

It is difficult to reach any firm conclusions about the relationship between the *Relación mercurina* and the *Nican mopohua*. Though most of the wording is different, the dialogues are similar. The affectionate and diminutive terms of the *Nican mopohua*, however, have been softened in the *Relación*. It may reflect a later or variant stage of the tradition, one that included an attempt to find a native name for the devotion, or it may simply have been a local retelling of the story. The *Relación* does not exalt the Indian or convey a sense of special election. It clearly shows, however, that by 1712 there was more than one version of the apparition story in circulation (something also shown by the *Inin huey tlamahuiçoltzin*, which dates from about the same time) and that the *Nican mopohua* had not yet become the *textus receptus*.

The Second Archdiocesan Inquiry

As was mentioned in chapter 8, the papers of the capitular inquiry of 1666 returned in some unknown way to New Spain, where they and the very existence of the inquiry fell into oblivion. In December 1720 they were discovered by José de Lizardi y Valle, later the majordomo of the ermita, who was inspired to renew the request to Rome for a proper mass and office.[9] In a report to José de Lanciego y Eguíluz, the archbishop of Mexico, he summarized the fate of the previous request as given by Florencia and painted an exuberant picture of the range and popularity of the devotion. "In this kingdom there is probably not a church, chapel, house, nor hut of Spaniard or Indian, in which images of Our Lady of Guadalupe are not seen and venerated. There is scarcely a person of any rank, age, or sex who does not have his mementos or medals. In the cathedrals of Mexico, Puebla, and Oaxaca they have sumptuous chapels and altars; in Querétaro and San Luis Potosí magnificent churches which are richly adorned and dedicated to their own copies [of the image]. I doubt, or better, I do not doubt that in all the world more copies have been made than of this Guadalupe of Mexico."[10]

The archbishop's response was slow in coming, for it was not until November 1722 that he appointed two teams of experts from the fields of medicine and art to inspect the picture. An interrogatory was drawn up and in May and June 1723 two witnesses were examined. These were Franciscan Antonio Margil de Jesús (1657–1726), founder of the missionary college of Our Lady of Guadalupe in Zacatecas, and Rodrigo García Flores de Valdés, dean of the cathedral chapter and former vicar at Guadalupe. The questions were by necessity general and referred in great part to the witnesses' knowledge of the 1666 inquiry. Nothing came of this new investigation, and it would not be until the epidemic of 1736 to 1737 that enthusiasm for the feast day and proper office would be rekindled.

The Tradition Institutionalized

The Patronato

In 1736 to 1737 there was another devastating epidemic of matlazahuatl, which some believed was the same disease as that of 1576 and in which as many as 200,000 Indians died.[11] Rumors circulated among the Indians that a fatal deity was killing them. A sick person in delirium saw the fever in the form of a woman on the causeway to Guadalupe who advised him to go there to be cured. An Indian woman shouted in the sanctuary at Tepeyac, "It is all right, Little Mother, that the Indians die, but let the Spaniards die also." Out of anger over the fact that the Spaniards were unaffected, some Indians began to dump corpses into the aqueducts and mix the blood of victims in bread.[12] Many images were invoked, including Guadalupe, but it was not the first.

The initiative was taken by the city council of Mexico. The steps taken resembled what William Christian called trial and error, whereby "saints were asked for help serially and the one that worked gained in devotion."[13] On 17 December 1736 the council agreed that there should be public prayers and sought the authorization of Archbishop-Viceroy Vizarrón y Eguiarreta to have a novena to the Virgin of Loretto.[14] When this brought no relief, the council turned to the Virgin of Remedios, whose image was brought to the city in January 1737.[15] A novena was held in the cathedral from 10 to 19 January, with the canónigo magistral Bartolomé de Ita y Parra, as the principal preacher.[16] This also proved ineffective. Remembering how the image of Guadalupe had been brought to the city during the flood of 1629, the council suggested to the archbishop on 23 January 1737 that this be repeated in order to stop the epidemic.[17] There was opposition in some quarters on the grounds that this was rash and that the image might be exposed to harm. The suggestion was then made that an oath be sworn to the Virgin of Guadalupe as principal patroness of the city. Such promises and bargaining were characteristic of religious practice at the time. The archbishop responded by saying that the city should go to Tepeyac instead for a novena and public prayers. On 26 January the cathedral chapter nominated the celebrants and preachers, including Ita y Parra, for the novena.[18]

The novena was held at the shrine, with Ita y Parra as the principal preacher. "Why does the image of Remedios come to the city and the city come to the image of Guadalupe?" The reason, he said, was that Remedios had come from

Europe and had no special or determined place in America, for all of America was her home. The Virgin of Guadalupe, in contrast, was born in New Spain, she was the queen of New Spain, and so the populace, like good vassals, must go to her.[19]

Still the epidemic did not abate and other saints were invoked. Cabrera y Quintero listed some thirty images of saints for whose help processions and novenas were held, but he may have been exaggerating in order to stress the eventual victory of Guadalupe. On 11 February the council agreed on the oath of the *patronato*, as the Guadalupan patronage came to be known. Both the civil and cathedral cabildos chose deputies to take the oath in their name.[20] The archbishop set the date for Saturday, 27 April, in the chapel of the viceregal palace. The formal ceremony took place at that time with much pomp. In addition to accepting the Virgin of Guadalupe as the patroness of the city, they also swore that the city would observe 12 December as her feast and that they would have recourse to Rome to confirm the feast day and patronato and to grant a proper office. Finally, they agreed to attempt to have the patronato extended to all of New Spain. On 26 May, after a solemn procession and during a mass in the cathedral, the publication of the oath and patronato took place. After giving a brief summary of how the oath came about, the archbishop proclaimed 12 December a holy day of obligation for the archdiocese. Almost immediately the epidemic began to abate and was soon over. With that began the final triumph of the Virgin of Guadalupe.

The next step was to extend the patronato. A call was sent out to all of New Spain and Guatemala to join Mexico City in accepting it. The civil and ecclesiastical cabildos of numerous cities quickly gave affirmative responses. The move, however, was not uncontested. When the ecclesiastical cabildo of Puebla accepted the feast, its master of ceremonies, Juan Pablo Cetina, wrote an opinion that it was not lawful to celebrate the feast.[21] He apparently had some scruples about the apparition story and also believed that the entire patronato was conditioned on approval by Rome. He managed to prevent the celebration in Puebla for one year. Eventually, the patronato triumphed, though it was not until 1746 that all the desired responses had come in from the farthest parts of New Spain. An edict was published that declared that on 11 December 1746 the archbishop would proclaim "the principal patronage of the Virgin of Guadalupe over the entire nation."[22] Until such time as Rome would grant the proper feast, the mass and office were to be those of the Nativity of the Virgin (8 September), with the change of name inserted where necessary. Because of the state of mourning required by the death of King Philip V, the celebrations were postponed to the following year. The formal religious proclamations were made in the cathedral on 4 December and at the church of Guadalupe on 12 December. The national patronato was very popular in New Spain, and celebrations were many and elaborate. In 1757 the city council of Ponce, Puerto Rico, also accepted the patronato.

The efforts to secure the proper mass and office took longer. The noted painter Miguel Cabrera made three copies of the image, which were compared with the original on 15 April 1752. One he kept for himself as a model for future copies. The second was given to the archbishop and the third was sent to Rome with the Jesuit Francisco López, who was going there as the representative of the Mexican province of the Jesuits. He was also empowered by the archbishop of Mexico and the bishop of Michoacan to seek papal confirmation of the patronato and the concession of a proper mass and office. It was during an audience with Pope Benedict XIV that López presented Cabrera's copy of the image and the pontiff supposedly responded with the famous quotation from Psalm 147. After a series of complex negotiations, the pope granted both the confirmation of the patronato and the proper mass and office by the brief *Non est equidem* (25 May 1754).[23] It fell short of being the kind of endorsement that was sought. The sixth or historical lesson of the second nocturn of matins was guarded in its language. "In the year 1531 a miraculously painted image of the Mother of God is said [fertur] to have appeared in Mexico; displayed in a magnificent church in a place near the city where she is said [dicitur] to have designated by a magnificent prodigy to a pious neophyte a house sacred to her, it is honored by large numbers of people and miracles."[24] The news of the confirmation, representing as it did a strong affirmation of criollismo, was received enthusiastically throughout New Spain, and the year 1756 saw numerous public celebrations. In the following year the proper feast and office were extended to all Spanish dominions to be celebrated on a day chosen by the local bishop.[25]

The granting of the office was considered to constitute Roman approval of the tradition. In 1770 Archbishop Lorenzana wrote, "Although we mourn the loss of the authentic documents with which the Venerable Señor Zumárraga verified this miracle, it is very much justified by the constant tradition from fathers to sons, and with the many relevant proofs that the universal Church considered sufficient to grant a proper office with octave and the universal patronage of all New Spain."[26] The guarded wording of the office proved disappointing, and in the late nineteenth century the bishops of Mexico would campaign for a stronger Roman endorsement.

It was the epidemic of 1736 to 1737, not the flood of 1629, that marked the triumph of Guadalupe over other devotions in New Spain and eventually Latin America. Except for the publication of Sánchez's and Laso de la Vega's books, these events—the epidemic, the patronato, and the papal grants—were the most important in the history of the devotion. It had been thoroughly incorporated into the institutional Church and the religious life of New Spain, and Guadalupe and the criollismo it represented were supreme.

The acceptance of the patronato throughout New Spain was the occasion for the publication in 1746 of the *Escudo de armas de Mexico* of Cayetano de Cabrera y Quintero (1698?–1775).[27] A professor of canon and civil law at the Royal and Pontifical University, Cabrera composed this work as a celebration of the Guadalupe devotion and the special status it gave to the city of Mexico. Long and rambling, it included almost all the standard materials on Guadalupe as they were known up to that time and contained little that was original. As was mentioned in chapter 2, it gave evidence of an early cultus for Juan Diego. Cabrera was also the first to mention the story of Mezquía and the account supposedly composed by Zumárraga that was in the archive of the Franciscan convent at Vitoria. With regard to the authorship of the "Relación" cited by Florencia, Cabrera agreed that it was written by a Franciscan but believed him to be Francisco Gómez, Zumárraga's secretary.[28] He was the only person to make this attribution, which was never widely accepted.

La Colegiata

In 1688 Florencia wrote that the chapel at Guadalupe had six endowed chaplaincies attached to it. The chaplains rotated the celebration of daily mass and had other minor liturgical duties. Florencia, however, hoped for more: the establishment of a chapter of canons that would add luster to the liturgical ceremonies and enhance the prestige of the chapel and the archdiocese of Mexico. "May God inspire it in someone who can do it, for I can do no more than point it out."[29] The inspiration came in 1707 when Andrés de Palencia, a wealthy citizen of Mexico, left the sum of 100,000 pesos in his will for the foundation of a convent of Augustinian nuns near the sanctuary. In the event that the foundation could not be made, the money was to be used for establishing a chapter of canons (*una colegiata*).[30] The negotiations that followed were tortuously complex and delayed the establishment for more than forty years. King Philip V refused permission for the convent on the grounds that there were already enough in the area.[31] Through a misunderstanding, however, he directed the viceroy, the duke of Alburquerque, to set up a junta to study the feasibility of a colegio, a school rather than a chapter. The viceroy's legal experts and all but one of the executors of the will agreed that the money should be used for the chapter. Because one of the executors protested the procedure, it was necessary to take further counsel. Finally, in 1714, the viceroy, the duke of Linares, submitted a request for a chapter consisting of one abbot and four prebendary canons. The proposal was approved with some modifications by the king in 1717. The pope sent the bull *Verificatis narratis* to this effect on 9 February 1725 to the archbishop of Mexico, José de Lanciego y Eguíluz, who died the following year before the bull arrived. This caused new delays, complicated by a lawsuit by the heirs of one of the executors, that even a new bull in 1729 could not resolve. After interminable discussions at various governmental levels, the king issued a cédula in 1738 that should have concluded the matter, but it was not implemented, partly because of the War of the Austrian Succession, which broke out in the following year. In 1744 the crown presented a new plan to the pope, who issued a bull of approval two years later. In order to prevent further delays, the newly appointed archbishop of Mexico, Manuel José Rubio y Salinas, who was in Spain when the bull arrived, brought it with him to New Spain and implemented it. The problems were still not over, since the new archbishop protested some of the clauses in the bull.

On 22 October 1750 the abbot and prebendaries finally took possession of their offices in the newly established collegiate church. At about this time the church was also named as a royal foundation. After taking possession the abbot and prebendaries joined in the efforts to obtain a proper feast and office, using the Jesuit López as their agent in Rome. As part of this request, there was a second inspection of the image by experts, beginning on 30 April 1751. On 24 June a royal decree renewed a previous decree of 18 December 1733 that apparently was never implemented, whereby the pueblo of Guadalupe was raised to the rank of *villa*, just below that of city (*ciudad*).

Criollo Sermons

The eighteenth century saw a flowering of sermons on Guadalupe by criollo preachers, often baroque in their extravagance. The preachers cited mythology and Roman poets (especially Horace and Vergil); they dealt at length with astrological lore and the significance of numbers, often in esoteric ways. The number of stars and rays on the image became the raw material for sometimes outlandish interpretations. In 1700, for example, a Franciscan, fray Juan Antonio Lobatto, published a sermon on Guadalupe, *El phenix de las Indias*, that began with a brief but flamboyant introduction that contained a great deal of astrology. Like the sermons of the previous century, it opened with a citation of the Gospel from the feast of the Nativity of the Virgin Mary, but a verse different from that used by other preachers. The text was "Judah was the father of Perez and Zerah, whose mother was Tamar" (Matthew 1:3). He developed an elaborate exegesis based on those persons. Juan Diego was mentioned only once, and Lobatto, like Sánchez, found meaning in the fact that Mary was the mother of John and James. His sources were Florencia and Becerra Tanco.

On 12 December 1731, the two hundredth anniversary of the traditional apparition date, Bartolomé de Ita y Parra preached a sermon that was published in the following year under the title *La imagen de Guadalupe*. Ita y Parra was an important and prolific preacher with at least twenty-two published sermons. He preached the funeral of Archbishop Lanciego and the Mexican obsequies for Philip V. Even prior to the epidemic and patronato he was emerging as a champion of Guadalupe and one of the devotion's main preachers. In an introduction José de Lizardi y Valle noted the rapid spread of the devotion, not just in the

Spanish empire but throughout all of Catholic Europe. Like other preachers of the century Ita y Parra was fond of finding cabalistic and mystic meanings in numbers, especially numbers associated with different aspects of the image. He pointed out that there were forty-six stars on the Virgin's clothing, which he connected with Adam, the father of humanity and the first name in Matthew's genealogy. The letters of Adam's name in Greek equaled forty-six (A=1, D= 4, A=1, M=40), and the four letters also stood for the four parts of the Greek world: Arctos, Dysis, Anatole, and Mesembria.[32] It is not surprising that amid such convoluted interpretations Juan Diego and the Indians would be overlooked.

Other sermons that have been consulted for this study reveal some interesting aspects of the tradition and devotion as it was accepted and preached in the eighteenth century.

The first is the spread of the devotion outside of Mexico City, even prior to the epidemic and patronato. The year 1701 saw the publication of a sermon titled *Sagrado retrato* by the Dominican Juan de San José that was given at the annual celebration of the feast by the Oratory of Sombrerete. Three sermons of special interest were preached at Zacatecas, which had become a major center of the devotion: *Sermon de Nuestra Señora de Guadalupe* by José Guerra (12 December 1709), *La imagen mas clara* by Cosme Borruel (12 December 1732), and *Sermon de rogativa* by José Alfaro y Acevedo (11 June 1758). All three were delivered at the Colegio de Nuestra Señora de Guadalupe, the Franciscan missionary seminary where missionaries were prepared for work on the northern frontier of New Spain. It had been founded in 1708 by Margil de Jesús to train mobile missionaries to work with Indians who were dispersed over a wide area and to bring new methods to bear on the task. Though the relationship of this college to the Guadalupe devotion needs more study, it seems that the colegio represented a strong criollo consciousness and was a center of Guadalupan devotion. The Franciscan Matías Sáenz de San Antonio preached at the dedication of the new church at the colegio and the placing of a copy of the image within it (*Conveniencia relativa*, 1720/1721). On 12 December 1725 Angel Maldonado, bishop of Oaxaca, preached at the consecration of a church dedicated to Guadalupe in Antequera. In 1758, after the papal confirmation, Manuel Antonio Martínez de los Ríos preached a devotional sermon in Cuernavaca, published with the title *Condescendencia de Christo*.

The devotion also reached Guanajuato, where on 12 December 1744 Joaquín Osuna preached a sermon, *El iris celeste*, in a church dedicated to the Virgin of Guadalupe. Like many others it was overburdened with numerology, anagrams, and other fancies. In an addition written in 1745 Osuna pointed out that it had been 214 years since the apparition. Giving numerical values to the five vowels, he work out that Asturias equaled 1531 and the prince of the Asturias, heir to the Spanish throne, equaled 214, thus giving the year 1745. His sermon is heavily dependent on Sánchez's *Imagen* but contains far more references to Juan Diego and Juan Bernardino than those of the previous century.

Guadalupe expanded not only geographically but also in its invocation. Recourse was had to the Virgin at Tepeyac for an increasing variety of reasons. One of the earliest indications was the sermon of Antonio de Ayala (*Deprecacion*, 20 December 1711), which was preached at the Augustinian convent in Mexico City, asking for the Virgin's help against earthquake, fire, and epidemic. The sermon of Manuel Ignacio Farías (*Eclypse del divino sol*, 12 December 1742 at Valladolid) sought her help against epidemic. She was also invoked for military success. In 1711, during the War of the Spanish Succession, thanksgiving services were held at the sanctuary to honor the victories of Philip V, the Bourbon candidate for the Spanish throne, at Birhuega (8 December 1710) and Villaviciosa (9 December 1710). One of the sermons on that occasion was preached by the Franciscan Manuel de Argüello. Guadalupe was also credited with a naval victory over the English in the Pacific. Though the captain's flagship was named María Señora del Rosario, he promised a novena to the Virgin of Guadalupe if he was victorious. The novena was celebrated at Tepeyac, where the first preacher, the Jesuit Juan de Goicoechea, spoke of Mary of Guadalupe as having been "substituted for Mary, the lady of the Rosary."[33] This sermon devoted far more attention to the miracle of the roses than most others did. In 1743, during the War of the Austrian Succession, her aid was invoked against the threat of Admiral Vernon's English fleet in a sermon in Mexico City by José Fernández de Palos at a novena commissioned by the audiencia and in another preached at San Luis Potosí by fray José Arlegui. In Antequera, Oaxaca, the *canónigo lectoral* (canon theologian) of the cathedral chapter, Jerónimo Morales Sigala, gave a sermon on 12 December 1756 that honored both the patronato and military victories.

The major shift was in the invocation of Guadalupe against drought rather than flood, something that made it a special devotion for farmers and ranchers. This appears to have occurred in the latter half of the century, and the first known cases are found in sermons by Luis Beltrán de Beltrán (*El poder sobre las aguas*, 23 June 1765 at Guadalupe) and Agustín de Bengoechea (*La gloria de Maria*, 15 May 1768 at Guadalupe), which invoked the Virgin against drought at the request of the ranchers (*hacendados*) of New Spain. Similarly, Guadalupe became a special devotion of the farmers and their guild and was celebrated in the spring at planting time. The farmers usually made a pilgrimage to Tepeyac for a mass and sermon. On 17 May 1772 the Franciscan Juan Agustín Morfi preached this event.[34] A very interesting sermon was delivered at Tepeyac on 27 May 1781 by Juan Gregorio de Campos, an Oratorian, for the benefit of the farmers' guild. In his introduction to the published sermon Campos stated that he wanted to reduce or specify the patronage of Guadalupe to one single object, "and thus I intend to make you see that the protection of Mary in her image of

Guadalupe is proper, special, and specific with regard to the successful cultivation of the land and the plentiful gathering of its fruits."[35] He also cited more sources than most other preachers for the story of the apparitions—Sánchez, Mateo de la Cruz, Florencia, and Nicoseli, but not Laso de la Vega. In 1782 Pablo Antonio Peñuelas preached the final sermon of the annual novena that the farmers sponsored "in order to obtain the benefit of rain." Peñuelas made an observation, which he probably borrowed from Uribe, that in the year that the Virgin had appeared, more than a million Indians were baptized.[36] His source for this was a letter written by Martín de Valencia to the superior general of the Franciscans on 12 June 1531. Apparently Peñuelas, like Uribe, was not bothered by the fact that the letter was written before the traditional date of the apparitions.

Even before the papal confirmation of the patronato opened the floodgates of unrestrained criollismo, triumphalism, and civic pride, these themes had been common among preachers. In 1720 the Mercedarian Juan Antonio de Segura preached a sermon on the apparition in which he offered a unique interpretation of the name Guadalupe. He said that it came from Quatope, which meant "mantle of the serpent." Thus Juan Diego overcame the serpent when he received the image.[37] He also identified Juan Diego with the constellation that some astronomers called Indus. The two hundredth anniversary of the traditional date of the apparitions in 1731 also brought about celebrations and sermons. In that year the Mercedarian Miguel de Aroche closely identified Guadalupe with the Immaculate Conception in a sermon published as *Flores de la edad*. The themes of criollismo and special election also appeared in a sermon, *La venerada y glorificada de todas las naciones*, preached by the Carmelite Andrés de la Santíssima Trinidad on 12 December 1755.

Criollismo appeared quite strongly in a sermon delivered by Ita y Parra on 12 December 1746 in honor of the patronato. He also referred to the image as that of "a modest woman of the Indies" [una modesta indiana], that is, a criolla.[38] In the course of the sermon he gave a classic exposition of the criollo appropriation of the devotion.

> I cannot omit the surplus of glory that because of this comes to the *indianos*, in that Mary becomes their adopted mother and that they become her adopted children. I will explain. Mary is, as it were, the necessary and natural mother of all the faithful because she is in the proper sense the mother of Christ and because the faithful are his members; in that sense she must be like their natural mother. This is the conclusion that Gilbert the Abbot ingeniously draws: Mater Christi, mater et membrorum Christi. The mother of Christ is also the mother of the members of Christ. In this the inhabitants of the Indies and the other Christian nations are equal, because all are part of that body of which Christ is the head. But their [the criollos'] surplus is in the fact that Mary wants to be their special mother by adopting them, because besides this common love of a

mother, there is this other particular one by which she chooses them as her special adopted children.[39]

As might be expected, there was no reference to the Indians, Juan Diego, or the
tradition of the apparitions.

The theme of criollismo was also strong in a sermon preached by Ita y Parra
on 12 December 1743. The introduction by Franciscan José Torrubio defended
the criollos against charges made by a peninsular priest, Manuel Martín de Alicante, who in his published Latin letters had disparaged the learning and culture of the indianos. According to Ita y Parra, "Mary favors all nations, granting
them images for their shelter, but none has the glory of being raised up in order
to form a copy of her together with the Lady herself; and for this very rare
exaltation Mary chooses among all others only the indiano. . . . Full of astonish-
ment I say, what is the indiano, my Lady, that leaving aside all other peoples
you raise him [sic] up so that he, and no other, joins in the formation of your
image?"[40] This was followed by a long and impassioned defense of the indianos.
"The honor and glory that no other people has—that Mary elevated you to
form with your spirit her image in this [image] of Guadalupe—places you
today in a category superior to all other nations."[41] Ita y Parra, however, did
devote more attention than previously to the Virgin as the patroness and protectress of the Indians.

In 1733, also before the epidemic and patronato, the Dominican Juan de
Villa preached a Guadalupan sermon on Saint Stephen's Day (26 December) in
the chapel of the hospital of Amor de Dios in Mexico City. It was not published,
however, until 1754, the year of the papal confirmation. It had strong criollo
sentiments; for example, as God gave Moses the law on the mountain, so he
gave Zumárraga the image on a hill. Unlike most of his predecessors, however,
Villa laid great stress on the importance of the devotion to the Indians. He
spoke at length of the image and apparitions as a means of bringing the Indians
to God.

> Now I turn to those rude and unbelieving natives, excited, astonished, beside
> themselves, at the sight of this most holy image. What would they say on
> seeing a picture so perfect, so beautiful, so finished, formed without any other
> brush, without any other colors, without any more art than contact with some
> roses? What, on seeing such a beautiful image that human hands did not paint,
> could not paint, on the coarse and rough surface of the peasant's tilma? What
> maid is this (they would say)? What itzpotzle [sic for ichpochtli, "young unmar-
> ried woman"]? What lady? What ruler, whose hueipil [sic for huipilli, a native
> woman's blouse] is the sun, whose catle [sic for cactli, "sandals"] is the moon,
> whose stones are the stars? It is necessary that their coarseness pass judgment
> on something that is more than human on seeing that that lady uses, as cloth-
> ing and shoes, that sun and moon that were their idolatrous deities.[42]

Another sermon that was preached in Querétaro was *La transmigracion de la iglesia a Guadalupe* by the Jesuit Francisco Javier Carranza on 12 December 1748. Like the others this began with Matthew 1. In an introduction Alonso Manuel Zorilla y Caro said that Fernando VI had asked Pope Benedict XIV for all the graces and indulgences that Rome enjoyed in its holy year for the sanctuary at Guadalupe. This sermon also came between the epidemic and the confirmation of the patronato.

It was, however, the oath of the patronato and its confirmation by the papacy that unleashed the preachers of New Spain to celebrate an unbridled criollismo. Although, as has been said, these preachers were more willing to acknowledge the role played by the Indians, their emphasis was still on the indianos, God's new chosen people, whom Mary had honored uniquely by painting her own portrait in the land, something no other area of the Catholic world could claim. *Non fecit taliter omni nationi.* Typical was the sermon preached by the Jesuit Nicolás de Segura in 1742. He gave a short account of the apparition tradition with Florencia as his source. He compared Juan Diego's mission to Zumárraga to that of the prophet Nathan to David about the construction of a temple (2 Samuel 7:1–17).[43]

In Mexico City the papal confirmation was celebrated with a variety of functions. On 11 November 1756 Cayetano Antonio de Torres preached a sermon as part of the solemnity. This was apparently sponsored by the city council, since two of its members wrote the introduction, which was emphatically criollo. Pointing out that Mary had chosen America for her wonders, they declared that the miracles that God worked for the Israelites were the same as those for the indianos. A *parecer* written by Fernández Vallejo noted that just as Mary went to visit her cousin Elizabeth in the mountains, so she came to visit Mexico. In the sermon itself Torres made some notable statements about the process of the papal approval.

> Who but Most Holy Mary of Guadalupe could smooth away all the serious difficulties that hindered the happy progress of the confirmation of her patronato . . . ? The difficulties in the ecclesiastical sphere are very well known to all those who have any knowledge of the rites of the Church because, even without pointing out other reasons, we unfortunately journey in this matter without the original notices or authentic documents of the miracle and apparition. Either through the misfortune of time they were not preserved in any archive or through the worst fatality they perished or through some negligence they do not appear until divine providence disposes otherwise through the patronage of the Lady.[44]

Later in that same year the celebration was continued with a solemn novena that began on 12 December. The first sermon, preached by Mariano Antonio de la Vega, contained no mention of the apparition story.

An important sermon celebrating the acceptance of the patronato through-out New Spain was that of José Ponce de León, delivered in Pátzcuaro 12 December 1756. As indicated in the title, he explicitly stated that there was no written testimony to the tradition. "We all understand that there is no testimony of the apparition of Our Lady of Guadalupe, and that is what the bull of her new patronato states; but I have come up with this strange argument: there is no testimony, then there is."[45] He was referring to the image, which in itself was a testimony. A good part of the sermon was dedicated to addressing the question, How can the image be a testimony to itself? He never answered it.

The confirmation of the patronato was celebrated with special enthusiasm in Querétaro. There were nine sermons preached during the celebration, with that of José Rodríguez Vallejo being the first on 8 October 1757. The final sermon was given by Ignacio Luis de Valderas Colmenero, who gave more attention to Juan Diego than did most other preachers. He, too, drew a comparison between Mary's greeting to Elizabeth and her greeting to Juan Diego. The approval was also celebrated in San Luis Potosí, where the devotion was becoming increasingly popular among miners. The event was celebrated for seven days in 1757, complete with a sermon each day. In one of the sermons the Jesuit Javier Evangelista Contreras spoke of the patronato as an espousal between Mary and New Spain. Exalting New Spain over all other nations, he spoke of a threefold glory that belonged to Mary, New Spain, and the city of San Luis Potosí. In Zacatecas the papal confirmation of the patronato brought special celebrations, including the presentation of comedies and bullfights and the preaching of sermons six days in a row.[46] The celebration reached as far as Yucatan, where the bishop, Ignacio de Padilla y Estrada, sponsored a service in the cathedral at Mérida during which Jesuit Pedro Uturriaga preached a sermon strongly tinged with criollismo on 14 February 1757.

During the celebration of the papal confirmation of the patronato in Puebla in 1755, the Jesuit Antonio Paredes preached a sermon in which he gave a detailed account of a miracle worked through the intercession of the Virgin of Guadalupe. A nun who was suffering from high fever, distension of the stomach, and other disorders and who was so sick that she was unable to take liquids was instantly healed after praying before an image of Guadalupe. After four years of investigation a canonical inquest declared that there was no natural explanation of the cure. This is the first known case of a canonical investigation of a cure attributed to Guadalupe and a verdict on it.

The general mood of elation was enhanced by the extension of the feast and mass to all the Spanish dominions. The Jesuit Francisco Javier Lascano, in a sermon preached at Guadalupe on 12 December 1758, spoke of the patronato as being extended over all North America. The introduction, written by the cathedral chapter of Mexico, mentioned that through the intercession of Ferdinand VI, the office of Guadalupe was extended to all his dominions "leading the most miraculous lady of Mexico in triumph, through the 7,000 leagues that his crown encompasses, more than fifty million vassals bending the knee before Mary of Guadalupe."[47] The sermon was also very strong on criollismo and civic pride. All other images of Mary, declared Lascano, no matter how ancient or venerable, were made by human beings. Guadalupe, in contrast, was made by Mary herself. He also testified to the strength of the Indian devotion and to the fact that native dances were still performed before the image. "She wished to be our countrywoman, to be a native and, as it were, born in Mexico, and as such to have the name of the Mexican Mary of Guadalupe, to be the *conquistadora*." King Philip V had established a congregation or order of Guadalupe with himself and all future kings as the *hermano mayor* (presiding officer). "And now in this present era and blessed epoch, by an apostolic rescript issued from the Vatican on 2 July of the year 1757 through the sovereign intercession of don Fernando VI, the miracle of Guadalupe is celebrated in the four corners of the entire world with the same office and mass as in this basilica."[48] A similar note was sounded by the Jesuit Sancho Reynoso in a sermon delivered at the Colegio de San Luis de la Paz at approximately the same time[49] during the festivities celebrating the papal confirmation, and again, the emphasis was strongly on criollismo and triumphalism. "Non fecit taliter omni nationi. This great king and prophet says that God, in having given us the princess of Guadalupe, does us a favor and grace so stupendous and singular such as he has not granted to any nation on earth. *Americanos*, you have heard it."[50] The sermon of Rodríguez Vallejo had indicated something similar, as had the sermon of Muñoz de Castiblanque. The sermon of Rodríguez Vallejo was given on 8 October 1757 and has already been mentioned. He took his account of the apparition from Becerra Tanco. He mistakenly said that all the cities of New Spain took the oath in 1737 and that it was repeated in Mexico City in 1746.[51]

Some preachers gave more attention to the place of the Indians in the devotion, especially in the latter half of the century. This appears in a sermon preached at Guadalupe by the Jesuit Juan José Ruiz de Castañeda on 12 December 1756. "Mary dressed herself in the native style, showing herself in the same clothing, with the same form as the natives of this kingdom. She left no doubt as to how she took their same nature and came down from heaven to become incarnate on that ayate [maguey cloth or cloak], as if being conceived and born again, in order to imprint on that canvas her second conception and birth."[52] After quoting the Virgin's words to Juan Diego, Ruiz de Castañeda apostrophized, "What are you saying, señora? That for Mexico was reserved the news that was not given in Jerusalem? That on the hill of Tepeyacac was seen what was not seen on Mount Calvary? A humble Juan Diego deserved to hear from your divine lips what the ears of a John the Evangelist did not?"[53] A similar note was sounded by the Discalced Carmelite Francisco de San Cirilo in a strongly criollo sermon delivered at La Colegiata on 12 December 1778. "Is it not an imponderable glory that the first dais, the first throne, the first altar that Mary chose for her image was a poor Mexican Indian?"[54]

The strongest statement of the natives' place in the Guadalupe devotion was made toward the end of the century by fray Antonio López Murto, a peninsular Franciscan. "Most happy Indians, blessed inhabitants of America, I cannot hide my feelings. I am European and I look on you with envy. I look on your land, this land that you are in, as a holy land, because it is an earth changed into heaven. . . . Happy are you, and a thousand times happy, because to the envy of other nations the Lord has chosen one of your mountains for the exaltation of Mary, his mother."[55] It may be premature to see in this an inchoate alliance of criollismo and *indianismo*, but the seed was being planted.

The sermons of the eighteenth century marked a great step forward in the devotion, if not in the actual formulation of the apparition tradition. The strongest element was criollismo and the sense of special election. There was a blending of Guadalupe with the Nativity of the Virgin and the Immaculate Conception—the latter perhaps because the image shows the Virgin without a child. The standard text was still the genealogy of Christ from Matthew 1, at least until 1754, when the papal grant of a special mass replaced it with Luke 1, the story of the visitation of Mary to Elizabeth. There were increasing citations of Psalm 147 and still some of Revelation 12. Even before the patronato the date of 12 December was beginning to emerge as at least equal to that of 8 September, though the latter continued to be observed. The apparition devotion spread throughout New Spain and even parts of Central America quite rapidly after the papal confirmation. It also expanded in invocation, with farmers and ranchers among the most devout. The invocation of Guadalupe against drought shows that she was eclipsing Remedios in the criollo mind. Sermons of the eighteenth century contained more detailed descriptions of the apparitions and allowed more room for the Indians. The sources of the tradition were Sánchez, Becerra Tanco, Florencia, and Nicoseli, but not Laso de la Vega. There is need for a thorough, systematic study of these sermons in order to describe more in detail their theology, hermeneutic, and criollo mentality.

Nahuatl Sermons

The Biblioteca Nacional de México has ten bound volumes of sermons in Nahuatl, mostly from the eighteenth century.[56] They contain only three sermons on Guadalupe. These sermons are (1) the *Inin huey tlamahuiçoltzin* discussed in chapter 3, which is actually titled "n.ra Señora de Guadalupe," in the *Santoral en mexicano*; (2) "Nican micuiloa in temachtilli in itechpatzinco tlatoa in totlaçomahuizmexicanantzin in tepeyacac ichpochtzintli in quimotocayotilia in caxtilteca: la Virgen de Guadalupe" [Here is written the sermon that tells about our precious, honored, Mexican mother, the Virgin of Tepeyac, who is called in Spanish: la Virgen de Guadalupe];[57] and (3) a sermon on Guadalupe and the

Eucharist to be delivered on the feast observed "by the natives."[58] This latter is the only one in which the account of the apparition is clearly borrowed from the *Nican mopohua*. This account, however, is rather brief, and most of the sermon is taken up with the Eucharist, the lesson being that just as Mary appeared to the Indians for their salvation, so God wants them to know about the Eucharist for the same purpose.

A fourth Guadalupan sermon in Nahuatl was that of the well-known Jesuit preacher Ignacio de Paredes. He was born at San Juan de los Llanos in 1703 and entered the Society of Jesus in 1722. Paredes was noted for his knowledge of Nahuatl and published a summary of Carochi's grammar in 1759.[59] In that same year he published a collection of sermons titled *Promptuario: manual mexicano*,[60] which included a notable sermon on Guadalupe. It contained a lengthy account of the apparitions, which in general followed the *Nican mopohua*, although the wording is different. Like many preachers Paredes took dramatic license with the story. The dialogues differed in wording from those in Laso de la Vega. Paredes retained the affectionate and familiar terms in the dialogues but not the inversions by which Juan Diego addressed the Virgin. The sermon contained the third apparition, the one omitted in the *Nican mopohua*. The sermon also located the Virgin's appearance to Juan Diego at the spring, after he had tried to avoid her, but omitted the consoling speech by which she reassured him. Paredes's version of the tradition ended with the placing of the tilma in the oratory. The lesson of the sermon is one of devotion to the Virgin Mary and her loving protection. In contrast with criollo sermons, that of Paredes did allow a special place for the Indians; "thus in a special way they have received mercy, they have been favored" [can nel in yehuantin oc cenca yê otlaocoliloque, oicneliloque]. He spoke of "this miraculous happening which your special and particular beloved, honored Mother, Saint Mary, wrought for you Indians" [inin tlamahuizollachihualli in amopampa in amehuantin in ammacehualtin oqui-mochilhuili in amixcoyan in amotlazomahuiznantzin Santa Maria]. At the same time, however, Paredes implied that the miracle was not widely known among the natives, "and there, in brief [and] clear language, is related step by step her perfectly marvelous apparition, her portrayal, the reproduction of her likeness on the cape of the Indian Juan Diego, so that all humble Indians may be instructed and so that you may be assured and informed of this very great heavenly miracle" [auh in oncan àmo hueyac chiahuacatâtoltica motec-pancapohua in cenquizcamahuizauhqui in inexilitzin, in Iîcuilocatzin, in icopin-catzin in itilmatitech in macehualtzintli Juan Diego inic machitilozque in ixquichtin in icnomacehualtzitzintin auh inic in itechcopa inin ca ça cenca huei ilhuicac tlamahuizolli ompachihuiz ihuan ommàciz in amoyollo]. Paredes's sermon supports the hypothesis of a conscious program of propagating the apparition devotion among the Indians.

The small number of these sermons is not necessarily indicative of the actual amount of preaching since they were models that were intended to help preachers in composing their own. In general the intent of the preachers was to enhance the Indians' devotion to the Virgin Mary, and there are few indications of the sense of special election and divine favoritism that characterized the criollo sermons.

Guadalupan Dramas

Another form in which the Guadalupe tradition was celebrated was that of dramas written in Nahuatl. What Ricard called "the edifying play" came into use in the sixteenth century during the first stages of the missionary enterprise.[61] The earliest ones were almost entirely Franciscan in origin and inspiration. These plays were often quite elaborate, involving numerous actors, music, and complex stage effects. There are two such plays on Guadalupe in the Monumentos Guadalupanos of the New York Public Library, Series 1, volume 2. It is impossible to date them accurately, though both appear to be from the eighteenth century.

The first is titled "Coloquios de la aparicion de la Virgen S.ta M.a de Guadalupe escritos en Mexicano copiados de un antiguo Ms."[62] The stage directions are written in Spanish in a hand different from that of the Nahuatl. There is also a Spanish translation made by Chimalpopoca Galicia. While adhering to the basic apparition tradition, it also uses dramatic license. In addition to Juan Diego, Juan Bernardino, and Zumárraga, the cast of characters includes María Lucía, some little angels (who appear on Tepeyac with the Virgin), a physician, a chaplain, two pages, and three sick persons. It begins with Juan Diego's proposal to his wife that they observe marital celibacy in a dialogue that is didactic and moralistic. In a soliloquy prior to the apparition the Virgin speaks of her intention to make the natives the special object of her love. Most of the dialogues between the Virgin and Juan Diego are taken verbatim from the *Nican mopohua*, and some of its narrative material has been incorporated into Juan Diego's speeches. There is additional dramatic license in the scenes at the bishop's palace. His chaplain does not try to hinder Juan Diego but rather brings him to the bishop. Zumárraga is presented in a kindly light when he addresses Juan Diego, who has knelt before him. "Get up, for although you are a humble person, which shows in your face, I know that you are good and virtuous" [Ximoquetza can macihui ticnotlacatzintli in yuh mixco neci Nonmati ca ticualli ca tiyectli]. On the other hand, when he hears the message, he replies, "In truth all of you are the same as you were formerly, you Indians believe what you dream or perhaps you are trying to deceive us and make fun of us" [ca nelli in anmehuantin yeppa amiyuhqui in amacehualtin huel anquineltoca in anquintemiquiz, auh intla yuhqui cuix no tehuatl toca timocayahua titech tla(p or y)olaltiz (tlapolottiz?)].

The "Coloquios" show a strong Spanish influence in some of the stage and character conventions. As in Spanish plays of the seventeenth century and later, the pages, who are vulgar and lower class, provide the comedy relief, though they do not try to hinder Juan Diego's interviews with the bishop. Another Spanish convention is that the physician is pictured as incompetent, deceitful, greedy, and quite literally the devil incarnate ("I recognize you, you are the physician, you are the devil, you go around killing people" [Ca nimitziximati, ca titicitl, ca tiDiablo in titemimictitinemi]). In one interview with the bishop Juan Diego gives a homily on the evils of drunkenness among the Indians. On returning to the mountain to ask the Virgin for a sign, Juan Diego encounters his father and mother, who tell him of Juan Bernardino's illness. It is they, not Juan Diego, who go in search of a physician. The sickroom scene of Juan Bernardino is given at some length. It is interesting that Juan Diego tells the Virgin that he is going to Tlatelolco to get a priest to hear Juan Bernardino's confession and "prepare him," not to give him the last rites. The play concludes not with the unfolding of the tilma but with the unmasking of the rascally physician.

The other play is titled "El Portento Mexicano, comedia original escrita en verso mexicano. Copiada de un antiguo Ms." It is written in Nahuatl verse with the stage directions in Spanish. There is also a Spanish translation by Chimalpopoca Galicia.[63] Botturini Benaduci attributed it to José Pérez de la Fuente, who was also the putative author of the *Relación mercurina*.[64] At the end of the Nahuatl version, Galicia has written that the original was in the library of the cathedral of Mexico and was moved to the National Museum by order of José Fernando Ramírez in 1856. In addition to the other characters, this includes two servants named María Cacahuatzin and Totopochtli, Juan Diego's aged father-in-law, three pages, and two Indians. The speeches are much more flowery, perhaps because they are written in verse, and the Spanish stage conventions are less obvious. Like the "Coloquios," the play opens with Juan Diego's resolve to live celibately, but it is part of a long, ornate speech in praise of the Virgin Mary, and as in the other play, there are soliloquies by the Virgin on her love and protection for the Indians. The dialogues show less dependence on the *Nican mopohua*, perhaps again because of the poetic form used. The pages are not the low comedy types of the "Coloquios." A major part of the drama is devoted to the two Indian servants, even more so than to Juan Diego. The "Portento" takes more dramatic license with the story. The Virgin's appearance to Juan Bernardino is dramatized. She reveals the name to him as Santa Maria Tecuantitalopan (the same name used in the *Relación mercurina*). This happens while Juan Diego is on the mountain collecting flowers, something that is also reminiscent of the *Relación mercurina*. The stage directions are more detailed. The play ends with the unfolding of the tilma, "here it is" ("can izcatqui").

These dramas are not important for their variations from the standard Guadalupe account, since that is the result of dramatic license. Both, for example, picture Juan Diego as a young man and María Lucía as still alive. They are, however, significant for other reasons. The dialogues of the "Coloquios" are clearly borrowed from those in the *Nican mopohua*, whereas those of the "Portento" are not. Both seem to reflect a knowledge of the *Relación mercurina*. The lesson they seek to impart is that of devotion to the Virgin, who has a special love for the Indians, and living a good Christian life. There is not, however, any strong sense of special election, such as is found in the criollo sermons. Though it is perilous to make generalizations on the basis of only two dramas, it does seem that they were part of an effort of deliberate evangelization.

11

La Criolla Challenged

In 1736, the year in which the great epidemic began, the last of the key figures in the history of the Guadalupe tradition arrived in New Spain: Lorenzo Botturini Benaduci, lord of La Torre and Hono and knight of the Holy Roman Empire.[1] He was born about 1702 at Sandrio in the duchy of Milan, a Spanish dominion at that time. A disciple of pioneering Italian historian Giambattista Vico, he received his early education in Italy. In 1735 he went to Madrid, where he made the acquaintance of the countess of Santibañez. She persuaded him to go to New Spain in the following year and subsidized his journey from a pension she received as a descendant of Moteucçoma II. He became deeply interested in the history of New Spain and especially the story of the Guadalupe apparitions. Aware of the lack of documents supporting the traditional account, he determined to find some. For the next six years he traveled throughout the colony, enduring hardships and dangers and gathering documents, pictures, and maps of every description. The result was a collection of some five hundred manuscripts, both pre- and postconquest, that dealt not only with the apparition but also with different aspects of Nahua history and culture.

It was against the background of the epidemic and the patronato that Botturini Benaduci's campaign to have a formal coronation of the image took place. In his devotion to the shrine and the tradition, he secured a papal bull authorizing the coronation of the image (papal permission was required for such coronations), but it came to New Spain without the clearance (*pase*) of the Council of the Indies. Because communications were hindered by a war between Spain and England, he secured approval from the audiencia. Since the coronation was to be at his own expense and he lacked money, he sent appeals throughout New Spain, but the returns were meager. At about the same time a new viceroy, the count of Fuenclara, arrived in Mexico and was concerned to find a foreigner taking up a collection. Botturini was arrested in 1743 and his collection of documents confiscated. He was sent back to Spain in the following year, but his ship was captured by English corsairs and more of his documents were stolen. He finally reached Spain, where he was befriended by Mariano Fernández de Echeverría y Veytia, the son of a colonial official.

To justify himself to the Council of the Indies, Botturini Benaduci wrote from memory a lengthy memorial, *Idea de una nueva historia general de la America Septentrional*, of which Benjamin Keen has said that it "must rank among the most prodigious *tours de force* of memory in the history of scholarship."[2] The work achieved its purpose, and Botturini was not only exonerated but also appointed official historian of the Indies as compensation for his losses. Despite a royal order, however, his collection of documents was not restored to him. He revised the *Idea* between 1744 and 1746. In 1749 he finished the first volume of his *Historia general de la América septentrional*, which was not published until 1948. This work dealt mostly with the preconquest history of the Aztecs, but he appended to it a *catálogo* of all the contents of his museo, that is, of all the documents that he had acquired. This was also done from memory. He died in Madrid around the year 1755.

While Botturini Benaduci was interested in the entire history of New Spain, he had a special interest in the Guadalupe tradition. Discussing its sources in his introduction, he sounded a refrain that had become commonplace: "I found their [the apparitions'] history founded on tradition alone, without there being any knowledge of where or in what hands the sources of such a rare portent had stopped."[3]

The Catálogo

Botturini Benaduci not only listed the books, manuscripts, and maps that were in his museo but also gave a brief commentary on each one. Paragraphs 34 through 36 describe those that deal with Guadalupe.[4] Among manuscripts he included "the history in the Nahuatl language of bachelor Luis Laso de la Vega, which . . . should be listed among the manuscripts by Indian authors" because he believed that Laso de la Vega was not the true author, a point that will be treated again below.[5] Three other manuscripts apparently were the same as some of the annals treated previously, but it is impossible, on the basis of his descriptions, to identify them with exactitude.

There was one manuscript that dealt with the history of the Virgin of los Remedios "and gives an account of the fifth apparition of [the Virgin] of Guadalupe to the cacique don Juan Bernardino de Tovar, *ce Quauhtzin Tequitlalo* [a tribute collector] of the said town of Remedios, which in pagan times was called Totoltepec. No Indian or Spanish author mentions the said fifth apparition, except Father Florencia."[6] The fifth apparition that Florencia related was to Juan Diego's uncle, Juan Bernardino, not the one to Juan Tovar at Guadalupe. Botturini said that this manuscript was the same as the history in verse which he had mentioned earlier.[7] That history was actually Angel Betancurt's poem (see chapter 6). Like Betancurt, Botturini confused the apparitions to

Juan Bernardino and Juan de Tovar and even the two persons themselves. He was clearly mistaken in saying that no one but Florencia had mentioned the fifth apparition to Juan Bernardino.

Botturini Benaduci accepted the identification of Valeriano as the author of an original, Nahuatl account of the apparitions. "By reason of some historical fragments [that is, notes] that I copied from the originals, belonging to the celebrated don Carlos de Sigüenza y Góngora, it is clear to me that don Antonio Valeriano . . . wrote the *Historia de las apariciones de Guadalupe* in the Nahuatl language."[8] As was mentioned in the previous chapter, he added later that "perhaps" this was the one published (but not authored) by Laso de la Vega, thus beginning the identification of Valeriano as the author of the *Nican mopohua*. He also had notes on the history of Guadalupe written in Spanish by Alva Ixtlilxochitl, "whose handwriting I am familiar with and which I am looking for with the greatest diligence."[9] He did not say why he did not compare his historical fragments with the *Nican mopohua*.

Botturini Benaduci was at pains to deny Laso de la Vega's authorship of the *Huey tlamahuiçoltica*. He claimed that no Spaniard could have had such close knowledge of Indian matters such as the struggle at Teotihuacan or the will of Francisco de Verdugo Quetzalmamalitzin. The Milanese also believed that if Laso de la Vega had been the true author, he would have mentioned that fact in his introductory letter to Sánchez's work, since the Nahuatl version would appear a mere six months later. Botturini Benaduci's reconstruction of what happened was that "by chance he found some ancient manuscript by an Indian author, and did nothing more than print it and affix his name, easily taking away from the natives the honor of having written it, but also the antiquity of the history."[10] These last words, of course, show Botturini Benaduci's real concern. If Laso de la Vega was truly the author he claimed to be, then there was no direct connection via Valeriano to Juan Diego and the problem of the lack of written sources remained. The Milanese's explanation is clearly arbitrary.

In his discussion of authors who had written about the apparitions, Botturini Benaduci criticized Becerra Tanco. "This author bases it [his account] on the records of the Indians, but he did not give an individual account of them, nor was he careful about including them in it and leaving the originals in a secure place, so that they could be examined."[11] With regard to the cantar that Francisco Plácido was said to have composed for the transfer of the image to Tepeyac, Botturini Benaduci cited Florencia's description of it and said that "it was found among the orderly papers of don Domingo de San Antón Muñón Chimalpahin, and it bothered me very much that the said father [Florencia] did not include it in his history, because it runs the risk of being lost."[12]

Aside from the listing in the *catálogo*, none of the originals of the documents Botturini claimed to have found has survived. Writing from memory, Botturini was obviously confused in his identification of some of the documents. For this reason his assertions cannot be taken at face value. As will now be seen, he introduced more than a little confusion into the history of the apparition tradition.

The Will of Juan Diego

According to an inventory of Botturini's papers made by Patricio Antonio López in 1745, these contained "a simple copy of the will of the fortunate Juan Diego. . . . It belongs to the town of San Juan Bautista, one of those nearest this court."[13] This is the only reference to any such will, and the copy, whatever it may have been, has not survived. Without further data it certainly cannot be cited as evidence of the apparitions.

The Wills of Cuauhtitlan

Botturini Benaduci was the first to mention a will drawn up by a relative of Juan Diego in which an account of the apparitions was included. Later in the eighteenth century Archbishop Francisco Antonio de Lorenzana described what he said was the same will, which today is often called the will of Juana Martín. Lorenzana's description, however, more closely resembles another will, sometimes called the will of Gregoria María mentioned by other writers. These so-called wills of Cuauhtitlan are a minefield of confusion and conjecture, and it seems almost impossible to arrive at any definitive conclusions concerning them. What follows are the essential facts to the extent that they are known.

In his catálogo Botturini Benaduci, writing from memory, twice described a will drawn up by a female relative of Juan Diego. In his first description he wrote:

> The original will on *metl* [maguey] paper and in the Indian language of a relative of the blessed Juan Diego, in which are mentioned the said apparitions in these words: "Sapa omonextitzino itlazocihuapilli Santa Maria, inoque cayotilique in itlazoteopixque Guadalope," that is, "On Saturday the very beloved Lady Saint Mary appeared, and the beloved pastor of Guadalupe was informed of it." There is also a bequest of three pieces of land that the said relative and cacique's wife left to the Most Holy Lady with the expression, "to axcatzin," which means, "that the Virgin belongs to us Indians." . . . There is also an account of the purity and chastity in which Juan Diego lived during his marriage with María Luisa [*sic*], who "omomiquili in ychpochtli," meaning, "she died a virgin," and "relativorum eadem est ratio [and his relatives' account is the same]" and the same thing is proven from the printed history of the said apparitions in the Indian language.[14]

In his second reference he wrote, "Mention is made that the Virgin of Guadalupe appeared on a Saturday and she [the testator] left to the blessed image by way of bequest some lands situated in the area of Cuauhtitlan, and there is an account of María Lucía, wife of the blessed Juan Diego, and of the conjugal chastity in which these two fortunate consorts lived."[15]

This testament has not survived and is known only from Botturini Benaduci's two descriptions. He called it a document of major importance. Since he did not know Nahuatl and was quoting phrases from memory, his quotations from that language were garbled.[16] Much ink has been spilled over the meaning of *teopixque* (a plural form) in the first citation, since the word properly does not mean pastor but priest or friar. To a certain extent this is beside the point, since all other sources are in agreement that Juan Diego went directly to Zumárraga, not to any priest or pastor. Since there was no resident priest at Tepeyac in 1531 this document is either mistaken or follows a tradition not found elsewhere. The assertion that the priest of Guadalupe was Zumárraga is gratuitous. The statement about the celibate marriage seems to be based solely on the phrase "omomiquili in ichpochtli," the exact meaning of which in context is ambiguous.

In 1770 Francisco Antonio de Lorenzana, archbishop of Mexico, in his work *Historia de Nueva-España* described a will that he had seen in the library of the Royal and Pontifical University.[17] He wrote that it was "original, of Juana Martín, Indian, a relative of the Indian V[enerable] Juan Diego, written on paper of metl, or maguey, in the Nahuatl or Mexican language, executed in the place called San Joseph de las Casas Texapa, before the civil notary Morales. It leaves some lands in the area of Cuauhtitlan to Our Lady and says that Juan Diego was raised in San José Millán, that he was married to Malintzin or María. It is not quoted here in full because the year was changed."[18] Lorenzana's description of this so-called will of Juana Martín included details not found in that of Botturini: the name of the testator (Juana Martín), the place of execution of the will (San Joseph de las Casas Texapa), the name of the notary (Morales), the fact that Juan Diego was raised in San José Millán, and the alteration of the date. On the face of it, it would seem that two different wills were being described.

In the inventory of Botturini's papers that was made by Patricio Antonio López in 1745, there is reference to a will written on ancient Indian paper, dated 1559, and executed before the notary Jerónimo Morales. "It is very ancient and many of the letters are crossed out, most of its contents are difficult to read."[19] López identified the testator with a certain "Gregoria María" and said that it was the will cited above by Botturini, though it more clearly resembled that described by Lorenzana.

According to Velázquez, Lorenzana had a translation of the will made by Carlos de Tapia y Centeno, who had held the chair of Nahuatl at the Royal and Pontifical University.[20] A copy of the will and the translation in the Bibliothèque Nationale, Paris, contains the following introduction.

Copy of a document done on maguey fiber, which the Indians used in the time of their heathenism and the first years of their conversion, which is found in the Royal University of Mexico in the museo of the knight d[on] Lorenzo Botturini, inventory 8, n. 67. In it, in the earliest written letters that the natives began writing, is contained a will apparently executed before Gerónimo de Morales, notary of their republic, by Gregoria María. In it she leaves a piece of land in Cuauhtitlan to Our Lady of Guadalupe of Mexico and mentions that the apparition of Our Lady took place on Saturday and gives an account of the most fortunate Juan Diego, as the same knight Botturini cites it in his *Idea de una Nueva Historia General de la América*, printed in Madrid in 1746, f. 90, h. 4ff. The translation was made by the bachiller don Carlos de Tapia at the order of the señor archbishop of Mexico and Toledo, don Francisco Lorenzana. It is found in the same inventory and number, and verified as exact by licenciado don José Julián Ramírez, both catedráticos and synodal examiners of the said archdiocese and university. It should be noted that the original Mexican [Nahuatl] is so old, torn, and the letters so worn that in many places the translators have been unable to decipher what was written, even with a magnifying glass.[21]

This description compounds the confusion because the will mentioned by Botturini Benaduci did not contain the names Gregoria Maria or Gerónimo de Morales. In fact, the version of the will that followed this introduction did not contain the name Gregoria María nor did it mention Saturday as the day of the apparition. Like Lorenzana, the author of this introduction (who wrote it after Lorenzana became archbishop of Toledo in 1772) confused what were seemingly two different wills.

The history of this manuscript of the so-called will of Gregoria María is difficult to reconstruct. According to an act of the cathedral chapter, 29 June 1817, Pedro Cantón, the Jesuit provincial, donated a series of papers to the archive of La Colegiata, among which was the will of Gregoria María.[22] An index that came with the papers contained the following entry: "A bound manuscript in folio . . . it contains the will of an Indian woman of Cuauhtitlan named Gregoria María, made before the notary Morales on 11 March 1559 and the Castilian translation of the same will. . . . All of this is a copy of a document made on maguey fiber, the original of which is kept in the Royal University of Mexico, in the museo of the aforesaid Botturini."[23] No date was given for this delivery, but it must surely have been prior to the expulsion of the Jesuits in 1767. This, however, is inconsistent with Lorenzana's statement that he saw the original in the university's library. According to Velázquez, the will and Tapia y Centeno's translation were removed from the university's library by José Patricio Fernández de Uribe for use in his *Disertacion historico-critica*.[24] According to Uribe, the document was "so ancient and worn out that even with strong lenses the translators have been unable to decipher it in many sections."

Velázquez further confused the issue by stating that after Uribe's death in 1796 the document passed to Juan Francisco de Castañiza, the bishop of Durango, who, at the instigation of Cantón, the Jesuit provincial, donated it to the archive of Guadalupe.[25] This, of course, was chronologically impossible.

In 1817 a canon of La Colegiata, Estanislao Segura, was commissioned to make an inventory of documents concerning the apparition. "So I found the original will that I mentioned earlier and also the notebook in which it is copied and translated into our language; but since the original is so torn, old, and erased in many sections that some words cannot be understood, even with the help of lenses, and it is written with many defects and mistakes in spelling, especially in the Mexican [Nahuatl], in which the scribe, who undoubtedly did not know the language, committed such barbarisms and solecisms that they alter the substance of what is said, making it partly unintelligible."[26] Segura made his own translation of the document as best he could in view of its ruined condition.

The copies of the so-called will of Gregoria María consulted for this study are to be found in the Monumentos Guadalupanos of the New York Public Library, series 1, volume 1, folios 24 through 26, and the Bibliothèque Nationale, Paris, Mexicains 317.[27] The two contain variations, and the latter seems to be a more accurate copy. The text, however, is so garbled and ungrammatical that it is impossible to translate it with total accuracy. What follows is a literal translation of the section that deals with Juan Diego and the apparition account.

> I am a native [quiçani, "one who comes from"] right here in the altepetl of Cuauhtitlan and the barrio of San José Millán, in which the young man Juan Diego grew up. Later he went to get married over at Santa Cruz Tlapac, next to San Pedro. He married the young woman named Malintzin. The young woman [ichpochtli] soon died. Juan Diego was left alone. Afterward . . . as if a few days . . . by means of him a marvel took place over at Tepeyac . . . where the beloved noble lady Saint Mary appeared. There we saw/moved [tictolique] her precious face [itlazoixcapinque]. It [or she] is our property right here in Cuauhtitlan.[28]

What can be said about this document? To begin with, it is clear that this was the will seen by Archbishop Lorenzana, not the one described by Botturini Benaduci. It is not impossible that Botturini, writing from memory at a later date, simply gave a very inaccurate or mistaken description. Still, it seems more plausible that there existed two wills that had many similarities and many differences.

The photocopy of this will reproduced by Cuevas in his *Album*, for which he gave no source, is filled with erasures, emendations, interlineations, and spaces for the insertion of words.[29] It looks less like a finished work than a draft. If the will is a draft, why does it carry the name of the notary but not that of the testator? Cuevas claimed that the copyist had copied the original exactly, even down to the changes and blottings. This is hardly credible, since it would have required him to reconstruct the scratched-out words. The hand is not similar to the notarial hand of the sixteenth century and, in fact, appears to be at least seventeenth or eighteenth century.

The text of the will in whatever form it has been preserved presents problems. The Nahuatl contains numerous grammatical errors and may have been written by an uneducated person or one not well versed in the language. At the beginning, for example, the scribe has written the unintelligible "copal cuauhtitlan," though later he wrote "copalquahuitl" (a resinous tree). The testator speaks initially of having only one surviving child but later uses the plural. There is inconsistency about whether the children were alive or not. The name of her father is given first as Juan García and later as Juan Martín. The name of the barrio is first given as San José Millo and then as San José Millán. Finally, the testator is not named. The names Gregoría María and Juana Martín applied to both wills are the inventions or conjectures of later writers.[30]

The reference to Juan Diego and the apparitions is not entirely clear and differs from the standard tradition. In this version he was a young man at the time of the apparitions, which took place shortly after his wife's death. The account telescopes the time of his marriage, his wife's death, and the apparitions. The phrase *omomiquili in ichpochtli* in strict grammar means that his wife died a young unmarried woman, but in the context it was probably intended to mean that she died young rather than a virgin. The meaning of the last lines concerning Cuauhtitlan's claim to the image is not at all clear, nor does anything similar occur in any other version of the apparition story.

From what can be reconstructed from the sketchy knowledge of this will and the one described by Botturini Benaduci, it is possible to find similarities and differences between them. The similarities include the description of the miracle, the bequest of lands, the unelided *to axcatzin* instead of *taxcatzin*, and probably the phrase *omomiquili in ichpochtli*. The differences are the statement of the testator's relationship to Juan Diego, the notification of the pastor, the name given to Juan Diego's wife, the specification of Saturday as the day of the apparition, and the amount of land bequeathed. There are a number of possible explanations for these differences: that two different wills are in question, that one will was an expansion of an earlier one, or that some unknown author was consciously writing or experimenting with wills in order to provide evidence for the apparition account. Cuevas has added to the confusion by assuming that there was only one will to begin with but without facing the question of the differences.[31]

The will or wills cannot be taken seriously as evidence of the apparition tradition. One suspicious aspect of the so-called will of Gregoria María is that it contains so much information about Juan Diego and Guadalupe, almost a brief history. There was no need in this will, for example, to mention Malintzin and her death. This is not a case of oral spontaneity, as is sometimes found in Nahuatl wills, since it has nothing to do with the bequests, but rather is a purposeful digression.[32] In fact, it does not follow the standard format of Nahuatl wills at all. There is no formal statement of intention, no careful itemization of bequests, no statement of belief in Christian teachings, no request for the intercession of the Virgin Mary on behalf of the testator's soul, no offering for masses, no naming of executors, and no signature or notarial formula.[33] On the basis of all the above, together with the fact that the author seems unfamiliar with Nahuatl, there are grounds for suspecting that both wills were crude seventeenth-century forgeries that were intended to make up for the lack of authentic documents or, more probably, to establish a claim by Cuauhtitlan over the image and devotion. In that respect they resemble the "titles," those documents written in Nahuatl in later times in imitation of earlier styles that were used to support land claims.

Mariano Fernández de Echeverría y Veytia

Botturini Benaduci's work was continued by his disciple, Mariano Fernández de Echeverría y Veytia, who was born in the city of Puebla in 1718 into a family with a long legal tradition.[34] His father was an official in New Spain who had given Botturini Benaduci a letter of recommendation to his son when the Milanese set out on his ill-fated trip to Spain. The son came under Botturini Benaduci's influence and the two became close friends. In general, though, he was not so exact as his mentor. He tended to be uncritical in his use of sources and, as Keen has said, "the Enlightenment had not seriously touched the spirit of this pious and romantic creole, who never understood the ideas of the man who awoke his interest in ancient Mexico."[35] He died at Puebla in 1780. He was the author of a number of books, one of which, *Baluartes de México*, published posthumously in 1820, dealt with the four principal Marian devotions in the area of Mexico City: Guadalupe, Remedios, Piedad, and Bala.[36]

Veytia, as he is commonly called, went beyond other writers of the seventeenth century in emphasizing that there was no written source for the Guadalupe apparitions, only the tradition. Before recounting the story of the apparitions, he wrote, "The authentic monuments that ought to exist for such a singular prodigy are entirely lacking today, not because of carelessness in having composed them in those primitive times in which it occurred, but because those who had custody of them in later times allowed them to perish." After recounting the story, he added, "This is exactly the tradition, handed on without change for more than two centuries, and if indeed no authentic instrument of that time concerning the prodigy has survived, it seems impossible to me that there could not have been some in those early days, since the greatness of the prodigy would justly require it, and there is not a total lack of documents that more than justify the truth of the tradition."[37] However, these latter documents, as he went on to explain, were the capitular inquiry of 1665 to 1666.

Significantly, he made no mention of the native accounts described by Becerra Tanco and Florencia, though he was clearly familiar with the works of both writers. In addition, there were no references to Laso de la Vega, Sigüenza y Góngora, or Antonio Valeriano. Why these omissions? This question cannot be answered with certainty, but it may indicate a devaluing of the "Relación" as testimony, perhaps because it was nowhere to be found.

With regard to the name Guadalupe, Echeverría y Veytia rejected the standard explanation of a misunderstanding of the Nahuatl original by Zumárraga. "I must say that I cannot agree with the theory of some writers who persuade themselves that the title or patronage of Guadalupe is not the same that Our Lady gave to this image of hers when she advised Juan Bernardino that in placing her image in the church they were to call it Saint Mary, Virgin of Guadalupe, but that when the Indian gave the word in his language and because the Spaniards could not pronounce it, they corrupted it, as they did with others in the Mexican language." On the contrary, he believed that Guadalupe was the word used by the Virgin. His principal reason was that a confusion of terms would have frustrated the will of the Virgin in assigning a name to the shrine. One of the reasons he gave why she chose that title borders on the ingenuous, that is, that since both the Extremaduran shrine and the Mexican were next to rivers, they should have the same name.[38]

Francisco Javier Clavigero

One of the true scholars of colonial Mexico, Francisco Javier Clavigero was born at Veracruz in 1731. He entered the Society of Jesus at Tepotzotlán in 1748 and taught at the Jesuit colegios in Valladolid (present-day Morelia) and Guadalajara. He tended to break away from the more encrusted ideas of the past and adopt the best aspects of the Enlightenment. Together with the more progressive of his fellow Jesuits, he attempted to fuse the best of the old with the best of the Enlightenment. After the expulsion of the Jesuits in 1767, he went to Bologna, Italy, where he remained after the suppression of the Society in 1773. He died there in 1787.[39]

Clavigero published in both Spanish and Italian. His works were marked by a meticulous commitment to accuracy and a good critical sense. His two most important works were *Storia antica della California* (Venice: 1789) and the *Historia antigua de México*, cited previously, still a valuable source for preconquest history. Like other Jesuits exiled from New Spain he had a strong devotion to the Virgin of Guadalupe and sought to spread it in Europe. In 1782 he published a short work, *Breve ragguaglio della prodigiosa e rinomata immagine della*

Madonna di Guadalupe di Messico, in which he sought to explain and popularize the devotion and tradition.[40]

In narrating the life of Juan Diego and the story of the apparitions, Clavigero mentioned the tradition of a celibate marriage, but, in contrast with those who said that it was celibate from the beginning, he wrote that Juan Diego and his wife decided after marriage to abstain from its use. In this he may have been following Becerra Tanco. Like him, Clavigero dated María Lucía's death in 1534. With regard to the name Guadalupe, he considered it plausible that the Virgin chose that name in order to make the devotion acceptable to the Spaniards, since so many of them were from Extremadura. He commented unfavorably on the fact that during the first century after the apparitions the Spaniards were unwilling to build a more ornate church for the image. He accepted the claim that Francisco Plácido composed some cantares for the solemn transferal of the image to Tepeyac, but he said that the custom of singing cantares died out after a century, though the dances remained. According to him, the epidemic of 1736 was very influential in spreading and increasing devotion to Guadalupe, and this led to her being proclaimed patroness of all New Spain.[41] In describing the flood of 1629, however, he made no reference to Guadalupe.

Clavigero spoke of two feast days that were celebrated at Guadalupe in his time. The first was on 12 December, with the viceroy and principal citizens of the city in attendance. Called "the feast day of the Spaniards," it was accompanied by illuminations and fireworks. The Indian feast was celebrated on one of the Sundays of November and brought as many as 25,000 Indians to the shrine, together with many Spaniards.[42] This is significant testimony to the different meanings that the devotion had for the two peoples and its growing popularity among the Indians.

Clavigero described the spread of the devotion, not only throughout New Spain, but also to Europe. To propagate the devotion Philip V established a special congregation in Spain which was not only under royal patronage but to which members of the royal family belonged.[43] The copy of the image that Jesuit Juan Francisco López brought to Pope Benedict XIV when pursuing the request for a special office, and about which the pope is supposed to have quoted Psalm 147, was at that time in the chapel of the Visitation nuns of Rome. In Bologna, where Clavigero was living, there were three altars dedicated to Guadalupe.[44]

José Ignacio Bartolache y Díaz de las Posadas

José Ignacio Bartolache y Díaz de las Posadas was a criollo born in Guanajuato in the year 1739 to a family of limited means. He studied at the Jesuit colegio of San Ildefonso and then at the conciliar seminary, but he did not continue on to the clerical state. In 1766 he obtained the degree of bachelor of medicine. He also studied mathematics and astronomy and taught those subjects. In 1766 he published *Lecciones matemáticas* and in 1772 received the degrees of licenciado and doctor of medicine. Under the influence of the Enlightenment, he sought to popularize new advances in medicine and physics and to that end began the publication of a journal, *Mercurio volante*, in 1773. He was also a believer in the Guadalupe tradition. After his death in 1790, his widow published *Manifiesto satisfactorio u opúsculo guadalupano* as a way of paying his debts.[45] Written in a charming, unaffected, and even conversational style, it was well organized and approached the subject in a logical and scientific spirit.

The introductory approbation, given by Doctor Juan Gregorio Campos of the Royal and Pontifical University, made a reference to the objections that had been brought against the apparition account. "Astronomers have discovered on the sun's disk some spots which render its rays opaque; also against that which surrounds Our Mother and Lady some heavy clouds have arisen, which, if they do not render it opaque, because this is not possible, can for those who have a less penetrating intellectual vision interfere with the rays with which it illuminates the heavenly picture and enlightens our entire hemisphere."[46] Bartolache made a similar reference when he listed the three classes of persons for whom he was writing the book: the largest number, those who believed in the ancient tradition without requiring further proof; not a few who out of timidity and distrust did not wish to do this; a few who, while accepting the tradition, would like to have more proof. Bartolache surveyed all the literature on Guadalupe that had appeared until his time and gave a critique of each. He took Miguel Sánchez to task for failing to identify his sources. "I wish that its pious author, in place of the many texts that he copies from Holy Scripture and the holy fathers . . . had given us a simple historic narration of the miracle, backed up with some good document."[47] Similarly, when citing Sánchez's claim that he found "some" among the Indians, he writes, "the bachelor Miguel Sánchez would have done very well in having said what papers those were that he found and where."[48] He blamed this on Sánchez's preoccupation with associating the Virgin of Guadalupe with the woman of Revelation 12. In discussing Laso de la Vega, Bartolache disagreed with Botturini Benaduci's claim that he was not the author of the *Nican mopohua*. A large part of the *Manifiesto satisfactorio* is devoted to a consideration of the image from a scientific point of view. The annals that Bartolache discovered in the library of the Royal and Pontifical University have been discussed in chapter 3.

According to Servando Teresa de Mier, when Bartolache was making his investigation of the images, word spread that he did not believe in the story of the miracle. Hence he wrote his *Manifiesto satisfactorio* to justify himself. Mier was convinced that Bartolache did not believe in the tradition but hid his disbelief out of fear. Part of his strategy was to dedicate his work to the canons of

Guadalupe, "whose heads were not very sharp" and who accepted the refutation as a defense.[49] In all likelihood Bartolache was a believer, though not an uncritical one. Most of the question revolves around his analysis of the image, not his use of sources.

There was at least one other person who was convinced that Bartolache was undermining the apparition tradition: Francisco Javier Conde y Oquendo (1733–1799), a canon of the cathedral chapter of Puebla. In 1794 he composed a lengthy treatise rebutting what he considered to be Bartolache's allegations against the tradition and the image, but it was not published during his lifetime.[50] Like Bartolache he evaluated the various writers who had dealt with Guadalupe. He dismissed Sánchez and Mateo de la Cruz as too concise, Nicoseli and Florencia as not concise enough, and Cabrera as too affected. His preferred account was that of Becerra Tanco, which he quoted at length. The treatise contained almost nothing that was new or original, depending in great part on Becerra Tanco, Florencia, and Sigüenza y Góngora. Conde y Oquendo was harsh in dealing with Bartolache, even going so far as to quote the Latin phrase for a snake in the grass.

Miguel Cabrera

In 1756 appeared one of the most important books on the image itself, Miguel Cabrera's *Maravilla americana*. In one of the introductions to this work, the Jesuit Francisco Javier Lascano observed the rapid spread of the devotion in the previous few years. Cabrera, who had been one of those who inspected the image in 1751, devoted eight chapters to the image, stressing the following. (1) Its survival in the climate of Mexico City in spite of having rosaries and sacred images pressed to it; also, it was of two pieces, sewed together with fragile cotton thread. (2) He said that the material was made from threads taken from palm trees, called in Nahuatl *ayatl* and in Spanish *ayate*, but not made from maguey fiber, which was coarser than that used in the painting. (3) The lack of all sizing on the material. His assertion was based partly on the 1666 investigation, in which the experts testified under oath that they could see the image from the back through the material. When Cabrera investigated the image, the back was covered with two layers of silver about two or three inches from the image, with a small fissure through which the image could be seen from the rear. (4) The perfection of the drawing. The image was eight and two-thirds heads in height (the approximate height of a well-proportioned young girl). (5) The image was done with four different styles never before used together: oil (the head and hands), tempera (the tunic, angel, and clouds), gouache (the mantle), and figured tempera or tempera on a solid surface (the background to the rays), which at first Cabrera had thought to be sizing or primer. (6) The rare quality of the gold on the image. His summary description was that the tilma was two yards and a twelfth high and a yard and a fourth wide. The picture depicted a girl of fourteen or fifteen years of age.

It is significant that Cabrera found it necessary to deal with some objections that were brought against the miraculous origin of the image. Most of these concerned the ways in which the image seemed to violate the accepted rules of art, for example, that the body was off the perpendicular, that the left leg from the knee down was too short, that the hands were out of proportion to the body, or that the lighting and use of outlines did not follow the rules of art. Most of these objections seem to have been minor, and Cabrera had little difficulty in rebutting them.[51] They are, however, indicative of the fact that not all experts were ready to accept the miraculous nature of the image.

In 1787 there was a third inspection of the image by five painters at the instigation of Bartolache and in the presence of the abbot and a canon of the chapter. Bartolache's purpose was to correct what he considered to be mistakes by Cabrera, for example, that the head and hands were painted in oil. They concluded that the material was not coarse maguey but fine palm. Contradicting Cabrera, they also said that it had been sized sufficiently so that the colors did not bleed through the tilma. Four years later, however, two of them testified that the artists had not seen the back of the image and so could not say whether it had been sized.[52] There is no clear explanation of how this confusion came about. The experts also denied that there were any outlines on the golden flowers on the Virgin's tunic. Asked if they considered the image miraculous, they replied, "Yes, with regard to the substantial and original that they see in our holy image; but no, with regard to certain retouchings and strokes which show beyond doubt that they were executed at a later date by presumptuous hands." They did not go into detail as to what these retouchings were, and it is only in recent times that these have been specified.[53]

The conclusions reached by Bartolache's experts aroused strong opposition. On 22 October 1795, when the image was removed to facilitate repairs to the frame, it was again inspected by Conde y Oquendo and the painter José de Alcíbar. Looking closely at the golden flowers on the tunic, they concluded that anyone with decent eyesight could tell that they were outlined. "We are very much taken aback by the rashness and lack of care of Bartolache in seeking to discredit the Guadalupan picture and to give the lie to Cabrera face to face and in public on a point of fact of which the eyes are the judges."[54]

The Tradition Challenged

Despite the rapid spread and growing popularity of the devotion, there was not universal acceptance of the traditional apparition account. In 1793 Ignacio

Carrillo y Pérez wrote *Pensil americano florido en el rigor del invierno la imágen de María Santísima de Guadalupe*, which was published four years later. The appendix contained a defense of the apparitions against critics who cited the silence of the early chroniclers. This silence was still a problem in the eighteenth century, as it had been in the seventeenth.

Juan Bautista Muñoz

This argument from silence was used in 1794 by Juan Bautista Muñoz in a dissertation read before the Real Academia de Historia in Madrid. Muñoz was born near Valencia, Spain, in 1745. He was a student of philosophy and theology, strongly influenced by the Enlightenment. In 1770 Charles III appointed him *cosmógrafo mayor* (official historian and supervisor of scientific and geographic studies) of the Indies and then tutor to Prince Francisco Javier. In 1779 he was given the task of revising the history of the New World that had been entrusted to the Real Academia. He had a modern sense of history and was a precise and critical thinker. In preparation for his revision of the history of the New World he was given free access to Spanish libraries and archives together with the privilege of taking papers and books for his personal use. Between 1783 and 1790 he received from New Spain copies or originals of the works of Morfi, fray Antonio Tello, Botturini, Clavigero, and Veytia.[55] It was these papers, specifically the manuscript of Veytia's *Baluartes de México*, that interested Muñoz in the Guadalupe apparitions.

His paper before the Real Academia was titled "Memoria sobre las apariciones y el culto de Nuestra Señora de Guadalupe de México."[56] After a brief summary of the theology of miracles and of the traditional account, Muñoz surveyed the various chroniclers and writers of the sixteenth and seventeenth centuries who were silent on the subject. These included Torquemada, Motolinía, and Mendieta. "Thus, either the tradition that we are dealing with did not exist in their time, or, if there was some rumor among the populace, [they] paid no attention, as sound reason says should be done with the populace's stories that do not have an ancient origin."[57] To these he added the silence of Zumárraga. He dismissed all the proofs based on cantares, maps, and manuscripts. The "Relación" mentioned by Sigüenza y Góngora he considered to be of a vastly later date than the apparitions. "And why has it never been published?"[58] He quoted the letter of Martín Enríquez, the first to do so and perhaps the first to find it, and the statement of Sahagún. He rejected the so-called will of Juana Martín because of its reference to a pastor at Guadalupe in 1531.

Muñoz believed that the story originated between 1629 and 1634 as a result of the prolonged stay of the image in Mexico City during the flood of those years. "That it was invented long after the fact is proved by the irrefutable testimonies of Father Sahagún and Viceroy Enríquez. It is the obligation of its defenders to exhibit more ancient and less suspicious documents than those that they have produced up to now."[59] He pointed out that the proper office that Rome granted for the feast was circumspect and sparing in its references to the devotion, using phrases like "it is said." Muñoz believed that the devotion had increased notably during the time of Moya de Contreras and cited the archbishop's desire to use the extra income for orphans' dowries. He also included a history of the church buildings at the site and the erection of the chapter. In his conclusion he made a clear distinction between the devotion, "which is reasonable and all right," and the apparitions.[60]

Muñoz's "Memoria" was relatively brief and ranged over a wide variety of topics with scant detail. His arguments were ones that would be used by later opponents of the Guadalupe tradition. His was not only the first public, or published, antiapparitionist work, but it was also the foundational one. Just as Becerra Tanco provided the fundamental approach of the apparitionists, Muñoz did the same for the antiapparitionists.

Servando Teresa de Mier

Because of its importance in the history of Mexico, mention should be made of the sermon delivered by fray Servando Teresa de Mier in the church at Guadalupe on 12 December 1794. Mier was one of the more extravagant figures in Mexican history. Born at Monterrey in 1763, he joined the Dominican order and made a reputation as both a scholar and a preacher. Because of the contents of his sermon he was arrested by the Inquisition and sent to Spain. After some years he escaped from the convent in which he had been imprisoned and fled to France. In Paris he made the acquaintance of Lucas Alamán, Humboldt, Chateaubriand, and other notable figures. He secured his secularization and returned to Spain but was arrested and imprisoned in Seville. He escaped again but was recaptured and imprisoned for three more years. After a number of other adventures, he returned to New Spain as a strong advocate of independence. After the separation of Mexico from Spain, he opposed the imperial pretensions of Agustín Iturbide and later was a signer of the constitution of 1824. He died in Mexico City in 1827.

Mier was a man of overwrought imagination. His Guadalupe sermon must be considered one of the more bizarre events to have occurred in colonial New Spain.[61] It wandered through a long excursus on the origins of the Indians of the New World. Like Sigüenza y Góngora and Echeverría y Veytia, he believed that the apostle Saint Thomas had first preached the Gospel in the New World and was the Quetzalcoatl of Indian myth. The Indians, he believed, had apostatized but had kept basic Christian ideas, though in a degenerate form. He identified Christ with the Mexica god Huitzilopochtli. His most remarkable assertion was that the tilma at Guadalupe was not the mantle of Juan Diego but of Saint Thomas/Quetzalcoatl, on which the Virgin had painted her image. The latter, then, dated from the first century of the Christian era, not 1531. The events at Tepeyac in that year were not a new impression of the image but a revelation of what had been hidden for centuries.

Mier's sermon proclaimed the religious and psychological independence of New Spain. In his mental construct, the New World owed nothing to the Old, not even Christianity.[62] Christianization had from the beginning been the key title of Spain to its domination of the New World. Everything had come before the Spaniards and so there was no title. It is easy to understand how the good friar drew down on himself the wrath of both Church and state. As important as the sermon is in the development of Mexican nationalism, it is not important as a source for the study of the apparition tradition. It added nothing new and actually moved in a divergent direction.

Much more important for the history of the controversy were the six letters that Mier wrote to Muñoz in 1797.[63] Included with a multitude of topics and amid much verbiage were cogent attacks on the Guadalupe tradition. His point of reference was still his contention that Christian evangelization of the New World antedated the coming of the Spaniards, with the alteration of the apparition story as an essential component. Each letter is less correspondence than a minor treatise. In his haste Mier was often inaccurate, but his arguments, like those of Muñoz, were to be very influential. He strongly denied that he did not believe in the apparitions, only that he believed that the cult of Tepeyac antedated the conquest.

Mier accepted Valeriano's authorship of the original Guadalupe account, though his writing is unclear. "Everything that I have said works against the tradition of Guadalupe and I will make it clear that in fact it did not exist for 117 years, until in 1648 it began to be born of printed authors; that these had no other basis than a Mexican manuscript of the Indian D. Antonio Valeriano, a native of Azcapotzalco, written some eight years after the time assigned to the apparition, and full of anachronisms, falsehoods, contradictions, mythological, and idolatrous errors."[64] Without explicitly saying so, he was apparently referring to the *Nican mopohua*, though it is difficult to see how his description applied to that account. Mier also offered a confused rendering of the story of the archbishop of Mexico who was discovered reading the original accounts, identifying the archbishop as Montúfar. He believed that the Virgin had chosen the name Guadalupe to show that her affection for Indians and Spaniards was equal.

Mier claimed to have in his possession a manuscript of Sigüenza y Góngora, written when the latter was administrator of the Hospital de Jesús in Mexico City, which contained the accounts of all the churches in the diocese but without any reference to Guadalupe. He cited the silence of writers, with special emphasis on Las Casas, Remesal, González Dávila, and other mendicants. He said that even in 1797 the Indians still celebrated 8 September as the feast day of Guadalupe, whereas the Spaniards celebrated 12 December. He cited

Torquemada as saying that all the images venerated in New Spain came from the school of painting established by Pedro de Gante for the Indians of New Spain. He denied any role to Guadalupe in relieving the flood of 1629, which he believed was the result of natural causes, and cited the differing story given by Florencia. He claimed that in 1531 no Indian had two names, citing Torquemada, who said that the custom of a second name was introduced at a later date because of confusion that had arisen.[65]

Despite his feverish writing style, Mier expanded on the original points made by Muñoz and added some of his own. These have remained the basic elements in the antiapparitionist stance down to the present day. With him it can be said that both the apparition tradition and the arguments against it had been fixed. Many authors would write about this in subsequent years and engage in often heated controversy, but they would not substantially change the question.

José Patricio Fernández de Uribe

Deeply upset by Mier's Guadalupan sermon, the chapter of La Colegiata looked for a defender and found him in José Patricio Fernández de Uribe. He was born in Mexico City in 1742 and received a doctorate in theology from the Royal and Pontifical University in 1765.[66] After serving in various parishes he was made a member of the cathedral chapter. He died at Tlalpan in 1796.

Uribe's first strong defense of the apparitions was in a sermon he preached at La Colegiata on 14 December 1777. It was defensive in tone and contained a strong attack on Enlightenment thought and attitudes, "an age whose favorite profession is a rashly free philosophy for which devotion is superstition, miracles illusions or fables, the most pious traditions ignorant concerns of childhood, with which we blindly follow the errors of our ancestors."[67] With regard to the documentary basis of the apparitions, he mentioned the various writings he had seen and which dated from 1640, especially two of them:

> the history of this same in the Mexican language [was] kept at that time in the archive of the Royal University. Its antiquity, although not known precisely, is known to date from times not very distant from the apparition, both by the quality of the handwriting and also by its material, which is maguey pulp, which the Indians used before the conquest; the testament of Gregoria Morales dated 1559, twenty-eight years after the apparition, in which there is precise reference to this prodigy, an instrument written on the same paper, so old and worn out that not even with the finest lenses have translators been able to decipher it in many places, all are respectable documents that testify to the antiquity of this cult.[68]

Uribe offered no clarification of the first document. With regard to the second, it is clear that he was referring to the so-called will of Gregoria María but confused the supposed name of the testator with that of the notary.

The sermon also contained strong criollo sentiments and no reference whatever to the Indians. "O year 1754! What a glorious place you will always oc-
cupy in the annals of America! Never has there dawned on our horizon a day
more beautiful and peaceful than the eleventh of May of the same year, when
His Holiness, Benedict XIV, confirmed and approved . . . the cult and choice of
Mary Most Holy under her image and invocation of Guadalupe as the principal
patroness of New Spain."[69]

The scandal resulting from Mier's sermon caused the archbishop of Mexico,
Alonso Núñez de Haro y Peralta, to commission Uribe and Manuel de Omana
y Sotomayor to draw up a critique or censure of it. Their report, which was
completed in 1795, was long and exhaustive. The two examiners claimed that
Mier had obtained most of his ideas from a certain Ignacio Borunda, a lawyer
of the audiencia who had written a manuscript called *Clave historial*. According
to Uribe and Sotomayor, Borunda's ideas about Guadalupe were delirious and
frenzied and smacked of don Quixote's delusions. If the excerpts they cited
truly represented his thought, they were correct. They devoted a large part of
their report to rebutting Borunda's claim that the Apostle Thomas had come
to the New World, while at the same time they offered a lengthy defense of
the apparition. It had, they claimed, spread to Italy, France, Austria, Germany,
Bohemia, Poland, Naples, Flanders, Ireland, and, of all places, Transylvania. As
in Uribe's sermon, blame was cast on the Enlightenment. "In this last century,
in which all respect and veneration owed to the Church and its pious traditions
has been lost and the proud erudition of the *philosophe* spirit has been unleashed
against them, pious traditions are characterized as common errors and belief in
any miracles as superstitious credulity . . . but up to now there has not been any
writer, national or foreign, who has dared to impugn this marvel publicly."[70]

Because of the success of Uribe's sermon and his reputation for scholarship,
the chapter of La Colegiata asked him on 16 December 1794 to respond to
Mier. He agreed, but for some unknown reason his *Disertacion historico-critica*,
which was an expansion of his sermon, was not published in his lifetime. After
his death the executor of his will, Juan Francisco de Castañiza, found both it
and the sermon among Uribe's papers. They were published together posthumously in 1801.

In the *Disertacion* Uribe said that the knowledge of the apparitions had been
maintained by tradition for a hundred years after the event and then began to
be published from 1640 (*sic* for 1648) onward. He considered Mateo de la
Cruz's version of the story to be entirely distinct from that of Miguel Sánchez.
In his narration of the apparitions he said that he had taken his information
from Sánchez, Laso de la Vega, and Becerra Tanco, though it seems to owe most
to the latter two. He admitted that Zumárraga had left nothing in writing
about the occurrence and attributed this to the fact that the bishop was too

busy and involved to have written a juridical instrument. "Recourse was had to ancient or contemporary historians or those immediately at that time and neither was there found in them clear and individual notices of the prodigy. These two points—the lack of the former and this silence—have always served, if not as stumbling blocks to piety, as reasons for bitter feelings."[71] Admitting the lack of early or contemporary documentation, Uribe also testified to the existence of arguments against the apparition. "We did not believe it opportune to omit what the opposing side has commonly asserted about this lack in order to cover the apparition with an unjust suspicion."[72] He countered by claiming that the fact that none had survived did not prove they had not been written. They could, he said, have been lost with the passage of time or during the many floods that Mexico City experienced.

Uribe repeated Sánchez's story of the paper shortage as a reason for the loss of the documents and of Alonso Muñoz's finding Archbishop García de Mendoza reading the original acts and processes of the apparition "with singular tenderness."[73] He also repeated the story of how Pedro de Mezquía found a copy of Zumárraga's original account in Vitoria. Uribe took this story from Cabrera's *Escudo de armas*, but it was he who added the detail that it had been lost in a fire that destroyed the convent's archives. "We owe this notice to Canon Doctor don Juan Joaquín Sopeña, who is still living, . . . who was one of those who spoke about this with Father Mezquía, and to whom he responded with what has been said."[74] Uribe went on to deal at length with the question of the silence of the early missionaries and the implications of an argument from silence. He dealt specifically with the silence of Torquemada and Díaz del Castillo and concluded that neither one was opposed to the devotion. He depended heavily on the argument from tradition and gave a summary of the 1665 to 1666 testimonies.

Beginning with chapter 8 Uribe attempted to prove the apparition tradition from authentic and indisputable documents. He cited Moya de Contreras and the constitutions that the archbishop promulgated on 1 December 1576 for the distribution of dowries to orphan girls. He had consulted this paper in the archive of La Colegiata. Though it carried no signature or seal, it was supported by numerous documents attesting to the presentation of dowries. Uribe remarked that these proved that the ermita had a large income at that time. In chapter 9 he discussed the various historians whose works proved the apparitions, but none of these antedated Sánchez. Like Becerra Tanco he criticized Sánchez for failing to give accurate notice of his sources.

> This respectable author would have done a great service for posterity if he had left us a precise notice of those documents that he used for his work. But either because he did not judge this useful work necessary for proving a tradition that he found universally accredited in the common and general concept of the miracle or because his design (as it is explained) was more to proclaim it as an orator

of the apparition than to detail it as a historian, he contented himself with just the common notice and with assurances that he had before him ancient and curious documents, examined well and at length, in agreement with the information in the most ancient and trustworthy and sufficient ones in order to go forward in security with the historic eulogy that he contemplated.[75]

Uribe did, however, consider Laso de la Vega's account to be a translation, literal or paraphrased, of a very ancient Nahuatl account. He then went on to make one of his most important and enduring assertions: "This [Nahuatl account] (as everyone has generally believed after Father Florencia) the bachelor Luis Laso copied and made known. . . . [Other authors] have worn themselves out in useless conjectures on the original author of this history, when it is evident who it was, enough to give it the greatest authority."[76] Uribe then summarized his thesis and subtheses. (1) It was morally certain that there was an account of the apparition by a contemporary and trustworthy author. (2) It was morally certain that the account in Nahuatl existed. (3) It was morally certain that the author was Antonio Valeriano. (4) It was morally certain that Valeriano was a contemporary of the apparitions and a creditable historian.[77] In listing the eyewitnesses who actually saw the document, he included Laso de la Vega, who "saw it, copied it, and published it, as Luis Becerra affirms."[78] In actual fact, of course, none of this was true.

Uribe's sermon and *Disertacion* are extremely important for two reasons. The first is that in his sermon he made the first clear references to the doubts and questions raised by opponents of the apparitions. He made explicit what had been implicit in the works of other authors. The second reason is that in his *Disertacion historico-critica* he was the first person positively to identify the so-called "Relación" of Antonio Valeriano with the *Nican mopohua* (the history of this attribution has been given in chapter 9). Uribe was highly critical of those who denied the apparitions, equating them with the skeptical and rationalistic spirits of the Enlightenment, and in general he followed the standard argumentation of the defenders of the traditional account.

The eighteenth century saw the triumph of Guadalupe as the preeminent Marian devotion of New Spain and Central America. The epidemic of 1736 to 1737, the patronato, and the subsequent papal grant of a proper office and feast—an unusual privilege—were the catalysts of this triumph. The Virgin of Guadalupe was now invoked for numerous causes in New Spain and Central America, while preachers found in her a rich source of material for their sermons. The fundamental reason for this popularity was criollismo. The association of Guadalupe with Mexican nationalism, so characteristic of the independence period, was now firmly established. In an inchoate way the shrine, the image, and the Virgin were now becoming associated with a burgeoning revolutionary consciousness. The same was also true of the Indians, though the process is not so easy to discern. There seems to have been an effort to evangelize the Dark Virgin among the natives, but their devotion still remained distinct from that of the criollos. Despite this triumph there was still opposition. The account of the apparitions still existed in differing versions, and the *Nican mopohua* was not yet the authoritative source. The tradition was attacked for scholarly and historical reasons, not just because of its association with paganism. By the end of the eighteenth century the position of the Virgin of Guadalupe in Mexican society, consciousness, and religious life was close to what it is today.

12

Conclusions

In terms of symbolism Mexico was not born at Tepeyac in 1531 but in Mexico City in 1648. In that year there suddenly appeared a cult legend, European in substance and form though with an Indian as protagonist, of which nothing had been recorded before. It was quickly embraced by the criollos, who found in it a legitimation of their aspirations and identity. They now had divine approval for regarding themselves as the new chosen people whom God had selected through the agency of the Virgin Mary. She was born a second time, not in Judea but in New Spain, her new homeland, whose people were specially favored by her. These people were unique because no other had an image of the Virgin painted by "brushes that were not from here below." She confirmed the identity of a people who resented their second-class status. Criollismo was well developed by 1648 and needed only a catalyst, a symbol on which the people could base their self-esteem and a tool that could be used to emphasize their uniqueness. It may be premature to see in this the seeds of revolution or independence, but it is possible to see in Guadalupe's inchoate rivalry with Remedios the formation of the "other," a symbol against which the criollos could direct their hostility and define themselves.

The fundamental question here is whether a sign or symbol can exist apart from an underlying reality. It is clear that for all writers on Guadalupe before Muñoz the symbol was not separate from the reality. True, criollo preachers relegated the Indian dimension to the background in order to advance their own agenda. Interpretation of a phenomenon can also be a means of appropriating and manipulating it. A narrative configuration of an experience can also be a refiguration or distortion of that experience. Miguel Sánchez was responsible for this refiguration. In doing so he turned criollismo in a particular direction and gave it an empowering symbol that has lasted to the present day. Though he was concerned with exalting Mexico City, he also laid the way for the expansion of Guadalupe throughout New Spain by his exaltation of criollismo. He thus created the single most important tool of Mexican nationalism. Hence the question of the reality of Guadalupe is more than an epistemological one. It touches the heart of Mexican identity and religion.

In considering the Guadalupe tradition, it is necessary to make a distinction between the devotion at Tepeyac and the story of the apparitions, for the two became identified only at a late period in the history of the devotion and the chapel. Both proponents and opponents of the apparitions have assumed that any mention of Guadalupe by sources prior to 1648 automatically referred to and supported the apparition account. This assumption lies behind the citation of the wills of Verdugo Quetzalmamalitzin and Esteban Tomelín and the comments of Bernal Díaz del Castillo and Suárez de Peralta as evidence for the Guadalupe tradition. One entire book, Vera's *Tesoro guadalupano*, is based on this premise.[1] A principal thesis of the present study is that the devotion at Tepeyac prior to 1648 and the apparition devotion after that year are two distinct entities.

The origins of the ermita at Tepeyac are shrouded in obscurity. Though there were claims that it dated back to the days of the conquest (Luis de Cisneros testified to this in 1621, and in 1665 Alfonso de Hita, former vicar of the chapel of Guadalupe, spoke of the chapel as having been founded "over 140 years earlier"),[2] the weight of evidence points to the years 1555 to 1556. The evidence also points to Archbishop Montúfar as its founder. The claim that he was given this title because he refurbished it around 1555 or 1556 lacks credibility. The all-important role assigned to Zumárraga in the *Huey tlamahuiçoltica* and in all subsequent accounts makes it highly improbable that the title of founder would be attributed to his successor merely because of improvements in the building. The midcentury founding, which coincides with the dates given for Remedios, reinforces the linkage or perhaps common origin of the two devotions.

The association of the Virgin of Guadalupe with the Mexica goddess Tonantzin, though widely accepted, is open to question. The only source for it is Sahagún's diatribe against the use of Tonantzin as a name for the Virgin Mary. Later writers drew their information, at times almost verbatim, from Sahagún. Francisco de Bustamante's failure to mention the association in 1556 in his emotional condemnation of Guadalupe as renascent idolatry casts doubt on it. The lack of any clear evidence of the identification from a source not ultimately dependent on Sahagún makes it questionable. What is clear is that there was never any deliberate substitution by the missionary friars, specifically the Franciscans. That assertion should be laid to rest once and for all.

From the beginning there was an image that was venerated in the ermita, but it is not clear what it was. In 1555 to 1556 there was a painting that Bustamante attributed to an Indian artist, perhaps named Marcos, but his assertion is weakened by the failure of any other sources to substantiate it. In 1566, on the occasion of a major procession to Tepeyac, Alonso de Villaseca donated a silver and copper statue of the Virgin, but it is impossible to say what it looked like. Within a decade, according to Miles Philips, that statue was the object of a cult. It remained in the ermita until the end of the seventeenth century, when, having been superseded by the present image, it was melted down to make candelabra. The assertion by Lafaye and Weckmann that the image at Tepeyac was a statue is based on a confusion with Villaseca's gift. From the beginning some people considered the image to be miraculous in the sense that it worked miracles, but it was only in 1634 that it was first and rather vaguely described as miraculous in origin. The one thing that is certain is that the present image was in the ermita by 1606, the year in which Echave Orio painted his picture of it.

With regard to the devotion that was originally centered at the ermita, Martín Enríquez cited a vague tradition that traced its origins to the cure of a herdsman around 1556. Later in the sixteenth century, the tradition of an apparition around 1555 to 1556 also developed, though some of the testimonies may refer only to the placing of the image in the ermita. There is no written evidence before 1648 for an apparition in 1531. Though the ermita at Tepeyac was called Guadalupe, its primary invocation in the sixteenth century was the Nativity of the Virgin Mary and its patronal feast was 8 September. Evidence, such as Cepeda's sermon, indicates that this was a true patronage, not just the result of using the mass of the Nativity for a devotion that lacked its own proper one. This association, as Florencia's story of the rescue of Francisco de Almazán indicates, continued well into the middle of the seventeenth century. The date at which 12 December, the anniversary of Zumárraga's appointment as bishop, began to be observed is not known. The first indication of the new date is the request by the cathedral chapter in 1662, though the earlier date continued to be observed as late as 1797, according to Mier. By 1556, the ermita and devotion had become associated in the popular mind with the Extremaduran Guadalupe. This means that the association comes early in the history of the shrine, perhaps at the beginning. The most reasonable hypothesis is that it arose from the resemblance between the image of Tepeyac and the secondary image in the choir of the shrine in Extremadura.

According to Lockhart, "the Virgin of Guadalupe was never an altepetl patron, but instead appealed to the populace of the general Mexico City area regardless of their unit affiliation."[3] One reason for the lack of unit identification was that Guadalupe did not become a strong native devotion until the eighteenth century. Until 1648 it was opposed by the mendicants, especially the Franciscans, on the grounds of neo-idolatry and so its impact on the Indians was blunted. From 1648 until the eighteenth century it appealed not to the natives but to the criollos of the Mexico City area. Despite claims to the contrary, there is no evidence of mass conversion of the Indians after 1531, only that some missionaries, especially Franciscans, baptized in large numbers after rudimentary instruction. The apparition devotion grew only after the publication of Miguel Sánchez's book and then almost exclusively among the criollos and their sympathizers. Guadalupe was not appropriated by the Spaniards in 1555 to 1556, as O'Gorman claims, but by the criollos beginning in 1648. Some criollo authors, such as Sánchez, Florencia, and Juan de Villa, did allow a place for the Indian, but criollismo remained paramount. Almost nothing is known about the devotion among the Indians in the seventeenth century.

It was the clergy, especially the diocesans, the Jesuits, and the Franciscans of the seventeenth and eighteenth centuries, who took the lead in associating *guadalupanismo* with criollismo. Of the fifty-nine criollo preachers whose published Guadalupan sermons were consulted for this work, more than two-thirds were diocesan (sixteen), Franciscan (thirteen), or Jesuit (eleven). It was in these groups that the strongest criollo sentiment was to be found. After their expulsion in 1767, the Jesuits continued to spread the devotion in Europe. Sánchez, Siles, Mateo de la Cruz, Becerra Tanco, Antonio de Gama, Sigüenza y Góngora, Florencia, and the diocesan, Jesuit, and Franciscan preachers from 1660 to 1800 were the evangelists of the new devotion. To them must go the principal credit for making Guadalupe the preeminent Mexican national symbol.

How did the peninsulars react to this? The archbishops of Mexico favored the devotion, if only because they needed the support of the predominantly criollo secular clergy. When Archbishop de la Serna took leave of his successor, Francisco Manso y Zúñiga in Madrid, he told him, "May Your Excellency go to Mexico with great consolation because in it and outside its walls you have three admirable jewels: the miraculous image of Our Lady of Guadalupe . . . Remedios . . . and Christ Our Lord, called Izmiquilpan."[4] The civil cabildo of Mexico City had a special relationship with Remedios, the peninsular devotion, that dated back to the sixteenth century. It is not clear if this bond was weakened by advancing criollismo and the criollo domination of city government. It is noteworthy, however, that the cabildo took the lead in the invocation of Guadalupe and the establishment of the patronato during and after the epidemic of 1736 to 1737. The testimonies of the capitular inquiry and Florencia in his *Estrella del norte* emphasize the devotion of the peninsular viceroys to Guadalupe: García Sarmiento de Sotomayor y Luna, count of Salvatierra (1642–1647), who donated a silver cover for the image; Luis Enríquez de Guzmán, count of Alva de Aliste y Villaflor (1649–1653), who on leaving New Spain to become viceroy of Peru in 1653 took a copy of the image with him and introduced the devotion there; the marquess of Mancera (1664–1673), who visited the shrine each Saturday and participated in the inspection of the image in 1666 and whose daughter took a copy of the image to Spain.[5] As with the devotion of the visitador Pedro de Gálvez (who also took a copy of the image to Spain, where it was placed in the chapel of the Augustinian college in Madrid) and the royal congregation founded by Philip V, the reasons for the viceroys' devotion are not clear. It may have been a way of forging an alliance with the criollos or blunting the political impact of the apparition tradition. Other peninsulars, however, were not favorable, like Manuel Martín de Alicante, Juan Bautista Muñoz, and the anonymous priest cited by Florencia. They may have seen the reversal of roles in the story and the glorification of the criollos as a threat to the unity and fabric of the empire.

García Icazbalceta believed that after an initial enthusiasm in the sixteenth century, the pre-apparition devotion became less popular; for example, Robles states that in 1648 in all New Spain there was only one convent that had a picture of Our Lady of Guadalupe in it.[6] This, however, is inconsistent with Miles Philips's description of the popularity of the shrine among Spaniards in the 1570s, the testimony of Suárez de Peralta in 1589, the opposition of Martín de León in 1611, and the invocation of the image against the flood of 1629. The use of the image to stop that flood did not, as Lafaye claims, mark its victory over all other protecting images and devotions in Mexico City. There is no evidence of the image's being brought to the city after that time. Remedios was invoked more often, perhaps because drought was more common than flood.

It was the epidemic of 1736 to 1737 that completed the emergence of the Guadalupe of the apparitions as the foremost devotion of New Spain. Loretto and Remedios were invoked first, and only after they failed was the intercession of Guadalupe sought. The image was not brought to the city, and there was opposition to invoking Guadalupe at all. The invocation of Guadalupe began with novenas and ended with the oath. When this ritual seemingly halted the epidemic, the patronato was extended to the rest of New Spain and then to all Spanish dominions, leading in turn to renewed requests for the proper office and feast. Papal approval of these and the patronato opened the floodgates of unrestrained criollismo. The idea of special election, especially as manifested in an image painted by Mary herself, accounts for the widespread jubilation over Benedict XIV's confirmation of the patronato. It seemed to the criollos that they had received a strong affirmation from heaven itself on the eve of Gálvez's *visita* and the expulsion of the Jesuits, two more "others" against which the criollos could define themselves. Though for the criollos of the eighteenth century Guadalupe was still their preserve, they were more willing than their predecessors of the previous century to admit a role for the Indians. The accelerating sense of national identity may also have played a role in the increased evangelization of the devotion among the Indians, though it is difficult to make a definitive statement in this regard. Eventually Guadalupe became identified with both a criollismo and an indianismo that embraced the entire future nation. It was the one thing that could unite criollos, Indians, and mestizos, even though they found different meanings in it.

After 1648 the chapel and the devotion at Tepeyac became inextricably bound to the story of the apparitions. The accepted account of these apparitions is not free of internal problems. Of these only two are substantial: the use of the name Guadalupe, which presupposes a preexisting shrine with a Spanish title, and the Cuauhtitlan-Tlatelolco question. Both are strong evidence that the apparition account, as an explanation for both the image and the devotion, was formulated at a date when the ermita was already in existence and when the Franciscan establishment at Tlatelolco had emerged as preeminent.

The overwhelming difficulty with the account of the apparitions of Our Lady of Guadalupe is, and always has been, the lack of any documentary evidence or unequivocal reference between 1531 and 1648. Some sources would not be expected to mention it because of the limitations of subject matter or the period of time treated, and so their silence has no special significance. This category includes the bishops at the *juntas apostólicas* and provincial councils, Acosta, Alva Ixtlilxochitl, Durán, Remesal, Talavera, and Tezozomoc. Others, such as the *Cantares mexicanos*, the native annalists, Díaz del Castillo, Diego de Santa María, and Suárez de Peralta, make references that are so vague, ambiguous, or self-serving that they are worthless in attempting to verify the account. Most striking is the total lack of mention by persons from whom it would logically be expected: Zumárraga in his will, the Franciscans of Cuauhtitlan, Garcés, Motolinía, Montúfar, Bustamante, Las Casas, Miles Philips, Sahagún, Martín Enríquez, Moya de Contreras, Pedro de Gante, Ponce, Dávila Padilla, Mendieta, Freire, the biographers of Valeriano, Martín de León, Cisneros, and the mendicant biographers of Zumárraga. This silence is incomprehensible unless they knew nothing of the story.

In history an argument from silence is not usually persuasive in itself, but it is very strong when the sources would logically be expected to say something. The Franciscan historian Francis Borgia Steck, who translated and edited an English edition of Motolinía's *Historia*, found himself facing the dilemma posed by that friar's silence about the Guadalupe apparitions. Steck's comment in this regard attests to the force of an argument from silence in the case of someone from whom a mention would ordinarily be expected.

> Nowhere, neither in his History nor in his Memoriales, does Motolinía even mention, much less recount, the apparitions of the Blessed Virgin to the Indian Juan Diego. This seems strange, especially in view of the fact that in the course of his narrative he repeatedly had occasion at least to mention or allude to the apparitions. He speaks of the great devotion the Indians practiced to the Blessed Virgin and how they invoked her intercession in time of need. Several times he refers to the town of Cuauhtitlán without saying that it was the birthplace of Juan Diego, who, when Motolinía was writing, must have been well known among the Indians.[7]

Sherlock Holmes's dog in the nighttime was significant precisely because of what it did not do.[8]

In the latter half of the sixteenth century there were abundant written references to the chapel and devotion, none of which even hint at the occurrence of an apparition in 1531. As a result, the defenders of the apparitions have relied on the concept of tradition, a constant, uniform, uncontested tradition passed down from father to son from 1531 onward. Yet that is precisely what is lacking. There is no evidence of a tradition prior to the capitular inquiry of 1666, and the testimonies given at that investigation, with their inconsistencies and improbabilities, do not inspire confidence.

Was the story of the apparitions known among the peninsulars and criollos of Mexico City prior to 1648? The evidence is inconclusive. There is no reason for doubting the assertions of Robles, Lara Mogrovejo, and Siles (who called Sánchez the "first Columbus" of the Guadalupan story)[9] that Miguel Sánchez's account came as a total surprise and that the story had been forgotten for over a century. Later indications that an oral tradition existed, perhaps as early as the beginning of the seventeenth century, may have some basis. Mendieta and Motolinía bear witness to the fact that many such stories were in circulation in the later sixteenth century. If the Guadalupe account was one of these, it was not outstanding enough to merit mention or notice by writers before 1648, nor did it have any known impact on the religious life of New Spain prior to that year. There is a strong possibility that later testimonies to an oral tradition, such as those given in 1666, were influenced by the sudden popularity of the shrine and devotion in the wake of Sánchez's book, literally a case of *post hoc, ergo propter hoc*.

All testimonies of the seventeenth and eighteenth centuries agree that there was no official, authoritative evidence in Church archives for the apparition account. Sánchez, Siles, Robles, and Sigüenza y Góngora testified to that. The capitular inquiry of 1665 to 1666 does not even seem to have considered the possibility. The explanations that have been given for this lack, such as the paper shortage or the carelessness of earlier generations, lack credibility, if only because the absence of official records is so total.

Was there any other kind of written account of the apparitions prior to 1648? For the sixteenth and seventeenth centuries the evidence, though far from conclusive, is that there was not. The *Inin huey tlamahuiçoltzin* cannot be cited as evidence because it is clearly an eighteenth-century sermon. Miguel Sánchez implied that there was not, although his wording is ambiguous. Laso de la Vega clearly said that the people of those times failed to write down an account at the time it happened. Becerra Tanco was the first to make reference to a written account that was formerly in the possession of Alva Ixtlilxochitl and written in Nahuatl with the Latin alphabet by an Indian whom he later identified as a graduate of Santa Cruz de Tlatelolco and who for him was clearly not Antonio Valeriano. Florencia cited another document that he attributed to Mendieta. Sigüenza y Góngora was the first to name Valeriano as author of a Nahuatl account, but his testimony is confused and unconvincing. Those who wrote biographical notices on Valeriano made no mention of his authorship of a "Relación." The evidence is much clearer in the eighteenth century. With the exception of Botturini Benaduci and Cabrera y Quintero, no author of that century mentioned any native document or written account as surviving into their time nor has any survived to the present. No authors of the eighteenth century who wrote about Guadalupe had an indisputably authentic account available to them, and they were almost unanimous in stating that there was none.

What, then, of the *Nican mopohua*? Is it contemporary or nearly contemporary with the apparitions and was it written by Antonio Valeriano? The answer to both questions is a clear no. At first Becerra Tanco identified a native account he had claimed to use with the *Nican mopohua* but then backed away from the identification. Was the "Relación" that Florencia borrowed from Sigüenza y Góngora the original of the *Nican mopohua*? Again, the answer is clearly negative. The citations and extracts that Florencia gave from this "Relación" indicate an account totally distinct from the *Nican mopohua*. Sigüenza y Góngora, whose testimony about this "Relación" is often considered the most weighty, did not identify it with the *Nican mopohua*. In addition, his description of the "Relación," specifically in regard to the miracle stories, shows that it was a distinct document. There is no good reason to reject Laso de la Vega's claim to substantial or supervisory authorship, even if most of the work was done by native assistants.

The Florencia/Sigüenza y Góngora "Relación" has disappeared. It is not clear if it was among the papers willed by Sigüenza y Góngora to the Jesuits at the time of his death in 1700. If it was among them, it had disappeared by 1752, when Eguiara y Eguren inspected the collection, or even earlier, in light of the silence of eighteenth-century authors. It is not among the papers in the *Documentos guadalupanos* in the New York Public Library, for the accounts of the apparitions in that collection are copies of the *Nican mopohua*. As a result, aside from the quotations by Florencia, it is impossible to form any clear idea of its contents, age, or provenance. All the alleged Guadalupe sources met similar fates. For all the claims made by various authors, no document that is identifiable as an original source is currently in existence. It is incomprehensible that a document as supremely important as this "Relación" should have been allowed to perish without having been published or without having been copied.

There is a clear progression in the sequential linking of Valeriano to the *Nican mopohua*. Until 1648 the apparitions were generally unknown or forgotten among the peninsulars and criollos of Mexico City, and there were no sure documentary sources. Becerra Tanco moved a step forward by testifying to the existence of a Nahuatl account by an unnamed Indian from the Colegio de

Santa Cruz de Tlatelolco that was in the possession of Alva Ixtlilxochitl and a separate oral tradition from Valeriano. Florencia testified to a similar "Relación," which he did not identify with the *Nican mopohua*. He cited another document, which he did not describe closely, as that published by Laso de la Vega. Sigüenza y Góngora inaugurated the association of Valeriano with the "Relación," though he also did not identify it with the *Nican mopohua*. Botturini Benaduci was the first to suggest a possible connection. Fernández de Uribe established this association in the late eighteenth century, and it was accepted by Guridi y Alcocer and Bustamante. Cuevas completed it with a fanciful construction of a link from Juan Diego to the *Nican mopohua*. All this is clearly a process of legitimation, a linkage of the *Nican mopohua* to the most famous native scholar of the sixteenth century, a man who was being surrounded by the mists of legend and whose family was still well known. Valeriano's authorship was an imprimatur for the authenticity of the apparitions, but it also required the denial of Laso de la Vega's authorship, even in a generic sense, of the *Nican mopohua*. Not only is the claim of Valeriano's authorship unfounded, but it has also been the single greatest error in the history of the Virgin of Guadalupe.

Why was this legitimation deemed necessary? The answer is clearly that from the beginning objections, implicit or explicit, were raised to the truth of the account on the basis of the lack of written evidence. These objections were implicit in the defenses mounted by almost every source in the seventeenth century. In the following century the challenges became explicit. It was only in the twentieth century that the *Nican mopohua* came to be considered an important, even primary source for the Guadalupe apparitions. It was Mariano Cuevas who in 1921 turned it into the *textus receptus*.

Where, then, did the *Nican mopohua* come from? García Icazbalceta theorized that it was a cult drama or auto sacramental that originated at the Franciscan college of Santa Cruz de Tlatelolco, perhaps from the Indian students there, an idea he may have gotten from Mier.[10] He pointed to the structure of the account, which can be easily divided into acts, and the extensive use of dialogue and the favorable references to Tlatelolco. If this theory is true, the story would have to be dated to the late sixteenth century, when the colegio was still active. It would also suppose the existence of a written manuscript, something that contradicts the majority testimony of the seventeenth and eighteenth centuries, and it would have the tradition originate in a milieu that was hostile to the devotion. This hypothesis is intriguing, but it is also arbitrary. Barring fortuitous new manuscript discoveries, it must remain a fanciful theory and no more.

The simplest and ultimately most convincing answer is found by returning to the statements of the man who first made the apparitions known, Miguel Sánchez. He said that in the absence of any official written account—and he never varied from his assertion that there was none—he had to appeal to the memories of the older Indians. There is ambiguity in his first statement on the matter, and he may have claimed to have found some sort of written testimony among the Indians. His primary source, however, seems to have been some form of oral tradition among the natives, a conclusion supported by Becerra Tanco, Florencia, and much of the testimony of the 1665 to 1666 interrogatory. This tradition had a more or less uniform core but varied in details, such as Juan Diego's age at the time of the apparitions, whether he lived a celibate marriage and when it began, the time of his wife's death, the number of apparitions, the number of interviews with Zumárraga, the proclamation of the miracle in Cuauhtitlan with drums and trumpets, and the day and year when the image was transferred to Tepeyac. Similarly, there were different versions about the miracles, some of which had assumed a clear form by 1615. Laso de la Vega took that tradition, either from Sánchez immediately or from a common source after reading Sánchez's book, and reworked it into classic Nahuatl, probably with the help of educated natives. With these two authors the story becomes more or less fixed, though the extent to which they embellished and added to this core will never be known with certainty. Hagiographers and spiritual writers of the seventeenth century had no hesitation about adding legends, stories, and speculations to their works.

In this hypothesis the story was a vague local cult legend that arose among Christian Indians, explaining the origin of a shrine that was perhaps associated with memories of the past, or it may have been a variation on the Remedios legend. Because of the consistent use of the Spanish name Guadalupe, the account must be subsequent to the establishment of the ermita or at least the popular attribution under that title. Since the earliest datable reference to the ermita is 1555 to 1556, at which time it was considered new, the story of the apparitions must have developed after that. If Sánchez's assertion that he spent half a century researching the account, the testimonies of Becerra Tanco's witnesses, and the witnesses in the capitular inquiry of 1665 to 1666 are reliable, it would be dated toward the end of the sixteenth or more probably the beginning of the seventeenth century. However, the silences of Mendieta (1596), Grijalva (1611), León (1611), and Cepeda (1622) argue for a later date. The Stradanus engraving (1615) gives the first hint of an apparition at the spring at Tepeyac, though it does not include the apparitions among the miracles worked at Tepeyac. It is not until the *Coplas* of 1634 that a miraculous origin was in any way attributed to the image. That would have meant a rapid development of the story prior to 1640, when Miguel Sánchez announced his intention to write a book on Guadalupe. If any oral account existed at an earlier time, it would have been extremely localized or just one of many such stories in circulation. This short time frame for the development of the story permits the suspicion that the apparition story, as it is now known, was largely the work of Miguel Sánchez.

Because there is no way of ascertaining how much Sánchez embellished the account (and the extravagance of his interpretations would certainly permit us to suspect that he added a great deal), we will never know what the core story was. The seed of the account may date to the mid–sixteenth century, that is, to the claim of a herdsman to have been cured at the ermita. There is also the possibility, implicit in some of the miracle stories, that the curative power attributed to the spring played a role in the development of the devotion. There is a strong possibility, reflected by Angel Betancurt, Agustín Vetancurt, and Botturini Benaduci, of a confusion between the stories that underlay the shrines of Guadalupe and Remedios. Betancurt's poem and Vetancurt's *Teatro mexicano* confuse Juan Diego and Juan Tovar, and Botturini Benaduci called the latter Juan Bernardino de Tovar. This opens the way for the speculation that the protagonists of Guadalupe evolved from the discoverer of Remedios. That would support my conjecture that the story of Juan Bernardino was a later addition to the original Guadalupe account. The story of the cure of Tovar at Guadalupe may reflect a relationship between the two. It could also have been an attempt to subordinate La Gachupina to La Criolla, just as Betancurt's poem may have been the opposite.

In this hypothesis the ermita was founded about 1555 and dedicated to the Nativity of Mary. An image of the Immaculate Conception, probably painted by an Indian, was placed there from the beginning. That image is the original, unretouched part of the one presently in the basilica. It followed the standard iconography of the time, that is, the Virgin without child, with hands folded, looking to her right, head slightly bowed, and usually a moon beneath her feet. The association with the Nativity and the allied devotion of the Immaculate Conception (which was very popular among Spaniards) remained throughout the colonial period.[11] A reputation for working miracles almost immediately grew up, perhaps because a herdsman claimed to have been cured there or perhaps of some less creditable claims. This reputation at various times attached to the image, the shrine in general, the spring, and the Villaseca statue. Almost from the beginning the ermita became associated with the Extremaduran Guadalupe, and the image was retouched to resemble the secondary image at that shrine. One motive may have been to make Tepeyac more attractive to the peninsular population of Mexico City, such as Alonso de Villaseca, in an effort to get them to patronize and support it. This change in emphasis was probably the work of Archbishop Montúfar, whose procession and placing of the image was changed by legend into that of Zumárraga of 26 December 1531.

In this explanation it is possible that an Indian named Juan Diego actually existed and somehow became the protagonist of the legend. If indeed he lived, he never experienced in reality the events narrated in the *Nican mopohua*. For all the attention given to him in the early accounts, no serious move toward his canonization was made until the twentieth century. The Indian witnesses at the 1665 to 1666 inquiry gave evidence of an incipient cultus: how the Indians sought Juan Diego's intercession for good harvests and how they regarded him as a holy and upright man who led a retired and penitential life at Tepeyac.[12] Why was there no move to canonize him? Obviously, because he was an Indian. A native saint would have been a rallying point for the natives that no peninsular or criollo wanted. Like the education of the Indians at Santa Cruz de Tlatelolco, it would have destroyed the myth of Indian inferiority and hence the economic basis of life in New Spain. This failure to promote Juan Diego to sainthood is even more notable when one remembers that there has been only one canonized saint in Mexican history: a Franciscan lay brother martyred in Japan.

Guadalupe still remains the most powerful religious and national symbol in Mexico today. The symbolism, however, does not rest on any objective historical basis. Despite that it will probably endure, if only because it can be interpreted and manipulated by succeeding generations to meet the needs of the Mexican people.

Chronology

1521	August. Tenochtitlan falls to Cortés.
1524	Arrival of Toribio de Motolinía and "The Twelve" in New Spain.
1527	12 December: Juan de Zumárraga appointed bishop of Mexico.
1530	Apparition of the Virgin at Tepeyac according to the Códice Gómez de Orozco.
1531	9–12 December: days of the apparitions according to Mateo de la Cruz (1660).
	26 December: traditional date for installation of image at Tepeyac.
	Year of the apparitions according to Miguel Sánchez and the *Nican mopohua.*
	Apparition of the Virgin at Tepeyac according to the Annals of Bartolache (eighteenth century).
1532	17 November: letter of Franciscans of Cuauhtitlan to Charles I.
1533	27 April: Juan de Zumárraga consecrated first bishop of Mexico in Valladolid, Spain.
1536	Cathedral chapter established in Mexico City.
1537	Garcés's *De habilitate et capacitate gentium.*
	2 June: *Sublimis Deus* of Paul III.
1541	Toribio de Motolinía's *Historia de los indios de la Nueva España.*
1544	Epidemic. Reputed procession of children to Tepeyac, according to the *Nican motecpana* (1649).
	Traditional date of death of Juan Bernardino.
	Cervantes de Salazar's *Dialogues.*
1547	Diocese of Mexico elevated to archdiocese.
	Publication of *Regla cristiana breve.*
1548	3 June: death of Zumárraga.
	Traditional date of death of Juan Diego.
	Death of Juan Diego according to the Annals of Bartolache (eighteenth century).

1551	Appointment of Alonso de Montúfar as archbishop of Mexico.
1553	Montúfar takes possession of the see of Mexico.
1555–1556	Time of founding of chapel at Tepeyac according to the report of Antonio Freire (1570).
	Time of founding of chapel at Tepeyac according to the report of Viceroy Martín Enríquez (1575).
1555	First Mexican Provincial Council.
	Apparition of Virgin at Tepeyac according to Annals of Juan Bautista.
	First recorded appointment of priest to ermita of Tepeyac.
1556	6 September: Guadalupan sermon of Archbishop Montúfar.
	8 September: responding sermon of fray Francisco de Bustamante.
	9 September: Archbishop Montúfar orders investigation of Bustamante sermon.
	Apparition of Virgin at Tepeyac according to Chimalpahin.
	Apparition of Virgin at Tepeyac according to the *Anales antiguos de Mexico y sus contornos* (ca. 1625).
1556–1562	Map of Uppsala, earliest depiction of ermita at Tepeyac.
1557	Beginnning of conflict between people of Teotihuacan and the Augustinians.
1557–1560	Time of founding of chapel at Tepeyac according to Juan de Velasco (1571–1574).
1560	Change of name of ermita at Tepeyac according to Diego de Santa María's second report (24 March 1575).
1562	1 July: *censo* of Martín de Aranguren and annuity for chapel at Tepeyac, describing Montúfar as its founder.
	Avila-Cortés conspiracy.
	Change of name of ermita at Tepeyac according to Diego de Santa María's first report (12 December 1574).
1563	2 April: will of Francisco de Verdugo Quetzalmamalitzin.
1564	Death of Bartolomé de las Casas.
1565	Alonso de Molina's *Vocabulario*.
1566	15 September: procession to Tepeyac organized by Archbishop Montúfar.
	Silver statue donated to ermita at Tepeyac by Juan de Villaseca.
1570	10 January: Antonio Freire's report on the status of the chapel at Guadalupe.
1571–1574	Report of Juan de Velasco on chapel at Guadalupe.
1571	Establishment of Inquisition in Mexico.
1572	7 March: death of Archbishop Montúfar.
	Pedro Moya de Contreras appointed archbishop of Mexico.
1573	Jubilee indulgences granted to chapel at Guadalupe.
	Miles Philips passes through Tepeyac.

1574	12 December: Diego de Santa María reports to Philip II about the chapel at Guadalupe. Annals of Juan Bautista.
1575	24 March: second report of Diego de Santa María on the chapel at Guadalupe. 28 March: Pope Gregory XIII extends jubilee indulgences for the chapel at Guadalupe for ten years. 15 May: Council of the Indies asks Viceroy Martín Enríquez and Archbishop Moya de Contreras for reports on the chapel at Guadalupe. 23 September: report of Enríquez on the chapel at Guadalupe. 25 September: report of Archbishop Moya de Contreras on chapel at Guadalupe. 17 December: Archbishop Moya de Contreras writes to Pope Gregory XIII to acknowledge extension of indulgences for the chapel at Guadalupe.
1576	Epidemic of matlazahuatl. Vision of Virgin by Miguel de San Jerónimo. Statue of Remedios brought to city. Archbishop Moya de Contreras issues a constitution allotting surplus income from the chapel at Guadalupe to orphans' dowries.
1577	Sahagún's condemnation of Guadalupe in the appendix on superstitions to his *Historia general*.
1579	Diego Valadés's *Retórica cristiana*.
1580	Diego Durán's *Historia de las Indias de Nueva España*.
1585	6 January–21 October: Third Mexican Provincial Council. 23 July: Alonso Ponce and companions pass near Guadalupe.
1588	Publication of José de Acosta's *De promulgatione evangelii apud barbaros*.
1589	Juan Suárez de Peralta completes *Tratado del descubrimiento de las Indias*.
1589–1596	*Anales antiguos de Mexico y sus contornos*.
1590	José de Acosta's *Historia natural y moral de las Indias*.
1596	Completion of Gerónimo de Mendieta's *Historia eclesiástica indiana*. Agustín Dávila Padilla's *Historia de la fundacion y discurso de la provincia de Santiago de Mexico, de la Orden de Predicadores*.
1597	Statue of Remedios brought to city to stop drought. Gabriel de Talavera's *Historia de N. S. de Guadalupe*.
1598	Putative date of Fernando Alvarado Tezozomoc's *Crónica mexicana*.
1600–1625	Annals of Chimalpahin.
1600	29 August: cathedral chapter transfers titular feast of chapel at Guadalupe from 8 September to 10 September.
1604	May: Death of Gerónimo de Mendieta.
1605	August: Death of Antonio Valeriano, supposed author of *Nican mopohua*.

1606	Earliest known reproduction of present image of Guadalupe by Baltasar de Echave Orio.

1609   Publication of Tezozomoc's *Cronica mexicayotl*.

1611   Juan de Grijalva's *Cronica de la orden de N. P. S. Augustin en las prouincias de la Nueva España*.
Antonio Daza's *Chronica general de S. Francisco y su apostolica orden*.
Alonso Fernández's *Historia eclesiastica*.
Martín de León's *Camino del cielo*.

1615   Juan de Torquemada's *Monarquía indiana*.
Samuel Stradanus's engraving of the present image of Guadalupe.

1616   Statue of Remedios brought to city at initiative of Archbishop Juan de la Serna to stop drought.

1620   Antonio de Remesal's *Historia general de las Indias occidentales*.

1622   8 September: Juan de Cepeda's sermon on the *vocación* of Guadalupe.
Luis de Cisneros's *Historia del principio . . . de Nuestra Señora de los Remedios*.
Dedication of the new church at Guadalupe by Archbishop de la Serna.

1625   Thomas Gage makes two references to Guadalupe in his *Travels*.

1629–1634   Great flood in Mexico City.

1634   *Coplas a la partida* and sonnet on return of image to Tepeyac.

1639   Statue of Remedios brought to city because of drought and threat of Dutch attack.

1641   Statue of Remedios brought to city because of drought.

1642   Statue of Remedios brought to city for safety of flota.

1643   13 September: rescue of Francisco de Almazán from charging bull through intercession of Guadalupe, according to Florencia.

1648   Miguel Sánchez's *Imagen de la Virgen María*.
Juan de Correa's *Tratado de la qualidad manifiesta, qve el Mercurio tiene*.

1649   Luis Laso de la Vega's *Huey tlamahuiçoltica*.

1653   Statue of Remedios brought to city because of drought.

1660   12 December: Guadalupan sermon of José de Vidal Figueroa at Guadalupe.
Mateo de la Cruz's *Relación de la milagrosa aparición de la Santa Virgen de Guadalupe*.

1661   April: Bishop Diego Osorio de Escobar y Llamas of Puebla becomes administrator of archdiocese of Mexico.

1662   Francisco de Siles undertakes move for feast and proper office on 12 December.
Publication in Spain of Mateo de la Cruz's *Relación de la milagrosa aparición de la Santa Virgen de Guadalupe*, sponsored by Pedro de Gálvez.

1663	Statue of Remedios brought to city for reasons unknown.
1664	Escobar y Llamas named viceroy.
1665	2 September: death of Archbishop Alonso Cuevas y Dávalos of Mexico.
	11–19 December: judges appointed for capitular inquiry into Guadalupe.
1666	3 January: appointment of interpreters for capitular inquiry.
	7 January: testimony of Marcos Pacheco.
	8 January: testimony of Gabriel Suárez.
	9 January: testimony of Andrés Juan.
	10 January: testimonies of Juan de la Concepción and Pablo Suárez.
	11 January: testimony of Martín de San Luis.
	19 January: testimony of Juan Suárez.
	22 January: testimony of Pedro Oyanguren.
	25 January: testimony of Bartolomé de Tapia.
	27 January: testimony of Antonio de Mendoza.
	18 February: testimony of Miguel Sánchez.
	28 February: testimonies of Juan de Herrera and Pedro de San Simón.
	2 March: testimony of Diego de Monroy.
	5 March: testimonies of Juan de San José and Pedro de San Nicolás.
	11 March: testimonies of Miguel de Cuevas Dávalos and Diego Cano Moctezuma.
	13 March: first inspection of the image by the viceroy, Poblete, and assorted clerics and artists.
	22 March: written testimony of Luis Becerra Tanco.
	28 March: inspection of the image by the *protomedicato* of New Spain.
	Becerra Tanco publishes his testimony as *Origen milagroso del santuario de Nuestra Señora de Guadalupe*.
1667	16 January: Archbishop of Mexico forbids opening of protective case around image for devotional purposes.
	2 March: suit by descendants of Andrés de Tapia.
	4 March: papers of the capitular inquiry arrive in Seville.
	10 June: preservation of family of Pedro de Quijada from lightning through intercession of Guadalupe, according to Florencia.
	Statue of Remedios brought to city for reasons unknown.
1668	Statue of Remedios brought to city for reasons unknown.
	Rescue of the vicar of Guadalupe in a mule accident, according to Florencia.
1669	Foundation of the Congregación Eclesiástica de María Santísima de Guadalupe in Querétaro.
	José López de Avilés: *Ueridicum admodum anagramma*.
1671	8 September: Guadalupan sermon of Juan de San Miguel at the cathedral in Mexico City.

1672 12 December: Guadalupan sermon of Juan de Mendoza at the convent of San Francisco in Mexico City.

Guadalupan sermon of José de Herrera at the convent of the religious of Saint Catherine of Siena, Mexico City.

1674 22 March: death of Miguel Sánchez. Obituary by Antonio de Robles.

1675 Republication of Becerra Tanco's *Origen milagroso* under title *Felicidad de Mexico*.

1678 Statue of Remedios brought to city for reasons unknown.

1679 16 April: Guadalupan sermon of Antonio Delgado y Buenrostro in the cathedral, Havana, Cuba.

1680 Bernardo de Riofrío's *Centonicvm Virgilianum*.

Sigüenza y Góngora's *Primavera indiana*.

Completion of church of Nuestra Señora de Guadalupe in Querétaro, the first one outside of Mexico City.

1681 12 December: Guadalupan sermon of Juan de Robles in Querétaro.

1682 12 December: Guadalupan sermon of Luis de Santa Teresa in Querétaro.

1683 Guadalupan sermon of José de Olivares.

1684 12 December: Guadalupan sermon of Lorenzo Benítez at convent of San Francisco in Mexico City.

Cure of María Altamirano Villanueva at Guadalupe, according to Florencia.

1685 Statue of Remedios brought to city because of drought.

Guadalupan sermon of Bartolomé de Navarro at Puebla.

1686–1687 Guadalupan sermon of Manuel de San José.

1688 Francisco de Florencia's *Estrella del norte*.

1689 Sigüenza y Góngora's *Piedad heroyca de Don Fernando Cortes*.

1690 12 November: edict of faith read in church at Guadalupe.

Guadalupan sermon of Pedro Manso.

Church of San Bernardo rededicated to Guadalupe.

1698 Agustín Vetancurt's *Teatro mexicano*.

1700 Guadalupan sermon of Juan Antonio Lobatto.

1701 8 December: Guadalupan sermon of Juan de San José at Sombrerete.

1708 Foundation of Franciscan missionary college at Zacatecas under patronage of Guadalupe.

1709 Guadalupan sermon of Juan de Goicoechea for dedication of new church at Tepeyac.

1710 Guadalupan sermon of Juan de Goicoechea at Guadalupe.

1711 20 December: Guadalupan sermon of Antonio de Ayala.

Guadalupan sermon of Manuel de Argüello at Guadalupe.

1712	6 May: copy of *Relación mercurina* signed by Joseph Pérez de la Fuente.
1720–1721	Guadalupan sermon of Matías Sáenz de San Antonio at Zacatecas.
1720	12 December: Guadalupan sermon of Juan Antonio de Segura.
1722–1723	Second archdiocesan inquiry into Guadalupe.
1725	12 December: Guadalupan sermon of Angel Maldonado, bishop of Oaxaca, at dedication of a church to Guadalupe in Oaxaca.
1731	12 December: Guadalupan sermon of Bartolomé de Ita y Parra. Guadalupan sermon of Miguel de Aroche.
1732	12 December: Guadalupan sermon of Cosme Borruel at Zacatecas.
1733	26 December: Guadalupan sermon of Juan de Villa in Mexico City.
1736	Second epidemic of matlazahuatl. Arrival of Lorenzo Botturini Benaduci in New Spain.
1737	Image of Remedios brought to city to end epidemic. 10–19 January: novena to end epidemic. 26 January: beginning of novena at Guadalupe to stop epidemic. 27 April: oath of patronato to Guadalupe. 26 May: publication of the oath and the patronato.
1738	Juan Pablo Cetina challenges celebration of the patronato in Puebla.
1742	12 December: Guadalupan sermon of Manuel Ignacio Farías at Valladolid. Guadalupan sermon of Nicolás de Segura.
1743	24 April: Guadalupan sermon of José Fernández de Palos in Mexico City. 12 December: Guadalupan sermon of Bartolomé de Ita y Parra. Guadalupan sermon of José Arlegui at San Luis Potosí. Arrest of Botturini Benaduci.
1744	12 December: Guadalupan sermon of Joaquín Osuna at Guanajuato.
1744–1746	Botturini Benaduci revises the *Idea de una nueva historia general de la America Septentrional*.
1746	12 December: Guadalupan sermon of Bartolomé de Ita y Parra. Patronato accepted by the cities of New Spain. Cayetano de Cabrera y Quintero's *Escudo de armas de Mexico*. Rome approves establishment of a collegiate chapter at Guadalupe.
1747	4 December: proclamation of the patronato over New Spain.
1748	12 December: Guadalupan sermon of Francisco Javier Carranza in Querétaro.
1750	Abbot and prebendaries take possession of their offices at La Colegiata.
1751	30 April: second inspection of the image by experts. 24 June: pueblo of Guadalupe raised to rank of villa.

1754   25 May: bull *Non est equidem* of Benedict XIV confirms patronato and proper mass and office.

1755   12 December: Guadalupan sermon of Andrés de la Santísima Trinidad.

12 December: Guadalupan sermon of José Rubio de Salinas in Mexico City.

1756   11 November: Guadalupan sermon of Cayetano Antonio de Torres in Mexico City.

12 December: Guadalupan sermon of José Ponce de León in Pátzcuaro.

12 December: Guadalupan sermon of Juan José Ruiz de Castañeda.

Guadalupan sermon of Jerónimo Morales Sigala in Oaxaca.

Miguel Cabrera's *Maravilla americana*.

1757   14 February: Guadalupan sermon of Pedro Uturriaga in Yucatan.

8 October: Guadalupan sermon of José Rodríguez de Vallejo in Querétaro.

9 October: Guadalupan sermon of Javier Evangelista Contreras in San Luis Potosí.

10 October: Guadalupan sermon of José de Gauna at San Luis Potosí.

11 October: Guadalupan sermon of Antonio Muñoz de Castiblanque at San Luis Potosí.

16 October: Guadalupan sermon of Ignacio Luis de Valderas Colmenero at Querétaro.

Ponce, Puerto Rico, accepts the patronato.

Proper feast and office of Guadalupe extended to all Spanish dominions.

1758   11 June: Guadalupan sermon of José Alfaro y Acevedo at Zacatecas.

September: Guadalupan sermons of Luis Beltrán de Beltrán, José Jorge de Alfaro, Manuel José Cassares, José Camacho, and Juan de Dios Ruiz, at Zacatecas.

12 December: Guadalupan sermon of Antonio de Paredes in Puebla.

12 December: Guadalupan sermon of Francisco Javier Lascano at Guadalupe.

Guadalupan sermon of Manuel Antonio Martínez de los Ríos at Cuernavaca.

1758(?)   Guadalupan sermon of Sancho Reynoso at the Colegio de San Luis de la Paz.

1759   Ignacio de Paredes's *Promptuario: manual mexicano*.

1765   23 June: Guadalupan sermon of Luis Beltrán de Beltrán at Guadalupe, against drought.

1767   Expulsion of Jesuits from New Spain.

1768   15 May: Guadalupan sermon of Agustín de Bengoechea at Guadalupe, against drought.

1771   17 May: Guadalupan sermon of Juan Agustín Morfi at Guadalupe, for
        pilgrimage of farmers.

1777   Guadalupan sermon of José Patricio Fernández de Uribe at
        Guadalupe.

1778   12 December: Guadalupan sermon of Francisco de San Cirilo at
        Guadalupe.

1781   27 May: Guadalupan sermon of Juan Gregorio de Campos at
        Guadalupe.

1782   12 May: Guadalupan sermon of Pablo Antonio Peñuelas at
        Guadalupe.
        Francisco Javier Clavigero's *Breve ragguaglio della prodigiosa e rinomata
        immagine della Madonna di Guadalupe di Messico.*

1787   Inspection of the image by five painters at the instigation of
        Bartolache.

1790   José Ignacio Bartolache's *Manifiesto satisfactorio.*

1791   7 May: Guadalupan sermon of López de Murto at San Luis Potosí.

1793   Ignacio Carrillo y Pérez's *Pensil americano.*

1794   12 December: Guadalupan sermon of Servando Teresa de Mier.
        Composition of Fernández de Uribe's *Disertacion historico-critica.*
        Juan Bautista Muñoz's "Memoria sobre las apariciones y el culto de
        Nuestra Señora de Guadalupe."

1795   22 October: inspection of the image by Conde y Oquendo and painter
        José de Alcíbar.

1797   June: six letters of Servando Teresa de Mier to Juan Bautista Muñoz.

1801   Publication of Fernández de Uribe's *Disertacion historico-critica.*

1804   José Miguel Guridi y Alcocer's sermon on Guadalupe.

1820   Posthumous publication of Fernández de Echeverría y Veytia's
        Baluartes de México.

Notes

Abbreviations

BNAH   Biblioteca Nacional de Antropología e Historia, Mexico City, Mexico

BNM   Biblioteca Nacional, Mexico City, Mexico

BNF   Bibliothèque Nationale de France, Paris, France

THG   *Testimonios históricos guadalupanos*. Ed. Ernesto de la Torre Villar and Ramiro Navarro de Anda. Mexico City: Fondo de Cultura Económica, 1982

Introduction

1. These are cited in Vera, *Tesoro guadalupano*, 69, 77–78, 113–15, 128–32, 201, 323–24.
2. Boban, *Document*, 2:197, n. 1.
3. *Investigación histórica y documental*, 18.
4. Cited by Taylor, "The Virgin of Guadalupe," 9.
5. Jiménez Moreno, *Estudios de historia colonial*, 120–21; Wolf, "The Virgin," 34–39; Campbell, "The Virgin of Guadalupe," 5; Paz, foreword to Lafaye, *Quetzalcoatl and Guadalupe*, xi.
6. Taylor, "The Virgin of Guadalupe," 9–10.
7. Peggy Liss, "A Cosmic Approach Falls Short: A Review of Jacques Lafaye's *Quetzalcoatl and Guadalupe: The Formation of Mexican National Consciousness, 1531–1813*," *Hispanic American Historical Review* 57, no. 4 (November 1977): 707–11. See also the more favorable review of the French version by John Leddy Phelan, *Hispanic American Historical Review* 55, no. 1 (February 1975): 104–7.
8. Rodríguez, *Guadalupe: ¿Historia o símbolo?*, 82.
9. O'Gorman, *Destierro de sombras*, 30, 35–38, 39–40, 43, 44, 48–49, 50, 145–48.
10. Kurtz, "The Virgin of Guadalupe," 195.
11. Ibid., 197.
12. Ibid., 203.
13. Ibid., 204, 205, 207. In support of these assertions Kurtz cites Chauvet, *Fray Juan de Zumárraga*, 113, where Chauvet says that Cortés helped in the collection

of funds, that in the five years after 1531 six times as many Indians were baptized as in the period 1524 to 1531, and that Zumárraga never again suffered serious opposition. All these statements are gratuitous and not in accord with known facts. In the same footnote Kurtz also cites Steck's translation of Motolinía's *Historia* but without citing a specific page. In actuality Steck makes no assertions like those in Kurtz's article. His primary concern is with Motolinía's silence about the apparitions.

14. Kurtz, "Guadalupe," 207.
15. Harrington, "Mother of Death," 26.
16. Ibid., 31. Harrington's source for these statements is Sahagún, *Florentine Codex*, ed. Anderson and Dibble, part 2, book 1, "The Gods," 4. Sahagún says that Teteoinnan was also called Heart of the Earth (Tlalli yollo) and Our Grandmother (Toci), but he makes no mention of Tonantzin or Tepeyac.
17. Harrington, "Mother of Death," 38.
18. Ibid., 47–48.
19. Campbell, "The Virgin of Guadalupe," 7.
20. Ibid.
21. Ibid., 12.
22. Ibid.
23. Ibid., 13.
24. Peterson, "The Virgin of Guadalupe," 39.
25. Ibid., 42.
26. Ibid., 45.
27. Taylor, "The Virgin of Guadalupe," 11.
28. Ibid., 14.
29. Ibid., 23.
30. Ibid., 15.
31. Ibid., 21.
32. In extenuation it should be noted that Cuevas's adult life coincided with the most difficult period of modern Mexican history, especially in relations between Church and state. Ernesto de la Torre Villar's evaluation is instructive. "That period, so critical for traditional values, in which many felt that the country was suffering shipwreck, impelled Mariano Cuevas to defend those aspects and men of our history who were being impugned and to fight in turn on various occasions, without mature reflection and sufficient evidence, those personalities and events that he considered opposed. 'It is my duty,' he once told me, 'to defend the authentic values of Mexico and the men to whom we owe our origins, freedom, and progress'" (Torre Villar, *Mexicanos ilustres*, 2:102).
33. This claim, which is frequently found in works on Guadalupe, is also cited in the process for the beatification of Juan Diego. See *Congregatio pro Causis Sanctorum*, viii, xvi. This is also called a *positio*, which is a combination of biography and evaluation of a candidate's fitness for canonization.
34. Vaillant, *Aztecs of Mexico*, 185; Weckmann, *La herencia*, 1:240, n. 12. The thesis that the friars were responsible for the devotion has been rejected by de la Maza, *El guadalupanismo mexicano*, 21.

35. Candelaria, *Popular Religion*, vii.
36. Pius XII, "Christifidelibus," 265–66.
37. The decree of beatification, 6 May 1990, is reproduced in the *Acta Apostolicae Sedis*, 4 September 1990, 853–55.
38. Elizondo, "Popular Religion," 39–40. Emphasis in original.
39. McKenzie, "¡Viva La Guadalupana!," 3.
40. *Acta Apostolicae Sedis*, 5 November 1990, 1405; Hebblethwaite, "Beatification," 8. For a good summary of the liberationist aspects of Guadalupe, see also Hoornaert, *Guadalupe*: "The truth of Guadalupe is the truth of the oppressed," for the oppressor cannot listen to the oppressed without being changed (18).
41. Hoornaert does this at some length (Hoornaert, *Guadalupe*, 14).
42. Gibson, *The Aztecs*, 498, n. 140.
43. Taylor, "The Virgin of Guadalupe," 25.

Chapter 1

1. Mexica (pronounced approximately Meh-SHEE-ca) is the more correct term for the people popularly but inaccurately known as Aztecs. In the colonial period the term *Mexicano* could mean (1) an inhabitant of Mexico City; (2) a Mexica Indian; (3) the Nahuatl, or Aztec, language. The term Nahua as used in this study refers to a linguistic and cultural grouping in the central Mexican plateau that shared a common language, Nahuatl, and a common culture associated with that language. Some of the material in this chapter is adapted from my "Iberian Catholicism."
2. In the Spanish imperial system the dependencies were divided into kingdoms (*reinos*), each one a constitutive part of the empire.
3. [Gage], *Thomas Gage's Travels*, 6; [Velasco], *Geografía y descripción*, cited in Israel, *Race, Class, and Politics*, 89. For a good survey of the criollos in the first century of Spanish rule, see Bacigalupo, *A Changing Perspective*.
4. Gibson, *The Aztecs*, 118.
5. Karttunen and Lockhart, *Nahuatl in the Middle Years*, 49–51; Lockhart, *The Nahuas after the Conquest*, 263–318, 428, table 10.1.
6. After his election as Holy Roman emperor, he was known as Charles V outside of Spain, a designation still favored by historians writing in English. Since the context of this work is entirely within the Spanish empire, the Spanish listing has been retained.
7. Ricard, *The Spiritual Conquest*, 307.
8. Halliczer, *The Comuneros of Castile*, 46.
9. The best single treatment of this in English is Christian, *Local Religion*; for a briefer summary, see Payne, *Spanish Catholicism*, chap. 2.
10. Taylor, "The Virgin of Guadalupe," 21.
11. Coudert, "The Myth," 85.
12. For an excellent treatment of this subject, see Burkhart, *The Slippery Earth*, throughout.
13. Dibble, "The Nahuatilization of Christianity," 225–33.

14. Burkhart, *The Slippery Earth*, 15.
15. Although there are many histories of individual apparitions and devotions, there are few of the apparition genre itself. In English the best is Christian, *Apparitions*, throughout; see also his *Local Religion*, chap. 3; and Staehlin, *Apariciones*, throughout.
16. Part of the apparition genre involved the finding of images by farm animals, especially bulls and oxen. "The bull is an appropriate intermediary between culture and nature; so too is the herdsman. . . . The herders are the society's interface with nature and know its ways best. They are the most 'wild' of the people" (Christian, *Apparitions*, 19).
17. Ibid., 73.
18. Christian, *Local Religion*, 82.
19. Christian, *Apparitions*, 6.
20. The summary given here is taken from Talavera, *Historia*, 13r–16v. A summary of the earliest known account contained in a manuscript dated 1440 in the Archivo Histórico Nacional, Madrid, is given by Christian, *Apparitions*, 88–92. See also Lafaye, *Quetzalcoatl and Guadalupe*, 221–22. A somewhat more detailed one can be found in Villafañe, *Compendio historico*, 264. For an interesting, brief treatment from a somewhat different perspective, see Montes Bardo, "Iconografía," 273–78.
21. A good summary of the various versions can be found in Fernández de Echeverría y Veytia, *Baluartes de México*, 565–77.
22. One version of the story says that on the Noche Triste the Virgin saved the fleeing Spaniards by appearing before the startled Mexica and throwing dust in their eyes. It was also said that Saint James, the patron saint of Spain, had appeared with her.
23. Ibid., 566.
24. The motif of the miraculous belt was to be found in many apparition stories. A chasuble that, according to legend, the Virgin Mary had given to Saint Leander of Seville became a holy belt in later versions, although other saints or holy persons were named as recipients. See Christian, *Apparitions*, 52–54.

Chapter 2

1. The *positio* of the process of beatification refers to Juan Diego as an Indian of the Chichimeca race and the peoples of Texcoco, Tlacopan, and Cuauhtitlan as Chichimecas, though no source is cited (*Congregatio pro Causis Sanctorum*, ix, 10). None of the early accounts of the Guadalupe apparitions actually gives his specific race—he was merely an *indio* or *macehual*. It is difficult to discern what the authors or editors of this document mean by Chichimeca. Gerhard says that prior to the Spanish conquest Cuauhtitlan had had Tepanec rulers and its language was Nahuatl (Gerhard, *Guide*, 127). The *Positio* also describes him as a *principal*, or "village leader," who was not just a farmer but also worked as a potter and businessman (ibid., ix, xxxvi, 12). No evidence for this assertion, supposedly based on recent research, is to be found in any early account of the apparitions.

2. In the *Nican mopohua*, the day of the month of the apparitions is not specified. The name of the hill is found in two forms, Tepeyac and Tepeyacac. The first is used in this work, except when Tepeyacac is found in a quotation.

3. Juan Diego's reference to pre-Christian tradition has proved baffling for many commentators. Edmundo O'Gorman regards it as an attempt by the author to distinguish the apparition of the Virgin from any preconquest devotion on the same site (*Destierro de sombras*, 57). Burkhart mentions that "land of flowers" (*xochitlalpan*) was a Nahuatl name for one of the paradises of preconquest belief (*The Slippery Earth*, 76).

4. "In ipalnemohuani, in teyocoyani in Tloque Nahuaque in ilhuicahua in Tlalticpaque." The text uses terms that were appropriated from preconquest deities, specifically Tezcatlipoca, and applied by the friars to the Christian god. See Burkhart, *The Slippery Earth*, 39; Clendinnen, *Aztecs*, 75.

5. In the accepted version of the account as it is commonly told today, Juan Diego returned on Sunday to inform the Virgin of his interview with Zumárraga. This is not in the *Nican mopohua*. Rather, the narrative leaps immediately to Monday morning.

6. "In nepapan caxtillan tlaçoxochitl." Most later versions simply say "roses." Roses were not native to New Spain, and it is uncertain when they were introduced. Miguel Sánchez, in his testimony before the archdiocesan inquiry of 1665 to 1666, said that the flowers were of the kind called "of Alexandria" in Castile, but "of Castile" in New Spain. These were roses. See Sada Lambretón, *Las informaciones jurídicas*, facsimile 113. Molina defines *xochitl* as "rose or flower" (*Vocabulario*, Nahuatl to Spanish, 160). See also Lockhart, *The Nahuas after the Conquest*, 276.

7. "Nahuas conceived of the sacred in terms of a 'flower world': a sunny garden filled with flowers, brightly colored tropical birds and precious stones like jade and turquoise. Characterized by light, heat, fragrant aromas and beautiful music, this garden was sometimes described as located on a mountain; this links it to Tonacatepec 'Sunshine Mountain' or 'Sustenance Mountain,' the mythological source of food crops" (Burkhart, "The Cult of the Virgin of Guadalupe," 210).

8. Carlos de Sigüenza y Góngora, writing in 1689, was the first to give a native name for Juan Diego (*Piedad heroyca*, 63).

9. Becerra Tanco, "Origen milagroso," in THG, 331; Clavigero, "Breve noticia," 589.

10. "The same Indians who frequented the sanctuary availed themselves of the prayers of their compatriot, whether living or dead or buried in that very place; they set him up as an intercessor before Mary Most Holy in order to attain their petitions" (Cabrera y Quintero, *Escudo de armas de Mexico*, 345, no. 682).

11. The *Congregatio pro Causis Sanctorum* states that Juan Diego's remains were hidden so as to prevent popular veneration in violation of canon law about premature public cultus (xii). There is no evidence of any such deliberate hiding.

12. García Icazbalceta, "Carta," 63–65. García Icazbalceta also questioned whether a Franciscan bishop-elect would have servants. In 1797 Servando Teresa de Mier made the same observation, citing Dávila Padilla as saying that Bishop Julián

Garcés of Tlaxcala, even after his consecration, had no servants. Mier also pointed to the well-known poverty and simplicity of Zumárraga's life ("Cartas del Doctor," 818). On the other hand, Velázquez argues persuasively that Zumárraga had other persons, especially fellow Franciscans, in his household (*La aparición*, 439–40).

13. In general, Spanish churchmen and the Inquisition of the sixteenth century were skeptical about witchcraft, regarding it as a delusion or mental aberration. See *Historia de la Inquisición*, ed. Pérez Villanueva and Escandell Bonet, 463–64, 647, 913–18.

14. García Icazbalceta, "Carta," 62. Mendieta seems to be the principal source for this assertion, though he attributes the reason to the shortage of priests (*Historia*, chap. 49, 307). On the other hand, Juan de Grijalva described how it was administered in the earlier days (Grijalva, *Cronica*, 155–56).

15. On indigenous naming patterns after the conquest, see Lockhart, *The Nahuas after the Conquest*, 119–22.

16. Gerhard, *Guide*, 127. Ricard says that it was one of the first villages outside Mexico City evangelized by the Franciscans and definitely before 1531 (*Spiritual Conquest*, 64–65). Motolinía cited it as one of the two towns first evangelized outside of Mexico City (*Memoriales*, part 1, chap. 35 [191], 116). The same assertion, in almost identical wording, is to be found in Motolinía's *Historia*, 218–19.

17. *Cartas de Indias*, 54–61.

18. [Puga], *Provisiones*, 1:96v. On the other hand, Gerhard says that the Franciscan parish at Tlatelolco was not established until perhaps 1543 (*Guide*, 181). Velázquez tried to show that there had been some sort of church in Tlatelolco as early as 1529 (*La aparición*, 221). He based this on Motolinía's statement that from 1529 onward the Indians began to convert in larger numbers and build churches (Motolinía, *Memoriales*, part 1, chap. 35 [191], 116). He coupled this statement with Motolinía's description of the church at Tlatelolco and drew the somewhat feeble conclusion that it was built at that time. It should be kept in mind that the Franciscan parish and house in Tlatelolco was named Santiago, whereas the colegio was called Santa Cruz.

19. Becerra Tanco says that the natives would have pronounced it Tetuatolope ("Origen milagroso," in THG, 321). In Nahuatl documents one finds Hualalope and Cuatalope. For a detailed study of Nahuatl pronunciation of Spanish loan words, see Karttunen and Lockhart, *Nahuatl in the Middle Years*, 1–15, esp. 3–4, which discusses intervocalic *d* pronounced as *t* or *l*.

20. "Origen milagroso," in THG, 320–21.

21. The difficulty of using *tlaza* in this regard is that it is not an active verb. See Karttunen, *Analytical Dictionary of Nahuatl*, 303. The initial *te-* may also stand for the Spanish *de*.

22. *Estrella del norte*, chap. 17, par. 205, fols. 100r–v. Florencia himself did not accept this hypothesis because there was no evidence that the natives had ever used the name.

23. Weckmann, *La herencia*, 1:240.

24. One of the foremost defenders of the apparitions, Primo Feliciano Velázquez, also

believed that it is futile to seek a Nahuatl substratum. He confessed that he does not know why the Virgin chose to be called by that name ("Comentario a la historia original guadalupana," in López Beltrán, *La protohistoria guadalupana*, 168). Jiménez Moreno regarded such attempts as "clearly absurd" (*Estudios de historia colonial*, 121). The argument in favor of the Nahuatl originals has most recently been advanced by Fidel de Jesús Chauvet, "Historia del culto guadalupano," 21.

Chapter 3

1. The significance of this date in the history of the Guadalupe apparitions is immediately apparent, especially since the original patronal date of the chapel at Tepeyac was 8 September.
2. See Greenleaf, *The Mexican Inquisition*, 74–75, and *Zumárraga and the Mexican Inquisition*, 14–15, 68–75.
3. *Regla cristiana breve*, ed. Almoina, 58. For data on the first edition, see the bibliography. For a study of this work, see Alejos-Grau, *Juan de Zumárraga y su "Regla Cristiana Breve."*
4. Cuevas attempted at great length to find a reference to the apparitions in an undated letter from Zumárraga to Cortés that he found in the Archivo General de Indias, Seville, estante 51, cajón 6, legajo 3 (old enumeration). The key line for him is "Tell the Señora Marquesa [Cortés's wife] that I wish to give the cathedral church the name of the Conception of the Mother of God because on that day God and his mother wanted to grant this favor to this land which you won." Cuevas dated the letter 24 December 1531, the day before the vespers of the great procession that according to tradition took place for the transfer of the image. Zumárraga, however, was clearly referring to the feast of the Immaculate Conception (8 December) and to the favor that he saw in the conquest and conversion of New Spain. Cuevas sought, unsuccessfully in my view, to show that the bishop-elect was speaking of an event that took place within the octave of the Immaculate Conception, that is, between 8 and 16 December (*Album*, 32–39). For a lengthy and negative evaluation of Cuevas's thesis, see Bravo Ugarte, *Cuestiones históricas guadalupanas*, 39–45.
5. The will can be found in García Icazbalceta, *Zumárraga*, 3:285–94. See also *Zumárraga and His Family*, throughout.
6. Sánchez made this assertion in his testimony before the capitular inquiry of 1666. See Sada Lambretón, *Las informaciones jurídicas*, facsimile 115. Bartolomé García was also the source of the story that a paper shortage was responsible for the destruction of the original accounts of the apparitions. See chap. 7.
7. THG, 442–43. The incident of the fire was related and rejected by García Icazbalceta, "Carta," 24, but he gave no source, nor is it in the transcription of Cabrera's work in the THG, 442–43, nor in the first edition of 1746 (*Escudo de armas de Mexico*, 328, par. 653). The story of the fire was supposedly told by Mezquía to Juan Joaquín Sopeña, who in turn related it to José Patricio Fernández de Uribe in the later eighteenth century. See chap. 11.

8. Gil, "Las 'juntas eclesiásticas,'" throughout.

9. Ibid., 6–11. Gutiérrez Vega speaks of four (*Las primeras juntas*, 53–54, 69–77). The differences depend ultimately on the definition of junta.

10. Gil, "Las 'juntas eclesiásticas,'" 15–16; Llaguno, *La personalidad*, 14–22.

11. Llaguno, *La personalidad*, 22–26; Gutiérrez Vega, *Las primeras juntas*, 124–27, 128–32. The New Laws of 1542 were an unusual combination of Christian humanitarianism and practical politics. Their primary purpose was to put an end to the encomienda, or, perhaps more correctly, bring all encomiendas under the control of the crown. This would both free the Indians from exploitation and prevent the growth of a new quasi-feudal class in the New World. Because of strong opposition, the laws were eventually amended. Some churchmen opposed them because they believed that some sort of compulsory labor system was necessary for the good of the Indians and the preservation of the Christian state.

12. Llaguno, *La personalidad*, 26–29; Gutiérrez Vega, *Las primeras juntas*, 141–80.

13. Gil, "Las 'juntas eclesiásticas,'" 23–24.

14. It is reproduced in García Icazbalceta, *Zumárraga*, 3:94–122.

15. Garcés, *De habilitate*, unpaginated.

16. García Icazbalceta, "Carta," 26.

17. See Keen, *The Aztec Image*, 110–14.

18. *Memoriales*, chap. 44, 139–41.

19. Cuevas, *Historia*, 1:290–91.

20. Cuevas, *Album*, 97. On Ramírez, see Torre Villar, *Mexicanos ilustres*, 2:221–53. After the defeat of Maximilian in 1867, in whose government he had served, Ramírez went to Europe, taking a considerable portion of the Sigüenza y Góngora collection with him. He put some 1,290 items up for sale. He died at Bonn, Germany, on 4 March 1871. Part of the remaining collection was shipped back to Mexico. Some of the items are now in the Bancroft Library of the University of California, Berkeley, and others in the section Méxicains of the BNF.

21. *Santoral en mexicano*, vol. 1, ms. 1475, BNM. Garibay identified this sermon as an earlier version of a sermon on the apparition of Guadalupe to be found in ms. 1493 ("Los manuscritos en lengua náhuatl," 8, 16). They are, in fact, two different sermons.

22. The Spanish translation by Chimalpopoca Galicia is not accurate and at times is all but incomprehensible. It can be found in THG, 24–25. The Nahuatl original contains what appear to be grammatical errors and defects.

23. *Macehual* had the original meaning of "commoner" or "subject" but in seventeenth-century documents was often synonymous with Indian.

24. Tumpline (*mecapalli*) and digging stick (*huictli*) were common terms of humility, probably with working-class connotations. In the *Nican mopohua*, Juan Diego describes himself as a tumpline (*ca nimecapalli*), which literally means the cord across the forehead with which cargo carrriers (*tamemes*) hauled loads.

25. *Altepetl* (from "in atl in tepetl," the water and the hills) referred to Nahua municipal districts, different in concept and structure from those of the Spaniards. Because of this difference the term is usually left in the Nahuatl form rather than translated as "city" or "municipality." "The minimum requirements for an

altepetl as the Nahuas mainly used the word (in reference, that is, to preconquest times) are a territory; a set (usually a fixed canonical number) of named constituent parts; and a dynastic ruler or *tlatoani* (pl. *tlatoque*)" (Lockhart, *The Nahuas after the Conquest*, 15). For a discussion of this complex subject, see ibid., chap. 2, "Altepetl," throughout.

26. The term "Christians" was often synonymous with "Spaniards" but in this context seems to be more inclusive.

27. This part of the manuscript is somewhat garbled because of erasures and additions.

28. *Toquichtin* (our man), which appears several times in the manuscript, is a plural form and hence means "our men." In all probability it is a scribal error for *toquichtzin*, the reverential form, analogous to *toquichtzintli*, which also appears.

29. Translation conjectured.

30. The original Nahuatl is:

N[uest]ra Señora de + Guadalupe

[fol. 51r]Ynin huey tlamahuiçoltzin tot[ecuiyo] Dios in quimochihuili yn inpampatzinco cemicacaichpochtli S[an]ta M[ari]a ca yehuatl: in anquimocuilizque, in anquimocaquilizque, in quenin tlamahuiçoltica, quimonequilti mocal quechilitzinoz, mochantlalitzinoz in quimotocayoltilia cihuapilli S[an]ta M[ari]a tepeacac. Ca iuhquin in mochiuh, ce icnotlatzintli, macehualtzintli, ànel huel ytlateomatcatzin ynin icnohuictzintli, icnomecapaltzintli, yn oncan tepeacac tepetozcac nenentinenca, ànel àço tlanelhuatzintli, quimotàtaquilitinenca, yn oncan quimottititzino in Dios ytlaçonantzin, quimonochili, quimolhuili noXocoyouh, tla xonmohuica in huey altepetl ytic Mexico xicmolhuili yn ompa teoyotica tepachoa, arçobispo, Ca noconnequi, notlanequiliztica ynic nican in tepeacac nechmochâtilizque, nechmoquechililizque nocaltzin ynic oncan [fol. 51v] nechoncenmatiquihui nechtlatlauhtiquihui in tlaneltocanime, Christianosme; huel oncan in canin ochihuaz [*sic*] yn ìquac nechmotepantlàtòcatizque niman yà ynin icnooquichtzintli ixpantzinco necito *in huey teopixcatlatoani arçobispo, quimolhuili tlàtoanie* [italicized words are marginal corrections in manuscript] macamo nimitznotlapolotili, ca y[?] onechalmihuah [*sic*] yn ilhuicac Cihuapilli, onechmolhuili ynic nimitznolhuiliquiuh yn queni [*sic*] quimonequilitia yn ompa tepeacac mochihuaz moquetzaz cētetl ycaltzin ynic oncan quimotlatlauhtilizque in Christianosme huel yuh onechmolhuili in ca huel iyoca oncan in ca mochiuhtzinoz yn ìquac oncan quimotlatlahtilizque: Auh yn arçobispo àmo quimoneltoquîti ça quilmohuili tla yn tiquitoa nopiltze àço otictemic ànoçe otihuītica, intlanelli, neltiliztli *in tlein quitoa xicmolhuili* [italicized words are in margin, replacing deleted words in text] yn on cihuapilli yn tlein omitzmohuili, ma ytla nezcayotl, mitzmomaquili, ynic toconneltocazque, yn ca ye nelli, neltiztli in tlein tiquitoa. [fol. 52r] Occeppa *hualmocuep in toquichtin tlà-tlaocoxtihuitz: auh in tlàtòcacihuapilli occeppa* [these words written in margin to replace deleted words in text] quimottititzino: auh in toquichtin yn oquimottili, quimolhuili, Cihuapille Ca onihuia yn ompa otinechmotitlani: auh àmo nechmoneltoquitia in tlàtoani, çan nechmohuilia àço onictemic, ànoce onihuintic,

yhuan onechmolhuili ynic quimoneltoquitiz, ma ytla nezcayotl xinechmoma-
quili, ynic noconnotquililiz; auh in tlàtòcacihuapilli in Dios ytlaçonantzin, niman quimolhuili maca ximotlaocolti notelpochtzin, tla xoconmocuìcuili, xocon-
motìtequili yn oncan on cuecuepocatoc [sic] xochitzintli; ynin xochitl çan
tlamahuiçoltica yn oncan cuecuepon auh yn iquac yca tlalli huàhuaqui àcan tle-
xochitl cueponia yn ocontètec in toquichtin ic concuexano yn itilmá Ompa ya
in Mexico, quimolhuilito in teopixca tlàtoani: [fol. 52v] tlatoanie ca nicâ niquit-
quitz [sic] in xochitl onechmomaquili in ilhuicac cihuapilli ynic timotlanelto-
quitiz, in ca ye neltiliztli, ca ytlàtoltzin, ytlanequilitzin, in tleyn onimitznol-
huilìco in ca ye nelli in ca yèhuatzin onechmohuili, Auh yn ìquac quiçouh yn
itilmà ynic quimottitiliz in xochitl in arçobispo, oncan yhuâ quimottili ytilmat-
itech yn toquichtin oncan ycuiliuhtoca [sic], ye oncàn omocopinca nezcayotitzi-
no in tlàtòcacihuapilli, tlamahuiçoltica, ynic ye quinemotlaneltoquiti in arçobispo,—ixpantzinco motlanquaquetzinòque, quimomahuiztililique; auh ca
huel ye ehuatl, yn ixiptlatzin in tlàtòcacihuapilli y[?] çan tlamahuiçoltica, yn
itilmàtitech yn icnotlacatzintli mocopincaycuilotzino yn axcan ompa momanil-
tia in mochi cemanahuàcatocatl: oncan quimomachiltitihuitz, in quihualmotlat-
lauhtilia; auh in yèhuatzin yn ica yhueytetlaocoliliznanyotzin [fol. 53r] oncan
quinmopalehuilia, quinmomaquilia in tlein quimitlànililia, ca nelli ca yn aquin
huel quimotepantlàtòcatitzinoz, quimoçenmacatzinoz, tetlàçòtlaliztica huel
ytlacauhtzin mochiutzinoz in Dios ytlaçònantzin ça nelli ca huel quimopalehuil-
iz, quimoteyttitiliz in ca quimotlaçotilia in ca ycehuallotitlantzinco yècauhyotit-
lantzinco ma quetztinemi.

31. He said, "End of the XVIth century" (Cuevas, *Album*, 98). It appears, however,
that he was speaking of the Spanish copy in the New York Public Library.

32. *Congregatio pro Causis Sanctorum*, lxx; Moreno, "Los manuscritos en náhuatl," 89.

33. Cuevas, *Album*, 99.

34. *Historia de la literatura náhuatl*, 2:262–67, though he does not mention González
by name; O'Gorman, *Destierro de sombras*, 155–59. Garibay also included this thesis in the article on Guadalupe that he wrote for the *New Catholic Encyclopedia*
s. v. Guadalupe.

35. O'Gorman lists them: Mario Rojas Sánchez, Luis Medina Ascensio, Jesús Jiménez, Manuel Robledo Gutiérrez, Ramón Sánchez Flores, Ernesto de la Torre Villar, and Ramiro Navarro (*Destierro de sombras*, 206, n. 72).

36. Ibid., 205–6, 165–72, which gives the biography of González. His reputation
for sanctity (there was a move to have him canonized) is given on 172–83. See
also Rivera, *El intérprete Juan González*, 7–10.

37. O'Gorman, *Destierro de sombras*, 183–85. The portrait shows González kneeling
before a picture of Our Lady of Guadalupe, whereas all others show him before a
crucifix. He had a special devotion to Christ crucified. Another reason given by
O'Gorman is that there is no mention of the portrait or its inscription in Vera's
exhaustive *Tesoro guadalupano*, nor is there an allusion in any source prior to 1895,

when it was mentioned in the album published on the occasion of the coronation of the image (ibid., 191–92).

38. *Autos que se siguen ante el Illmo. y Rmo. Señor Arzobispo D. F. Joseph de Lanciego para las informaciones ad perpetuam en preparatorio juicio, para ocurrir a la Sta. Sede e implorar letras remisoriales cerca de la buena fama, y opinion del Vr. sacerdote Señor Doctor D. Juan Gonzalez*, Benson Latin American Collection, University of Texas at Austin General Libraries, G. 161 ms., fol. 45r; O'Gorman, *Destierro de sombras*, 181; *Congregatio pro Causis Sanctorum*, 170, 257. The reference given is from Castañeda and Autrey, *Guide*, México: Ciudad de México 1223, p. 103.

39. The accuracy of O'Gorman's statement can be questioned. In 1797 Servando Teresa de Mier wrote that Zumárraga did not know Nahuatl. See "Cartas del Doctor," 802.

40. O'Gorman, *Destierro de sombras*, 188–89. O'Gorman adds another factor, that is, that the Mexican bishops at that time were seeking a new proper office for the feast from Rome. The second nocturn of the office then in use employed the term *fertur* (it is said) in reference to the apparitions. The bishops were seeking a stronger endorsement. In an effort to thwart this, Vicente de Paúl Andrade and Antonio Icaza published a Latin translation of García Icazbalceta's letter to Labastida y Dávalos. O'Gorman gives a detailed description of the attempt to secure the new office (ibid., 190–91). He believes that against this background the identification of González as the interpreter was an attempt to make the Guadalupe tradition more concrete and credible. I am inclined to agree with this thesis.

41. *Cinco cartas*, 126–27; Franco, *Segunda parte*, 115–18.

42. O'Gorman's conclusions are (1) that the *Inin huey tlamahuiçoltzin* comes from the seventeenth century and that there was no older original; and (2) that the author was a Jesuit, probably Baltasar González (*Destierro de sombras*, 209–12). His reasons for the latter identification are based on what he perceives to be similarities of thought between González's introduction to Laso de la Vega's history of the apparitions and the contents of the *Inin huey tlamahuiçoltzin*: (1) the fact that González speaks not of the history of the apparitions but of "the miraculous appearance of the image," thus suppressing the antecedent wondrous appearances to Juan Diego, just as the *Inin huey tlamahuiçoltzin* does; (2) González does not use the name Guadalupe in reference to the image, just as the *Inin huey tlamahuiçoltzin* does not, but uses terms such as "Most Holy Virgin Mother of God" and "Queen of Heaven," just as the *Inin huey tlamahuiçoltzin* does; (3) González wanted to see devotion to the image popularized, but since a book like Laso's, printed in relatively few numbers, could not achieve this, he wrote his own account based on the *Nican mopohua*. I leave it to the reader to go to O'Gorman's book to evaluate his reasons, which I find very weak. It should also be noted that the version of the *Inin huey tlamahuiçoltzin* in the Monumentos Guadalupanos of the New York Public Library refers to it as a sermon, "Sermon de Santa Maria de Tepeyac" (series 1, vol. 2, fols. 240–53).

43. On native songs, see Garibay, "Temas guadalupanos III," 244–45; Lockhart, *The Nahuas after the Conquest*, 392–401.

44. Durán, *Historia*, 2:233.
45. BNM, ms. 1628bis.
46. Brinton, *Ancient Nahuatl Poetry*; [Peñafiel], *Colección de documentos*, 38–39; Garibay, "Temas guadalupanos III. El problema de los cantares (prosigue)," 381–420; *Cantares Mexicanos*.
47. Burkhart calls Bierhorst's interpretation "somewhat fanciful" but adds that his assertion "that the texts are not exact renditions of pre-Conquest compositions is a valid point" (*The Slippery Earth*, 57). For a critique of Bierhorst's thesis, see Lockhart, *Nahuas and Spaniards*, 141–57.
48. Garibay, "Temas guadalupanos III. El problema de los cantares (prosigue)," 392. Brinton, *Ancient Nahuatl Poetry*, 144, says that the poem was probably written by Zumárraga for his neophytes. This hardly seems credible.
49. *Cantares Mexicanos*, 220. Garibay also has a transcription, "Temas guadalupanos III," 394. Garibay omits the last line, both in the transcription and in his translation.
50. Garibay, "Temas guadalupanos III," 395.
51. *Cantares Mexicanos*, 221.
52. Cuevas, *Album*, 7, 22; "El 'Pregón del atabal,'" 23.
53. Chauvet, "Historia del culto," 23.
54. Garibay, "Temas guadalupanos III," 408.
55. *Cantares Mexicanos*, 62.
56. Florencia, *Estrella del norte*, chap. 15, par. 195, fol. 95v.
57. *Cantares Mexicanos*, 115.
58. Beristáin de Sousa dates the placing of the image in 1535 (*Biblioteca*, 2:146). The little information he gives on Plácido is taken from Florencia.
59. The date 1550 is given by Beristáin de Sousa, *Biblioteca*, 2:97.
60. Keen, *The Aztec Image*, 85–86; Díaz-Thomé, "Francisco Cervantes de Salazar," 17–41.
61. Moya de Contreras to Philip II, 25 March 1573, in *Cinco cartas*, 124–25.
62. Cervantes de Salazar, *Life in the Imperial and Loyal City of Mexico*, 75. In the sixteenth century the Spaniards began calling this site Tepeaquilla to distinguish it from Tepeaca in Tlaxcala.
63. Most of this material is drawn from Toussaint, "El Plano Atribuído a Alonso de Santa Cruz," 135–46. An ermita, or chapel of ease, was not a parish church in the technical sense but a chapel, with or without a resident priest, to which the faithful could go to hear mass (except on Easter Sunday) and go to confession. Ordinarily baptisms, confirmations, marriages, and funerals were not allowed in them.
64. Ibid., 140–43, 145–46.
65. It is reproduced in enlarged form in Pompa y Pompa, *Album*, 14.

Chapter 4

1. For a detailed analysis of the native annalists, see Lockhart, *The Nahuas after the Conquest*, 376–92; a briefer account is Garibay, "Temas guadalupanos I," 37–46.

Aztec paper was not usually made of maguey (*metl*), as is often thought and was asserted even in the colonial period, but of the inner bark of the wild fig tree. See Lenz, *El papel indígena mexicano*, and Vaillant, *Aztecs of Mexico*, 198–99. I wish to thank Professor Robert Ryal Miller for calling this to my attention.

2. For a detailed study of these annals, see Garibay, "Temas guadalupanos II," 155–69. This annalist should not be confused with the Juan Bautista, a contemporary, who was a Franciscan on the faculty of the college of Santa Cruz de Tlatelolco.

3. These dates are taken from Garibay, "Temas guadalupanos I," 53–54. In his later article, "Temas guadalupanos II," 157, he said that it covered the years 1528 to 1582. The author of the "Aditamentos" in *Investigación histórica y documental*, 170, said that he had consulted the document in the Biblioteca Real de Historia in Mexico City, whatever that may have been. The original manuscript of the annals is in the library of the basilica of Guadalupe and so was not available to me (Medina Ascensio, "Las fuentes esenciales," 101; Velázquez, *La aparición*, 65). There used to be a copy in the BNAH, but it disappeared in 1975. I have used the reproductions in Pompa y Pompa, *Album*, 50, and Velázquez, *La aparición*, 65–66.

4. Villaseca came to New Spain about ten years after the conquest and soon became wealthy. He donated heavily to religious causes and was especially devoted to Guadalupe. After his death his body was taken to the ermita, where a three-day vigil was held. He was also instrumental in bringing the Jesuits to New Spain and contributed so much to the Colegio de San Pedro y San Pablo that he was called its founder. For data on him, see Florencia, *Historia de la provincia*, 84–85, 115–17, 124–30, 150, 198–205, 297–321, 322–35. On his contributions to Remedios, see Florencia, *La milagrosa invencion*, 41.

5. Garibay, "Temas guadalupanos II," 163.

6. Cited in Velázquez, *La aparición*, 8.

7. Ibid., 11, n. 26.

8. Florencia, *Estrella del norte*, 191v–92r.

9. On Chimalpahin, see Schroeder, *Chimalpahin*, esp. chap. 1; Lockhart, *The Nahuas after the Conquest*, 387–89.

10. Chimalpahin, *Annales*, 278.

11. Ibid., 252.

12. CATA 373, no. 2.

13. Cuevas, *Album*, 46–49.

14. *Anales antiguos de Mexico*.

15. Medina Ascensio, "Las fuentes esenciales," 101; García Icazbalceta, *Apuntes*.

16. Garibay, "Temas guadalupanos I," 52.

17. Chimalpopoca Galicia's Spanish translation reads "12 Pedernal. Bajó la reina señora a Tepeyacac (*punto de los cerros, ò la entrada de ellos*) e igualmente entonces exhaló vapor la estrella (cometa)." The words in italics were inserted by Chimalpopoca Galicia and are not in the Nahuatl.

18. Cuevas, *Album*, 47. Garibay finds the same, or nearly the same, wording in two other annals. The one, which he identifies as Anónimo A, has "Za ye icuac popoca citlalin," and the *Anales de Tecamachalco* has "ipan xihuitl in citlalin popoca." He

claims that there is no source that speaks of a comet for 1556 but that there was definitely one in 1531 ("Temas guadalupanos I," 55).

19. Cuevas, *Album*, 53–55.

20. Garibay, "Temas guadalupanos I," 52–53. This may be the same one that López Beltrán calls the *Anales de Cuetlaxcoapan* (the Nahuatl name for Puebla), the original of which he said was in the Archivo Histórico of the Instituto Nacional de Antropología e Historia, Mexico (*La historicidad de Juan Diego*, 59). All that I was able to find was a typewritten Spanish translation, with the full title of Colección Gómez de Orozco, no. 184, "Traducción de los Anales de Tlaxcala y Puebla, 1524–1691. Lengua Española." The museum does not have the original Nahuatl manuscript. This appears to be the same as the one under consideration here. There is also the "Anales mexicanos: Puebla, Tepeaca, Cholula, 1524–1645" that once belonged to Alfredo Chavero. It is in Nahuatl but is not the same as that cited by Cuevas and Garibay. It says nothing about Guadalupe.

21. Velázquez, *La aparición*, 68–70.

22. "Las fuentes esenciales," 100.

23. Velázquez, *La aparición*, 69. Velázquez's transcription is more correct than that of Cuevas, *Album*, 53.

24. Cuevas, *Album*, 53. His Spanish translation of the Nahuatl is somewhat free: "Y también en este año (del nuevo-bien-venido sacerdote gobernante), siendo obispo Juan de Zumárraga, padre franciscano, se apareció la nuestra muy amada Madre de Guadalupe." Cuevas reproduces a photocopy of the original in his *Historia*, 1:273, and his transcription, 272, no. 1, has a slightly different orthography: "Nican ipan xihuitl huala presidente yancuican tlatocatica Mexico. Zanno ipan xihuitl in huel yancuican hualmoihuac teopixcatlatoani Obispo intocatzin Juan de Sumarraga, teopixqui de San Francisco, in huel icuac monextizino intotlasonantzin de Guadalupe." He cites Mariano Rojas, professor of Nahuatl at the Museo Nacional de México, as saying that the construction and vocabulary "son *propios* y *exclusivos* de la época raíz de la conquista," though he cites no evidence (ibid., emphasis in original). It should be noted that the photocopy puts all this material under the year 1530, a fact that Cuevas for some strange reason believes authenticates the document. The Spanish translation in the BNAH, Colección Gómez de Orozco, no. 184, 1, carries the date 13 caña 1531, but this is apparently an interpretation by the translator.

25. Garibay, "Temas guadalupanos I," 53. De la Maza says that it has been corrected to 1530 (*El guadalupanismo mexicano*, 29).

26. BNAH, Colección Gómez de Orozco, 8, 10.

27. Garibay, "Temas guadalupanos I," 53.

28. Quoted in Velázquez, *La aparición*, 70.

29. Cuevas, *Album*, 50. He is incorrect in asserting that García Icazbalceta passed over in silence the annals of Juan Bautista. Cuevas's most extraordinary statement is that if the midcentury dates were correct, it would make the documents all the more valuable because they would be evidence for a second apparition that confirmed the first! (ibid., 50–51).

30. Garibay, "Temas guadalupanos I," 60–62.

31. Ibid., 62.

32. Bartolache, "Manifiesto satisfactorio," 618, 630–31.

33. Ibid., 631. See also Velázquez, *La aparición*, 68.

34. García Icazbalceta, "Carta," 55. Garibay identified 1531 as being flint year ("Temas guadalupanos I," 53).

35. Velázquez, *La aparición*, 66–67.

36. Ibid., 71.

37. Ibid., 71–72.

38. "Las fuentes esenciales," in *Album conmemorativo*, 102.

39. *Anales de Tlatelolco; Anales de Cuauhtitlan.*

40. *Congregatio pro Causis Sanctorum*, 228–30, 234.

41. Sylvest, *Nuestra Señora de Guadalupe*, 77–78.

42. Cuevas, *Album*, 50.

43. Glass and Robertson, "A Census," 195, entry 282.

44. There is little biographical data available on Montúfar. For a good summary, see O'Gorman, *Destierro de sombras*, 115–16, Velázquez, *La aparición*, 19–21, and Dávila Padilla, *Historia*, book 2, chap. 47.

45. Cabildo to king, 14 February 1561, in *Epistolario*, 9:109–18. According to O'Gorman, this is the first known mention of the shrine in any correspondence with the king (*Destierro de sombras*, 244).

46. O'Gorman attaches great importance to this (*Destierro de sombras*, 21, 118, n. 10). I do not. The reference to a local devotion centered in Mexico City would not have fitted in with the needs of the Church of New Spain at that time, nor would it have been an appropriate agenda for a provincial council such as this one. This is clear from the fact that despite Montúfar's own devotion and the possibility of using it as a lever against the mendicants, the council said nothing. Neither did the Second Provincial Council ten years later, which accomplished relatively little, outside of formally accepting the decrees of the Council of Trent.

47. Velázquez, *La aparición*, 24–25.

48. Cuevas, *Historia*, 2:71–73.

49. Biographical information on Bustamante can be found in Mendieta, *Historia*, book 5, part 1, chap. 52, 701–2. Other data are in book 4, chap. 52, 541, 543; book 3, chap. 58, 347; book 5, part 1, 669.

50. Cervantes de Salazar, *Life in the Imperial and Loyal City of Mexico*, 55. For the sake of clarity it should be noted that the index to this translation refers this description to Blas Bustamante, a professor at the Royal and Pontifical University. The context, however, which is a description of the chapel of San José de los Naturales at the Franciscan convent, leaves no doubt that Francisco de Bustamante was being described. Also Cervantes de Salazar's description is quite different from that given of Blas de Bustamante by Archbishop Pedro Moya de Contreras in 1575. See Moya de Contreras to Philip II, 24 March 1575, in *Cinco cartas*, 134. In addition, Blas de Bustamante did not receive tonsure until 1554 and was not ordained to the priesthood until 1569. See *Descripción del arzobispado de México*, 385–86.

51. There is no such decree by any of the Lateran councils. The reference is probably to Leo X's constitution, *Supernae majestatis*, which was promulgated at the Fifth

Lateran Council, 19 December 1516. It regulated the licensing of preachers and leveled penalties for excesses in preaching, especially in attacks on bishops and the propagation of false miracles and prophecies. See *Sacrorum Conciliorum nova et amplissima collectio*, 32:944–47.

52. The references to the presence of the viceroy, Luis de Velasco I, are few and ambiguous. It hardly seems possible, however, that he would not have been present at such an important occasion.

53. This can be found in the *Investigación histórica y documental*, 91–136, hereafter cited as *Información 1556*. I have also made use of the printed edition, which is also called *Información* and in these notes is cited as *Información 1891*. The original documents of the inquiry are in the archive of the basilica of Guadalupe and hence inaccessible.

54. Velázquez says that Bustamante claimed that most of the income for the hospital had been taken from it, but I have been unable to find this in the original inquiry (*La aparición*, 49).

55. Ibid., 24–25.

56. Some historians, including Antícoli (*Historia*, 1:203–28), José de Jesús Cuevas (*La santísima virgen de Guadalupe*, 14:54–55, 22:119), and Chauvet ("Historia del culto guadalupano," 30–34), believe that this was a formal canonical process designed to bring serious charges against Bustamante, but that out of magnanimity or charity Montúfar did not pursue the matter. O'Gorman devotes an entire appendix to showing that the inquiry lacked the necessary canonical formalities (*Destierro de sombras*, 231–37). The debate seems academic and does not affect the significance of the testimonies given.

57. *Información 1556*, 99; *Información 1891*, 10.

58. *Información 1556*, 106; *Información 1891*, 18.

59. *Información 1556*, 106–7; *Información 1891*, 18.

60. O'Gorman makes a good case for the fact that through witnesses such as these Montúfar was protecting himself from the accusation of having encouraged idolatry and preached false miracles (*Destierro de sombras*, 97–107).

61. *Información 1556*, 101, 104; *Información 1891*, 12, 15.

62. On Huete, see Mendieta, *Historia*, book 5, part 1, chap. 46, 679–80.

63. *Información 1556*, 120; *Información 1891*, 33.

64. *Información 1556*, 120–21; *Información 1891*, 33.

65. *Información 1556*, 131; *Información 1891*, 46–47. This was probably fray Luis Cal, the guardian of the Franciscan house of Tlatelolco. See Velázquez, *La aparición*, 19.

66. *Información 1556*, 109, 114, 123, 134–35; *Información 1891*, 20, 26, 36, 51.

67. *Información 1556*, 127; *Información 1891*, 50.

68. *Información 1556*, 115; *Información 1891*, 27.

69. Díaz del Castillo, *Historia verdadera*, chap. 91, 1:328; chap. 209, 2:460.

70. There is also the possibility that Bustamante may have been speaking of another Indian artist, Marcos Cipac. He was known to have been active in the years 1564 to 1565 as a member of a studio of artists. There is a question, however, as to whether he was skillful enough to have painted the image of Guadalupe. For a discussion of this, see Velázquez, *La aparición*, 55–57.

71. The literature on Las Casas is too voluminous for even a small part of it to be cited here. The reader is referred to some of the principal works: Wagner and Parish, *The Life and Writings of Bartolomé de las Casas*; *Bartolomé de las Casas in History*; Giménez Fernández, *Bartolomé de las Casas*; Bataillon and Saint-Lu, *El Padre Las Casas*. A good summary of Las Casas and his works and of the entire humanitarian movement is Hanke, *The Spanish Struggle for Justice*, throughout.

72. Díaz del Castillo, *Verdadera historia*, 2b, chap. 150, 59.

73. Ibid., 2:463. Velázquez dates this notice from before 1550 (*La aparición*, 5).

74. Some mention should be made of Juan Focher. Little is known about his life other than that he was French; came to New Spain after the conquest; learned Nahuatl, for which he composed a grammar, now lost; and died in 1572. He was author of an important missionary treatise *Itinerarium Catholicum* that, because it was intended to be a guide for missionaries, was not concerned with Guadalupe.

75. *Congregatio pro Causis Sanctorum*, 258.

76. *Tres conquistadores*, 202.

77. Velázquez, *La aparición*, 8, n. 23; *Congregatio pro Causis Sanctorum*, 272–73. This sort of arrangement was quite common. Repayment of the principal was often delayed so long that there was no thought of actually redeeming it. The interest payments constituted an annuity.

78. García Icazbalceta, "Carta," 26.

79. *Papeles de Nueva España*, 9:109–18.

80. A marginal note to Freire's dimissorial letter in García Pimentel's edition of the *Descripción* says that he was very old in 1570. He was the first abbot of the Congregación de San Pedro, a sodality of diocesan clergy (in their disputes with the religious the diocesans claimed Saint Peter as their founder). Freire died about 1586, and his will was probated 6 October of that year (Archivo General de la Nación, Mexico City, Bienes Nacionales 391, exp. 15). However, neither Freire nor Guadalupe were mentioned in Archbishop Moya de Contreras's listing of the clergy of Mexico of 24 March 1575 (Moya de Contreras to Philip II, 24 March 1575, in *Cinco cartas*, 121–51). He left 2,000 pesos for the construction of a new sanctuary at Tepeyac, with the implication that the previous one had not been well constructed. I wish to thank Professor John F. Schwaller for this information.

81. Carreño insisted that Montúfar made a full parish of the ermita, not just a chapel of ease. This, however, does not agree with the testimony of Martín Enríquez, to be seen in the next chapter, that Archbishop Moya de Contreras wanted to erect it into a full parish. See Carreño, "Don Fray Alonso de Montúfar," 280–95. According to Juan Bautista Muñoz, the ermita did not become a full parish until 1706 ("Memoria," 698). Chauvet claims that Montúfar was called the founder of the ermita only in the sense that he refurbished it and established a residential benefice there ("Historia del culto," 26). Velázquez claims the same, on the grounds that there was already a primitive ermita at Tepeyac when Montúfar arrived in New Spain (*La aparición*, 6).

82. *Geografía y descripción universal de las Indias*, 190.

83. The *Congregatio pro Causis Sanctorum*, 323, states that in 1571 a copy of the image of Guadalupe, a gift from Montúfar to Philip II and from the king to Andrea

Doria, accompanied the combined Christian fleet at the battle of Lepanto, 7 October 1571, and that it now hangs in the parish church of San Stefano d'Aveto, province of Genoa, in Italy. The only source for the story is Rossi's, *La B. V. di Guadalupe in S. Stefano d'Aveto*, which is quite unreliable. The story may have arisen from confusion with another account. In 1674 a Jesuit, Juan Zappa, had a copy of the Mexican Guadalupe image painted that he sent to the widowed princess Violante Lomelín Doria, mother of another Andrea Doria, in Genoa. During a bombardment the copy was credited with saving the Doria palace. See Vera, *Tesoro guadalupano*, 203–4.

84. Prem, "Disease Outbreaks in Central Mexico," 38–42.

Chapter 5

1. See Greenleaf, *The Mexican Inquisition of the Sixteenth Century*, 166–67.
2. Philips's account was reprinted by Richard Hakluyt in his *Voyages*, of which there are numerous editions. This quotation is taken from the edition by Richard Davis, 414.
3. On Enríquez, see García Abásolo, *Martin Enriquez*, throughout; Poole, *Pedro Moya de Contreras*, throughout.
4. On satellite shrines, and those of Guadalupe in particular, see Christian, *Apparitions*, 87–93.
5. Santa María's letters were discovered by Cuevas in the Archive of the Indies in Seville and sections published by him in his *Historia*, 2:493–96. The heading of the second letter says that it was addressed to the emperor Charles V, a clear error.
6. Ibid., 2:493–94. Cuevas accuses Santa María of an error in saying that there was no drinking water at Tepeyac (*Album*, 499). Philips, however, noted that the water was brackish and that its healing power seemed to be more in washing than drinking. Undoubtedly, however, the friar was exaggerating.
7. Tantalizingly, he also spoke of *la verdadera relacion* of the business of the ermita that he was sending along with his letter. This has not yet been found.
8. Cuevas writes, "Together with Hernán Cortés, Zumárraga went out to seek alms and did not fail to visit it, as is clear from the information given by the Viceroy Enríquez. . . . This viceroy could not say that 'the archbishops have always visited it,' if we excluded Zumárraga from this account" (*Album*, 16). Aside from the misquotation, Cuevas seems to have misunderstood the meaning of *visitar*, which in this context clearly denotes supervision, not devotion.
9. *Cartas de Indias*, 1:310.
10. San Joseph, *Historia universal*, chap. 21, 144–45.
11. Moya de Contreras to Philip II, 25 September 1575, in Paso y Troncoso, *Epistolario*, 11:266.
12. Ibid. Unfortunately, this account has not yet been found. I was unable to find it while researching Moya de Contreras's life. Given the archbishop's habitual meticulousness and accuracy, this report would be of surpassing importance.
13. Fernández de Echeverría y Veytia, *Baluartes de México*, 545–46. He says that he saw the auto in the archive of the basilica of Guadalupe (which is closed at this

time). See also Velázquez, *La aparición*, 9, especially n. 24, where he cites one of the cases in which the dowry was actually paid.

14. Everard Mercurian, Jesuit superior general, to Pedro Sánchez, 31 March 1576, in *Monumenta Historica Societatis Iesu*, 1:192–93.

15. Mercurian to Moya de Contreras, 12 March 1576, quoted in Zambrano and Gutiérrez Casillas, *Diccionario*, 1:203. See also Churruga Peláez, *Primeras fundaciones Jesuitas*, par. 374.

16. The brief can be found in *America Pontificia*, 2:no. 335.

17. Moya de Contreras to Gregory XIII, 17 December 1576, in Zambrano and Gutiérrez Casillas, *Diccionario*, 1:205.

18. Gregory XIII, *Dum praecelsa meritorum*, 20 October 1576, in *America Pontificia*, 2:no. 340.

19. Sánchez Baquero, *Fundación*; *Relación Breve de la Venida*.

20. For information on Sahagún, see *Sixteenth-Century Mexico*, throughout; d'Olwer, *Fray Bernardino de Sahagún*, throughout.

21. Sahagún, *Historia*, 3:352.

22. Ibid., 1:46; Clavigero, *Historia antigua de Mexico*, 2:82. Soustelle refers to Centeotl as a male divinity (*The Daily Life of the Aztecs*, 104). Andrews and Hassing say that in classical times Tonantzin was identified with Centeotl, who was a male deity (Ruiz de Alarcón, *Treatise on the Heathen Superstitions*, 221, 240).

23. Schendel, *Medicine in Mexico*, 28.

24. Burkhart, *The Slippery Earth*, 154.

25. Burkhart, "The Cult of the Virgin of Guadalupe," 208.

26. Ibid. Contrast this with the statement by Campbell: "On the other hand, the Indian population accepted her [Guadalupe] as the miraculous incarnation of the Aztec earth and fertility goddess Tonantsi [*sic*]" ("The Virgin of Guadalupe," 7).

27. Lockhart, *The Nahuas after the Conquest*, 351. The Còdice de Teotenantzin in the BNAH, uncataloged, shows two cliff carvings and a chapel on a hill. An inscription reads: "These two pictures are drawings of the goddess whom the Indians named *Teotenantzin*, which means Mother of the Gods, whom they worshiped during their paganism on the hill of Tepeyac, where today the Virgin of Guadalupe is." In an unpublished manuscript Alfonso Caso said that the images were of Chalchiuhcueitl and Tonantzin. Glass says that the codex was drawn by a European in the eighteenth century. See Glass, *Catálogo*, 1:140, n. 90. The images no longer exist, and a local oral tradition says that they were destroyed during road construction. Though the codex seems to support the idea of the worship of Tonantzin at Tepeyac, the proof is not conclusive. Why, for example, would it show the chapel on top of the hill and not the church at the bottom?

28. De la Maza, *El guadalupanismo mexicano*, 19; Velázquez, *La aparición*, 5; O'Gorman, *Destierro de sombras*, 158; Bravo Ugarte, *Cuestiones históricas guadalupanas*, 31.

29. Bravo Ugarte, *Cuestiones históricas guadalupanas*, 294.

30. Garibay, *Historia de la literatura náhuatl*, 2:265.

31. O'Gorman refers to another mention of Guadalupe by Sahagún but does not specify it (*Destierro de sombras*, 158). He may mean the citation by García Icazbalceta, "Carta," 29–30. On this, see chap. 6, n. 47.

Chapter 6

1. The information on Acosta has been taken from Acosta, *Historia natural y moral de las Indias*, 15–27.

2. For details on Tezozomoc, see Lockhart, *The Nahuas after the Conquest*, 389–91; Garibay, *Historia de la literatura náhuatl*, 2:299–308.

3. Some biographical information can be found in Beristáin de Sousa, *Biblioteca*, 5:83–85; García Icazbalceta, *Bibliografía mexicana del siglo XVI*, 475.

4. Cervantes de Salazar, *Life in the Imperial and Loyal City of Mexico*, 62.

5. Gibson, *The Aztecs*, 169–70. As part of an attempt to keep the Indians separated from harmful Spanish influence, the crown divided Mexico City into four barrios, each with its own government.

6. García Icazbalceta, *Bibliografía mexicana*, 475; Torquemada, *Monarquía indiana*, book 5, chap. 10; book 15, chap. 43.

7. This assertion about his translating in the style of Cato was made by Torquemada, *Monarquía indiana*, book 15, chap. 43, 114–15.

8. Suárez de Peralta, *Tratado del descubrimiento de las Indias*, 161.

9. Burkhart believes that this may refer to a tradition that existed before or along-side that of the apparitions ("The Cult of the Virgin of Guadalupe," 206–7). It is my belief that the apparition story did not exist at the time that Suárez de Peralta was writing.

10. Garibay, *Historia de la literatura náhuatl*, 2:228–29, 308–13.

11. Keen, *The Aztec Image*, 198.

12. It can be found included in Bernardino de Sahagún, *Historia*, 4:189–276.

13. "Al tener asiento y principio." This appears to be a mistranslation of the Nahuatl "Yn oc itzinècan, in oc ipeuhyan" (At the origin, at the beginning).

14. Cuevas, *Album*, 93–95. Cuevas does not identify the source where the document can be found. He says that he saw it and that it was not in the hand of Ixtlilxochitl but surmises that it might be in that of his son. It is not included in the THG.

15. Mendieta, *Historia*, book 3, chap. 59, 347–52. A truncated version of Mendieta's story can be found in *Nueva colección de documentos para la historia de México*, 1:85–90; see also Gibson, *The Aztecs*, 111; Torquemada, *Monarquía indiana*, 3:320. The Augustinians had the reputation for building large and sumptuous monasteries, a fact that may have prompted the Indians' preference for the Franciscans. Lockhart sees the Indians' preference for particular orders as something associated with the identity of the altepetl. "The Nahuas may also have detected the Franciscan strength within the Spanish establishment from the conquest forward, and that perception may have made them especially resistant when Spanish policy called (as it sometimes did to correct the early imbalance) for the removal of the Franciscans from a given altepetl in favor of another order or, later, secular priests. We would be naïve to believe, as the friars maintained and as Ricard tended to accept, that indigenous actions and reactions in the matter of order affiliation had primarily to do with the order's popularity or an indigenous

group's devotion to it or to certain of its members" (*The Nahuas after the Conquest*, 208).

16. Vera, *Tesoro guadalupano*, 1:35–37.

17. Laso de la Vega, *Hvei tlamahuiçoltica*, fols. 14r–v.

18. BNF, Mexicains, 243. Quoted with permission.

19. This will is in the BNF, Mexicains, 243, and is quoted in Cuevas, *Album*, 96. See also Vera, *Tesoro guadalupano*, where the full text of the Verdugo Quetzalmamalintzin will can be found in 1:5–11 (appendix) and the Tomelín will in 1:18–22 (appendix).

20. Méndez Plancarte, "Fray Diego Valadés," 265–82.

21. *Relación breve y verdadera*, 1:107.

22. Mendieta, *Historia*, book 5, part 1, chaps. 27–29.

23. Ibid., book 4, chaps. 24–28 incl.

24. Ibid., book 4, chap. 24, 453–54.

25. Ibid., book 4, chap. 25, 454–57.

26. Ibid., book 4, chap. 24, 451.

27. Ibid., book 4, chap. 26, 458–60; chap. 27, 461–66; Motolinía, *Memoriales*, 140; Mendieta, *Historia*, book 4, chap. 28, 465–69.

28. Grijalva, *Cronica*, book 2, chaps. 14–15.

29. Ibid., 269 and book 1, chap. 24.

30. Fernández, *Historia eclesiastica*, 58–59.

31. León, *Camino del cielo*, 96r. García Icazbalceta quotes a remarkably similar statement that he said he found in a manuscript in the BNM entitled *Cantares de los mexicanos*, in a paragraph that deals with the calendar ("Carta," 29–30). He attributed the manuscript to Sahagún. It reads: "La tercera disimulación es tomada de los nombres de los ídolas que allí se celebraban, que los nombres con que se nombran en latín ó en español significan lo que significaba el nombre del ídolo que allí adoraban antiguamente. Como en esta ciudad de México, en el lugar donde está Santa María de Guadalupe se adoraba un ídolo que antiguamente se llamaba Tonantzin; y entiéndolo por lo antiguo y no por lo nuevo." The document then goes on to speak of Santa Ana in Tlaxcala. It seems strange that García Icazbalceta made no comment on the similarity of the two passages, both of which he quotes in close proximity in his letter. In actual fact the citation is found in the *Santoral en mexicano*, referred to in chapter 3, the latter part of which is a paraphrase of Sahagún's *Historia*, book 4.

32. León, *Camino del cielo*, 96v.

33. Ibid., 98r.

34. These themes are taken from Keen, *The Aztec Image*, 181. On Torquemada's debt to Mendieta, see Phelan, *Millennial Kingdom*, 112–17.

35. Torquemada, *Monarquía indiana*, book 10, chap. 8, 245–46.

36. Lafaye, *Quetzalcoatl and Guadalupe*, 242.

37. Talavera, *Historia de Nvestra Senora de Gvadalvpe*, fols. 444v–45r. Velázquez gives a different wording, which he copied from the editors of the Montúfar-Bustamante inquiry: "La devoción de los conquistadores arraigóse y comenzaron a levantar

iglesias y santuarios con el título de Nuestra Señora de Guadalupe especial en la ciudad de México de nueva España" (Velázquez, *La aparición*, 17).

38. *Historia*, quoted in *Investigación histórica y documental*, 181. For brief biographical data on Cisneros, see Beristáin de Sousa, *Biblioteca*, 2:116.

39. [Gage], *Thomas Gage's Travels*, 67, 108.

40. *Sermon de la Natividad*, quoted in Vera, *Tesoro guadalupano*, 1:25–26 (appendix).

41. De la Maza, *El guadalupanismo mexicano*, 41–42. See also Velázquez, *La aparición*, 58–59. The original of the poem is in the Archivo General de la Nación, Mexico City.

42. Botturini Benaduci, *Idea*, par. 35, no. 4, 85. García Gutiérrez says that Botturini discovered the poem (*Cancionero histórico guadalupano*, 14).

43. Joaquín Peñalosa, *Flor y canto*, 55–56. Eight sections of the poem are also in García Gutiérrez, *Cancionero histórico guadalupano*, 11–14.

44. Alegre, *Historia*, 2:402.

45. A contemporary account of the flood and the drainage projects that followed can be found in Cepeda, *Relacion vniversal*, fols. 1r–17r, 27r–42r. For an excellent study of the flood from the point of view of its impact on civic government, see Hoberman, "Bureaucracy and Disaster," 211–30.

46. Alegre says that it was brought in September and that by the 22nd, after thirty-six hours of rain, the city was totally inundated (*Historia de la Compañía*, 2:404–5). Baltasar de Medina says that it was the 27th (*Chronica*, 122v). Hoberman gives the 24th ("Bureaucracy and Disaster," 218). Manso y Zúñiga was archbishop from 1629 until 1635. He was consecrated in the church of Remedios but was also responsible for repairing the church at Guadalupe and establishing a hospice there. He died in 1656 as archbishop of Burgos (Beristáin de Sousa, *Biblioteca*, 3:188).

47. Alegre, *Historia de la Provincia*, 2:405; meeting of the cathedral chapter, 4 October 1629, in *Actas del Cabildo de Mexico, años 1626–1632*, in Family History Library, Salt Lake City, microfilm 0645731.

48. Medina, *Chronica de la Santa Provincia de San Diego*, 123r.

49. Miguel Sánchez said that the waters subsided little by little (*Imagen de la Virgen Maria*, fol. 88r). Vetancurt said that it lasted five years (*Teatro mexicano*, tratado 5, nn. 28–29, p. 121); Miguel de Cuevas Dávalos, who claimed to have been an eyewitness, in his testimony before the capitular inquiry (see chapter 8) said three years; Velasco said four (*Exaltacion de la divina misericordia*, 46r–49v). Velasco was the curate at Guadalupe. He credited the Virgin of Guadalupe with stopping the flood but also reproduced Florencia's story about the vision of Sister Inés de la Cruz (see chapter 9).

50. García Gutiérrez, *Cancionero*, 17.

51. Ibid., 23–24.

52. In a manuscript titled *Continuación*, 303, cited by Bancroft, *History of Mexico*, 3[11]:87, n. 24. This work is not now in the Bancroft Library.

53. Florencia, *Estrella del norte*, chap. 20, pars. 238–40, fols. 120v–22v.

54. These are listed by Florencia, *La milagrosa invencion*, 58–95. Guijo mentioned only the procession to stop a drought and an accompanying epidemic of smallpox

in 1653 and for other droughts in 1661 and 1663 (*Diario*, 1:214–15; 2:149–51, 198).

55. Muñoz, "Memoria," 699.
56. Mier y Noriega, "Cartas del Doctor," 780–81.
57. Lafaye, *Quetzalcoatl and Guadalupe*, 254.

Chapter 7

1. For information on Sánchez, see López Beltrán, *La primera historia*, 9–16. A brief biography, heavily dependent on earlier sources, can be found in Gutiérrez Dávila, *Memorias historicas*, part 1, book 4, par. 619, 253–55. The oratory was not a religious order, like the mendicants or the Jesuits, but a union of diocesan clergy.
2. This claim was made in an obituary of Sánchez by Robles, *Diario*, 1:144–46. It was repeated by Gutiérrez Dávila, *Memorias historicas*, 254.
3. Quoted by de la Maza but without further details (*El guadalupanismo mexicano*, 49).
4. The work is reprinted in THG, 153–267, and, with some omissions, in López Beltrán, *La primera historia*, 39–190. It is very difficult to find copies of the first edition today. The one used for this chapter is in the John Carter Brown Library, Providence, R.I. The first edition contains a well-executed engraving of Juan Diego opening the tilma before a kneeling Zumárraga, an engraving later used also by Laso de la Vega. To my knowledge this is the first known illustration of the apparition account.
5. López Beltrán makes references to these approbations but does not include them in *La primera historia*.
6. Sánchez, *Imagen de la Virgen María*, unpaginated; THG, 153.
7. Sánchez, *Imagen de la Virgen María*, unpaginated; THG, 155.
8. Sada Lambretón, *Las informaciones jurídicas*, facsimile 112.
9. Sánchez, *Imagen de la Virgen María*, unpaginated; THG, 158. López Beltrán does not include this in the prologue in his reprint of Sánchez's work, nor can this sentence be found anywhere in that reprint. López Beltrán asserts categorically that he scrupulously reprinted the original, "word by word and line by line without adding or removing even a tittle" (*La primera historia*, 19). The conclusion seems inescapable that López Beltrán deliberately omitted the *fundamento*. De la Maza refers to this as "mala fe" (*El guadalupanismo mexicano*, 56). Actually, López Beltrán took a number of liberties with the text.
10. Sada Lambretón, *Las informaciones jurídicas*, facsimile 115.
11. The scarcity of paper was mentioned in the viceregal approval for Luis de Cisneros's history of Remedios. See Beristáin de Sousa, *Biblioteca*, 2:116.
12. Sánchez, *Imagen de la Virgen María*, f. 26r; THG, 186.
13. It is unclear whether a bishop-elect, with special faculties, could celebrate such a mass.
14. Sánchez, *Imagen de la Virgen María*, fol. 92r; THG, 255.
15. Sánchez, *Imagen de la Virgen María*, fols. 77v–78r; THG, 240.

16. Sánchez, *Imagen de la Virgen María*, unpaginated; THG, 261. López Beltrán places these two letters at the beginning of his version of Sánchez's book.

17. Genesis 2:23–24.

18. Laso de la Vega has a confused translation here. *Virago* in classical Latin means a manlike woman but in this context in the Vulgate simply means woman. "She shall be called woman because she has been taken from man (haec vocabitur virago quoniam de viro sumpta est)." This was an attempt to translate the original pun and popular etymology of the Hebrew into Latin. Laso de la Vega seems to have taken it literally and translates *virago* as *varonil*.

19. Sánchez, *Imagen de la Virgen María*, unpaginated; THG, 263–64.

20. Lafaye, *Quetzalcoatl and Guadalupe*, 246.

21. Revelation [Apocalypse] 12:1, 2, 7, 6, 14, 15, 17. The arrangement of verses given by Sánchez is out of order with the original.

22. Sánchez, *Imagen de la Virgen María*, fol. 93r; THG, 257.

23. Sánchez, *Imagen de la Virgen María*, fol. 19r; THG, 179.

24. Sánchez, *Imagen de la Virgen María*, fol. 69r; THG, 231.

25. Sánchez, *Imagen de la Virgen María*, fol. 57v; THG, 219.

26. Robles, *Diario*, 1:145. Writing in the following century, Gutiérrez Dávila, who borrowed much of his material verbatim from Robles, was surprised that such a great event could have been forgotten. "The forgetting of such a great benefit that the Empress of Heaven did for our America, and especially for Mexico, was certainly something worthy to be pondered" (*Memorias historicas*, 254).

27. Wood, "Christian Images," 275. Since it is Nahua wills that are dealt with, there is little doubt that the Mexican image, not the Extremaduran one, was bequeathed.

28. Sánchez, *El David seraphico*, 26v.

29. Quoted in García Icazbalceta, "Carta," 112, n. 5.

30. Ibid.

31. The only reprints that I have been able to verify personally are those in THG, 153–267, and López Beltrán, *La primera historia*.

32. De la Cruz, *Relación*, 267–81.

33. Ibid., 281.

34. Gálvez was fiscal of the council from 1654 until 1657 and a *consejero* (councillor) from 1657 until 1662. See Schäfer, *El real y supremo consejo*, 1:361, 368.

35. A *racionero* was a member of the chapter who received a salary for his participation in the liturgy but did not have a specific administrative function. A *medio racionero* received half the salary of a racionero. Ascensión H. de León-Portilla says that Laso de la Vega had studied at the University of Mexico and that he was fluent in Nahuatl, in which he preached (*Tepuztlahcuilolli*, 93). Unfortunately, she does not give a source for these statements, which I have been unable to verify.

36. Laso de la Vega, *Hvei tlamahviçoltica*, unpaginated; *Hvei tlamahvicoltiça* [*sic*], 20; also in THG, 288. González was a devotee of the Guadalupan devotion and supposedly composed a history of the apparitions in Nahuatl. See Velázquez, *La aparición*, 100; Beristáin de Sousa, *Biblioteca*, 2:372. For a discussion as to whether this was the same as the *Nican mopohua* or whether González had helped Laso de

la Vega in its composition, see Zambrano and Gutiérrez Casillas, *Diccionario*, 7:324–26.

37. Laso de la Vega, *Hvei tlamahviçoltica*, unpaginated; *Huey tlamahuicoltiça* [*sic*], 20.

38. Garibay considered Laso de la Vega to be the author of the introduction, the description of the image, the concluding section (*Nican tlantica*), and the final version of the *Nican motecpana* (*Historia de la literatura náhuatl*, 2:258).

39. Ibid., 2:257; Lockhart, *The Nahuas after the Conquest*, 250.

40. Laso de la Vega, *Hvei tlamahviçoltica*, unpaginated.

41. Velázquez's translation of the *Nican mopohua* includes the third apparition in a Spanish version but not in a Nahuatl one. He does not identify its source, saying only that it came from "a translation from a torn and very old piece of paper, written in Mexican," made by licenciado D. Joseph Julián Ramírez. Velàzquez included it because it filled the vacuum of the third apparition (*Hvei tlamahvicolt-çia* [*sic*], 100–1, n. 94). Ortiz de Montellano says that this translation comes from the beginning of the nineteenth century and that the full title was "Translation from a very old and torn piece of paper, written in Mexican, which was found among the books, maps, and other writings from the antiquities of the Indians, and which the lord archbishop of Toledo, don Franco [*sic* for Fran.co] Antonio Lorenzana gave to the archive of this royal university and they belonged to the knight don Lorenzo Boturini Benaduci, inventario 8, n. 7, made by the licenciado don Joseph Julián Ramírez, catedrático and synodal examiner of the said language in this royal university and archdiocese." A copy of Ramírez's translation, with this note included, can be found in the BNF, Mexicains, 317. The Nahuatl version that is occasionally found was a retranslation by Mario Rojas Sánchez. See Ortiz de Montellano, *Nicā mopohua*, 101–2.

42. Laso de la Vega, *Hvei tlamahviçoltica*, unpaginated.

43. *The Nahuas after the Conquest*, 250.

44. Laso de la Vega, *Hvei tlamahviçoltica*, unpaginated.

45. Ibid., unpaginated.

46. Ibid., unpaginated.

47. Andrews, "Directionals in Classical Nahuatl," 2.

48. León-Portilla, *Tepuztlahcuilolli*, 93.

49. Burkhart, "The Cult of the Virgin of Guadalupe in Mexico," 204.

50. Lockhart, *The Nahuas after the Conquest*, 250.

51. Siller, *La evangelización guadalupana*, 5. He also says that it is written in different styles but does not specify them.

52. *Cantares Mexicanos*, 430.

53. Monumentos Guadalupanos, Rare Books and Manuscripts Division, The New York Public Library, Astor, Lenox and Tilden Foundations, all quotations with permission.

54. "It features the frequent but haphazard usage of the letter *h* to represent glottal stops, an orthographic convention typical of Franciscan and Jesuit texts of the late sixteenth and very early seventeenth centuries, later superseded by the Jesuit convention of using diacritics for that function" (Burkhart, "The Cult of the Virgin," 223, n. 18).

55. Burrus, *The Oldest Copy*, 3–4. Burrus believed that Antonio Valeriano wrote the *Nican mopohua* between 1540 and 1545.

56. Ibid., 5. In addition to the manuscripts noted in this section, there is a third copy in volume 1 of the second series, but it is clearly from the eighteenth century or even later.

57. Pichardo was pastor of San Felipe Neri church in Mexico City for twenty-three years and famed as a linguist.

58. De la Maza, *El guadalupanismo mexicano*, 74; Garibay, *Historia de la literatura náhuatl*, 2:257.

59. *El milagro de la Virgen del Tepeyac*, cited by Velázquez, "El gran acontecimiento," 286–87.

60. BNF, Mexicains, 317. Quoted with permission. The introductory note speaks of Lorenzana as archbishop of Toledo, thus dating the copy after 1772.

61. Laso de la Vega, *Hvei tlamahviçoltica*, fol. 8r.

62. Velázquez, *La aparición*, 134–35.

63. Prem, "Disease Outbreaks," 31–34.

64. Mendieta, *Historia*, book 4, chap. 36, 515.

65. Processions of children who flagellated themselves as a means of averting epidemics were rather common in the apparition folklore of Spain. According to Christian, "In the fifteenth and sixteenth centuries, Barcelona children were prominently situated in penitential processions. In 1427 boys and girls . . . flagellated themselves in a penitential procession because of an earthquake. . . . The Augustinian friars organized a procession in which 'small boys . . . barefoot in shirts walked whipping themselves between men who carried lighted candles'" (*Apparitions*, 217–18). The miracle related here seems to belong very much to that genre.

66. This miracle was also related by Baltasar de Medina in a biographical note on Valderrama. Threatened with the amputation of his foot, he asked to be taken to Guadalupe, where he was cured. Medina mentions that there was no documentary evidence for the miracle, but that it was well attested in a *lienzo* (picture on a canvas) that was still conserved at the ermita. That may possibly refer to the Stradanus engraving of 1615. Medina did not give a date for the cure but said that Valderrama was professed in Mexico in 1601 and had been in religion for twenty-nine years at the time of his death (*Chronica*, 121r–22v).

67. Florencia mentioned a Luis de Castilla, a regidor of Mexico and a knight of Santiago, who made donations to the first Jesuits who came to New Spain (*Historia de la provincia*, 117). He made no mention of a miraculous cure, however.

68. The earliest reproduction of the present image that I know of is a painting by the Basque artist Baltasar de Echave Orio. See Ortiz Vaquero, "Notas sobre la pintura," 29–30. The picture is reproduced on p. 31. The original is in a private collection.

69. "Samuel Stradanus (1523–1605), Indulgence for Donation of alms towards building a church to the Virgin of Guadalupe, the Metropolitan Museum of Art, New York City, Gift of H. H. Behrens, 1948." The dates given are incorrect and are based on a confusion of this Stradanus with another member of the famed family of engravers. On Stradanus and this engraving, see Conde-Cervantes de

Conde, "Nuestra Señora de Guadalupe en el arte," 124–26; Peterson, "The Virgin of Guadalupe," 40. Peterson's article also has a full-page reproduction of the engraving on page 41.

70. Florencia gave the man's name as Granado (*Estrella del norte*, chap. 25, par. 279, fol. 143v).

71. Laso de la Vega, *Hvei tlamahviçoltica*, fol. 14v.

72. Becerra Tanco, "Origen milagroso," in THG, 330; Clavigero,"Breve noticia," in ibid., 581.

73. "Auh ca yeppa yuhque in tlalticpac tlaca, iz çan huel ìquac, quimahuiztilia, quitlaçòcamati in iteicneliltzin TlatòcaÇihuapilli, intla oquimomàçehuìque, auh in moztla, in huiptla ca ye intlalcahualizpan contlaztihui inic aocmo inpan hual àçi, iz çatepan hualhui, quihualmomàçehuia in itlanextzin, in itonatiuhtzin Totecuiyo Auh ca huel ye yèhuatl in, in ipampa achi opoliuhca, omocauhca in iteicneliltzin ilhuicac Çihuapilli, inic çenca huei tlamahuiçoltica omonexiti in nican ichantzino Tepeyacac; inic àmo çenca in iuh monequia quihualmomachiltia, quihualmocuitìtzinoa in imaçehualtzitzinhuā in huel inpampa oncan omocaltìtzino inic oncan quinmocaquililiz in innetoliniliz in inpatzmiquiliz, in inchoquiz, in intlaìtlaniliz, auh quinmomaquiliz, quimocneliliz in itepalehuiliztzin" (Laso de la Vega, *Hvei tlamahviçoltica*, fols. 15v–16r).

Chapter 8

1. González Dávila, *Teatro eclesiástico*, 1:92.

2. Guijo, *Diario*, 1:214–15; 2:149–50, 151, 198–200.

3. Siles's letter, the sonnets, and the introduction are all unpaginated. The first number of the date of Lomelín's letter is lost in the binding of the copy in the BNM. It was (?)5 August 1648. The license for printing was given on 2 September 1648.

4. Florencia, *Estrella del norte*, chap. 13, par. 102, fol. 45v. It is difficult to tell from Florencia's account whether Siles contacted the viceroy or that Escobar y Llamas was viceroy. Leyva y de la Cerda, the marquess of Labrada and count of Baños, was viceroy from 1660 to 1664. On 19 March 1664 Escobar y Llamas, on the basis of some cédulas that he had heard were coming from Madrid, deposed the viceroy and assumed the position temporarily. A period of conflict and instability followed until late June and early July, when Escobar y Llamas triumphed. He remained interim viceroy until the arrival of the marquess of Mancera in September. Siles was archbishop-elect of Manila at the time of his death.

5. This term refers to the canonical hours, which were prayed in choir by religious orders and chapters and in private by clerics in major orders. There were seven of these hours: Matins/ Lauds, Prime, Tierce, Sext, None, Vespers, and Compline.

6. Vera, *Informaciones*, 7. A Latin account of the apparitions was sent to Rome and was translated and published by Anastasio Nicoseli in 1681. See Medina Ascensio, "Las informaciones guadalupanas," 1339. Vera includes a partial translation of Nicoseli's work in *Tesoro guadalupano* 2:87–90. He also gives the names of all those who signed the petition to Rome (ibid., 90–108).

7. Antícoli theorized that the original request was an ordinary process, that is, one that came only from the local bishop or his representative. For the Holy See to be involved, it was necessary that it have a bishop or other dignitary acting as its delegate and using a questionnaire drawn up in Rome (*Historia de la aparición de la Sma. Virgen*, 354–58).

8. At this time the see of Mexico was vacant. Cuevas Dávalos held office for only a few months, November 1664 to September 1665. Eighteenth-century copies of the documentation of the interrogatory, formerly in the archive of the archdiocese of Mexico, are now in the library of the basilica of Guadalupe, which is closed. Fortunately, they have been reproduced in photostatic form in Sada Lambretón, *Las informaciones*, facsimiles 1–426. They have also been transcribed and published in Vera, *Informaciones*. Medina Ascensio gives summaries and partial quotations in "Las informaciones guadalupanas," 1339–40.

9. Sada Lambretón, *Las informaciones*, facsimiles 6–7; Vera, *Informaciones*, 4, 7–8. Medina Ascensio says that the date was 19 December ("Las informaciones guadalupanas," 1340). Later he says that it was 11 December (ibid., 1344). The appointments were made on the 11th and accepted on the 19th.

10. Sada Lambretón, *Las informaciones*, facsimile 253.

11. Florencia, *Estrella del norte*, chap. 13, par. 102, fol. 45v; Medina Ascensio, "Las informaciones guadalupanas," 1340.

12. It can be found in Sada Lambretón, *Las informaciones*, facsimiles 14–19; Vera, *Informaciones*, 11–14.

13. Sada Lambretón, *Las informaciones*, facsimiles 14–15; Vera, *Informaciones*, 11.

14. Sada Lambretón, *Las informaciones*, facsimiles 125–26; Vera, *Informaciones*, 12.

15. Pacheco's testimony is in Sada Lambretón, *Las informaciones*, facsimiles 22–36; Vera, *Informaciones*, 16–23; Medina Ascensio, "Las informaciones guadalupanas," 1345–47. The *Congregatio pro Causis Sanctorum* gives his age as more than ninety (lxxvii).

16. Sada Lambretón, *Las informaciones*, facsimile 33; Vera, *Informaciones*, 21.

17. Sada Lambretón, *Las informaciones*, facsimile 26; Vera, *Informaciones*, 18. All other witnesses gave the name of the barrio as Tlayacac.

18. Sada Lambretón, *Las informaciones*, facsimile 29; Vera, *Informaciones*, 18.

19. Sada Lambretón, *Las informaciones*, facsimile 35; Vera, *Informaciones*, 23.

20. Suárez's testimony is in Sada Lambretón, *Las informaciones*, facsimiles 36–47; Vera, *Informaciones*, 22–29.

21. Sada Lambretón, *Las informaciones*, facsimile 38; Vera, *Informaciones*, 24. Medina Ascensio conjectures that this was Alonso de Escalona, who left New Spain for Guatemala in 1554 ("Las informaciones guadalupanas," 1348).

22. Sada Lambretón, *Las informaciones*, facsimile 39; Vera, *Informaciones*, 25.

23. Sada Lambretón, *Las informaciones*, facsimile 39; Vera, *Informaciones*, 24.

24. This part about Juan Diego's later life is not in Medina Ascensio, "Las informaciones guadalupanas."

25. Andés Juan's testimony is in Sada Lambretón, *Las informaciones*, facsimiles 47–59; Vera, *Informaciones*, 29; Medina Ascensio, "Las informaciones guadalupanas,"

1348–50. Medina Ascensio erroneously states that Andrés Juan was from the barrio of San Juan Atempan, which was actually that of his parents ("Las informaciones guadalupanas," 1348).

26. Her testimony is in Sada Lambretón, *Las informaciones*, facsimiles 59–70; Vera, *Informaciones*, 35–40; Medina Ascensio, "Las informaciones guadalupanas," 1350–52.

27. Vera gives the date as 1569, a clear impossibility (*Informaciones*, 36).

28. Florencia gives the father's name as Aztatzontli, which seems to be more accurate.

29. Sada Lambretón, *Las informaciones*, facsimile 62; Vera, *Informaciones*, 36.

30. His testimony is in Sada Lambretón, *Las informaciones*, facsimiles 70–81; Vera, *Informaciones*, 40–46; Medina Ascensio, "Las informaciones guadalupanas," 1352–53.

31. Sada Lambretón, *Las informaciones*, facsimiles 72–73; Vera, *Informaciones*, 42; Medina Ascensio, "Las informaciones guadalupanas," 1352.

32. Martín de San Luis's testimony is in Sada Lambretón, *Las informaciones*, facsimiles 81–90; Vera, *Informaciones*, 46–52; Medina Ascensio, "Las informaciones guadalupanas," 1354.

33. Juan Suárez's testimony is in Sada Lambretón, *Las informaciones*, facsimiles 90–101; Vera, *Informaciones*, 52–59; Medina Ascensio, "Las informaciones guadalupanas," 1354–56.

34. Sada Lambretón, *Las informaciones*, facsimile 91; Vera, *Informaciones*, 53.

35. Sada Lambretón, *Las informaciones*, facsimile 93; Vera, *Informaciones*, 53, 54.

36. Her testimony is in Sada Lambretón, *Las informaciones*, facsimiles 101–9; Vera, *Informaciones*, 59–65; Medina Ascensio, "Las informaciones guadalupanas," 1356–58.

37. At this point Florencia inserts a highly abbreviated version of Luis Becerra Tanco's testimony from the *Origen milagroso* of 1666 (*Estrella del norte*, chap. 13, pars. 114–20, fols. 51v–53v).

38. Sánchez's testimony is in Sada Lambretón, *Las informaciones*, facsimiles 110–21; Vera, *Informaciones*, 66–73; Medina Ascensio, "Las informaciones guadalupanas," 1362–64.

39. Sada Lambretón, *Las informaciones*, facsimile 112; Vera, *Informaciones*, 67.

40. Sada Lambretón, *Las informaciones*, facsimile 114; Vera, *Informaciones*, 68.

41. Oyanguren's testimony is in Vera, *Informaciones*, 73–80; Medina Ascensio, "Las informaciones guadalupanas," 1366–68.

42. Sada Lambretón, *Las informaciones*, facsimile 124; Vera, *Informaciones*, 75.

43. Tapia's testimony is in Sada Lambretón, *Las informaciones*, facsimiles 131–38; Vera, *Informaciones*, 80–84; Medina Ascensio, "Las informaciones guadalupanas," 1368.

44. Sada Lambretón, *Las informaciones*, facsimile 134; Vera, *Informaciones*, 82.

45. Mendoza's testimony is in Sada Lambretón, *Las informaciones*, facsimiles 138–51; Vera, *Informaciones*, 85–90; Medina Ascensio, "Las informaciones guadalupanas," 1368–69.

46. An Antonio Maldonado was oidor of Guadalajara from 1578 to 1585, then alcalde del crimen of Mexico from 1585 until 1589, and finally oidor of Mexico

from 1589 to 1602. He retired from the last-named position. This is the only person of that name listed as an oidor by Schäfer (*El real y supremo consejo*, 2:453, 459, 494). This Maldonado could not possibly have been even a near contemporary of the apparitions.

47. Sada Lambretón, *Las informaciones*, facsimiles 148–49; Vera, *Informaciones*, 89.

48. Herrera's testimony is in Sada Lambretón, *Las informaciones*, facsimiles 151–59; Vera, *Informaciones*, 90–95; Medina Ascensio, "Las informaciones guadalupanas," 1369.

49. San Simón's testimony is in Sada Lambretón, *Las informaciones*, facsimiles 159–71; Vera, *Informaciones*, 95–99; Medina Ascensio, "Las informaciones guadalupanas," 1369. Florencia says that San Simón had been in New Spain for thirty-five years (*Estrella del norte*, chap. 13, par. 129, fols. 57r–v). Cuevas gives his first name as Diego (*Album*, 136).

50. Monroy's testimony is in Sada Lambretón, *Las informaciones*, facsimiles 171–83; Vera, *Informaciones*, 99–104; Medina Ascensio, "Las informaciones guadalupanas," 1369–70. According to Zambrano and Gutiérrez Casillas, Monroy was a criollo, born in Colima (*Diccionario*, 10:101). Velázquez says that the forty years refers to the length of time that Monroy had been hearing the story of the apparitions (*La aparición*, 266). Monroy, however, said that he had heard it since he had the use of reason, a period of time much longer than forty years (Vera, *Informaciones*, 100).

51. Florencia said fifty-six years (*Estrella del norte*, chap. 13, par. 131, fol. 58r). San José's testimony is in Sada Lambretón, *Las informaciones*, facsimiles 183–96; Vera, *Informaciones*, 104–9; Medina Ascensio, "Las informaciones guadalupanas," 1370.

52. San Nicolás's testimony is in Sada Lambretón, *Las informaciones*, facsimiles 197–209; Vera, *Informaciones*, 109–14; Medina Ascensio, "Las informaciones guadalupanas," 1370.

53. Cerdán's testimony is in Sada Lambretón, *Las informaciones*, facsimiles 209–22; Vera, *Informaciones*, 114–19; Medina Ascensio, "Las informaciones guadalupanas," 1370.

54. Cuevas Dávalos's testimony is in Sada Lambretón, *Las informaciones*, facsimiles 222–36; Vera, *Informaciones*, 119–24; Medina Ascensio, "Las informaciones guadalupanas," 1370–71. Florencia identified him as the brother of Archbishop Cuevas Dávalos of Mexico (*Estrella del norte*, chap. 13, par. 133, fol. 58v), but this is not in the original testimony.

55. Moctezuma's testimony can be found in Sada Lambretón, *Las informaciones*, facsimiles 236–51; Vera, *Informaciones*, 124–30; Medina Ascensio, "Las informaciones guadalupanas," 1371. Florencia says only that he was a descendant of the emperor (*Estrella del norte*, chap. 13, par. 135, fol. 60r). In 1681 Anastasio Nicoseli, in an Italian translation of the Latin version of the inquiry, wrote that Moctezuma was a great-grandson of the emperor, but this seems to have been his own solution to the dating problem. See *Dos relaciones*, 23.

56. It is in Sada Lambretón, *Las informaciones*, facsimiles 274–357; Vera, *Informaciones*, 138–67. Medina Ascensio, "Las informaciones guadalupanas," 1371–73 gives

only a summary, as does Florencia, *Estrella del norte*, chap. 13, pars. 114–20, fols. 51v–53v.

57. For the history of this congregation and Siles's part in it, see Sigüenza y Góngora, *Glorias de Queretaro*.

58. Florencia, *Estrella del norte*, chap. 13, par. 101, fol. 44v.

59. "In ipsa item catholica ecclesia magnopere curandum est ut id teneamus, quod ubique, quod semper, quod ab omnibus creditum est" (*Patrologiae Cursus Completus*, ed. J. P. Migne, *Series Latina*, 50:639; Rouët de Journel, *Enchiridion Patristicum*, 2168).

60. Spaniards of the colonial period believed that the Indians were inclined in a particular way toward perjury. See Velázquez, *La aparición*, 345. That was why the Third Mexican Provincial Council (1585), book 2, chap. 5, par. 10, had forbidden Indians to give testimony against pastors.

61. Gerhard makes no mention of this barrio in reference to Cuauhtitlan (*Guide*, 127–28).

62. In the BNF, Mexicains 388, there is a pictographic record of the Cano family that seeks to connect it to Mexica royalty. One line shows a don Diego Moctezuma who was a grandson of Moteucçoma II. The Cano side, however, which claimed descent from Acamapichtli, shows no one named Diego. Israel says that the Cano Moctezuma family was descended from Gonzalo Cano Moctezuma, the mestizo son of the "Aztec princess" Isabel Moctezuma, and identifies Diego de Cano Moctezuma y Contreras as a knight of Santiago and captain in the militia (*Race and Class*, 81).

63. García Icazbalceta, "Carta," 57. Emphasis in original.

64. Medina Ascensio says that "the books of Sánchez, Lasso, Becerra Tanco, published from 1648 to 1649 [*sic*], would have been for them [the witnesses] a dead letter; they did not know how to read. Only one was able to sign his name" ("Las informaciones guadalupanas," 1358–59). What he is overlooking is that books in the native languages were given public readings to groups of Indians by individuals who knew how to read. In addition, both word of mouth and sermons would have circulated the story. Eighteen years was ample enough time for it to spread.

65. Sada Lambretón, *Las informaciones*, facsimiles 258–74; Vera, *Informaciones*, 132–38. The artistic experts were Juan Salguero, a cleric of fifty-eight years of age who had been a master of painting for more than thirty years; Tomás Conrado, twenty-eight years of age and a master for eight years; Sebastián López de Avalos, fifty and a master for more than twenty years; Nicolás de Angulo, over thirty and master for over twenty years; Juan Sánchez, thirty and master for more than fifteen years; Alonso de Zárate, more than thirty and with experience of more than fourteen years.

66. Sada Lambretón, *Las informaciones*, facsimiles 375–404; Vera, *Informaciones*, 172–83. The doctors were Luis de Cárdenas Soto, Jerónimo Ortiz, and Juan de Melgarejo.

67. Florencia's account of the subsequent history of the inquiry is in *Estrella del norte*, chap. 13, pars. 144–49, fols. 64v–68v.

68. The receipt was notarized by Franciscan Sebastián Rodríguez, who received it from Captain Jacinto del Pino, a citizen of Seville. See *Dos relaciones históricas*, 22.

69. Letter of approval for López de Avilés, *Ueridicum admodum anagramma*, fol. 195v.

70. According to Beristáin de Sousa, very few copies were printed and he himself knew of none still existing (*Biblioteca* 1:238–39).

71. According to José Ignacio Bartolache, "Manifiesto satisfactorio," 607.

72. The editors of THG have confused the matter by giving their reprint of the work the title "Origen milagroso del Santuario de Nuestra Señora de Guadalupe," though what they have printed is the *Felicidad de Mexico* of 1675 (THG, 310–33).

73. Sada Lambretón, *Las informaciones*, facsimile 275; Vera, *Informaciones*, 138–39.

74. Sada Lambretón, *Las informaciones*, facsimile 276; Vera, *Informaciones*, 139.

75. Sada Lambretón, *Las informaciones*, facsimile 277; Vera, *Informaciones*, 139.

76. Sada Lambretón, *Las informaciones*, facsimile 277; Vera, *Informaciones*, 139.

77. Sada Lambretón, *Las informaciones*, facsimile 295; Vera, *Informaciones*, 145.

78. "Origen milagroso," in THG, 320.

79. For a detailed listing of these differences, see Velázquez, *La aparición*, 125–26.

80. According to de la Maza, Becerra Tanco concluded after studying maps and personally visiting the sites that the route from Cuauhtitlan to Tlatelolco would not have led Juan Diego by way of Tepeyac but through Tlalnepantla and Azcapotzalco (*El guadalupanismo mexicano*, 84–85). This would explain why Becerra Tanco gives a different location for Juan Diego's actual living place. Tolpetlac was near Cuautitlan and had originally been subject to Tlatelolco (Gerhard, *Guide*, 226). It was on the shore of the lake, about ten miles northeast of Mexico City (Gibson, *The Aztecs*, 48–49).

81. "Origen milagroso," in THG, 315, 331.

82. Sada Lambretón, *Las informaciones*, facsimile 288; Vera, *Informaciones*, 143; "Origen milagroso," in THG, 317.

83. "Origen milagroso," in THG, 318–19.

84. Sada Lambretón, *Las informaciones*, facsimiles 298–99; Vera, *Informaciones*, 146; "Origen milagroso," in THG, 323.

85. Sada Lambretón, *Las informaciones*, facsimiles 305–6; Vera, *Informaciones*, 149.

86. "Origen milagroso," in THG, 325.

87. Sada Lambretón, *Las informaciones*, facsimiles 306–7; Vera, *Informaciones*, 149. The words in brackets were omitted by the scribe. See "Origen milagroso," in THG, 326.

88. Sada Lambretón, *Las informaciones*, facsimiles 307–8; Vera, *Informaciones*, 149–50. Quoted also, with slightly different wording, in de la Maza, *El guadalupanismo mexicano*, 75; Junco, *Un radical problema guadalupano*, 12. It is interesting that Becerra Tanco identified Laso de la Vega as the publisher, not the author, of the account.

89. "Origen milagroso," in THG, 326.

90. *El guadalupanismo mexicano*, 75.

91. "Origen milagroso," in THG, 311.

92. Ibid., 315.

93. "Origen milagroso," in THG, 331. This is not in the testimony of 1666.
94. Mercado is not mentioned in Becerra Tanco's 1666 testimony.
95. *Informaciones*, 154; "Origen milagroso," in THG, 330.
96. "Origen milagroso," in THG, 320–21.
97. Sada Lambretón, *Las informaciones*, facsimiles 326–27; Vera, *Informaciones*, 155–56.
98. "Origen milagroso," in THG, 330.
99. Ibid., 332. This part is not in the testimony of 1666.
100. According to de la Maza, *El guadalupanismo mexicano*, 82.
101. See Smith, *Preaching in the Spanish Golden Age*, 29, 30, 31, 34, 40, 56.
102. This figure, which is only an approximation, comes from the forthcoming Guadalupan bibliography of Professsor W. Michael Mathes. I wish to express my thanks to him for sharing this information with me.
103. Robles, *Sermon*, unpaginated. The devotion to Guadalupe first came to Querétaro through the agency of a priest named Lucas Guerrero Rodea, who was actively helped by Francisco de Siles. In 1669 he and some other priests founded a congregation of secular clergy called the Congregación eclesiástica de María Santíssima de Guadalupe, which received royal approval in 1671. The church to the Virgin of Guadalupe was built between 1671 and 1680 by Caballero y Ocio at his own expense. See Sigüenza y Góngora, *Glorias de Queretaro*, throughout; Robles, *Oracion fvnebre*, dedication, unpaginated.
104. San Joseph, *Florido aromático*, unpaginated. In the pre–Vatican II liturgy, this quotation from Psalm 147 was used as the communion antiphon for the mass of Our Lady of Guadalupe.
105. San Miguel, *Sermon*, 9, 26. Note again the association of Guadalupe with the Nativity of the Virgin.
106. Mendoza, *Sermon*, 11.
107. Delgado y Buenrostro, *Accion de gracias*. García de Palacios had endowed a chapel to Guadalupe in 1660 in the cathedral of Puebla. This was occasion for Mateo de la Cruz's publication of the Guadalupe story, which was published in Puebla and dedicated to García de Palacios, at that time a canon in the cathedral chapter.
108. Olivares, *Oracion panegyrica*, fol. 1r.
109. Santa Teresa, *Sermon*, fol. 1v.
110. Benítez, *Sermon panegyrico*, unpaginated.
111. Besides Manso the other preachers were Alonso Rodríguez de Vargas, Manuel de Argüello, Juan de Rueda, Matías de San Juan Bautista, Luis Méndez, and Antonio Muñoz. All were criollos.
112. Herrera, *Sermon*, 8r–v.
113. This was not the first such Latin poetic work. Some time prior to 1669 Becerra Tanco invited some of the principal writers of Mexico City to contribute poems, anagrams, acrostics, and similar literary devices in both Latin and Spanish for publication. The result was López de Avilés's *Ueridicum admodum anagramma*, which contained contributions by Miguel Sánchez, López de Avilés, and Becerra Tanco himself.

114. Rivera, *Sermon de la publicacion de el edicto del Santo Tribunal de la Inquisicion*, 15.
115. Ibid., unpaginated.
116. Florencia claimed that Guadalupan sermons were preached at Tepeyac, especially by Jesuits, on major feasts (*Estrella del norte*, 619–20). To my knowledge none of these was published nor have any survived.

Chapter 9

1. The data given here are taken from Zambrano and Gutiérrez Casillas, *Diccionario*, 6:703–12. Zambrano's work merely collates and publishes data found in a variety of sources, even when these data are inconsistent or contradictory.
2. Florencia, *Estrella del norte*, unpaginated.
3. Ibid., unpaginated.
4. Ibid., unpaginated.
5. Ibid., unpaginated.
6. Ibid., chap. 7, par. 46, fol. 18r.
7. His discussion of this document is in ibid., chap. 13, pars. 160–80, fols. 75v–88v.
8. Ibid., par. 160, fol. 75v. Florencia mingles his descriptions of the two documents in such a way that it is difficult to know precisely which one he is talking about.
9. Ibid., par. 162, fol. 76v.
10. Ibid.
11. Ibid.
12. Ibid. Vetancurt did not seem as sure about Mendieta's authorship as Florencia made him out to be. He seemed to accept the possibility of Ixtlilxochitl's authorship (*Teatro mexicano*, tratado 5, n. 8, p. 55).
13. Florencia, *Estrella del norte*, par. 164, fol. 78r.
14. Ibid., par. 167, fol. 79r.
15. Ibid., par. 170, fols. 81r–v.
16. Ibid., chap. 16, par. 199, fols. 97r–v.
17. "Tuve noticia," in ibid., par. 200, fols. 97v–98r.
18. Ibid., chap. 21, pars. 241–43, fols. 123r–24v. He says that he obtained the story of Valderrama's cure from Medina's *Crónica de San Diego de Mexico*.
19. Florencia, *Estrella del norte*, chap. 25, par. 279, fol. 143v.
20. Ibid., chap. 22, pars. 248–55, fols. 226v–231r.
21. Ibid., chap. 25, par. 280, fols. 143v–44r; par. 281, fol. 144r; par. 283, fol. 144v; par. 284, fols. 144v–45r; par. 285, fols. 145r–v; par. 286, fols. 145v–46r.
22. Ibid., chap. 21, par. 244, fol. 124v.
23. Ibid., fols. 124r–v.
24. Ibid., chap. 19, par. 236, fols. 118v–19r; chap. 20, throughout.
25. De la Maza says that this story was invented to prove that Guadalupe had saved the city. "It is clear that later it was found necessary to justify the 'miracle' of the flood and *it was said* that Archbishop Cuevas y Dávalos *related* that a nun had seen Christ indignant against Mexico, for which reason he had sent it the calamity of

the flood, but that through the prayers of Saint Catherine and the Virgin of Guadalupe, had lifted his wrath and withdrawn [the waters]" (*El guadalupanismo mexicano*, 46–47, emphases in original). Unfortunately, de la Maza gives no source or evidence for his statement, which hardly seems likely in view of Cuevas y Dávalos's short term as archbishop. The story may have been one of many in circulation among the populace. Florencia's version does not mention Guadalupe, though it is possible that it received credit in popular belief. De la Maza's assertion should be viewed with some skepticism.

26. Florencia, *Estrella del norte*, chap. 10, par. 75, fols. 30r–v; Callahan, *The Tilma under Infra-Red Radiation*, 6–21.

27. Florencia, *Estrella del norte*, chap. 18, par. 223, fols. 111r–14r.

28. The story that Juan Diego had a son is mentioned, seemingly with approval, in the *Congregatio pro Causis Sanctorum*, vi:320; vii:344; viii:397. In 1739 a certain María Antonia de Escalona y Rojas, a novice in the Discalced Franciscans, claimed to be a direct descendant of Juan Diego. Botturini Benaduci wrote a refutation of this claim in which he defended the perpetual celibacy of Juan Diego. The document is quoted in full in *Congregatio pro Causis Sanctorum*, 623–31.

29. Florencia, *Estrella del norte*, chap. 29, par. 312, fol. 164r.

30. Ibid., pars. 316–20, fols. 166r–69r.

31. Ibid., chap. 11, par. 84, fol. 35v.

32. Ibid., chap. 15, par. 195, fol. 95v. Florencia said that Sigüenza y Góngora had found the cantar among the papers of Chimalpahin and was guarding it like a treasure. It was among the papers that Sigüenza y Góngora lent to Florencia for inclusion in his history and which Florencia promised to insert. In a final note, however, Florencia said that he had not included the cantar or the "antigua relación" because his book was longer and bulkier than anticipated (ibid., fol. 241v). In view of the fact that Florencia included large amounts of extraneous material of far lesser importance, it is difficult to accept this assertion at face value.

33. Florencia, *La milagrosa invencion*, 116–17.

34. The standard reference for his life is Leonard, *Don Carlos de Sigüenza y Góngora*.

35. It is reproduced in THG, 335–58.

36. Siguenza y Góngora, *Piedad heroyca*, 63.

37. There is some question as to how Sigüenza y Góngora would have obtained these papers, since he would have been no more than six years old at the time of Alva Ixtlilxochitl's death. See Velázquez, *La aparición*, 106. The papers may have come to Sigüenza y Góngora through Ixtlilxochitl's son, Juan de Alva y Cortés.

38. This was the edition of *Felicidad de Mexico* published in Seville in 1685. See "Origen milagroso," in THG, 326.

39. Siguenza y Góngora, *Piedad heroyca*, 65.

40. This was one of the factors that led Garibay to be skeptical about Sigüenza y Góngora's attribution of the authorship to Valeriano. "Confusions such as this at least make the testimony very suspect, if they do not totally invalidate it" (*Historia de la literatura náhuatl*, 2:264).

41. Icazbalceta, "Carta," 48. The date of Valeriano's death can be found in fray Juan Bautista's prologue to his collection of sermons in Nahuatl, quoted in García Icazbalceta, *Bibliografía mexicana del siglo XVI*, 475, "murió el año pasado de mil seiscientos y cinco, por el mes de agosto." Bautista had studied Nahuatl with Valeriano.

42. Botturini Benaduci, "Catálogo de obras guadalupanas," 408.

43. Mier y Noriega, "Cartas del Doctor," 791, n. 2.

44. "Sermón de Nuestra Señora de Guadalupe," 872, nota primera.

45. Guridi y Alcocer, "Apología de la aparición de Nuestra Señora de Guadalupe," 903.

46. Ibid., 904. See also the identification on 949–50.

47. Bustamante, "Elogios y defensa guadalupanos," 1020, 1021. Emphasis in original.

48. *Informe critico-legal*, 6. Emphases in original. The other two commissioners were Father José Ortigosa and licenciado Luis González Movellán.

49. Cuevas, *Historia*, 1:278, n. 8. He gave a somewhat more detailed account in "Documentos," 101–3. Pompa y Pompa also accepts this story and repeats it (*Album*, 32).

50. Burrus, *A Major Guadalupan Question*.

51. Burrus gives the year 1520 but cites no source (ibid., 59).

52. Gibson, *The Aztecs*, 382.

53. O'Gorman conjectures that Valeriano wrote the *Nican mopohua* in 1556, some time before Bustamante's sermon of 8 September. He considers this dating "not only valuable but a new contribution to the historiography of Guadalupe" (*Destierro de sombras*, 50).

54. Garibay, *Historia de la literatura náhuatl*, 2:104. It is remotely possible that it was the same as the cantar discussed in chapter 3. This will never be known for sure.

Chapter 10

1. Vetancurt, *Teatro mexicano*, tratado 5, n. 57, p. 128.

2. Taylor, "The Virgin of Guadalupe," 14–15. The data given by Wood show a great increase in the number of household Guadalupan images passed on by wills. The increase is especially notable after 1732 (Wood, "Christian Images," 275–76). One aspect of the increased devotion was an interest in finding Juan Diego's burial place and his remains.

3. The original is in the BNF, Mexicains, 303. All quotations are made with permission. The Nahuatl and Spanish are in parallel columns. Both are the work of a copyist. A copy of the Spanish translation of the *Relación* bound together with papers on the dispute over the patronato in Puebla and a dispute over whether the feast had an octave can be found in the BNAH, Papeles varios. Vera refers to this (*Tesoro guadalupano*, 2:393–94), as does Beristáin de Sousa (*Biblioteca*, 2:309–10). This may also be the account referred to by Botturini Benaduci ("Catálogo de obras guadalupanas," 409).

4. Fol. 1v, fol. 4r, fol. 6v, fol. 9r.

5. Fol. 98v. Emphasis in original. "Amo omitalhuitzino in impampatillotl" is retained in the Nahuatl in the Spanish translation.

6. I wish to express my thanks to Doctor Barry Sell and Professor James Lockhart for their observations on these points.

7. Karttunen has a brief discussion of Zohuatl as an alternate form of Cihuatl (*An Analytical Dictionary of Nahuatl*, 348).

8. "Huetzcatihuitz ohualihzac in tlahuizcallehualli in Martes, ca opohualloque: Zeyo ihuan ome in metztlicayotl icayo Diciembre in Xihuicayotl cemilpilli macuilmatlactlayotililiztli yeiya ihuan ce; auh iquac on yuh oneztca in cahuitl Oconhualxochipantlazaya in chalchiuhpapac tonalice nechiltonolizyotl inin quayollohualloyocayoca cemhueihuacatillotl, yuhqui macazan Oconhualtoton Xochitla cemmampan in papaquiltiloncayotl: ipampa ca centlallimotecatoc, yn yoltetlamachtillotl; . . . iquac oneziaya ca in Ilhuicatl inin tlalpolhuicancayotl concem papaquiltimallohuaya in tlacnellillotl ca in cemheicayotl icayotzin (in Teotl, in Tlatohuani) Dios, oquihualmotlazochachayhuiliaya; auh mochtin in tlachihualtzitzintim quinmoyollehuiliayah in tlalticpac tlacah quimoyhecteneuhcayotilitzinozque in iteyocoyanicatzin" (fol. 7v).

9. Vera, *Informaciones*, 195–215.

10. Ibid., 202.

11. For a listing of the sources and description of the symptoms, see Gibson, *The Aztecs*, 450.

12. Cabrera y Quintero, *Escudo de armas de Mexico*, 69, 70, 71. These incidents are also recounted by de la Maza, though he gives no sources (*El guadalupanismo mexicano*, 152–53).

13. Christian, *Apparitions*, 15. Harrington observes, "Spaniards of the sixteenth century believed God actively intervened in human affairs and the natural order when he was angered, and most vows promised devotion at a chapel in exchange for the cessation of the affliction" ("Mother of Death, Mother of Rebirth," 40).

14. Cabrera y Quintero, *Escudo de armas de Mexico*, book 2, chap. 1; Pompa y Pompa, *El Gran Acontecimiento Guadalupano*, 81.

15. Cabrera y Quintero, *Escudo de armas de Mexico*, book 2, chap. 2; Ita y Parra, *La Madre de la salud*, 3.

16. Ita y Parra, *Los pecados unica causa de las pestes*.

17. Ibid., 4.

18. Meeting of 26 January 1637, Actas del cabildo eclesiàstico de Mèxico, Family History Library, Salt Lake City, microfilm 0645755.

19. Ita y Parra, *La Madre de la salud*, 4.

20. Meeting of 20 February 1737, Actas del cabildo eclesiàstico de Mèxico, Family History Library, Salt Lake City, microfilm 0645755. Ita y Parra was one of the deputies. On 2 April the cabildo solemnly voted to accept the patronato.

21. Cetina, *Parecer*. It is known only through citations in *El patronato disputado*. The author of this work was Antonio Bera Cercada, a member of the cathedral chapter of Mexico. There was a great deal of rivalry between Mexico City and Puebla. See Lafaye, *Quetzalcoatl and Guadalupe*, 10, 87.

22. Velázquez, *La aparición*, 284.

23. It is quoted in ibid., 290–91. The *Congregatio pro Causis Sanctorum* quotes a decree of 24 April 1754 by which the pope granted his approval of the requests (641–42). This may have been just a preliminary formality.

24. *Officium in festo B. V. Mariae de Guadalupe Mexicanae*, ad matutinum.

25. Morelli, *Fasti novi orbis*, Ordinatio DCI, p. 627 (2 June 1757). The editor does not include the 1754 bull in this collection. A new set of constitutions for the confraternity at Guadalupe, the *Nuevas constituciones y reglas*, was also issued at about this same time.

26. Lorenzana, *Oracion á Nuestra Señora de Guadalupe*, vii.

27. For data on Cabrera, see THG, 413. Selections from the book can be found in 414–79.

28. Cabrera y Quintero, *Escudo de armas de Mexico*, 331, par. 659; 334, par. 663.

29. Florencia, *Estrella del norte*, chap. 32, par. 349, fols. 188v–89r.

30. A collegiate church is one that has a chapter of canons without at the same time being a cathedral. Until recent times the church at Guadalupe was called La Colegiata.

31. Carrillo y Pérez, *Pensil americano*, 55. For a detailed account of the negotiations that accompanied the establishment, see Echeverría y Veytia, *Baluartes de México*, 558–62.

32. Ita y Parra, *La imagen de Guadalupe*, 67. Miguel Sánchez made a similar interpretation of the number of stars.

33. Goicoechea, *La rossa por la rossa*, fol. 3r. The year before Goicoechea had preached the eighth day of the novena for the dedication of the new church at Tepeyac (*La maravilla immarcesible*).

34. On Morfi, see Robles, *Fray Agustín de Morfi y su obra*.

35. Camos, *Oracion panegyrica*, 3, 5. Campos later wrote an introduction to Bartolache's *Manifiesto satisfactorio* and the introduction to the published version of Morfi's sermon.

36. Peñuelas, *Panegirico a nuestra señora de Guadalupe*, 10.

37. Segura, *Milagro de la pintura y belleza de milagro*, 4r.

38. Ita y Parra, *El circulo de amor*, 18.

39. Ibid., 27.

40. Ita y Parra, *La imagen de Guadalupe*, 22.

41. Ibid., 28.

42. Villa, *Sermon de la milagrosa imagen de N. S. de Guadalupe de Mexico*, 26.

43. Segura, *Platica de la milagrosa imagen de Nuestra Señora de Guadalupe de Mexico*, 6–7, 11, 12, 13.

44. Torres, *Sermon de la santissima virgen de Guadalupe*, 18–19. On the latter page there is a Latin footnote that apparently is a quotation of some notations that were supplements to the papal bull. After explaining how Jesuit Francisco López had collected and arranged all the known documents, he "offers them to Your Holiness and regrets that authentic documents by eyewitnesses have not been found. It is assumed that they formerly existed, for now the archive is defective, with the result that no writing of our first bishop is to be found in it. Rather, when he

finds that the truth of this miracle had already been proposed in this [Roman] Curia, none of the documents produced at that time can now be found" (ibid., 19, n. 43).

45. Ponce de León, *El patronato que se celebra*, 5.

46. *Breve noticia de las fiestas*. Only five of the preachers are identified: Luis Beltrán de Beltrán, a diocesan priest of Guadalajara; José Jorge de Alfaro, also a diocesan priest; Manuel José Cassares, a Franciscan; José Camacho, an Augustinian; and Juan de Dios Ruiz, a Jesuit.

47. Lascano, *Sermon panegyrico*, unpaginated.

48. Ibid., 17, 26. The church at Guadalupe did not become a basilica in the strict sense of the term until the twentieth century.

49. Reynoso, *La injusticia por derecho justificada*, 4.

50. Ibid., 18.

51. Rodríguez Vallejo, *Sermon*, 4.

52. Ruiz de Castañeda, *Sermon panegyrico en glorias de Maria Santissima*, 6.

53. Ibid., 17.

54. San Cirilo, *El mas noble desempeño de la promesa mas generosa*, no pagination.

55. López Murto, *Maria Santissima exaltada en la América*, 9.

56. *Santoral en mexicano*, 2 vols. (mss. 1475–76); Pláticas en mexicano (ms. 1479); Sermones en mexicano, 4 vols. (mss. 1484–85, 1487–88); Manuscritos mexicanos, 2 vols. of model sermons (mss. 1481, 1493); Sermones y ejemplos en mexicano (ms. 1480).

57. Ms. 1493, 302–30.

58. Ms. 1481, 175–86.

59. Beristáin de Sousa, *Biblioteca*, 4:103; Zambrano and Gutiérrez Casillas, *Diccionario bio-bibliográfico*, 16:338–39.

60. I wish to thank Doctor Barry Sell for his help with the translation and his comments on the content of the sermon. The quotations are from his annotated copy.

61. Ricard, *Spiritual Conquest*, part 2, chap. 12. For a description of the postconquest Nahuatl theater, see Lockhart, *The Nahuas after the Conquest*, 401–10.

62. The Spanish is on fols. 17–49, the Nahuatl on fols. 50–80. Monumentos Guadalupanos, Rare Books and Manuscripts Division, The New York Public Library, Astor, Lenox and Tilden Foundations, all quotations with permission. Garibay deals with both plays in his *Historia de la literatura náhuatl*, 1:133–34. He considers the "Coloquios" as dating from the first third of the eighteenth century or at most from the end of the seventeenth. Horcasitas dated *El portento mexicano* as "1690 (?)" and the *coloquios* as "1718 (?)" (*El teatro nahuatl*, 79–80). There is an incomplete copy of the Nahuatl of the Coloquios made by Mexican priest-scholar José Pichardo in the BNF, Mexicains, 301, and a copy of "El portento" in Mexicains, 303. See also Brinckmann, "Coloquios de la Virgen de Guadalupe," 163–70. There is also a third play in the Monumentos Guadalupanos, the "Poema cómico-historial: El Yndio mas venturoso y milagro de milagros: La aparicion de Nuestra Señora de Guadalupe" by Mariano González de Avila y Uribe, but it is impossible to date it even approximately and so it has not been considered here.

63. The Nahuatl original is in fols. 81–119, the Spanish translation by Chimalpopoca Galicia in fols. 120–55v. Monumentos Guadalupanos, Rare Books and Manuscripts Division, The New York Public Library, Astor, Lenox and Tilden Foundations, all quotations with permission.

64. Botturini Benaduci, "Catálogo de obras guadalupanas," 409.

Chapter 11

1. For information on Botturini Benaduci, see Keen, *The Aztec Image*, 227–37; García Icazbalceta, "Don Lorenzo Boturini Benaduci." The legal proceedings against him have been reproduced in Glass, *The Boturini Collection*.

2. Keen, *The Aztec Image*, 228. As will be seen, his memory may not have been as good as Keen believes.

3. Botturini Benaduci, *Idea*, 2–3.

4. Ibid., 80–94; Botturini Benaduci, "Catálogo de obras guadalupanas," 407–12.

5. Botturini Benaduci, *Idea*, par. 34, no. 3, 81; Botturini Benaduci, "Catálogo de obras guadalupanas," 407–8.

6. Botturini Benaduci, *Idea*, par. 35, no. 4, 85–86; Botturini Benaduci, "Catálogo de obras guadalupanas," 408.

7. Botturini Benaduci, *Idea*, par. 333, no. 11, 79.

8. Ibid., par. 35, no. 5, 86; Botturini Benaduci, "Catálogo de obras guadalupanas," 408.

9. Botturini Benaduci, *Idea*, par. 35, no. 5, 86; Botturini Benaduci, "Catálogo de obras guadalupanas," 408.

10. Botturini Benaduci, *Idea*, par. 34, no. 3, 82; Botturini Benaduci, "Catálogo de obras guadalupanas," 406; de la Maza, *El guadalupanismo mexicano*, 75–76.

11. Botturini Benaduci, *Idea*, par. 35, no. 5, 83; Botturini Benaduci, "Catálogo de obras guadalupanas," 406–7.

12. Botturini Benaduci, *Idea*, par. 35, no. 7, 87; Botturini Benaduci, "Catálogo de obras guadalupanas," 408.

13. *Congregatio pro Causis Sanctorum*, 89, which says that the inventory is in the BNAH, Sección Manuscritos, Colección Antigua, no. 236, fol. 65. A copy of the testament was listed in Botturini's inventory of 1743 but was listed as missing in that of 1823. See Glass, *The Boturini Collection and a Concordance of the Inventories*, 39.

14. Botturini Benaduci, *Idea*, 157–58. This quotation from the will is not in the THG. Note the use of *sapa* to indicate Saturday. The full form is *sapato*, a Spanish loan word. Karttunen and Lockhart list *sabadotica* as a Spanish loanword under the year 1547. Joining the Spanish word to the Nahuatl enclitic was the common method of indicating days in the sixteenth century (Karttunen and Lockhart, *Nahuatl in the Middle Years*, 55). The variant of María Luisa for María Lucía is also found in Florencia's quotation from the *Relación*. The phrase "inoque cayotilique" is meaningless. The "printed history" appears to be the *Nican mopohua*.

15. Botturini Benaduci, *Idea*, 90; Botturini Benaduci, "Catálogo de obras guadalupanas," 410.

16. For an explanation of this, see Velázquez, *La aparición*, 73.
17. [Lorenzana], *Historia de Nueva-España*, 36, n. 1.
18. Ibid.
19. Quoted in Velázquez, *La aparición*, 74. According to Glass, the original, a copy, and a translation by Carlos de Tapia Centeno were in the inventories of 1743, 1746, and 1771 but were missing from the inventory of 1823 (*The Boturini Collection and a Concordance of the Inventories*, 39).
20. Velázquez, *La aparición*, 76–77.
21. BNF, Mexicains, 317. Quoted with permission.
22. Velázquez, *La aparición*, 74. This would explain why it was not in the inventory of 1823.
23. Ibid., 74–75.
24. Ibid., 76.
25. Ibid.
26. Quoted in ibid., 76.
27. A Spanish translation made by J. H. Cornyn and published in *El Universal*, 10 July 1928, can be found in Velázquez, *La aparición*, 79, n. 27.
28. The word *tictolique* is unintelligible. Tapia Centeno, Segura, and Chimalpopoca Galicia all translated it as "we have seen," though the correct form would be *tiquittaque*. Velázquez suggests that the intended form was *ticolinique*, "we have moved or transferred" (*La Aparación*, 81–82).

The complete Nahuatl text from the BNF is as follows and is reproduced with permission.

M.a IHS. JPH.
Ica in itocatzin Dios tetatzin Dios ipiltzin Dios Espiritu Santo yei persona ihuan in zan huel centetzintli Dios ixquich ihueli.

Axcan sabado à 11 de Marzo de 1559 años inimachiotia itech nitlatoa in nochan copal Cuauhtitlan onech mocahuilili in notatzin Juan Garcia, in nonantzin Maria Martina, ca huel nican notlacatian in itic altepetl San Buenaventura Quauhtitlan notlaxilacal S.n Joseph Millo cate in nohueltehuatzin D.a Ynes Martina inamictzin Bentura Morales in no teicatzin Gregorio Martin, ye omomiquilique zan nocel onocauh in notlacatocain notlazotatzin Juan Martin mochintin omomiquilique ic nopilhuan; zan çe omocauh notelpoch itoca Francisco Martin, azo nemi, anozo amo intla nemiz intla oniezque ipilhuan: cemixquich quicuizque ceme ixlta matizque mozcalizque, ipan tlatozque inin amatl tlacuiloz yacaque quitlatoz in notlatol ayac aquinquimaxcatiz in notlal . . . ihuan in quenin niquizani in nican ipan altepetl Quauhtitlan; ihuan tlaxilacalli S.n Joseph millan in nican omohuapauhtzino in telpochtli Juan Diegotzin quin tepan omonamictizinoto in ompa S.ta Cruz Tlacpac inahuac S.n Pedro quimonamicti in ichpochtli itoca Malintzin iciuhca omomiquili in ichpochtli, ca icel omocauh in Juan Diego zatepan . . . yuhqui quitzihuitl . . . in ipaltzinco omochiuh itlamahuizolli in ompa Tepeyacac . . . campa monexiti in tlazocihuapilli S.ta Maria, in oncan tictolique itlazoixcopinque Guadalupe; ca huel nican toaxcatzin in ipan toaltepeuh Quauhtitlan ahui inin axcan huel mochi ca huel . . . cà in noyolia in anima in notlanequiliz nicnonemactilia yehuatzin toaxca copalquahuitl in mochi mani tlateltozca icac ce quahuitl ma aciticani caltitlani imochi nicmomaquilia [*sic*] in ichpochtli tepeyacac, in huel nicaqui tlaixmayan in quimochihuililizque, cà xacatl izca nicanquiquimocentemanitilizque in nopilhuayo noxhuihuan in tlà onyezque, ye matia quimoyeyantilizque in tlazocihuapilli amo quimocuiquilizque in itlaltzin. Nicnomemactilitzinoa izampa n[or:x]oyocoxca . . . quimotequipanilhuizque . . . ihuan inic quitoa ninomazoaltili . . . zazo ac[or: oc] yehualtzin . . . moyezitiez quimotlapieliz in ipan altepetl Quautitlan, ipan motlatoltiz noce xeyehuantin in tlaxilacaleque, auh ac tehuatzin in tipilli, in titeuhtli, in timaltepehualiz in Cuauhtitlan, ma niman tecuantin ticmotlaxiliz in inemactzin tlazocihuapilli, ma ipati timotactloctitzinoz zatepan . . . yehuatzin mopantzinco motlatoltitzinoz in iquac timomiquiliz . . . ihuan ontlamantli notlahuitl inic mocacqui itech calliuhtica ontlamantli intotatzin San Joseph: ihuic copa in huehue octli ocotlama . . . otli oquimocahuilili inonamictzin itocactzin Bentura Mariano, S.n Joseph Caltitlan mochica in calli inic mextimani ome copalquahuitl, ihuan ce tapacatlatili ca yaxcatzin S. Joseph ayacaquin quimaxcatiz miec ac tlacatl imixpan omopopohuiz inin amatl . . . itotacocac S.n Joseph Caltitlan Texapa. Escribano Morales.

29. It is reproduced between pages 88 and 89 in Cuevas's *Album*. He does not cite the source from which he got the copy. The orthography differs from that of the copy in the BNF.

30. Velázquez believed that Segura was responsible for Juana Martín when he mistranslated "in notlacatoca in notlazotatzin Juan Martin" as "que me llamo Juana Martin." He added that "Canon Segura was the only one who understood that she was named Juana Martin" (*La Aparición*, 80). He overlooked the fact that Lorenzana had made the same identification. It is impossible to tell where the name Gregoria María came from.

31. Bravo Ugarte also accepted this identification (*Cuestiones históricas guadalupanas*, 29–30).

32. On oral spontaneity in Nahuatl testaments, see Lockhart, *The Nahuas after the Conquest*, 364–66.

33. On the structure of postconquest Nahuatl wills, see ibid., 251–55, 468–74.

34. For a summary of his life and work, see Keen, *The Aztec Image*, 237–40.

35. Ibid., 240.

36. The text of this work that deals with Guadalupe and Remedios can be found in THG, 530–77. See also Velázquez, *La aparición*, 337.

37. Fernández de Echeverría y Veytia, *Baluartes de México*, 532, 536.

38. Ibid., 539.

39. For a good summary of Clavigero's life and work, see Ronan, *Clavigero*.

40. Reproduced in a Spanish translation, "Breve noticia sobre la prodigiosa y renombrada imagen de Nuestra Señora de Guadalupe de México," in THG, 579–96. The original work was published anonymously but was well known as Clavigero's. See Ronan, *Clavigero*, 332.

41. "Breve noticia," 581, 585, 589, 590, 592.

42. Ibid., 593.

43. Ibid., 594.

44. Ibid.

45. Reprinted in THG, 597–651.

46. Ibid., 600.

47. Ibid., 603.

48. Ibid., n. 4.

49. Mier y Noriega, "Cartas del Doctor," 802–3.

50. According to Ignacio Manuel Altamirano, this work was printed in two volumes in 1852 under the title *Disertación histórica sobre la aparición de la portentosa imagen de María Santísima de Guadalupe de México* by the press of the Voz de la Religión ("La fiesta de Guadalupe," 1164). Since I have been unable to locate any copy of this work I have consulted a manuscript copy in the Bancroft Library, Mexican Manuscript 71, 2 vols., titled "Obra del S. D. Francisco Xavier Conde y Oquendo, canonigo de la Sto(a,-) Yglesia de la Puebla de los Angeles." These volumes came from the collection of J. M. Andrade.

51. Velázquez, *La aparición*, 239–40.

52. Ibid., 246.

53. Bartolache, "Manifiesto satisfactorio," 648; Velázquez, *La aparición*, 246. Velázquez believed that they were referring to the covering noted by the protomedicato in 1666 and the additions cited by Florencia, though these latter would have been removed by 1787. According to Callahan, these retouchings included the angel, the extension of the mantel to touch the angel's hand, the sunburst, the golden grid laid over the Virgin's dress (which does not follow the folds of the garment), the belt, the cuffs, and the repositioning of the hands (Callahan, *The Tilma under Infra-Red Radiation*, 6–21).

54. Quoted in Velázquez, *La aparición*, 247.

55. Ibid., 337; Robles, *Fray Agustín de Morfi*, 11–13.

56. Reprinted in THG, 691–701.

57. Ibid., 692.

58. Ibid., 693.

59. Ibid., 699.

60. Ibid., 701.

61. "Sermon guadalupano," 730–52.

62. See Keen, *The Aztec Image*, 304.

63. Mier y Noriega, "Cartas del Doctor," 757–861.

64. Ibid., 768.

65. Ibid., 772, 780–81, 790. Mier did not specify where this was to be found in Torquemada, and I have been unable to locate it. One of the proposals presented to the Third Mexican Provincial Council of 1585 was that Indians should be forbidden to have Old Testament names or double names.

66. For data on Uribe, as he is generally called, and the background of his *Disertacion*, see García Gutiérrez, *Apuntamientos*, 99–101.

67. Fernández de Uribe, *Sermon de Nuestra Señora de Guadalupe de Mexico*, 3.
68. Ibid., 17–18.
69. Ibid., 20–21.
70. "Critique d'un sermon sur N. D. de Guadalupe et divers autres sujets (1794–1795)," BNF, Mexicains 270, fol. 29r. Quoted with permission.
71. Fernández de Uribe, *Disertacion historico-critica*, 16.
72. Ibid., 21.
73. Ibid., 23.
74. Ibid. In a footnote Uribe says Sopeña died in June 1792 at the age of seventy-nine.
75. Ibid., 71.
76. Ibid., 77.
77. Ibid., 78.
78. Ibid., 79. It should be noted that Uribe must have taken this from Becerra Tanco's *Origen milagroso* rather than the *Felicidad de Mexico*.

Chapter 12

1. Typical of this confusion is the statement made by Jesuit Esteban Antícoli that in 1556 Francisco de Bustamante "denied the apparition" and that Montúfar had preached in favor of it (*Defensa*, 87, 225).
2. Cited in Taylor, "The Virgin of Guadalupe," 26, n. 6.
3. Lockhart, *The Nahuas after the Conquest*, 246.
4. Florencia, *Estrella del norte*, chap. 30, par. 344, fol. 185r.
5. The sermon by a peninsular priest that helped provoke Florencia's book was delivered at a Guadalupan celebration sponsored by Mancera's daughter in 1683 (*Estrella del norte*, unpaginated). According to Francisco de Siles, when Mancera was preparing to enter Mexico City, he replaced the Immaculate Conception with Guadalupe on his standards (letter of approval for López de Avilés, *Ueridicum admodum anagramma*, 195v).
6. García Icazbalceta, "Carta," 41.
7. Steck, *Motolinía's History*, 103, n. 1.
8. "'Is there any point to which you would wish to draw my attention?' 'To the curious incident of the dog in the night-time.' 'The dog did nothing in the night-time.' 'That was the curious incident,' remarked Sherlock Holmes" ("The Adventure of Silver Blaze").
9. In his letter of approval for López de Avilés, *Ueridicum admodum anagramma*, fol. 195v.
10. García Icazbalceta, *Carta*, 67–69; Mier y Noriega, "Cartas del Doctor," 5, 823–24.
11. In 1669 Francisco de Siles identified Guadalupe with the Immaculate Conception, "in which [God] wanted to give testimony in favor of the mystery of the Immaculate Conception of his mother" (approbation for López de Avilés, *Ueridicum admodum anagramma*, fol. 195v). In 1672 Ignacio de Santa Cruz Aldana concluded a sermon with a prayer of praise to "Virgin Mary of Guadalupe, conceived

without sin" (*Sermon en la festividad de la presentacion*, unpaginated).

12. This must not, however, be given undue importance. The Indians of Cuauhtitlan were answering a question about the goodness of Juan Diego's life that was presented to them by the judges. The uprightness of his life was viewed as important in showing the authenticity of his revelation.

A Note on Sources

The standard historical distinction of primary and secondary sources is difficult to apply to the Mexican Guadalupe legend. The only sources of the apparition account, which originated with Miguel Sánchez (1648) and Luis Laso de la Vega (1649), are printed or published ones. As has been indicated throughout this study, however, there are manuscript materials to be found in some archives, though ultimately they are of meager help. The most important repository, of course, is the archive and library of the basilica of Guadalupe in Mexico City. It is truly regrettable that it is closed to researchers at the present time. Among other items, it contains the original of the capitular inquiry of 1666, a copy of the will of Gregoria María, the original of the annals of Juan Bautista, and the papers of Archbishop Moya de Contreras concerning the payment of dowries. Fortunately, most of these materials are accessible elsewhere. What else the library may contain is not clear.

The Biblioteca Nacional and the Archivo General de la Nación in Mexico City have no manuscripts. The Biblioteca Nacional de Antropología e Historia in Mexico City has copies of the *Anales antiguos de Mexico y sus contornos* and a copy of the Códice Gómez de Orozco, but these are not autographs. A third item, a copy of the annals of Juan Bautista, has disappeared from the collection. The archive of the cathedral of Mexico City has the minutes of the meetings of the ecclesiastical cabildo, but these are more accessible in the microfilm copies in the Family History Library, Salt Lake City, Utah. The cabildo, which never dealt with the story of the apparitions, was concerned with the administration of the ermita, such as the payment of salaries and the appointment of preachers for special occasions. The Archivo General de Indias in Seville has the two letters of Diego de Santa María that were published by Cuevas but nothing touching the origins of the apparition account. It is to be hoped that the report on the ermita sent to the Council of the Indies by Moya de Contreras in 1575 may still be there and may yet be found. It could alter the entire history of the shrine and the apparition tradition. I was unable to find it when I was researching the archbishop's life.

Two repositories that are of more help are the Monumentos Guadalupanos in the New York Public Library, which were originally part of the Ramírez papers, and the Fonds Mexicains in the salon of Oriental manuscripts in the Bibliothèque Nationale de France in Paris. Because of their fragile condition, the papers in both places can be consulted only on microfilm. I wish to thank Professor John Frederick Schwaller for allowing me to use his survey of the documents in the New York Public Library.

The Monumentos Guadalupanos contain the following materials that are pertinent to this study: copies of all or parts of the *Nican mopohua*, though none earlier than the late seventeenth century (piece 1, ser. 1, vol. 1; piece 2, ser. 1, vol. 1; ser. 2, vol. 1); "Celestial reina y Señora," by Laso de la Vega (a Spanish translation of his introduction to the *Huey tlamahuiçoltica*, ser. 1, vol. 20); "Colloquios de la Aparición de la Virgen S.ta M.a de Guadalupe escritos en Mexicano traducidos por el Lic. D. Faustino Galicia," both the Spanish translation (ser. 1, vol. 2, fols. 17–49) and the Nahuatl (ibid., fols. 50–80); "El portento mexicano" (ibid., fols. 81–119); "Sermon de Santa Maria de Tepeyac," which is actually the *Inin huey tlamahuiçoltzin* (ibid., fols. 240–53); "Oracion con que debe suplicarse o que de dirigirse a nuestra celestial reina y señora Madre de Guadalupe," a Spanish translation of the concluding prayer of the *Huey tlamahuiçoltica* (ibid., 258v); a copy of the so-called will of Gregoria María in parallel columns of Nahuatl and Spanish (ser. 1, vol. 1, fols. 24–26); the 1722 testimony of Lizardi y Valle (ibid., fols. 77–152); copies of the will of Sebastián Lomelín (ser. 2, vol. 1, fols. 9–14v, published by Vera); and the so-called will of Gregoria María (ibid., fol. 24).

The Bibliothèque Nationale has the following materials of interest: the will of Francisco de Verdugo Quetzalmamalitzin (Mexicains, 243, published by Vera); "Del famoso idolo de la Toci o cibeles Mexicana que estaba en Guadalupe," 5 August 1898, ten folios, not very informative (Mexicains, 260); "Critique d'un sermon sur Notre-Dame de Guadalupe et divers autres sujets (1794–1795)," eighty pages, the official report by two censors, Patricio Fernández de Uribe and Manuel de Omana y Sotomayor on Mier's Guadalupan sermon; not important in the history of the tradition but invaluable for anyone studying Mier or his work (Mexicains, 270); "Coloquio de la aparicion de la Virgen Santa Maria de Guadalupe," copied by Pichardo, the same as in the New York Public Library (Mexicains, 301); "Fragment d'une histoire de N. D. de Guadalupe (Nahuatl)," copied by Pichardo, same as in the New York Public Library (Mexicains, 302, fols. 1v–23r); Nahuatl of the so-called will of Gregoria María (ibid., 26r–27v); fragment of the *Nican mopohua* (ibid., fols. 28v–33r); "Relacion Mercurina de la aparicion de Nuestra Señora la Virgen Maria de

Guadalupe en la lengua mexicana genuina y traducido en castellano, por Dn
Joseph Perez de la Fuente en Amecameca, a 6 dias del mes de mayor de 1712
años," copied by Pichardo (Mexicains, 303); "El portento mexicano," the same
as in the New York Public Library, copied by Pichardo (ibid.); the will of Gregoria María (Mexicains, 317, in Nahuatl, fols. 2r–3r, in Spanish translation,
fols. 3v–4r); translation of the *Nican mopohua* made by order of Archbishop Lorenzana by Carlos Tapia y Centeno, followed by a vocabulario (ibid.); "Recueil
de notes de Gama sur l'image de N. D. de Guadalupe," undated (Mexicains,
320).

Bibliography

Acosta, José de. *Historia natural y moral de las Indias*. Introduction, appendix, and anthology by Barbara G. Beddal. Valencia: Valencia Cultural, 1977.

————. *De Procuranda Indorum Salute: pacificación y colonización*. By L. Pereña V., Abril C. Baciero, A. García, D. Ramos, J. Barrientos, and F. Maseda. Corpus Hispanorum de Pace 23. Madrid: Consejo Superior de Investigaciones Científicas, 1984.

Album conmemorativo del 450 aniversario de las apariciones de Nuestra Señora de Guadalupe. Mexico City: Ediciones Buena Nueva, 1981.

Alegre, Francisco Javier. *Historia de la provincia de la Compañía de Jesús de Nueva España*. New ed. by Ernest J. Burrus, S.J., and Félix Zubillaga, S.J. Bibliotheca Instituti Historici S.J., 9. Rome: Institutum Historicum S.J., 1956.

Alejos-Grau, Carmen José. *Juan de Zumárraga y su "Regla Cristiana Breve."* Pamplona: Servicio de Publicaciones de la Universidad de Navarra, 1991.

Alfaro y Azevedo, José Jorge de. *Sermon de rogativa, . . . que se hizo en la muy noble y leal ciudad de Zacatecas . . . decia . . . el r. p. fr. Joseph George de alfaro y Azevedo*. Mexico City: N.p., 1758.

Altamirano, Ignacio Manuel. La fiesta de Guadalupe (1884). In *Testimonios históricos guadalupanos*. Ed. Ernesto de la Torre Villar and Ramiro Navarro de Anda. Mexico City: Fondo de Cultura Económica, 1982, 1127–1210.

Alva Ixtlilxochitl, Fernando de. *Obras históricas de don Fernando de Alva Ixtlilxóchitl*. Ed. Alfredo Chavero. 2 vols. Mexico City: Editorial Nacional, 1965.

America Pontificia Primi Saeculi Evangelizationis, 1493–1592: documenta Pontificia ex registris et minutis praesertim in Archivo Secreto Vaticano existentibus collegit, edidit Josef Metzler mandatu Pontificii Comitatus de Scientiis Historicis. 2 vols. Vatican City: Libreria Editrice Vaticana, 1991.

Anales antiguos de Mexico y sus contornos compilados por J. Fernando Ramírez. Anales Mexicanos no. 1. Anonymous work in the Mexican language, translated into Spanish by Licenciado Faustino Chimalpopoca Galicia. 4 vols. Mexico City: Biblioteca Aportación Histórica, 1948.

Anales de Cuauhtitlan. Noticias históricas de Mexico y sus contornos compiladas por D. José Fernando Ramírez y traducidas por los señores Faustino Galicia Chimalpopoca,

Gumesindo Mendoza y Felipe Sanchez Solis. Publication of the annals of the Museo Nacional. Mexico City: Imprenta de Ignacio Escalante, 1885.

Anales de Tlatelolco. Some historical annals of the Mexican nation and the Codex Tlatelolco. Version prepared and annotated by Heinrich Berlin, with a summary of the annals and an interpretation of the codex by Robert H. Barlow. Sources for the history of Mexico. Collection published under the direction of Salvador Toscano. 2. Mexico City: Antigua Librería Robredo, de José Porrúa e Hijos, 1948.

Andrews, J. Richard. Directionals in Classical Nahuatl. *Texas Linguistic Forum* 18 (1981): 1–16.

[Antícoli, Esteban]. *El Magisterio de la Iglesia y la Virgen de Tepeyac.* By a priest of the Society of Jesus. Querétaro: N.p., 1892.

[————]. *Defensa de la aparicion de la Virgen Maria en el Tepeyac, escrita por un sacerdote de la Compañia de Jesus contra un libro impreso en Mexico el año de 1891.* Puebla: Imprenta del Colegio Pio de Artes y Oficios, 1893.

[————]. *Historia de la aparición de la Sma. Virgen María de Guadalupe en México desde el Año de MDXXXI al del MDCCCXCV por un sacerdote de la Compañía de Jesús.* 2 vols. Mexico City: Tip. y Lit. "La Europea" de Fernando Camacho, 1897.

Argüello, Manuel de. *Accion de gracias a la soberana reyna del cielo Maria SS. de Guadalupe en su magnifico templo con que solemnizò el Real Acuerdo de esta Corte, en virtud de real Orden, las victorias que consiguiò personalmente la Magestad del Rey nuestro Señor Don Philippo V (que Dios guarde) en Viruega, y Villaviciosa los dias 8. y 11. de Diziembre del año de 1710 . . . Predicola El M. R. P. Fr. Manvel de Argvello.* Mexico City: Viuda de Miguel de Ribera, 1711.

Arlegui, José. *Sagrado paladion del americano orbe. Sermon que en la rogativa publica, que hizo a Maria S.ma de Guadalupe, la muy noble, ê ilustre, ciudad de San Luis Potosi por el feliz sucesso de las catholicas armas de nuestro catholico monarcha el señor d. Phelippe V . . . Predicò el R. P. fr. Joseph Arlegui.* Mexico City: Viuda de J. B. de Hogal, 1743.

Aroche, Miguel de. *Flor de la edad de la milagrosissima imagen de Maria Santissima en su concepcion en gracia. Sermon, que a la celebridad de los dos siglos de su aparicion en Guadalupe, predicó El M. R. P. M. Fr. Miguel de Aroche del Sagrado, Real, y Militar Orden de Nuestra Señora de la Merced, Redempcion de Cautivos.* Mexico City: Por Joseph Bernardo de Hogal, 1732.

The Art of Nahuatl Speech: The Bancroft Dialogues. Edited with a preliminary study by Frances Karttunen and James Lockhart. UCLA Latin American Studies vol. 65. UCLA Latin American Center Publications. Los Angeles: University of California, Los Angeles, 1987.

Ayala, Antonio de. *Deprecacion que por los temblores de tierra, fuego, y enfermedades . . . hizo el p. fr. Antonio de Ayala.* Mexico City: N.p., 1712.

Bacigalupo, Marvyn Helen. *A Changing Perspective: Attitudes Toward Creole Society in New Spain (1521–1610).* London: Tamesis Books, 1981.

Bancroft, Hubert Howe. *History of Mexico.* 5 vols. In *The Works of Hubert Howe Bancroft.* 39 vols. San Francisco: A. L. Bancroft & Company, Publishers, 1883–1890.

Bartolache y Díaz de las Posadas, José Ignacio. Manifiesto satisfactorio u opúsculo guadalupano (1790). In *Testimonios históricos guadalupanos.* Ed. Ernesto de la Torre

Villar and Ramiro Navarro de Anda. Mexico City: Fondo de Cultura Económica, 1982, 597–651.

Bartolomé de las Casas in History: Toward an Understanding of the Man and His Work. Ed. Juan Friede and Benjamin Keen. DeKalb: Northern Illinois University Press, 1971.

Bataillon, Marcel, and Saint-Lu, André. *El Padre Las Casas y la defensa de los indios.* Spanish translation by Javier Alfaya y Barbara McShane. Barcelona: Editorial Ariel, 1976.

Becerra Tanco, Luis. *Origen milagroso del santuario de Nuestra Señora de Guadalupe.* Mexico City: Viuda de Bernardo Calderón, 1666. Rev. ed. published in 1675, 1685, 1745, with the title *Felicidad de Mexico.*

———. Origen milagroso del santuario de Nuestra Señora de Guadalupe (1666). In *Testimonios históricos guadalupanos.* Ed. Ernesto de la Torre Villar and Ramiro Navarro de Anda. Mexico City: Fondo de Cultura Económica, 1982, 309–33.

Beltrán, Luis. *El poder sobre las aguas, dado a Nuestra Patrona la Virgen Santissima en su divina imagen de Guadalupe . . . Predico el dr. d. Lvis Beltran.* Mexico City: N.p., 1765.

Bengoechea, Agustín de. *La gloria de Maria en sus gracias para con los americanos . . . dixo el r. p. fr. Augustin de Bengoechea.* Mexico City: N.p., 1768.

Benítez, Lorenzo. *Sermon panegyrico qve en la solemn fiesta con que celebra la Aparicion de N. Señora de Gvadalvpe de Mexico, su Illustre Archi-Cofradia, cita en el Convento de N. P. San Francisco de Mexico: Predicò el P. Fr. Lorenço Benitez Maestro de Estudiantes de Theologia en dicho Convento, el dia doze de Diziembre de el año passado de 1684.* Mexico City: Viuda de Francisco Rodriguez Lupercio, 1685.

[Bera Cercada, Antonio]. *El patronato disputado, dissertacion apologetica, Por el Voto, Eleccion, y Juramento de Patrona, a Maria Santissima, venerada en su imagen de Guadalupe de Mexico, e invalidado para negarle el rezo del Comun (que à Titulo de Patrona electa, y jurada, segun el Decreto de la Sagrada Congregacion de Ritos) se le ha dado en esta Metropoli, por el Br. D. Jvan Pablo Zetina Infante, Mro. de ceremonias en la Cathedral de la Puebla.* Mexico City: Imprenta Real del Superior Gobierno, y del Nuevo Rezado de doña Maria de Rivera, 1741.

Beristáin de Sousa, José Mariano. *Biblioteca hispanoamericana septentrional.* 5 vols. Mexico City: Ediciones Fuente Cultural, 1883.

Bierhorst, John. *A Nahuatl-English Dictionary and Concordance to the Cantares Mexicanos. With an Analytical Transcription and Grammatical Notes.* Stanford, Calif.: Stanford University Press, 1985.

Boban, Eugène. *Document pour servir a l'histoire du Mexique: catalogue raissoné de la collection de M. E.-Eugène Goupil (ancienne collection J.-M.-A. Aubin).* 2 vols. Paris: Ernest Leroux, Editeur, 1891.

Borruel, Cosme. *La imagen mas clara de lo mas oculto de Maria. Sermon, que en el dia de Nuestra Señora de Gvadalvpe, en su Colegio apostolico de Zacatecas . . . predicò el Padre fr. Cosme Borruel.* Mexico City: N.p., 1733.

Botturini Benaduci, Lorenzo. *Idea de una nueva historia general de la America Septentrional fundada sobre material copioso de figuras, symbolos, caractères, y geroglificos, cantares, y manuscritos de autores indios ultimamente descubiertos. Dedicala al Rey n.tro Senor en su real y supremo consejo de las Indias el cavallero Lorenzo Boturini Benaduci, Señor de la Torre y de Hono.* Madrid: En la Imprenta de Juan de Zunniga, 1746.

————. *Historia de la América Septentrional por el caballero Lorenzo Boturini Benaducci, señor de la Torre y de Hono, cronista real en las Indias, edición, prólogo y notas por Manuel Ballesteros Gabrois.* Madrid: N.p., 1948.

————. Catálogo de obras guadalupanas. In *Testimonios históricos guadalupanos.* Ed. Ernesto de la Torre Villar and Ramiro Navarro de Anda. Mexico City: Fondo de Cultura Económica, 1982, 407–12.

Bravo Ugarte, José. *Cuestiones históricas guadalupanas.* 2d ed., expanded. Mexico City: Editorial Jus, 1966.

Breve noticia de las fiestas, en que la muy ilustre ciudad de Zacatecas explicó su agradecimiento en la confirmacion del patronato de Nrâ. Srâ. de Guadalupe, el mes de Septiembre del año de 1758 por N. SS. P. El Señor Benedicto XIV. Y Sermones predicados en dicha funcion. Siendo sus Comisarios Diputados los Señores D. Joseph de Joaristi, Theniente de Capitàn General, y D. Francisco Xavier de Aristoarena, y Lanz, Theniente de Infanterìa Miliciana. Por un apassionado de dicha Ciudad de Zacatecas. Mexico City: Imprenta de los Herederos de dona Maria de Rivera, 1759.

Brinckmann, Bärbel. Coloquios de la Virgen de Guadalupe. *Revista Española de Antropología Americana.* Departamento de Antropología y Etnología de América, Facultad de Geografía e Historia Universidad Complutense de Madrid (1978): 163–70.

Brinton, Daniel G. *Ancient Nahuatl Poetry, containing the Nahuatl text of XXVII ancient Mexican poems.* With a translation, introduction, notes, and vocabulary. Brinton's Library of Aboriginal American Literature, no. 7. Philadelphia: Ams Press, 1896.

Burkhart, Louise. *The Slippery Earth: Nahua-Christian Moral Dialogue in Sixteenth-Century Mexico.* Tucson: University of Arizona Press, 1989.

————. The Cult of the Virgin of Guadalupe in Mexico. In *South and Meso-American Native Spirituality: From the Cult of the Feathered Serpent to the Theology of Liberation.* Ed. Gary H. Gossen in collaboration with Miguel León-Portilla. Vol. 4 of *World Spirituality: An Encyclopedic History of the Religious Quest,* 198–227. New York: Crossroad Publishing Company, 1993.

Burrus, Ernest J., S.J. *A Major Guadalupan Question Resolved: Did General Scott Seize the Valeriano Account of the Guadalupan Apparitions?* CARA Studies on Popular Devotion, 2. Guadalupan Studies, 2. Washington, D.C.: N.p., 1979.

————. *The Oldest Copy of the Nican Mopohua.* CARA Studies on Popular Devotion, 4. Guadalupan Studies, 4. Washington, D.C.: N.p., 1981.

————. La continuidad y congruencia de los documentos de la Historia Guadalupana. *Congreso Mariológico.* Mexico City: N.p., 1982.

————. La copia más antigua del Nican Mopohua. *Histórica: Organo del Centro de Estudios Guadalupanos* (1986): 5–27.

Bustamante, Carlos María. Elogios y defensa guadalupanos (1831–1843). In *Testimonios históricos guadalupanos.* Ed. Ernesto de la Torre Villar and Ramiro Navarro de Anda. Mexico City: Fondo de Cultura Económica, 1982, 1009–91.

Cabrera, Miguel. *Maravilla americana y conjunto de raras maravillas observadas con la direccion de las reglas del Arte de la Pintura en la prodigiosa imagen de N.ra Señora de Guadalupe de Mexico por D. Miguel Cabrera, pintor del Ilustrisimo Señor D. D. Manuel Josef Rubio y Salinas, dignisimo Arzobispo de Mexico, y del Consejo de su Magestad, etc., a quien se la consagra.* Mexico City: Imprenta del Real y Más Antiguo Colegio de San Ildefonso, 1756.

Cabrera y Quintero, Cayetano de. *Escudo de armas de Mexico: celestial proteccion de esta nobilissima ciudad, de la Nueva-España, y de casi todo el Nuevo Mundo, Maria Santissima en su portentosa imagen del Mexicano Guadalupe, milagrosamente apparecida en el palacio arzobispal el Año de 1531. y jurada su principal patrona el passado de 1737. En la angustia que ocasionò la Pestilencia, que cebada con mayor rigor en los Indios, mitigò sus ardores al abrigo de tanta sombra: describiala de orden, y especial nombramiento ... D. Cayetano de Cabrera, y Quintero, Presbytero de este arzobispado.* Mexico City: Por Viuda de D. Joseph Bernardo de Hogal, 1746.

———. Escudo de armas de Mexico (1746). In *Testimonios históricos guadalupanos*. Ed. Ernesto de la Torre Villar and Ramiro Navarro de Anda. Mexico City: Fondo de Cultura Económica, 1982, 413–79.

Callahan, Philip Serna. *The Tilma under Infra-Red Radiation*. CARA Studies on Popular Devotion, 2. Guadalupan Studies, 3. Washington, D.C.: N.p., 1981.

Campbell, Ena. The Virgin of Guadalupe and the Female Self-Image: A Mexican Case History. In *Mother Worship: Theme and Variations*. Ed. James J. Preston. Chapel Hill: University of North Carolina Press, 1982, 5–24.

Campos, Juan Gregorio de. *Oracion panegyrica a Maria Santisima en su portentosa imagen de Guadalupe, Pronunciada en su Santuario el dia 27. de Mayo de este año de 1781. Por el P. Dr. y Mrô. D. Juan Gregorio de Campos, Presbytero de la Real Congregacion del Oratorio de N. P. S. Felipe Neri en la anual fiesta que celebran los Caballeros Labradores del Reyno.* Mexico City: Por D. Felipe de Zúñiga y Ontiveros, 1781.

Candelaria, Michael R. *Popular Religion and Liberation: The Dilemma of Liberation Theology.* Albany: State University of New York Press, 1990.

Cantares Mexicanos: Songs of the Aztecs. Translated from the Nahuatl with an introduction and commentary by John Bierhorst. Stanford, Calif.: Stanford University Press, 1985.

Carranza, Francisco Javier. *La transmigracion de la iglesia a Guadalupe. Sermon, que el 12. de Diciembre de 1748. años Predicò, en el templo de N. S. de Guadalupe de la Ciudad de Santiago de Queretaro, el P. Prefecto Francisco Xavier Carranza, Professo de quarto voto de la Sagrada Compañia de Jesus.* Mexico City: En el Colegio Real, y Mas Antiguo de S. Ildefonso de Mexico, 1749.

Carreño, Alberto María. Don Fray Alonso de Montúfar, the Second Archbishop of Mexico, and the Devotion to Our Lady of Guadalupe. *Americas* 2, no. 3 (January 1946): 280–95.

Carrillo y Pérez, Ignacio. *Pensil americano florido en el rigor del invierno la imágen de María Santísima de Guadalupe, Aparecida en la Corte de la Septentrional América México, en donde escribia esta Historia Don Ignacio Carrillo y Perez, hijo de esta Ciudad y Dependiente de su Real Casa de Moneda, año de 1793.* Mexico City: Por D. Mariano Joseph de Zúñiga y Ontiveros, 1797.

Cartas de Indias. Publícalas por primera vez el Ministerio de Fomento. Madrid: Imprenta de M. G. Hernández, 1877.

Castañeda, Carlos, and Dabbs Jack Autrey. *Guide to the Latin American Manuscripts in the University of Texas Library.* Cambridge, Mass.: Harvard University Press, 1939.

Cepeda, Fernando de. *Relacion vniversal legitima y verdadera del sitio en qve esta fvndada la muy noble, insigne, y muy leal Ciudad de Mexico, cabeça de las Provincias de toda la Nueva España . . . Dispuesta, y ordenada por el Licenciado Don Fernando de Cepeda Relator della.* Mexico City: En la Imprenta de Francisco Salbago, 1637.

Cervantes de Salazar, Francisco. *Life in the Imperial and Loyal City of Mexico in New Spain and the Royal and Pontifical University of Mexico as Described in Dialogues for the Study of the Latin Language.* Trans. Minnie Lee Barrett Shepard. Ed. Carlos Eduardo Castañeda. Austin: University of Texas Press, 1953.

Chauvet, Fidel de Jesús. *Fray Juan de Zumárraga, O.F.M.* Mexico City: N.p., 1948.

———. Historia del culto guadalupano. In *Album conmemorativo del 450 aniversario de las apariciones de Nuestra Señora de Guadalupe.* Mexico City: N.p., 1981.

Chimalpahin, Domingo Francisco de San Antón Muñón. *Annales de Domingo Francisco de San Anton Muñon Chimalpahin Quauhtlehuanitzin. Sixième et septième relations (1258–1612).* Published and translated from the original manuscript by Remi Siméon. Paris: Maisonneuve Ch. Leclerc, Editeurs, 1889.

Christian, William. *Apparitions in Late Medieval and Renaissance Spain.* Princeton, N.J.: Princeton University Press, 1981.

———. *Local Religion in Sixteenth Century Spain.* Princeton, N.J.: Princeton University Press, 1981.

Churruga Peláez, Agustín, S.J. *Primeras fundaciones Jesuitas en Nueva España, 1572–1580.* Mexico City: Editorial Porrúa, S.A., 1980.

Cinco cartas del Illmo. y Excmo. Señor D. Pedro Moya de Contreras arzobispo-virrey y primer inquisidor de la Nueva España. Precedidas de la historia de su vida segun Cristobal Gutierrez de Luna y Francisco Sosa. Biblioteca Tenanitla. Libros Españoles e Hispanoamericanos, 3. Madrid: Ediciones José Porrúa Turanzas, 1962.

Cisneros, Luis de. *Historia del principio, origen, progresos, venidas a Mexico y milagros de la Santa Imagen de Nuestra Señora de los Remedios, que se venera en su santuario a tres leguas de aquella Capital.* Mexico City: N.p., 1621.

Clavigero, Francisco Javier. *Breve ragguaglio della prodigiosa e rinomata immagine della Madonna di Guadalupe di Messico.* Cesena, Italy: Per Gregorio Biasini, 1782.

———. Breve noticia sobre la prodigiosa y renombrada imagen de Nuestra Señora de Guadalupe (1782). In *Testimonios históricos guadalupanos.* Ed. Ernesto de la Torre Villar and Ramiro Navarro de Anda. Mexico City: Fondo de Cultura Económica, 1982, 578–96.

———. *Historia antigua de México.* Ed. and prologue by Father Mariano Cuevas. Colección de Escritores Mexicanos. 4 vols. Mexico City: Editorial Porrua, S.A., 1958.

Clendinnen, Inga. *Aztecs: An Interpretation.* Cambridge: Cambridge University Press, 1991.

Colección de documentos para la historia mexicana publicados por el Dr. Antonio Peñafiel: Cantares Mexicanos. Mexico City: Oficina Tipográfica de la Secretería de Fomento, 1899.

Conde, José Ignacio, and María Teresa Cervantes de Conde. Nuestra Señora de Guadalupe en el arte. In *Album conmemorativo del 450 aniversario de las apariciones de Nuestra Señora de Guadalupe*. Mexico City: Ediciones Buena Nueva, 1981, 124–26.

Congregatio pro Causis Sanctorum Officium Historicum, 184: Mexicana: Canonizationis Servi Dei Ioannis Didaci Cuauhtlatoatzin viri laici (1474–1548) Positio super fama sanctitatis, virtutibus et cultu ab immemorabili praestito ex officio concinnata. Rome: N.p., 1989.

Constituciones de la real Congregacion de Nuestra Señora de Guadalupe de México, fundada en la Iglesia de S. Felipe el real de esta corte. Madrid: J. Ibarra, Impresor de Cámara de S.M., 1780.

Contreras, Javier Evangelista. *Desposorio feliz, o el dichoso vinculo de tres glorias; la plausible confirmacion Que hizo la Santidad del Sr. Benedicto XIV. Papa Reynante, del Patronato, antes jurado por todo el reyno, de Maria Santissima Señora nuestra, en su prodigiosa Imagen de Guadalupe. Sermon panegyrico Que el Domingo 9. de Octubre de 1757. en que la Noble Ciudad de S. Luis Potosi dió principio al Octavario de los pomposos festivos aplausos, Predicó En su Santa Iglesia Parrochial El P. Xavier Evangelista Contreras de la Compañia de Jesus*. Mexico City: Imprenta de la Biblioteca Mexicana, 1758.

Coplas a la partida, qve la Soberana Virgen de Guadalupe, hizo de esta Ciudad de Mexico, para su hermita. Compuestas por vn devoto suyo. Mexico City: Por Francisco Rodriguez Lupercio, 1634.

Correa, Juan de. *Tratado de la qualidad manifiesta, qve el Mercurio tiene; prueese ser frio, y humedo en segundo grado, con graues autores, y quarenta y ocho razones. Añadido vn discvrso de vna enfermedad que padeció en esta Ciudad vna persona grauisima, con las particularidades que se vieron quando se embalsamó. Dirigido a la Santissima Virgen Maria de Guadalupe. Compvesto por el maestro Iuan de Correa, Cirujano del Santo Oficio de la Inquisicion desta Nueua Espana, y Ministro de la Cathedra de Anothomia, por la Real Vniversidad de la muy noble, y muy leal Ciudad de Mexico, de donde es natural*. Mexico City: Por Hipolito de Ribera, 1648.

Coudert, Allison P. The Myth of the Improved Status of Protestant Women: The Case of the Witchcraze. In *The Politics of Gender in Early Modern Europe*. Ed. Jean R. Brink, Allison P. Coudert, and Maryanne C. Horowitz. Sixteenth Century Essays and Studies 12. Charles G. Nauert, gen. ed. Kirksville, Mo.: Sixteenth Century Journal Publishers, 1989, 61–89.

[Cruz, Mateo de la]. *Relación de la milagrosa aparición de la Santa Virgen de Guadalupe de México, sacada de la historia que compuso el Br. Miguel Sánchez*. Puebla de los Angeles: Viuda de Borja, 1660.

Cuevas, José de Jesús. *La santísima virgen de Guadalupe*. Mexico City: N.p., 1897.

Cuevas, Mariano, S.J. *Historia de la Iglesia en México*. 4 vols. Tlalpam, D.F.: Impr. del Asilo Patricio Sanz, 1921–1924.

———. *Album histórico Guadalupano del IV centenario*. Mexico City: N.p., 1930.

———. Documentos escritos en pro de la historicidad de las apariciones guadalupanas: su autenticidad. Su valor. In *Memoria del Congreso Nacional Guadalupano: discursos, conclusiones, poesías*. Mexico City: Escuela Tipográfica Salesiana, 1931.

Dávila Padilla, Agustín. *Historia de la fundacion y discurso de la provincia de Santiago de*

Mexico, de la Orden de Predicadores. 3d ed. Prologue by Agustín Millares Carlo. Mexico City: Editorial Academia Literaria, 1955.

Delgado y Buenrostro, Antonio. *Accion de gracias a Nuestra Señora la Virgen Maria concebida en gracia trasuntada en su Florida Milagrosa Imagen de Guadalupe aparecida en la Imperial Corte, y Ciudad de Mexico. Por el Feliz viaje, que hizo de la nueva España á la Isla de Cuba, el Ilustrissimo Señor Doctor D. Garcia de Palacios, Obispo suyo, y de la Havana, en cuya Iglesia Mayor se celebrò. Y predico El Licenciado Don Antonio Delgado y Buenrostro . . . en 16 de Abril . . . Año de 1679.* Seville: Thomas Lopez de Haro, 1679.

Descripción del arzobispado de México hecha en 1570 y otros documentos. Ed. Luis García Pimentel. Mexico City: José Joaquín Terrazas e Hijos Imprs., 1897.

Díaz del Castillo, Bernal. *La verdadera historia de la conquista de la Nueva España.* Edited by Miguel León-Portilla. Crónicas de América. 2 vols. Mexico City: N.p., 1984.

Díaz-Thomé, Jorge Hugo. Francisco Cervantes de Salazar. In *Estudios de historiografía de la Nueva España.* Ed. Ramón Iglesia. Mexico City: N.p., 1945, 17–41.

Dibble, Charles E. The Nahuatilization of Christianity. In *Sixteenth Century Mexico: The Work of Sahagún.* Ed. Munro S. Edmonson. Albuquerque: University of New Mexico Press, 1974, 225–33.

d'Olwer, Lluis Nicolau. *Fray Bernardino de Sahagún (1499–1590).* Mexico City: Departamento del Distrito Federal, 1990.

Dos relaciones históricas de la admirable aparicion de la Virgen Santisima y soberana Madre de Dios baxo el título de Santa Maria de Guadalupe, Acaecida en esta Corte de México el año de mil quinientos treinta y uno. Mexico City: En la Imprenta de d. Felipe de Zúñiga y Ontiveros, 1781.

Durán, Diego. *Historia de las Indias de Nueva España.* Paleographic ed. of the autograph manuscript in Madrid, with introduction, notes, and vocabulary of native and archaic words. Prepared and published by Angel Ma. Garibay K. 2 vols. Mexico City: Editorial Porrua, S. A., 1967.

Elizondo, Virgil. Popular Religion as Support of Identity: A Pastoral-Psychological Case-Study Based on the Mexican-American Experience in the USA. In *Popular Religion.* Ed. Norbert Greinacher and Norbert Mette. Edinburgh: T. and T. Clark, Ltd., 1986, 36–43.

El milagro de la Virgen del Tepeyac, por Antonio Valeriano, alumno y catedrático del Colegio de Santiago Tlatelolco en año de 1554, con un prólogo del Ilmo. Sr. Obispo de Cuernavaca, Dr. D. Fortino Hipólito Vera. Puebla, Mex.: N.p., 1895.

Enchiridion Patristicum. Loci SS. Patrum, Doctorum Scriptorum Ecclesiasticorum, quos in usum scholarum colligit M. J. Rouët de Journel S.I. Barcelona, Fribourg, Rome, New York: Herder, 1962.

Epistolario de Nueva España, 1505–1818. Ed. Francisco del Paso y Troncoso. 16 vols. Mexico City: Editorial Porrua, S.A., 1939–1943.

Farías, Manuel Ignacio. *Eclypse del divino sol, causado por la interposicion de la Immaculada Luna Maria sra. nuestra. Sermon, que . . . predicò el r. p. fr. Manvel Ignacio Farias.* Mexico City: N.p., 1742.

[Fernández, Alonso]. *Historia eclesiastica de nuestros tiempos, que es compendio de los excelentes frvtos qve en ellos el estado Eclesiastico y sagradas religiones han hecho y hazen, en la conuersion de idolatras y reducion de hereges. Y de los ilustres martirios de varones Apostol-icos, que en estas heroicas empressas han padecido. Por el P. F. Alonso Fernandez, de la Orden de Santo Domingo, de la Prouincia de España, del insigne Conuento de S. Vicente Ferrer de Plazencia.* Toledo: Por la Viuda de Pedro Rodriguez, 1611.

Fernández de Echeverría y Veytia, Mariano. Baluartes de México (1775–1779). In *Testimonios históricos guadalupanos.* Ed. Ernesto de la Torre Villar and Ramiro Navarro de Anda. Mexico City: Fondo de Cultura Económica, 1982, 529–77.

Fernández de Palos, José. *Triumpho obsidional que implora, y se anuncia la Real Audiencia Gobernadora de este Reyno de la Nueva-España, Por medio de la Virgen Maria N. Señora en su portentosa Imagen de Guadalupe. Sermon, Que el dia 24. de Abril de este Año de 1742. ultimo de la Novena, que le celebrò en su magnifico Templo, à sus expensas la misma Real Audiencia, con assistencia de sus Tribunales, y Nobilissima Ciudad. Predico El Dr. D. Joseph Fernandez de Palos.* Mexico City: En la Imprenta Real del Superior Gobierno, y del Nuevo Rezado de doña Maria de Rivera, 1743.

Fernández de Uribe, José Patricio. *Sermon de Nuestra Señora de Guadalupe de Mexico, predicado en su santuario el año de 1777 dia 14 de diciembre en la solemne fiesta con que su ilustre congregacion celebra su aparicion milagrosa, por el señor Doctor y maestro D. Joseph Patricio Fernandez de Uribe, Colegial Real de Oposicion en el mas antiguo de San Ildefonso, Cura propio de la Catedral, y despues Canónigo Penitenciario de la misma Met-ropolitana Iglesia de Mexico. El que dió motivo para escribir la adjunta Disertacion, como en ella misma se expresa. Sale á luz á expensas de dicha I. y V. Congregacion año de 1801.* Mexico City: En la Oficina de d. Mariano de Zúñiga y Ontiveros, 1801.

———. *Disertacion historico-critica en que el autor del sermon que precede sostiene la celestial imagen de Maria Santísima de Guadalupe de México, milagrosamente aparecida al hu-milde neófito Juan Diego escribiase por el año de 1778.* Mexico City: En la Oficina de d. Mariano de Zúñiga y Ontiveros, 1801.

Florencia, Francisco de, S.J. *La milagrosa invencion de un thesoro escondido en un campo, que hallò un venturoso cazique, y escondiò en su casa, para gozarlo à sus solas: patente ya en el Santuario de los Remedios en su admirable imagen de ntra. Señora; señalada en milagros, invocada por patrona de las lluvias, y temporales; defensora de los españoles, avogada de los indios, conquistadora de Mexico erario universal de las misericordias de Dios, ciudad de refugio para todos, los que à ella se acogen.* Seville: Imprenta de las Siete Revueltas, 1745.

———. *La estrella del norte de Mexico aparecida al rayar el dia de la luz Evangelica en este Nuevo Mundo, en la cumbre del cerro de Tepeyacac, orilla del mar Tezcucano, à un Natural recien convertido; pintada tres dias despues milagrosamente en su tilma ò capa de lienzo delante del Obispo y de su familia, en su casa Obispal, para luz en la fé à los Indios; para rumbo cierto à los Españoles en la virtud, para serenidad de las tempestuosas inundancias de la Laguna. En la historia de la milagrosa imagen de nuestra Señora de Guadalupe de Mexico Que se apareció en la manta de Juan Diego Compusola el Padre Francisco de Floren-cia de la Compañia de Jesus.* Mexico City: Viuda de Juan de Ribera, 1688.

———. *Historia de la provincia de la Compañia de Jesvs de Nueva España.* 2d ed. Prologue by Francisco Gonzalez de Cossio. Mexico City: Editorial Academia Literaria, 1955.

Focher, Juan. *Itinerario del misionero en America: texto latino con versión castellana, introducción y notas del P. Antonio Eguiluz, O.F.M.* Madrid: Librería General Victoriano Suárez, 1960.

Franco, Alonso. *Segunda parte de la Historia de la Provincia de Santiago de Mexico Orden de Predicadores en la Nueua España, por el Padre Fr. Alonso Franco, predicador general del real convento de Santo Domingo de la insigne ciudad de Mexico, hijo del dicho convento, y natural de la misma ciudad mexicana. Año de 1645 en Mexico. Publicada en 1900 por cuenta del Supremo Gobierno á solicitud del R. P. Fr. Secundo Martinez.* Mexico City: Imprenta del Museo Nacional, 1900.

Fuenlabrada, Nicolás de. *Oracion evangelica, y panegyrica relacion de las glorias, y maravillas grandes de la Soberana Reyna de los Angeles Maria Santissima Señora N. en su milagrosissima Imagen, del Español Gvadalvpe, en la Extremadura. Por el P. Fr. Nicolas de Fvenlabrada . . . Lector de Theologia en el Convento de N. P. S. Augustin de Mexico.* Mexico City: Viuda de Bernardo Calderon, [1681].

[Gage, Thomas]. *Thomas Gage's Travels in the New World.* Ed. and with an introduction by J. Eric. S. Thompson. Norman: University of Oklahoma Press, 1958.

[Garcés, Julián]. *De habilitate et capacitate gentium sive indorum novi mundi nu{n}cupati ad fidem Christ capessandum, & qua{m} libenter suscipiat.* Rome: N.p., 1537.

García Abásalo, Antonio F. *Martín Enríquez y la reforma de 1568 en Nueva España.* Seville: Publicaciones de la Excma. Diputación Provincial de Sevilla bajo la Dirección de Antonia Heredia Herrera, 1983.

García Gutiérrez, Jesús. *Apuntamientos para una bibliografía crítica de historiadores guadalupanos.* Zacatecas, Mex.: N.p., 1939.

―――. *Cancionero histórico guadalupano.* Mexico City: Editorial Jus, 1947.

García Icazbalceta, Joaquín. Carta acerca del origen de la imagen de Nuestra Señora de Guadalupe de México. In *Investigación histórica y documental sobre la aparición de la Virgen de Guadalupe de Mexico.* Mexico City: Ediciones Fuente Cultural, n.d., 21–70.

―――. D. Lorenzo Boturini Benaduci. In *Diccionario geográfico, histórico y biográfico de los Estados Unidos Mexicanos.* Ed. Antonio García Cubas. 5 vols. Mexico City: Antigua Imprenta de Murguia, 1888, 1:329–31.

―――. *Don Fray Juan de Zumárraga, primer obispo y arzobispo de México.* Ed. Rafael Aguayo Spencer and Antonio Castro Leal. 4 vols. Mexico City: Editorial Jus, 1947.

―――. *Bibliografía mexicana del siglo XVI.* New ed. by Agustín Millares Carlo. Mexico City: Fondo de Cultura Económica, 1954.

―――. *Apuntes para un catálogo de escritores en lenguas indígenas de América.* New York: Burt Franklin, 1970.

Garibay K., Angel María. Temas guadalupanos I. Los anales indígenas. *Abside* 9, no. 1 (1945): 37–46.

―――. Temas guadalupanos II. El diario de Juan Bautista. *Abside* 9, no. 2 (1945): 155–69.

―――. Temas guadalupanos III. El problema de los cantares. *Abside* 9, no. 3 (1945): 243–59.

————. Temas guadalupanos III. El problema de los cantares (prosigue). *Abside* 9, no. 4 (1945): 381–420.

————. La maternidad de María en el mensaje guadalupano. In *La maternidad espiritual de María*. Mexico City: N.p., 1961, 187–202.

————. *Historia de la literatura náhuatl.* 2 vols. Mexico City: Editorial Porrúa S. A., 1961.

————. Los manuscritos en lengua náhuatl de la Biblioteca Nacional de México. *Boletín de la Biblioteca Nacional* 17 (January–June 1966): 5–19.

————. Guadalupe, Our Lady of. *New Catholic Encyclopedia.* New York: N.p., 1967.

Gauna, José de. *Sermon de Nuestra Señora Maria Santissima de Guadalupe, Que el dia diez de octubre de este Año de 1757 en la Iglesia Parroquial de la Ciudad de San Luis Potosi, y Fiesta, que hizo el Comercio, en demostracion de aver confirmado nuestro Santissimo Padre Benedicto XIV . . . el Juramento, que la hizo este Reyno de su General Patronato. Predicó El reverendo P. F. Joseph de Gauna.* Mexico City: Imprenta de la Bibliotheca Mexicana, 1758.

Geografía y descripción universal de las Indias recopilada por el cosmógrafo-cronista Juan López de Velasco desde el año de 1571 al de 1574, publicada por primera vez en el Boletín de la Sociedad Geográfica de Madrid, con adiciones é ilustraciones por don Justo Zaragoza. Madrid: Establecimiento Tipográfico de Fortanet, 1894.

Gerhard, Peter. *A Guide to the Historical Geography of New Spain.* Cambridge, Eng.: Cambridge University Press, 1972.

Gibson, Charles. *The Aztecs under Spanish Rule: A History of the Indians of the Valley of Mexico, 1519–1810.* Stanford, Calif.: Stanford University Press, 1964.

Gil, Fernando. Las "juntas eclesiásticas" durante el episcopado de Fray Juan de Zumárraga (1528–1548): algunas precisiones históricas. *Teologia* (offprint) 26, no. 54 (1989): 3–30.

Giménez Fernández, Manuel. *Bartolomé de las Casas: I. Delegado de Cisneros para la reformación de las Indias. II. Capellán de S. M. Carlos I, Poblador de Cumaná.* Madrid: Consejo Superior de Investigaciones Científicas, Escuela de Estudios Hispanoamericanos, 1984.

Glass, John B. *Catálogo de la colección de códices Museo Nacional de Antropología e Historia.* 2 vols. Mexico City: N.p., 1964.

————. *The Boturini Collection and a Concordance of the Inventories, 1742–1918.* Indian Museum of Lorenzo Boturini, vol. 2, pt. 1. Contributions to the Ethnohistory of Mexico, number 6. Lincoln Center, Mass.: Conemex Associates, 1978.

————. *The Boturini Collection and the Text of the Legal Proceedings in Mexico, 1742–1743.* Indian Museum of Lorenzo Boturini, vol. 1, chap. 4. Contributions to the Ethnohistory of Mexico, number 8. Lincoln Center, Mass.: Conemex Associates, 1979.

Glass, John B., in collaboration with Donald Robertson. A Census of Native Middle American Pictorial Manuscripts. In *Guide to Ethnohistorical Sources, Part Three.* Vol. ed. Howard F. Cline, assoc. vol. eds. Charles Gibson and H. B. Nicholson. Vol. 14 of *Handbook of Middle American Indians.* Austin: University of Texas Press, 1975, 81–252.

Goicoechea, Juan de. *La rossa por la rossa Maria SSma. de Guadalupe substituida a Maria Señora del Rosario En el Naval Triumpho de la Argos China, conseguido por su Jasson el General D. Fernando de Angulo, de tres fragatas Inglesas, en el Mar Pacifico. Sermon que Predicó el Padre Juan de Goicoechea, Professo de la Compañia de Iesvs, primero dia del novenario, que en accion de gracias de su victoria le celebró en su Magnifico Templo, y Santuario de Mexico.* Mexico City: Francisco de Ribera Calderon, 1710.

———. *La maravilla immarcesible, y milagro continuado de Maria Santissima Señora Nvestra en su prodigiosa imagen de Guadalvpe de Mexico, Compite firnegas con su nuevo Templo, que la copía . . . Sermon en el dia octavo del Novenario â la Dedicacion de su Magnifico Templo, con el mysterio de la Pvrificacion, y dia de la Aparicion de San Migvel . . . predicôlo El R. P. Iuan de Goycoechea.* Mexico City: Imprenta de los Herederos de Iuan Ioseph Guillena, 1709.

González Dávila, Gil. *Teatro eclesiástico de la primitiva iglesia de la Nueva España en las Indias Occidentales por el maestro Gil González Dávila cronista de su Magestad.* 2d ed. 2 vols. Colección Chimalistac de libros y documentos acerca de la Nueva España 3. Madrid: J. Porrúa Turanzas, Editor, 1959.

Greenleaf, Richard E. *Zumárraga and the Mexican Inquisition: 1536–1543.* Washington, D.C.: Academy of American Franciscan History, 1961.

———. *The Mexican Inquisition of the Sixteenth Century.* Albuquerque: University of New Mexico Press, 1969.

Grijalva, Juan de. *Cronica de la orden de N. P. S. Augustin en la prouincias de la Nueua España. En quatro edades desde el año de 1533 hasta el de 1592. Por el P. M. F. Ioan de Grijalua prior del conuento de N. P. S. Augustin de Mexico dedicada a la prouincia del SSo nombre de Iesus de Mexico.* Mexico City: N.p., 1626; repr. Mexico City: Imprenta Victoria, 1924.

Guerra, José. *Sermon de Nuestra Señora de Guadalupe, que en el dia de Sv aparicion en su Colegio de missioneros de la ciudad de Zacatecas predico el p. fr. Joseph Guerra.* Mexico City: N.p., 1709.

Guijo, Gregorio M. de. *Diario 1648–1664.* 2 vols. Ed. and prologue by Manuel Romero de Terreros. Mexico City: Editorial Porrua, S.A., 1953.

Guridi y Alcocer, José Miguel. Apología de la aparición de Nuestra Señora de Guadalupe de México in respuesta a la disertación que la impugna. In *Testimonios históricos guadalupanos.* Ed. Ernesto de la Torre Villar and Ramiro Navarro de Anda. Mexico City: Fondo de Cultura Económica, 1982, 874–974.

Gutiérrez Dávila, Julián. *Memorias historicas de la Congregacion de el Oratorio de la Ciudad de Mexico . . . recojidas, y pvblicadas por el P. Julian Gutierrez Davila, Presbytero Preposito, que fue, de dicha Congregacion del Oratorio de Mexico.* Mexico City: En la Imprenta Real del Superior Govierno, y del Nuevo Rezado, de doña Maria de Rivera, 1736.

Gutiérrez Vega, Cristóforo. *Las primeras juntas eclesiásticas de México (1524–1555).* Rome: Centro de Estudios Superiores, 1991.

Halliczer, Stephen. *The Comuneros of Castile: The Forging of a Revolution, 1475–1521.* Madison: University of Wisconsin Press, 1981.

Hanke, Lewis. *The Spanish Struggle for Justice in the Conquest of America.* Boston, Toronto: Little, Brown and Company, 1965.

Harrington, Patricia. Mother of Death, Mother of Rebirth: The Mexican Virgin of Guadalupe. *Journal of the American Academy of Religion* 56, no. 1 (Spring 1988): 25–50.

Hebblethwaite, Peter. Beatification of Juan Diego Affirms Liberation Theology. *National Catholic Reporter*, 11 May 1990, 8.

Herrera, José de. *Sermon qve predico el R. P. Lector Regente F. Joseph de Herrera del Orden de Predicadores en la solemne fiesta, qve se celebra este Año de 1672. En el convento de Religiosas de Santa Catalina de Sena desta Ciudad: a la aparicion milagrosa de la Santa Imagen de Gvadalvpe, dentro de las Octavas de la Immaculada Concepcion de la Virgen Santissima Nuestra Señora. Dedicalo E. R. P. Fr. Thomas Mexia, Procurador General de la Provincia de Santiago de Predicadores de Nueva-España al Nobilissimo Consulado de Mexico.* Mexico City: Viuda de Bernardo Calderon, 1673.

Historia de la Inquisición en España y América. Ed. Joaquín Pérez Villanueva and Bartolomé Escandell Bonet. Vol. 1. *El conocimiento científico y el proceso histórico de la Institución (1478–1834).* Madrid: Biblioteca de Autores Cristianos: Centro de Estudios Inquisitoriales, 1984.

Historia general de la América Septentrional por el caballero Lorenzo Boturini Benaducci, señor de la Torre y de Hono, cronista real en las Indias. Ed., prologue, and notes by Manuel Ballesteros Gabrois. Madrid: Imprenta y Editorial Maestre, 1948.

Hoberman, Louisa. Bureaucracy and Disaster: Mexico City and the Flood of 1629. *Journal of Latin American Studies* 6 (1974): 211–30.

Hoornaert, Eduardo. *Guadalupe: evangelización y dominación.* Lima: Centro de Estudios y Publicaciones, 1975.

Horcasitas, Fernando. *El teatro nahuatl: épocas novohispana y moderna.* Mexico City: Universidad Nacional Autónoma de México, Instituto de Investigaciones Históricas, 1974.

Hvei tlamahvicoltiça [sic] . . . Libro en Lengua Mexicana, que el Br. Luis Lasso de la Vega hizo imprimir en Mexico, el año de 1649 ahora traducido y anotado por el Lic. Don Primo Feliciano Velazquez. Lleva un prólogo del Pbro. Don Jesus Garcia Gutierrez Secretario de la Academia. Academia Mexicana de Santa María. Mexico City: Carreño e Hijos, Editores, 1926.

"Información por el sermón de 1556," por fray Francisco de Bustamante y fray Alonso de Montúfar. In *Testimonios históricos guadalupanos.* Ed. Ernesto de la Torre Villar and Ramiro Navarro de Anda. Mexico City: Fondo de Cultura Económica, 1982, 36–141.

Información que mandó practicar con motivo de un sermon que en la fiesta de la Natividad de Nuestra Señora (8 de Septiembre de 1556) predico en la capilla de San José de los Naturales del Convento de San Francisco de Méjico, el Provincial Fray Francisco de Bustamante acerca de la devoción y culto de Nuestra Señora de Guadalupe. 2d ed. Mexico City: Imprenta, Litografia y Encuadernacion de Irineo Paz, 1891.

Las informaciones guadalupanas de 1666 y de 1723. Ed. Luis Medina Ascensio, S.J. In *Testimonios históricos guadalupanos.* Ed. Ernesto de la Torre Villar and Ramiro Navarro de Anda. Mexico City: Fondo de Cultura Económica, 1982, 1338–77.

Informaciones sobre la milagrosa aparicion de la Santísima Virgen de Guadalupe, recibidas en

1666 y 1723. Published by the priest Bachiller Fortino Hipólito Vera. Amecameca, Mex.: "Imprenta Católica," a Cargo de Jorge Sigüenza, 1889.

Informe critico-legal dado al muy Ilustre y Venerable Cabildo de la Santa Iglesia Metropolitana de Mexico por los comisionados que nombró para el reconocimiento de la Imagen de nuestra Señora de Guadalupe de la Iglesia de San Francisco, pintada sobre las tablas de la mesa del Illmo. Sr. Obispo D. Fr. Juan de Zumárraga, y sobre la que puso su tilma el venturoso Neófito Juan Diego, en que se pintó la Imagen de nuestra Señora de Guadalupe, que se venera en la Colegiata de la Ciudad de Hidalgo. Mexico City: Imprenta de la Testamentaria de Valdés á Cargo de José Maria Gallegos, 1835.

Investigación histórica y documental sobre la aparición de la Virgen de Guadalupe de Mexico. Mexico City: Ediciones Fuente Cultural, n.d.

Israel, J. I. *Race, Class and Politics in Colonial Mexico: 1610–1670*. Oxford, Eng.: Oxford University Press, 1975.

Ita y Parra, Bartolomé Felipe de. *La imagen de Guadalupe, señora de los tiempos, sermon panegyrico, que predico en la Iglesia de su santuario, patente el Santissimo Sacramento, Al cumplimiento de los dos Siglos de su Apparicion Milagrosa, El dia 12. de Diziembre de 1731. años. El Dr. y Mrò. D. Bartholome Phelipe de Yta y Parra*. Mexico City: Imprenta Real del Superior Govierno de los Herederos de la Viuda de Miguel de Rivera, 1732.

———. *La Madre de la salud, la milagrosa imagen de Guadalupe. Sermon que predicò El Doctor y Maestro Don Bartholomé Phelipe de Itta y Parra . . . en la Iglesia de su santuario . . . el dia 7. de Febrero, Año de 1737. ultimo del novenario, que se celebrò en su dicho Santuario, suplicandola, cessasse con su Patrocinio la Epidemia que se padecìa*. Madrid: Imprenta de Antonio Marin, 1739.

———. *Los pecados unica causa de las pestes: Sermon moral, que predicò en la Santa Yglesia Cathedral de Mexico . . . El Doctor, y Maestro Don Bartholome Phelipe de Ytta y Parra . . . Sabado 19. de Enero del Año de 1737. ultimo dia del novenario, que por la Epidemia que se padecia, le celebrò dicha Santa Iglesia à la milagrosa Imagen de Nuestra Señora de los Remedios, venerada extramuros de esta Ciudad, y en solemne Procession traìda à ella para pedirle su salud*. Madrid: Imprenta de Antonio Marin, 1740.

———. *La Imagen de Guadalupe, Imagen del Patrocinio: sermon panegyrico Que Predicò en el dia de su Apparicion, en que se celebra como Patrona, 12. de Diciembre, Año de 1743. El Dr. Y Mrô. D. Bartholome Phelipe de Yta y Parra*. Mexico City: Por la Viuda de D. Joseph Bernardo de Hogal, 1744.

———. *El circulo de amor formado por la America septentrional jurando a Maria Santissima en su imagen de Guadalupe, la imagen del patrocinio de todo su reyno. Sermon panegyrico, Que Predicò en el dia de su aparicion 12. de Diciembre de 1746. en que se celebrò dicho juramento El Dr. Y Mrò. D. Bartholomé Phelipe de Ita y Parra*. Mexico City: Imprenta de la Viuda de D. Joseph de Hogal, 1747.

Iturriaga, Pedro. *Profecia de raras, e inauditas felicidades del mexicano reyno, la celestial portentosa imagen de la Soberana Reyna Maria Señora de Guadalupe. Sermon, Que el dia 14. de Febrero de este año de 1757. en que celebró el Universal Patronato de la Señora el Ilmô. y Rmô. Sr. Dr. y Mrô D. Fr. Ignacio de Padilla, y Estrada, del Orden de San Augustin, Arzobispo Obispo de Yucatan del Consejo de S. Mag. en la Santa iglesia Cathedral de Merida. Predicó el Padre Pedro Iturriaga, Professo de la Compañia de Jesus*. Mexico City: En la Imprenta de la Biblioteca Mexicana, 1757.

Jiménez Moreno, Wigberto. *Estudios de historia colonial*. Mexico City: Instituto Nacional de Antropología e Historia, 1958.

Junco, Alfonso. *Un radical problema guadalupano*. Mexico City: Editorial Jus, 1953.

Kamen, Henry. *Spain: 1469–1714, a Society of Conflict*. London and New York: Longman, 1986.

Karttunen, Frances. *An Analytical Dictionary of Nahuatl*. Austin: University of Texas Press, 1983.

Karttunen, Frances, and James Lockhart. *Nahuatl in the Middle Years: Language Contact Phenomena in Texts of the Colonial Period*. Berkeley, Los Angeles, London: University of California Press, 1976.

Keen, Benjamin. *The Aztec Image in Western Thought*. New Brunswick, N.J.: Rutgers University Press, 1971.

Kurtz, Donald. The Virgin of Guadalupe and the Politics of Becoming Human. *Journal of Anthropological Research* 38 (1982): 194–210.

Lafaye, Jacques. *Quetzalcoatl and Guadalupe: The Formation of Mexican National Consciousness, 1531–1813*. Trans. Benjamin Keen. Chicago: University of Chicago Press, 1976. [Original French ed.: *Quetzalcóatl et Guadalupe: la formation de la conscience nationale au Mexique (1531–1813)*. Paris: Editions Gallimard, 1974.]

La primera historia guadalupana impresa. Obras Guadalupanas de Lauro López Beltrán, 4. Mexico City: Editorial Tradición, 1981.

Lascano, Francisco Javier. *Sermon panegyrico al inclyto patronato de Maria Señora Nuestra en su milagrosissima Imagen de Guadalupe, Sobre la universal Septentrional America, que . . . predicó El P. Francisco Xavier Lascano de la Compañia de Jesus . . . En el Augusto Templo, dedicado á la misma Soberana Reyna, en la magnifica annual solemnidad, que con assistencia del Excelentissimo Señor Virrey, Real Audiencia, Superiores Tribunales, y Corte, celebra la muy Ilustre Nobilissima Imperial Ciudad de Mexico En el dia Martes 12 de Diziembre de 1758*. Mexico City: Imprenta de la Bibliotheca Mexicana, 1759.

Laso de la Vega, Luis. *Huey tlamahuiçoltica omonexiti in ilhuicac tlatocacihuapilli Santa Maria totlaçonantzin Guadalupe in nican huey altepenahuac Mexico itocayocan Tepeyacac*. Mexico City: Imprenta de Iuan Ruiz, 1649.

Lenz, Hans. *El papel indígena mexicano*. Mexico City: Sep/Setentas, 1973.

León, Martín de. *Camino del cielo en lengva mexicana, con todos los requisitos necessarios para conseguir este fin, co{n} todo lo que vn Xpiano deue creer, saber, y obrar, desde el punto que tiene vso de razon, hasta que muere. Co{m}puesto, por el P. F. Martin de Leo{n}, de la Orde{n} de Predicadores*. Mexico City: En la Emprenta de Diego Lopez Daualos y a Costa de Diego Perez de los Rios, 1611.

León-Portilla, Ascensión H. de. *Tepuztlahcuilolli: Impresos en náhuatl, historia y bibliografía*. Vol. 1. Mexico City: Universidad Nacional Autónoma de México, 1988.

Leonard, Irving A. *Don Carlos de Sigüenza y Góngora, a Mexican Savant of the Seventeenth Century*. University of California Publications in History, 18. Berkeley: University of California Press, 1929.

Llaguno, José A., S.J. *La personalidad jurídica del indio y el III Concilio Provincial Mexicano (1585): ensayo histórico-jurídico de los documentos originales*. Biblioteca Porrua 27. Mexico City: Editorial Porrua, S.A., 1963.

Lobatto, Juan Antonio. *El phenix de las Indias vnico por inmaculado floreciendo en vna tilma de palma Maria en sv concepcion pvrissima aparecida en Gvadalvpe Trasuntada en Thamar, y aplaudida de Judas Pharès, y Zaràn con emblemas, empresas, ò heroglificos. Sermon Que en la plausible fiesta de la Concepcion predicò . . . E. R. P. Presentado Fr. Ioan Antonio Lobatto.* Mexico City: Por doña Maria de Benavides, Viuda de Iuan de Ribera, 1700.

Lockhart, James. *Nahuas and Spaniards: Postconquest Central American History and Philology.* Stanford, Calif.: Stanford University Press, 1991.

———. *The Nahuas after the Conquest: A Social and Cultural History of the Indians of Central Mexico, Sixteenth through Eighteenth Centuries.* Stanford, Calif.: Stanford University Press, 1992.

López Beltrán, Lauro. *La historicidad de Juan Diego.* Obras Guadalupanas de Lauro López Beltrán, 5. Mexico City: Editorial Tradición, 1981.

———. *La protohistoria guadalupana.* 2d ed. Mexico City: Editorial Tradición, 1981.

López de Avilés, José. *Ueridicum admodum anagramma, epigramma obseqviosvm, unaque cum acrostichide Uirgilio centuncvlvs rigorosvs, in Lavdem Pvrissimae, Immacvlataeqve Conceptionis Sanctissimae Virginis Dei-genetricis Mariae . . . humiliter affert, refert, offert, & dicat: Bacchalavrvs Iosephvs Lopez de Abiles.* Mexico City: Ex Typographia Vidue Bernardi Calderon, 1669.

López Murto, Antonio. *Maria Santissima exaltada en la América por el cielo, la tierra y el infierno. Sermon panegirico que en funcion de Accion de Gracias, despues del solemne Novenario con que el M. Ilustre Ayuntamiento de San Luis Potosí celebra annualmente á su jurada Patrona Maria Santissima de Guadalupe, Predicó el dia 7 de Mayo de 1791 en la Iglesia Parroquial de dicha Ciudad el R. P. Fray Antonio Lopez Murto.* Mexico City: Por D. Felipe de Zúñiga y Ontiveros, 1791.

Lorenzana, Francisco Antonio de. *Oracion á Nuestra Señora de Guadalupe compuesta por el Ill.mo Señor D. Francisco Antonio de Lorenzana arzobispo de México.* Mexico City: Imprenta del Superior Gobierno del Br. D. Joseph Antonio de Hogal, 1770.

[———]. *Historia de Nueva-España, escrita por su esclarecido conquistador Hernan Cortes aumentada con otros documentos, y notas, por el Ilustrisimo Señor Don Francisco Antonio Lorenzana, Arzobispo de Mexico.* Mexico City: En la Imprenta del Superior Gobierno del Br. D. Joseph Antonio de Hogal, 1770.

Maldonado, Angel. *Oracion evangelica, Que predicò el Illmo. y Rmo. Señor Mrô. Don Fr. Angel Maldonado, del Consejo de su Magestad, Obispo de la Santa Iglesia de Antequera, en el dia que se dedicò el Templo de Nuestra Señora de Gvadalvpe, en el Convento de Bethlehemitas de esta Ciudad de Antequera dia 12. de Diziembre de 1725.* Mexico City: Por Joseph Bernardo de Hogal, 1726.

Manso, Pedro. *Sermon panegyrico qve en la celebridad de la Dedicacion del Templo Nuevo de San Bernardo titvlo Maria de Gvadalvpe; dia segundo de la octaua, qve cupo â la esclarecida familia de los Predicadores, dixo el Reverendo Padre Lector Fr. Pedro Manso Maestro en Sagrada Theologia por la Real Universidad de Mexico.* Mexico City: Por la Viuda de Francisco Rodriguez Lupercio, 1690.

Martínez de los Ríos, Manuel Antonio. *Condescendencia de Christo a nuestras peticiones por gloria de su soberana Madre Maria Señora Nuestra; En que su Magestad Eterna se acredita de verdadero Hijo del Hombre. Sermon, que en la Solemne Jura, que hizo la muy noble Villa de Quauhnahuac, de venerar por Patrona à la Reyna Purissima en su imagen*

Milagrosissima de Guadalupe de Mexico. Predicó El R. P. Fr. Manuel Antonio Martinez de los Rios. Mexico City: Por los Herederos de la Viuda de D. Joseph Hogal, 1758.

Maza, Francisco de la. *El guadalupanismo mexicano.* Mexico City: Fondo de Cultura Económica, 1981.

McKenzie, Sabra. ¡Viva la guadalupana! *Catholic Worker* 59, no. 8 (December 1992): 1, 3.

Medina, Baltasar de. *Chronica de la Santa Provincia de San Diego de Mexico, de Religiosos Descalços de N. S. P. S. Francisco en la Nueva-España. Vida de ilvstres, y venerables Varones, que la han edificado con excelentes virtudes. Escrivelas, y consagralas al glorioso San diego de alcalá Patron, y Tutelar de la Misma Provincia, F. Balthassar de Medina.* Mexico City: Por Juan de Ribera, Impressor, 1682.

Medina Ascensio, Luis. Las fuentes esenciales de la historia guadalupana. In *Album Conmemorativo del 450 aniversario de las apariciones de Nuestra Señora de Guadalupe.* Mexico City: Ediciones Buena Nueva, 1981, 83–113.

————. Las informaciones guadalupanas de 1666 y de 1723. In *Testimonios históricos guadalupanos.* Ed. Ernesto de la Torre Villar and Ramiro Navarro de Anda. Mexico City: Fondo de Cultura Económica, 1982, 1339–77.

Méndez Plancarte, Gabriel. Fray Diego Valadés: humanista franciscano del s. XVI. *Abside* 10, no. 3 (1946): 265–82.

Mendieta, Gerónimo de. *Historia eclesiástica indiana: obra escrita a fines del siglo XVI.* 3d facsimile ed. Mexico City: Editorial Porrua, S.A., 1971.

Mendoza, Juan de. *Sermon qve en el dia de la Apparicion de la Imagen Santa de Gvadalvpe, doze de diziembre del Año de 1672. Predicò el P. Fr. Ioan de Mendoza Commissario Visitador de la Orden Tercero de Penitencia, en el Convento de N. Padre S. Francisco de Mexico.* Mexico City: Francisco Rodriguez Lupercio, 1673.

Mier y Noriega, fray Servando Teresa de. Cartas del Doctor Fray Servando Teresa de Mier al cronista de Indias Doctor D. Juan Bautista Muñoz, sobre la tradición de Ntra. Sra. de Guadalupe de México, escritas desde Burgos, Año de 1797. In *Testimonios históricos guadalupanos.* Ed. Ernesto de la Torre Villar and Ramiro Navarro de Anda. Mexico City: Fondo de Cultura Económica, 1982, 757–861.

————. Sermón guadalupano. In *Testimonios históricos guadalupanos.* Ed. Ernesto de la Torre Villar and Ramiro Navarro de Anda. Mexico City: Fondo de Cultura Económica, 732–57.

Molina, Alonso de. *Vocabulario de la lengua castellana y mexicana y mexicana y castellana.* Introductory study by Miguel León-Portilla. 2d ed. Mexico City: Editorial Porrua, S. A., 1977.

Montes Bardo, Joaquín, O.F.M. Iconografía de Nuestra Señora de Guadalupe. In *Doctrina y piedad mariana en la España del siglo XVI: rasgos de su historia.* Estudios Marianos, vol. 44. Madrid: Sociedad Marialógica Española, 1979, 273–78.

Monumenta Historica Societatis Iesu a patribus eiusdem Societatis edita. Vol. 77. Monumenta Mexicana 1 (1570–1580). Ed. Félix Zubillaga, S. I. Rome: N.p., 1956.

Morales Sigala, Jerónimo. *Sermon que en el dia doze de diciembre de esta año proximé [sic] passado de 1756. en la Festividad de la Aparicion Milagrosa de N. Sra. de Guadalupe patrona jurada universal de este Reyno, y juntamente discurida Señora de los Exercitos de España, en la Dominica infraoctavam de la Immaculada Concepcion, en q. concurriò la*

Accion de gracias por las Victorias conseguidas en Biruega, y en el Campo de Villaviciosa . . . Predicò en la Iglesia Cathedral de esta Ciudad de Antequera Valle de Oaxaca El Sr. D. Geronymo Morales Sigala Espinos de los Monteros. Mexico City: Imprenta del Real y Mas Antiguo Colegio de San Ildefonso, 1757.

Morelli, Cyriacus [Domingo Muriel, pseud.]. *Fasti novi orbis et ordinationum apostolicarum ad Indias pertenentium breviarium cum adnotationibus opera D. Cyriaci Morelli presbyteri, olim in universitate neo-cordubensis in Tucumania professoris.* 2 vols. Venice: N.p., 1776.

Moreno, Roberto. Los manuscritos en náhuatl de la Biblioteca Nacional de México. *Boletín de la Biblioteca Nacional* 17, no. 1–2 (January–June 1966): 33–199.

Morfi, Juan Agustín. *La seguridad del Patrocinio de Maria Santisima de Guadalupe. Sermon panegyrico que en la Fiesta, que anualmente hacen los Señores Labradores, implorando su Proteccion dixo el dia 17. de Mayo de este presente año en la Iglesia de su Santuario El R. P. Fr. Juan Agustin Morfi.* Mexico City: Imprenta de la Bibliotheca Mexicana del Lic. D. Joseph de Jauregui, 1772.

Motolinía, Toribio de. *Motolinía's History of the Indians of New Spain.* Trans. and annotated with a biobibliographical study of the author by Francis Borgia Steck. Washington, D.C.: Academy of American Franciscan History, 1951.

————. *Memoriales o libro de las cosas de la Nueva España y de los naturales de ella.* Ed., notes, and analytical study by Edmundo O'Gorman. Mexico City: Universidad Nacional Autónoma de México, Instituto de Investigaciones Históricas, 1971.

————. *Historia de los indios de la Nueva España.* Ed., introduction, and notes by Georges Baudot. Madrid: Clásicos Castellanos, 1985.

Muñoz, Juan Bautista. Memoria sobre las apariciones y el culto de Nuestra Señora de Guadalupe (1794). In *Testimonios históricos guadalupanos.* Ed. Ernesto de la Torre Villar and Ramiro Navarro de Anda. Mexico City: Fondo de Cultura Económica, 1982, 689–701.

Muñoz de Castiblanque, Antonio Cristóbal. *La mina de la Virgen tapada en Nazareth, y descubierta en el cerro de Guadalupe, para ser universal patrona de los americanos, y muy principal de los mineros. Y por mina de oro, de los de la mineria del Potosi. Oracion panegyrica, que en la universal celebridad que hizo la Ciudad de S. Luis Potosi, y sus gremios, en su Iglesia Parroquial, por siete dias continuos, en Aplauso, y gracias â la Santissima Virgen, por la confirmacion, que N. SS. P. y Sr. Benedicto XIV. se dignò conceder, del Jurado Patronato de esta America . . . Predicó el dia 11. de Octubre del año de 1754. El M. R. P. Mrô. Fr. Antonio Christoval Munoz de Castiblanque Ayerve y Aragon de Ayora y Chirino.* Mexico City: Imprenta de la Bibliotheca Mexicana, 1758.

Navarro, Bartolomé. *Sermon qve en la festividad este año de 85 transferida de la aparicion de Nvestra Señora de Gvadalvpe Predicó el Iueves infraoctavo de la Purissima Concepcion en el Convento observantissimo de Señoras Religiosas de Santa Theresa de la Puebla de los Angeles El P. Fr. Bartholomé Navarro, de San Antonio de el Orden de Predicadores, y Lector de Prima de theologia en el Collegio Real de San Luis de dicha Ciudad.* Puebla, Mex.: Diego Fernandez de Leon, 1686.

Nueva colección de documentos para la historia de México. Cartas de religiosos de Nueva España, 1539–1594. Ed. Joaquín García Icazbalceta. 3 vols. Mexico City: Editorial Salvador Chávez Hayhoe, 1941.

Nuevas constituciones y reglas, que la ilustre, y venerable Congregacion de Nuestra Señora de Guadalupe Fundada canonicamente en su Santuario, extra muros de esta Ciudad, y erigido oy en insigne, y real colegiata, Ofrece à sus Congregantes. Mexico City: Imprenta de la Bibliotheca Mexicana, 1758.

Officium in festo B. V. Mariae de Guadalupe Mexicanae. Mexico City: Typis Sacror, Librorum apud Héredes D. Mariae de Rivera, 1755.

O'Gorman, Edmundo. *Destierro de sombras: luz en el origen y culto de Nuestra Señora de Guadalupe de Tepeyac.* Mexico City: Universidad Nacional Autónoma de México, 1986.

Olivares, José de. *Oracion panegyrica qve a la festiva solemnidad de la nueva Capilla, que se consagrò à N. Señora de Gvadalvpe . . . Predicò El P. M. Fr. Joseph de Olivares, de dicha Orden, Maestro en Sagrada Theologia por la Real Vniversidad de Mexico.* Mexico City: Viuda de Bernardo Calderon, 1683.

Ortiz de Montellano, Guillermo. *Nicā mopohua.* Mexico City: Universidad Ibero-americana, Departamento de Ciencias Religiosas, Departamento de Historia, 1990.

Ortiz Vaquero, Manuel. Notas sobre la pintura: guadalupana de 1606 de Baltazar de Echave Orio. *Imágenes Guadalupanas Cuatro Siglos* (Mexico City) (November 1987–March 1988): 29–31.

Osuna, Joaquín. *El iris celeste de las catolicas españas, la Aparicion, y Patrocinio de N. S. de Guadalupe en las Indias occidentales. Predicado en su Santuario de Guanajuato, dia 12. de Diciembre, año de 1744. Por el r. P. Fr. Joachin Ossuna, Natural de Mexico.* Mexico City: Por D. Francisco Xavier Sanchez, 1745.

Papeles de Nueva España publicados de orden y con fondos del gobierno mexicano por Francisco del Paso y Troncoso. Segunda serie. Geografía y estadística. Vol. 3. *Descripción del arzobispado de México. Año 1571.* Madrid: Est. Tipográfico «Sucesores de Rivadeneyra», 1905.

Paredes, Antonio. *Sermon panegyrico que predicò El Muy Rdo. P. Antonio Paredes de la Sagrada Compañia de Jesus, Rector de el Colegio de el Espiritu-Santo de la Puebla de los Angeles en la solemne accion de gracias, que el dia 14. de Octubre de 1759. hizo el Religioso Convento de Stà. Catharina de Sena de la misma Ciudad. A Nra. Jurada Patrona Maria Sant.ma de Guadalupe Por un manifiesto milagro probado, y juridicamante declarado, que se dignó obrar la misma Srâ. el dia 12. de Diciembre de 1755. en una Religiosa de aquel Convento.* Mexico City: Imprenta de Real, y Mas Antiguo Colegio de S. Ildefonso, 1761.

Paredes, Ignacio de. *Promptuario: manual mexicano, que à la verdad podrá ser utilissima à los parrochos para la enseñanza; à los necesitados indios para su instruccion; y à los que aprenden la lengua para la expedicion . . . Añadese por fin un sermon de Nuestra Santissima Guadalupana Señora, con una breve narracion de su historia; y dos indices, que se hallarán al principio de la obra.* Mexico City: Bibliotheca Mexicana, 1759.

Patrologiae Cursus Complete: Series Latina. Ed. J. P. Migne. 231 vols. Paris: N.p., diverse dates.

Payne, Stanley G. *Spanish Catholicism: An Historical Overview.* Madison: University of Wisconsin Press, 1984.

Peñalosa, Joaquín Antonio. *Flor y canto de poesía guadalupana: siglo XVII*. Mexico City: Editorial Jus, 1987.

Peñuelas, Pablo Antonio. *Panegirico a nuestra señora de Guadalupe, que predicò en el famoso templo de su santuario de Mexico El Br. D. Pablo Antonio Peñuelas . . . El dia 12. de Mayo de 1782. y último del Novenario, con que anualmente imploran su Patrocinio, para conseguir el beneficio de las lluvias, los Señores labradores del Reyno*. Mexico City: En la Imprenta de D. Felipe de Zúñiga y Ontiveros, 1782.

Peterson, Jeannette Favrot. The Virgin of Guadalupe: Symbol of Conquest or Liberation? *Art Journal* (Winter 1992): 39–47.

Phelan, John L. *The Millennial Kingdom of the Franciscans in the New World: A Study of the Writings of Gerónimo de Mendieta (1525–1604)*. 2d ed., rev. Berkeley and Los Angeles: University of California Press, 1970.

[Philips, Miles]. *Hakluyt's Voyages*. Selected and ed. by Richard David. Boston: Houghton Mifflin Company, 1981.

Pius XII. Christifidelibus datus die XII mensis octobris A. MCMXLV, ob marialem conventum ad santuarium B. Mariae V. Guadalupensis mexicopoli coadunatis. *Acta Apostolicae Sedis: Commentarium Officiale*, ser. 2, vol. 12. Vatican City: Typis Polyglottis Vaticanis, 1945, 265–66.

Pompa y Pompa, Antonio. *Album del IV centenario guadalupano*. Mexico City: Talleres de la Editorial "Cvltvra," 1938.

———. *El Gran Acontecimiento Guadalupano*. Colección México Heroïco, no. 68. Mexico City: Editorial Jus, 1967.

Ponce de León, José. *El patronato que se celebra, suplemento del testimonio, que no ay, de la aparicion de la Santissima Virgen de Guadalupe Nuestra Señora. Sermon panegyrico, Que el dia doce de Diciembre de este año de 1756, en la Magnifica Funcion con que celebrò su declarado Patronato en la Iglesia de la misma Señora la Nobilissima Ciudad de Paztquaro [sic], Predicò Don Joseph Antonio Eugenio Ponze de Leon*. Mexico City: Imprenta de la Bibliotheca Mexicana, 1757.

Poole, Stafford. *Pedro Moya de Contreras: Catholic Reform and Royal Power in New Spain, 1571–1591*. Berkeley: University of California Press, 1987.

———. Iberian Catholicism Comes to America. In *Christianity Comes to the Americas*. A Giniger Book. New York: Paragon Press, 1992.

El "Pregón del atabal" (1531). In *Testimonios históricos guadalupanos*. Ed. Ernesto de la Torre Villar and Ramiro Navarro de Anda. Mexico City: Fondo de Cultura Económica, 1982, 23.

Prem, Hanns J. Disease Outbreaks in Central Mexico during the Sixteenth Century. In *"Secret Judgments of God": Old World Disease in Colonial Spanish America*. Ed. Noble David Cook and W. George Lovell. Norman and London: University of Oklahoma Press, 1992, 20–48.

[Puga, Vasco de]. *Prouisiones, cedulas, instrucciones de Su Magestad ordenanças de difuntos y audiencia para la buena expedicion de los negocios y administracion de justicia y gouernacion de esta Nueua España y para el buen tratamiento y conseruacion de los indios desde el año de 1525 hasta este presente de 63*. 2 vols. Mexico City: En Casa de Pedro Ocharte, 1563.

Relación Breve de la Venida de los de la Compañía de Jesús a la Nueva España. Año de 1602.

Ed. Francisco González de Cossío. Mexico City: Imprenta Universitaria, 1945.

Relación breve y verdadera de algunas cosas de las muchas que sucedieron al Padre Fray Alonso Ponce en las provincias de la Nueva España siendo comisario general de aquellas partes. Trátanse algunas particularidades de aquella tierra, y dícese su ida á ella y vuelta á España con algo de lo que en el viaje le aconteció hasta volver á su provincia de Castilla. Escrita por dos religiosos sus compañeros. 2 vols. Madrid: Imprenta de la Viuda de Calero, 1875.

Remesal, Antonio de. *Historia general de las Indias occidentales y particular de la gobernación de Chiapa y Guatemala.* Prologue by Licenciado Antonio Batres Jáuregui. 3d ed. Guatemala City: Editorial "José de Pineda Ibarra," 1966.

Reynoso, Sancho. *La injusticia por derecho justificada por gracia; Sermon que predicò El P. Sancho Reynoso, Professo de la Compañia de Jesus, en el Colegio de S. Luis de la Paz, dia tercero del festejo, con que se aplaudiò confirmada Patrona con oficio, y missa la Virgen Maria en su Milagrosa Imagen de Guadalupe.* Mexico City: Imprenta de la Bibliotheca Mexicana, 1759.

Ricard, Robert. *The Spiritual Conquest of Mexico: An Essay on the Apostolate and the Evangelizing Methods of the Mendicant Orders in New Spain, 1523–1572.* Trans. Lesley Byrd Simpson. Berkeley and Los Angeles: University of California Press, 1966.

Riofrío, Bernardo de. *Centonicvm Virgilianum monimentum* [*sic*] *mirabilis apparitionis pvrissimæ Virginis Mariæ de Gvadalvpe extramvros civitatis mexicanæ: avthore licito D. Bernardo de Riofrio michoacanensis ecclesiæ canonico doctorali: Ad Illustrissimum, Reverendissimum, & Excellentissimum Principem, M. D. D. Fr. Payum de Ribera Enriquez, Archiepiscopus Mexicani Antistitem, novique Indiarum Orbis Proregem nunc Conchensis Ecclesiæ præsulem designatum.* Mexico City: Apud Viduam Bernardi Calderon, 1680.

Rivera, Agustín. *El intérprete Juan Gonzalez es una conseja.* Pamphlet written by Agustín Rivera and dedicated to his learned physician and friend Sr. Dr. D. Eugenio Moreno. Lagos de Moreno: Ausencio Lopez Arce e Hijo Tipografos, 1896.

Rivera, Luis de. *Sermon de la publicacion de el edicto del Santo Tribunal de la Inquisicion, que se publicò, y leyò en la Iglesia de N. Señora de Guadalupe dia de la Presentacion de Nuestra Señora en el templo à 21 de Noviembre de 1694. Años (en ocasion) que aviendo bajado la ymagen de N. Señora, y en el Sagrario de el Altar mayor estaba la Santa Imagen en la grada inferior de el Arco Toral en Altar formado al proposito, y prevenido el valdoquin para descubrir el Santissimo sacramento que estaba en el Sagrario immediato á el Altar (dixolo) el P. Fr. Luys de Rivera.* Mexico City: Herederos de la Viuda de Bernardo Calderon, 1695.

Robles, Antonio de. *Diario de sucesos notables (1665–1703).* Ed. and prologue by Antonio Castro Leal. 2 vols. Mexico City: Editorial Porrua, 1964.

Robles, Juan de. *Sermon qve predico El P. Ivan de Robles, Theologo de la Compañia de Jesvs, en la civdad de Queretaro, su patria, el dia doze de Diziembre de 1681 en la Iglesia de N. Señora de Gvadalvpe, a la Annual memoria de la milagrosa Aparicion de su prodigiosa Imagen, que se Venera en el serro de Guadalupe mexicano.* Mexico City: Por Juan de Ribera, 1682.

———. *Oracion fvnebre elogio sepvcral en al anniversario de la mvy ilustre Señora, y Venerable Madre Antonia de San Jacinto . . . dixola el P. Jvan de Robles, Theologo de la Compañia de Jesvs, a 20. de Noviembre de 1684. Dedicala al Bachiller D. Jvan Cavallero, y Ocio.* Mexico City: Viuda de Juan de Ribera, 1685.

Robles, Vito Alessio. *Fray Agustin de Morfi y su obra. Liminares de la edición de la obra "Viaje de Indios y Diario de Nueva Mexico" por Fray Juan Agustín de Morfi.* Mexico City: Antigua Librería de Robredo de José Porrúa e Hijos, 1935.

Rodríguez, Mauro. *Guadalupe, ¿historia o símbolo?* Mexico City: Editorial Edical, S.A., 1980.

Rodríguez Vallejo, José. *Sermon que el dia ocho de Octubre del año de mil setecientos cincuenta y siete, primero de los nueve con que la Nobilissima, y siempre Leal Ciudad de Queretaro, y sus Sacratissimas Religiones celebraron la Confirmacion, que del Titulo de principal, y Universal Patrona del Reyno de la America, hizo la Santidad del Sr. Benedicto XIV. en la portentosa imagen de la Virgen Maria de Guadalupe de Mexico Predicò D. Joseph Rodriguez Vallejo.* Mexico City: Imprenta de la Bibliotheca Mexicana, 1758.

Ronan, S.J., Charles. *Francisco Javier Clavigero, S.J. (1731–1787): Figure of the Mexican Enlightenment: His Life and Works.* Bibliotheca Instituti Historici S.I., vol. 40. Rome: Institutum Historicum S.I. Chicago: Loyola University Press, 1977.

Rossi, Anton Domenico. *La B.V. di Guadalupe in S. Stefano d'Aveto.* Chiavari, It.: 1910.

Ruiz de Alarcón, Hernando. *Treatise on the Heathen Superstitions That Today Live Among the Indians Native to This New Spain, 1629.* Trans. and ed. J. Richard Andrews and Ross Hassing. Norman: University of Oklahoma Press, 1975.

Ruiz de Castañeda, Juan José. *Sermon panegyrico en glorias de Maria Santissima bajo el titulo de Guadalupe, Que en su Santuario dia 12. de Diciembre de 1756. años . . . predicó el P. Juan Joseph Ruiz de Castañeda, de la Compañia de Jesus.* Mexico City: En la Imprenta del Superior Gobierno, n.d. [Introductory letters are dated 1766.]

Sacrorum Conciliorum nova et amplissima collectio cujus Joannes Dominicus Mansi et post ipsius mortem florentinus et venetianus editores ab 1758 ad annum 1798, priores triginta unum tomos ediderunt nunc autem continuata et, deo favente, absoluta. 36 vols. Paris: Hubert Welter, 1802.

Sáenz de San Antonio, Matías. *Conveniencia relativa entre el termino de vn templo Apostolico, sujeto, que se dedica, y la Imagen de Gvadalvpe, Predicado, que se coloca. Proposicion que predicò el R. P. Fr. Mathias Saenz de San Antonio, Predicador Apostolico . . . Guardian del Collegio de Nra. Señora de Guadalupe, de la Ciudad de Nra. Sra. de los Zacatecos, en la solemne fiesta de la Dedicacion del nuevo Templo de Nuestra Señora de Guadalupe de dicho collegio.* Mexico City: Por Francisco de Rivera Calderon, 1721.

Sahagún, Bernardino de. *Florentine Codex. General History of the Things of New Spain.* 13 pts. Trans. with notes and illustrations by Arthur J. O. Anderson and Charles E. Dibble. Santa Fe, N.M.: School of American Research and University of Utah, 1958.

———. *Historia general de las cosas de la Nueva España escrita por Bernardino de Sahagún y fundada en la documentación en lengua mexicana recogida por los mismos naturales; la dispuso para la prensa en esta nueva edición, con numeración, anotaciones y apéndices,* Angel María Garibay K. 4 vols. 4th ed. Mexico City: Editorial Porrúa, 1981.

Sánchez, Miguel. *Imagen de la Virgen Maria, Madre de Dios de Guadalupe. Milagrosamente aparecida en la ciudad de Mexico. Celebrada en su historia, con la profecia del capitulo doce del Apocalipsis.* Mexico City: Imprenta de la Viuda de Bernardo Calderón, 1648.

————. Imagen de la Virgen María Madre de Dios de Guadalupe (1648). In *Testimo-nios históricos guadalupanos*. Ed. Ernesto de la Torre Villar and Ramiro Navarro de Anda. Mexico City: Fondo de Cultura Económica, 1982, 152–281.

————. *El David seraphico, de la solemne fiesta, qve la Real vniversidad de Mexico celebro a la Immacvlada Concepcion de la Virgen Maria, Madre de Dios; en qve ratifico el jvramento de Sv defensa: a deuocion del Bachiller Miguel Sanchez presbytero*. Mexico City: Biuda de B. Calderon, 1653.

Sánchez Baquero, Juan, S.J. *Fundación de la Compañía de Jesús en Nueva España, 1571–1580*. Ed. Félix Ayuso, S.J. Mexico City: Editorial Patria, 1945.

San Cirilo, Francisco de. *El mas noble desempeño de la promesa mas generosa; Sermon panegir-ico de nuestra Señora de Guadalupe, que en su Insigne y Real Colegiata dixo el dia de la celebridad de su Aparicion 12. de Diciembre de 1778. El R. P. Fr. Francisco de S. Cyrilo, Carmelita Descalzo*. Mexico City: Por D. Felipe de Zúñiga y Ontiveros, 1779.

San José, Juan de. *Sagrado retrato, è idea panegyrica de la soberana imagen de Maria SS. de Gvadalupe de Mexico*. Mexico City: N.p., 1701.

San José, Manuel. *Florido aromático panegyris, qve en el dia de la milagrosa Aparicion de Nuestra Señora de Gvadalvpe patente el Santissimo Sacramento orò El R. P. Fr. Manuel de San Joseph, Carmelita Descalzo Lector, que fue, de Sagrada Escriptura, y de theologia Mystica, en su Colegio de S. Angel*. Mexico City: Por doña Maria de Benavides, Viuda de Juan de Ribera, 1687.

San Joseph, Francisco de. *Historia universal de la primitiva y milagrosa imagen de nuestra Señora de Guadalupe, fundacion, y grandezas de su santa casa, y algunos de los milagros que ha hecho en este presente siglo. Refierense las historias de las plausibles imagenes de nues-tra Señora de Guadalupe de Mexico . . . Escrita por el Rmo. P. Fr. de S. Joseph, Ex-Prior de la Santa, y Real Casa de nuestra Señora de Guadalupe*. Madrid: Por Antonio Marin, 1743.

San Miguel, Juan de. *Sermon qve predicò el R.do P. Ivan de San Migvel, Religioso de la Com-pañia de Iesus, Rector del Colegio de Santa Ana de esta Ciudad de Mexico. Al nacimiento de N. Señora, y Dedicacion de su capilla de Gvadalvpe, en la Santa Iglesia Cathedral, á expensas de la Arch-Cofradia del Santissimo Sacramento*. Mexico City: Francisco Rodriguez Lupercio, 1671.

Santa Cruz Aldana, Ignacio de. *Sermon en la festividad de la presentacion de Nvestra Señora. Qve predicò el Sabado 21. de Noviembre de 1671. años en el conuento de Religiosis del Señor San Lorenço de esta Corte el Br. Don Ignacio de Santa Cruz Aldana*. Mexico City: Iuan Ruyz, 1672.

Santa Teresa, Luis de. *Sermon qve predico El R. P. Fr. Lvis de Santa Theresa, Religioso Car-melita Descalço en la Civdad de Santiago de Querétaro el dia 12 de Diziembre de 1682 en el templo de N. S.ra de Gvadalvpe à la milagrosa Aparicion de su sacratissima, y prodi-giosa Imagen*. Mexico City: Por Juan de Ribera, 1683.

Santissima Trinidad, Andrés de. *La venerada, y glorificada en todas las naciones, por haverse aparecido en estos reynos. Sermon de Nuestra Madre, y Señora Maria Santissima de Gua-dalupe, Que en el dia 12. de Diciembre de 1755. En que se estrenò su nuevo Oficio, con Missa Pontifical, que cantò El Illmô. Sr. Dr. D. Manuel Joseph Rubio de Salinas . . . Predicò en dicha Santa Iglesia El P. Fr. Andres de la Santissima Trinidad, Religioso Car-melita Descalzo*. Mexico City: Imprenta de la Bibliotheca Mexicana, 1759.

Schäfer, Ernst. *El real y supremo consejo de las Indias: su historia, organización y labor administrativa hasta la terminación de la casa de Austria*. 2 vols. Seville: Imp. M. Carmona, 1935–1947.

Schendel, Gordon. *Medicine in Mexico: From Aztec Herbs to Betatrons*. Austin: University of Texas Press, 1968.

Schroeder, Susan. *Chimalpahin and the Kingdoms of Chalco*. Tucson: University of Arizona Press, 1991.

Segura, Juan Antonio de. *Milagro de la pintura y belleza de milagro. Sermon panegyrico, Que en el dia de la Milagrosa Aparicion de la Imagen de Guadalupe, predicò E. R. P. P. Fr. Juan Antonio de Segura, Comendador del Convento Grande de Nuestra Señora de la Merced Redempcion de Captivos; En la Solemnissima Fiesta de la muy Ilustre, Noble, y Devota Arch-Cofradia de la Purissima Concepcion y el Santissimo Sacramento, fundada con Authoridad Apostolica en la Iglesia de dicho Convento*. Mexico City: Por los Herederos de la Viuda de Miguel de Ribera, [1720].

Segura, Nicolás de. *Platica de la milagrosa imagen de Nuestra Señora de Guadalupe de Mexico. Sacada del tomo nono de los sermones de el P. Nicolas de Segura de la Compañia de Jesus, Prefecto, que fue de la M. Ilustre Congregacion de la Purissima, Preposito actual de la Casa Professa de Mexico, y Calificador del Santo Oficio*. Mexico City: En la Imprenta de la Viuda de D. Joseph Bernardo de Hogal, 1742.

Sigüenza y Góngora, Carlos de. *Glorias de Queretaro en la nueva Congregacion Eclesiastica de Maria Santissima de Guadalupe, con que se ilustra: y en el sumptuoso templo, que dedicò à su obsequio D. Juan Cavallero, y Ocio Presbytero, commissario de Corte del Tribunal del Santo Oficio de la Inquisicion. Escrivelas D. Carlos de Siguenza, y Gongora natural de Mexico, Cathedratico proprietario de Mathematicas en la Real Universidad de esta corte*. Mexico City: Por la Viuda de Bernardo Calderon, 1680.

————. *Piedad heroyca de Don Fernando Cortes*. Ed. and study by Jaime Delgado. Coleccion Chimalistac de Libros y Documentos acerca de la Nueva Espana, 7. Madrid: José Porrúa Turanzas, Editor, 1960.

Siller a., Clodomiro I. *La evangelización guadalupana: Cuadernos de Estudios Indígenas n. 1*. Mexico City: CENAMI, December 1984.

Simpson, Lesley Byrd. *Many Mexicos*. 4th ed. Berkeley, Los Angeles, London: University of California Press, 1966.

Sixteenth-Century Mexico: The Work of Sahagún. Ed. Munro S. Edmonson. Albuquerque: University of New Mexico Press, 1974.

Smith, Hilary Dansey. *Preaching in the Spanish Golden Age*. Oxford: Oxford University Press, 1978.

Soustelle, Jacques. *The Daily Life of the Aztecs on the Eve of the Spanish Conquest*. Trans. Patrick O'Brian. Stanford, Calif.: Stanford University Press, 1970.

Staehlin, Carlos María. *Apariciones*. Madrid: Razón y Fe, 1954.

Suárez de Peralta, Juan. *Tratado de descubrimiento de las Indias (Noticias históricas de Nueva España). Testimonios mexicanos: historiadores 3*. Preliminary note by Federico Gómez de Orozco. Mexico City: Secretaría de Educación Pública, 1949.

Sylvest, Edwin E., Jr. *Nuestra Señora de Guadalupe: Mother of God, Mother of the Americas*. Elizabeth Perkins Prothro Galleries, Bridwell Library, Perkins School of Theology, Southern Methodist University, Dallas, Texas, 1992.

Talavera, Gabriel de. *Historia de Nvestra Señora de Gvadalvpe consagrada a la Soberana magestad de la Reyna de los Angeles, milagrosa patrona de este santuario por Fray Gabriel de Talavera prior de la misma casa.* Toledo: Thomas de Guzman, 1597[?].

Taylor, William B. The Virgin of Guadalupe: An Inquiry into the Social History of Marian Devotion. *American Ethnologist* (1986): 9–33.

Testimonios históricos guadalupanos. Ed. Ernesto de la Torre Villar and Ramiro Navarro de Anda. Mexico City: Fondo de Cultura Económica, 1982.

Tezozomoc, Hernando Alvarado. *Crónica mexicana escrita por D. Hernando Alvarado Tezozómoc hacia el año de MDXCVIII. Anotada por el Sr. Lic. Manuel Orozco y Berra, y precedida del Códice Ramírez, manuscrito del siglo XVI intitulado: relación del origen de los indios que habitan esta Nueva España según sus historias, y de un examen de ambas obras, al cual va anexo un estudio de la cronología mexicana por el mismo Sr. Orozco y Berra.* 2d ed. Mexico City: Editorial Porrua, S.A., 1975.

———. *Cronica mexicayotl.* Direct translation from the Nahuatl by Adrián León. Mexico City: Universidad Autónoma de México, 1976.

Torquemada, Juan de. *Monarquía indiana.* Introduction by Miguel León-Portilla. 3 vols. Mexico City: Editorial Porrua, S. A., 1969.

Torres, Cayetano Antonio de. *Sermon de la santissima virgen de Guadalupe, predicado En la Sta. Iglesia Metropolitana de Mexico en la solemnissima celebridad, que se hizo por la Confirmacion Apostolica del Patronato Principal y Universal de la Misma Señora en su Sagrada Imagen. El Dia Jueves 11. de Noviembre de este presente año de 1756 . . . Por el Dr. y Mrô. D. Cayetano Antonio de Torres.* Mexico City: Por los Herederos de la Viuda de D. Joseph Bernardo de Hogal, 1757.

Torre Villar, Ernesto de la. *Mexicanos ilustres.* 2 vols. Mexico City: Editorial Jus, 1979.

Toussaint, Manuel. El plano atribuído a Alonso de Santa Cruz: estudio histórico y analítico. In *Planos de la ciudad de Mexico siglos XVI y XVII: estudio histórico, urbanistico y bibliográfico.* Ed. Manuel Toussaint, Federico Gómez de Orozco, and Justino Fernández. Mexico City: XVI° Congreso Internacional de Planificación y de la Habitación, 1990, 135–46.

Tres conquistadores y pobladores de la Nueva España: Cristóbal Martín Millán de Gamboa, Andrés de Tapia, Jerónimo López. Paleographic version, notes, and alphabetic index by Francisco Fernández del Castillo. Publicaciones del Archivo General de la Nación, 12. Mexico City: Talleres Gráficos de la Nación, 1927.

Vaillant, George C. *Aztecs of Mexico: Origin, Rise and Fall of the Aztec Nation.* Revised by Suzannah B. Vaillant. Harmondsworth: Penguin Books, 1975.

Valadés, Diego, trans. *Retórica cristiana.* Introduction by Esteban J. Palomera; remarks by Alfonso Castro Pallares; preface by Tarscicio Herrera Zapién. Mexico City: Universidad Nacional Autónoma de México, 1989.

Valderas Colmenero, Ignacio Luis de. *Sermon de Nuestra Señora de Guadalupe de Mexico, Que en su Iglesia de la Ciudad de Queretaro, Domingo 16 de Octubre de 1757. dia ultimo del Solemnissimo Novenario que se celebrò en ella, por la Confirmacion Pontificia de el Patronato universal y primario de la misma Señora en su Aparecida Imagen . . . Predicó el Lic. D. Ignacio Luis de Valderas Colmenero.* Mexico City: Imprenta Nueva de la Bibliotheca Mexicana, 1758.

Varón de Berieza, José. *Fragrantiori paradiso toti florido immo flagrantiori coelo toti sidereo*

Santis.mae Virgini Mariae de Gvadalvpe hvic Sacro novi terrarum orbis, tvtoqve confvgio omnivm in se corda allicienti: angelica natura pro pedum fulcimento decoratae, & divina pro capitis fastigio redimitae. . . Defendentur in regia ac Pontificia Divi Caroli Academia a . . . D. Iosepho Varon de Berieza. Guatemala City: Antonio de Pineda & Ybarra, 1691.

Vega, Mariano Antonio de la. *Sermon panegyrico que en el dia 12 de diciembre de 1756, primero del solemne novenario, con que se celebrò la confirmacion del universal Patronato en la Nueva España, de Maria Santissima Señora nuestra, en su marabillosa imagen de Guadalupe de Mexico, concedida por breve de N. Bmô. P. Benedicto XIV . . . predicò el doctor don Mariano Antonio de la Vega.* Mexico City: En la Imprenta de Bibliotheca Mexicana, 1757.

Velasco, Alonso de. *Exaltacion de la divina misericordia en la milagrosa renovacion de la Soberana Imagen de Christo Señor N. crvcificado qve se venera en la Iglesia del Convento de San Ioseph de Carmelitas Descalzas de esta Ciudad de Mexico que consagra a la Madre de la Misericordia Maria Santissima de los Dolores El Doctor Alonso Alberto de Velasco, Cura mas antiguo desta Santa Iglesia Cathedral Metropolitana, Abogado de la Real Audiencia, y de pressos del Santo Officio de la Inquisicion de esta Nueva España, y su consultor, y del Colegio Seminario de Dicha Santa Iglesia, Capellan del mismo convento.* Mexico City: Por donna Maria de Benavides Viuda de Iuan de Ribera, 1699.

Velázquez, Primo Feliciano. *La aparición de Santa María de Guadalupe.* Facsimile reproduction of the 1st ed. of 1931. Introduction and bibliography by J. Jesús Jiménez López. Mexico City: Editorial Jus, 1981.

———. Comentario a la historia original guadalupana. In Lauro López Beltrán, *La protohistoria guadalupana.* 2d rev. ed. Obras Guadalupanas de Lauro López Beltrán, vol. 3. Mexico City: Editorial Tradición, S.A., 1981, 140–73.

Vera, Fortino Hipólito. *Tesoro guadalupano. Noticia de los libros, documentos, inscripciones &c. que tratan, mencionan ó aluden á la Aparición y devoción de Nuestra Señora de Guadalupe.* 2 vols. Amecameca: Imprenta del "Colegio Católico," 1887–1889.

Vetancurt, Agustín. *Teatro mexicano: descripción breve de los sucesos ejemplares, históricos, y religiosos del nuevo mundo de las Indias.* 1st facsimile ed. Mexico City: Editorial Porrua, S.A., 1971.

Vidal de Figueroa, José. *Theorica de la prodigiosa Imagen de la Virgen Santa Maria de Gvadalvpe de Mexico en vn discvrso theologico qve predicó el Doctor Ioseph Vidal de Figveroa, Colegial de Nra. Señora de todos Santos, Cura Beneficiado de la Iglesia Parroquial de Texopilco, feligresia de Indios de la Metropolitana de la Nueua España. El dia 12 de diziembre, en la fiesta anual de su Milagrosa Aparición en su Hermita. Fvndado en vn texto de San Pablo nueuamente illustrado por la Conuersion de los Indios à la fè del euangelio, y prueba deste milagro.* Mexico City: Iuan Ruyz, 1661.

Villa, Juan de. *Sermon de la milagrosa imagen de N. S. de Guadalupe de Mexico, en la Festividad, que le celebran sus Devotos, el dia del Proto-Martyr San Esteban, segundo de la Pasqua del Sagrado Nacimiento del Señor, en la Iglesia del Hospital del Amor de Dios de la misma Ciudad . . . Predicabalo el M. R. P. Fr. Juan de Villa . . . el Año de 1733.* Mexico City: Imprenta Real del Superior Govierno de doña Maria de Rivera, 1754.

Villafañe, Juan de. *Compendio historico de que se da noticia de las milagrosas y devotas imagenes de la Reyna de Cielos, y tierra Maria Santissima . . . de España.* Madrid: M. Fernandez, 1740.

Wagner, Henry Raup, in collaboration with Helen Rand Parish. *The Life and Writings of Bartolomé de las Casas.* Albuquerque: University of New Mexico Press, 1967.

Weckmann, Luis. *La herencia medieval de Mexico.* 2 vols. Mexico City: El Colegio de México, 1984.

Wolf, Eric. The Virgin of Guadalupe: A Mexican National Symbol. *Journal of American Folklore* 71 (1958): 34–39.

Wood, Stephanie. Christian Images in Nahua Testaments. *Americas* 47, no. 3 (January 1991): 259–93.

Zambrano, Francisco, S.J., and José Gutiérrez Casillas, S.J. *Diccionario Bio-Bibliográfico de la Compañía de Jesús en México.* 16 vols. Mexico City: Editorial Jus, S.A., 1961–1977.

[Zumárraga, Juan de]. *Regla christiana breue: para ordenar la vida y tiempo del xpiano que se quiere saluar y tener su alma dispuesta: para que Jesuxpo. more en ella. Impressa por mandado del reuerendissimo Señor don fray Juan de Çumarraga primer obispo de Mexico.* Mexico City: N.p., 1547.

[———]. *Regla cristiana breve.* Ed., introduction, and notes by José Almoina. Mexico City: Editorial Jus, 1951.

Zumárraga and His Family: Letters to Vizcaya, 1536–1548: A Collection of Documents in Relation to the Founding of a Hospice in His Birthplace. Transcribed and ed. by Richard E. Greenleaf. Trans. Neal Kaveny, O.F.M. Washington, D.C.: Academy of American Franciscan History, 1979.

Index

About the Author

Reverend Stafford Poole, C.M., a member of the Congregation of the Mission (Vincentian Community), was ordained a Roman Catholic priest in 1956. He received his Ph.D. in United States and Mexican history from Saint Louis University (1961), where he studied under John Francis Bannon, S.J., and Ernest J. Burrus, S.J. From 1956 until 1989 he taught at college seminaries in Missouri and California. He was president and rector of Saint John's Seminary College in Camarillo, California, 1980–1984. At the present time he is archivist for the Western Province of the Vincentian Community, a full-time research historian, and the editor of *Vincentian Heritage*. His primary research interests have been the Church in colonial Mexico and the history of the Vincentian Community. His recent works have included *Pedro Moya de Contreras: Catholic Reform and Royal Power in New Spain, 1571–1591* (Berkeley: University of California Press, 1987) and *In Defense of the Indians* (DeKalb: Northern Illinois University Press, 1992). At the present time, in collaboration with Lisa Sousa, he is preparing a translation and commentary on Luis Laso de la Vega's *Huey Tlamahuiçoltica* (1649), the first Nahuatl account of the Guadalupe apparitions. Professor John Frederick Schwaller and he are preparing an annotated edition of the *Directorio para confesores* of the Third Mexican Provincial Council of 1585. Father Poole is also working on a biography of Juan de Ovando, president of the Council of the Indies under Philip II.